MANCHESTER MARATHONS

1908 - 2002

by

Ron Hill

and

Neil Shuttleworth

To Philip + Carol,

best wishes,

Ron Hill Running Enterprises

British Library Cataloguing in Publication Data
A catalogue record for this book is available from the British Library.

ISBN: 0 9507882 4 4

Published by Ron Hill Running Enterprises

Printed by Litho Press, Midleton, Co. Cork, Ireland.

Cover Design by Rhino Design, Ashton-U-Lyne.

Other Titles By Ron Hill

The Long Hard Road - Part I: Nearly to the Top, 1981.
The Long Hard Road - Part II: To the Peak and Beyond, 1982.

By Neil Shuttleworth

The Best of British - a review of fell running champions, 1990.

Contents

PREFACE

The writing of this book was inspired by the visit of the 17th Commonwealth Games to Manchester in the year 2002.

Almost all of the research work has been carried out by co-author Neil Shuttleworth and many interesting new facts on individual characters and races have been unearthed.

There have been a total of 35 marathons in Manchester including the 2002 female and male Commonwealth Marathons.

The first "marathon" was in 1908 over a distance of 19 miles. This was before the official length of 26 miles 385 yards was laid down, and was one of the trials for the London Olympics. It was at this Games that the now-universally accepted, but rather odd, distance was established. We explain how. That particular Olympic Marathon is given a full account, perhaps one of the most detailed from a British perspective.

Manchester also had the privilege of organising the first amateur marathon in the UK over the new official distance, which we claim led to a new amateur world best time.

Many of the early race stories are lifted straight from the newspapers of the time. We make no apologies for this as the accounts give a real feel for these times.

Producing this book has taken a long time for both of us. It has been a labour of love and an attempt to illuminate some of the history and heritage of marathon running in the Manchester region.

Protocols

Timing: up until the mid-1930s timing was to the nearest fifth of a second.
  e.g. 0.2 is one fifth, and 0.4 is two fifths of a second.
Times: these are hours:minutes:seconds
  i.e. 3 hours one minute and one second is 3:01:01
Clubs: a person's club is recorded in brackets after their name.
  Runners not in a Club are shown as 'Unatt'.
Abbreviations: "Poly" is short for Polytechnic or Polytechnic Marathon;
  "RRC" is short for Road Runners Club; and
  "dnf" is short for "did not finish."
First person: where "I" is printed in the text, it refers to co-author Ron Hill.

ACKNOWLEDGEMENTS

Our thanks are due to all those athletes, running club members, and family associates of the characters in this book who have assisted us by answering questions and providing archive material and photographs. Some who have helped us are:

Bill Adcocks, Coventry Godiva Harriers; Mike Bateman, Honorary Secretary of Morpeth Harriers; Trevor Baxter, journalist; Wendy and Graham Beal, (niece of Arthur Cyril Chamberlain); George J Birchall, son of George P Birchall; Charles Arthur Bourne, Life Member of Liverpool Pembroke AC; Sandra Brown, Surrey Walking Club and Centurion 735; Bill Clapham, Blackheath Harriers; Dave Cooper (Road Runners Club); John Cooper, Sutton-in-Ashfield Harriers; Peter Downing, photographer; Geoff Doggett, President of Salford Harriers; Malcolm Dowthwaite, Hallamshire Harriers; Tony Duffy, Bolton United Harriers & AC; Roddy Fisher, Editor of Road Runners Club Newsletter (www.roadrunnersclub.org.uk); Charlotte Florkiweicz, Bradford, Yorkshire; Geoff Garnett, Bingley Harriers; Roger Gynn, marathon statistician and author; Chris Hallinan, Leigh Harriers; Harry Hardaker, initially with Wibsey Park, and now Life Member Bingley Harriers; Roy Henning, son of John Henning, MBE; Robert Hilton, Urmston; Ken Lucas, Hindley; Hugh Marsden, Exmouth Harriers; Graham Marshall, Sale Harriers; Dick Maxwell, President of Lancashire Walking Club; Brenda McCormick, Northern Ireland Athletic Federation; Paul Mee, Manchester Leisure; Wilf Morgan, Birchfield Harriers; Audrey Murden, Kirkby-in-Ashfield; Joe Salt, President of Rochdale Harriers & AC; Harry Smith, Clayton-le-Moors Harriers; Randell Tassell, Race Director, White Peak Marathon; John Taylor, Archivist for Leigh Harriers; Hamish M Thomson, Stockport Harriers; Peter Trainor, Ranelagh Harriers; Tom Tyrrell, journalist; Chris Vigrass, son-in-law of Mrs Marjorie Ferris; Arthur Walsham, President of Northern Veterans Athletic Club; John Walshe, Ballycotton '10' Race Director; Roy Wood, son of Harold Wood; and Frank Wood, Horwich RMI Harriers.

Special thanks are due to Allied Newspapers for their permission to use contemporary accounts verbatim and newspaper photographs of the time. Excerpts from The Manchester Guardian have also proved valuable.

The following magazines and newspapers have been important in providing vital leads and facts to make our story as complete as possible:
Athletics Weekly ("the Runners' Bible"); Road Runners Club Newsletter; Manchester Evening News; Bolton Evening News; Sheffield Star; and Bradford Telegraph and Argus.

The following libraries and archive collections have been really helpful:
National Centre for Athletics Literature at the University of Birmingham; Bolton Archive and Local Studies Collection; Crewe Library, Cheshire; Greater Manchester County Record Office; Hyde Library, part of Tameside Leisure Services; Kendal Local Studies Collection; Liverpool Libraries and Information Services; Manchester Central Reference Library; John Rylands University of Manchester Library; Salford Local Studies Collection; Sheffield Local Studies Collection; Warrington Library; Westhoughton Library, part of Bolton Leisure Services; and Wigan Local Studies Collection, The History Shop.

This book could not have been produced without the help given by www.realrunner.com and Steven Hill, Up + Running, Ltd, both of whom provided valuable assistance in producing the text .

Every effort has been made to acknowledge all copyright holders of photographs, but should there be any errors or omissions the publisher undertakes to rectify these at the earliest opportunity. Any errors or omissions are unintentional and will be similarly rectified.

INTRODUCTION

The Manchester area has a long history of running and it is only natural that the marathon event should have featured on many occasions during the last century and will continue to test runners during the new Millennium. The most prestigious Manchester Marathons of them all took place in July 2002, when the Commonwealth Games were contested by both men and women, on the streets of central Manchester and Salford.

The Origin of the Marathon Race

The Greek Historian Herodotus, who lived from approximately 484 to 425 BC, tells us that in 490 BC King Darius of Persia landed a force of 100,000 men near the small town of Marathon, around 35 kilometres over the mountains from Athens, intent on conquering the Greeks, whose army numbered only 10,000 under the command of General Miltiades.

Using superb tactics the Greeks routed the Persians, driving them into the sea, with a loss of only 192 soldiers compared with 6,400 Persians slaughtered. Legend has it that a young soldier named Pheidippides, famed for his running abilities, was despatched to Athens to convey the good news. Despite being exhausted from battle, Pheidippides delivered the victorious message, "Rejoice, we conquer." Having spoken these words, Pheidippides fell down dead. Herodotus, who was alive at the time of the battle and would have been able to converse with survivors makes no mention of this messenger.

Plutarch, another Greek Historian, writing more than 500 years later, describes a messenger from the battle, but does not name him Pheidippides. So this legend may indeed be a myth.

What Herodotus does describe in his story is a run from Athens to Sparta by a professional foot courier called Phillipedes (Pheidippides is probably an interpretation of this name), a distance of some 150 miles (250 kilometres) over mountainous terrain, and completed in less than 48 hours. His mission was to request the help of the Spartans in repelling the Persian invaders. His run was in vain as the extremely superstitious Spartans would not march until the moon was full, and that was several days away. Phillipedes set out the next day, once more delivering his message in less than 48 hours. A prodigious feat by any standards. There is now an annual race from Athens to Sparta: the Spartathlon.

The foundation of the Modern Olympics is usually attributed to a Frenchman, Baron Pierre de Coubertin. De Coubertin first proposed a revival of Games at a banquet in France in 1892, but the idea was only sceptically received.

However, Dr William Penny Brookes of Much Wenlock in Shropshire organised a multi-sport Games in his village in 1850. The same year he formed an Olympic Class "to promote the moral, physical and intellectual improvement of the inhabitants of the town and neighbourhood of Wenlock." The Games became an annual event and in 1860 the "Class" was renamed the Wenlock Olympian Society. In 1861 Penny Brookes founded the Shropshire Olympian Society, and over the years petitioned Greece to revive the Olympics.

In 1890 Dr Brookes invited Baron de Coubertin to England and organised a Wenlock Olympian Games in his honour. The two men shared their ambitions for a revival of the Olympics in Athens and returning to France de Coubertin wrote, "If the Olympic Games that Modern Greece has not yet been able to revive still survives today, it is due, not to a Greek, but to Dr W P Brookes."

Still determined, in 1894 de Coubertin hosted an International Congress of Amateurs, again in France, by the end of which he had formed an "International Olympic Committee" with plans to hold an Olympic Games in Athens in 1896. At this same conference was another Frenchman, Michel Bréal, who inspired by the legend of Pheidippides, suggested a marathon race, to run from the town of Marathon to Athens. The Greeks took warmly to this idea, and the race was the final event of the Games finishing in the newly reconstructed marble Panathenaikon Stadium, a distance of around 40 kilometres (25 miles).

In the Ancient Olympics, which had come to an end 1500 years previously, the longest event run was in the stadium, at a distance of around 3 miles.

The 1896 Olympic Marathon was contested by thirteen Greek runners, an Australian, living in London, an American, a Frenchman and a Hungarian. The Greeks had not had a winner in all the preceding events and expectations and hopes were high. In the end, to the joy of the whole of Greece, the race was won by a Greek, Spiridon Louis in a time of 2:58:50. All of the foreigners dropped out except the Hungarian Kellner, who finished third. Ten runners finished the course, but one Greek was disqualified for completing part of the course in a carriage.

It is probable that the enthusiasm which followed the Marathon victory of Spiridon Louis, gave the momentum for the Games to continue in the 20th and 21st centuries.

Chapter 1

The First Manchester Marathon
Saturday 21st March 1908

THE NORTHERN MARATHON TRIAL

In view of Baron de Coubertin's initiating the resurrection of the Olympics it was only fitting that the 1900 Games should take place in Paris. The Marathon winner here was Michel Théato of Luxembourg in a time of 2:59:45 over a distance of 40.26 kilometres.

The 1904 Olympics were held in St. Louis (USA), the English-born Thomas Hicks, now representing USA, taking victory in 3:28:53 for the 40 kilometre race.

In 1906 an "Interim" Olympic Games was held back in Athens. The marathon course from Marathon to the Panathenaikon stadium had been lengthened from 40 to 40.96 kilometres, a Canadian William Sherring succeeding in 2:51:23.6.

Great Britain had the honour of staging the 1908 Olympics, which were held in July, the marathon being run on the 24th.

Rome had originally been awarded the 1908 Olympic Games, but the eruption of Mount Vesuvius in 1906 led to great economic difficulties, and the Italians had to withdraw. The same year Great Britain volunteered to organise the Games in London, and this was accepted.

The performance of British marathon runners in previous Olympics had been practically non-existent. We had no starters in Athens in 1896. In Paris in 1900, three of the 16 starters were Britons, but none finished. The team had been selected as a result of finishing first three in the 1899 London to Brighton race, the first running event on the famous Brighton road and more than twice the distance of the marathon. Britain sent no athletes to the 1904 Games in St. Louis, and in the 1906, Athens Games only one Briton, J N Cormack (Transvaal AA, London AC and Edinburgh H), started of the 52 runners, and he finished in 14th place out of 15 finishers.

The excitement of an upcoming Olympic Marathon on home soil spawned a series of "marathon" races, sometimes referred to as "trials," presumably organised to identify the best long-distance athletes to represent Great Britain and Ireland on Friday 24th July.

The first of these trials, over a distance of "20 miles" was held in Manchester on the 21st March, 1908; the first Manchester Marathon. Salford Harriers was at that time one of the top six athletic clubs in the country, with an excellent cross-country record. Club membership peaked at an all-time high in the 1908/09 season at 520. The minutes of their 1907 annual general meeting states, *"In view of the marathon race in the Olympic Games next year it was proposed that the committee consider the desirability of holding a twenty miles road race in the winter programme."* The proposal was carried.

There was no exact distance for the marathon at that time and 20 miles was considered to be an adequate test. A course was devised, starting and finishing at the Saracens Head public house in Heatley, Warburton, four miles west of Altrincham, South Manchester and measured from an Ordnance Survey map. The cost to the club of organising this Northern Trial was £26.

The Start of the Northern Marathon Trial 1908. No. 22 was Wyatt, runner-up and No. 7 Perkin, third. (Courtesy Salford Harriers.)

Notes from Salford Harriers' minutes book at the time record:

"With regard to the 20 miles Road Race the following resolutions were agreed upon viz:

'that the prizes be value 7 guineas, 4 guineas, 3 guineas, 2 guineas, 1 guinea & half a guinea to the first six in the race. An 18 ct gold, 9 ct gold and

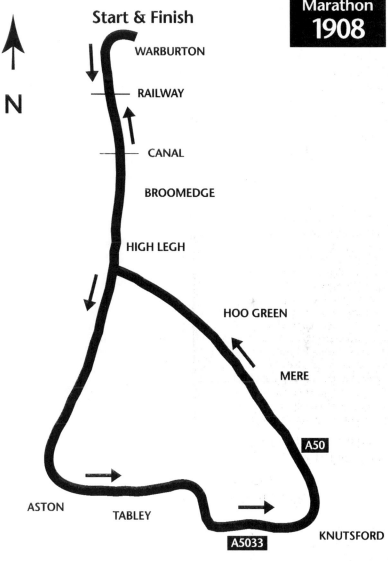

Start & Finish

WARBURTON

N

RAILWAY

CANAL

BROOMEDGE

HIGH LEGH

HOO GREEN

MERE

A50

ASTON

TABLEY

KNUTSFORD

A5033

0   1 Mile

Route map for 1908 Marathon. (Prepared by Tony Duffy)

gold centre medals to the first three Salford Harriers. And gold centre medals to the first novice of the Salford Harriers and the first novice of any other club,'

'that for the purpose of this race a novice shall be understood to mean one who has never won a first prize for running at any distance over a mile,'

'that the entry fee be 2/- each with the reduced fee of 1/- for members,'

'that a Hot Meat Tea at 2/- per head be arranged for, at which the prizes should be presented,'

'that the thanks of the club be accorded to the Oxo Company for supply of Oxo for Northern team, and also for prize of mounted Horses for winner of 20 miles Race.'"

We reproduce two accounts of the race, firstly from The Sporting Chronicle (Monday 23rd March 1908):

SALFORD HARRIERS' MARATHON RACE
VICTORY FOR F LORD

"The Salford Harriers Marathon trial, decided over the highways of Cheshire, proved a rare sporting event on Saturday. Out of an entry of 37 only seven failed to appear. The weather was beautiful, and the roads perfect. The pace set by the leaders was fast, and the field was soon broken up. At Tabley, 9^1/$_2$ miles, Duncan, Lord, Wyatt and Perkin led. The position was the same at Mere, 13^1/$_2$ miles. Just beyond, Duncan fell behind, leaving Lord and Wyatt together in front, with Perkin next, and Day forging ahead. With one mile to go, Lord made his effort, leaving Wyatt some ten yards. Lord won comfortably in 1 hr 50 min 23 sec. Wyatt was second, Perkin third, and Day fourth.

The surprise of the race, after his forward running, was the collapse of A Duncan, the English four mile champion, at Hoo Green, a distance of 14 miles having been covered. Much has been expected of the winner - F Lord - for he has been placed several years in the Northern Junior[1] Cross-Country Championship; and in fact he has shown his full powers. A Wyatt, who ran second, also occupied that position in this year's junior race to F Melville, a runner who was entered in this contest, but preferred to represent his club in the North-Eastern Counties C C Championship. From the times of the runners in this Marathon trial it would appear that the course was short. Fifteen men finished the distance, and many others preferred to arrive at the finishing point in one of the numerous motor cars which were lending assistance."

A more comprehensive report was given by *The Manchester Guardian* (Monday 23rd March 1908) and its account appears in full:

MARATHON RUNNERS -
SALFORD HARRIERS BIG RACE

"With its object of discovering candidates best able to represent the North in the great Marathon contest to be decided at the Olympic Games, the Salford Harriers offered valuable prizes for competition in a twenty miles road race open to all amateurs. The event was decided

[1] Junior Championships up to 1910 were not based on age, but were for Clubs which had not previously won medals.

at Warburton on Saturday. An admirable course was chosen with the start and finish at the Saracens Head Inn. The route lay past the old church and over the railway crossing at Heatley station. Thence through Broomedge, past the schools at High Legh (four miles), and on to the well at Aston (seven miles). Turning sharp to the left, the road was followed to Tabley and Knutsford (11^1/$_2$ miles), rounding by the Heath, and crossing the Chester highway at Mere corner (13^1/$_2$ miles). Going past the "Kilton" at Hoo Green, the outward course was again reached at High Legh Park (15 miles). There was an entry of 37 and only six failed to start. The most notable absentees were F Melville, of the Elswick Harriers, the winner of the Morpeth to Newcastle 14 miles race, and the holder of the Northern Junior Championship, and W H Whittingslow, the ten miles champion of the promoting club. The latter had met with an accident during training, and Melville had been called upon to represent his club in the North-eastern Counties Championship. Two of the most fancied runners were W H Day, the ex-Midland Counties 10 miles and cross-country champion, and A Duncan, the holder of the English, Scottish and Northern Counties four miles Championships. Neither, however, ran as expected, though up to the half distance Duncan did well.

A fast pace was set at the start, and when four miles was reached H S Perkin (Salford), F Lord (Wibsey), A Duncan (Salford), A Wyatt (Radcliffe), G W Crossley (Wibsey), J W Daniels (Rochdale) and D Fowden (Salford) were in close company. Then followed at various intervals J R Hall (Lancaster), H Cale (Birmingham), J R Johnson (Salford), W Swindells (Rochdale), E Cullen (Bury), W Mountey (Birmingham), J A McCracken (Moss Side), and W H Day (Birmingham), the rear now being brought up by three Salfordians, F Holt, W F Adshead and A Trippier. Another of the last named club's representatives, W C Wilde, retired early. Amongst the leading batch Fowden first began to feel the effects of the pace; then Daniels dropped in the rear, and he was followed by Crossley. At the end of seven miles Duncan, Lord, Wyatt and Perkin were running practically level, whilst Cale and Day, the two Midlanders, were placed tenth and eleventh.

When Knutsford Corner was reached Perkin was thirty yards in the rear of Duncan, Lord and Wyatt, Crossley, fourth, being 200 yards further behind. Then came Daniels, Hall, Day, McCracken, Rowbottom and Johnson. At this point H Mountey (Birmingham) and F Bridge gave up, and before another two miles had been covered W Mountey, Cale, Daniels, and E R Voigt[2] (Manchester AC) retired. The next feature of the race was Daniel's signals of distress, when 14 miles had been traversed. Meanwhile Lord and Wyatt were showing splendid form, running side by side until nearing the last mile. The Yorkshireman, then made his effort, and drawing away, won amidst cheers by 150 yards. The order of finish and times are as follows:-

1	F Lord	Wibsey Park	1:50:23	6	G Rowbottom Salford H	2:01:05	11	H C Dawson Salford H	2:21:17
2	A Wyatt Radcliffe H		1:50:46	7	J McCracken Moss Side	2:04:10	12	A Trippier Salford H	2:22:35
3	H S Perkin Salford H		1:57:43	8	W Brade Salford H	2:06:06	13	J Rose Castle H	2:26:10
4	W H Day Birchfield H		1:59:49	9	G W Crossley Wibsey Pk	2:15:38	14	J Shaw Salford H	2:31:35
5	A Duncan Salford H		2:01:05	10	A Johnson Salford H	2:16:37	15	C Oddy Rochdale H	2:37:10

The course, measured from the Ordnance Survey map, was said to be about 300 yards short of the required distance. Though the roads were in excellent going order, the times accomplished

[2] Voigt later won the Olympic 5 mile title in London.

7

suggest that the shortage was more than that stated. The world's record for 20 miles (1 hour 51 min. 54 sec.) was made by G Crossland (Salford H) at Stamford Bridge Grounds, London, in 1894. The prizes totalled £25 in value. The first was a silver cup value seven guineas. There were prizes for the next five to finish, with special medals to the first three members of the club. The medal to the first novice of the Salford Harriers was won by Rowbottom, and a similar medal went to the first novice of any other club went to Crossley. In more than one respect the race was noteworthy. It gave further proof of the advantage by Yorkshire long-distance runners at the present over others in the North and the marked abilities of junior runners. In the Northern Junior Cross-Country Championship, held at Haydock Park last month, Wyatt and Lord finished second and third, the former beating his Saturday's conqueror by 24 sec. After the race the prizes were presented by the President of the Salford Harriers, Mr E W Parry, who acted as starter and referee."

E W Parry was no mean athlete himself, having won the Northern Cross-Country Championships three times and the National Cross-Country title in 1888, 1889 and 1890.

Of the 37 who entered the Northern Trial, 30 started and 15 finished, eight of these from the host club Salford Harriers.

Shortly after the race the course was re-measured using a large scale map and was found to be exactly 19 miles. Thus Lord's time of 1:50:23 compared favourably with the World Record for 20 miles of 1:51:54 set on the track at Stamford Bridge, London in 1894 by George Crossland (Salford Harriers).

Fred Lord, Wibsey Park Harriers (Picture: Sporting Chronicle)

Frederick Thomas Lord, 29 years old, was born on 11th February 1879 in Cleckheaton, Yorkshire, and competed for Wibsey Park Harriers AC., Wibsey being a small village south of Bradford. In 1907 he had become Bradford and

District Cross-Country Champion, and in 1908 led Wibsey to silver team medals in the Northern "Junior" Cross-Country Championships at Haydock Park Racecourse finishing third (42:57) to F Melville, Elswick (42:27) and A Wyatt, Radcliffe Harriers (42:33). He was a stoker in a chemical works.

"Lord is a well built youth, tall and sinewy, without any superfluous flesh. He has a fine turn of speed and he has shown his staying powers and abilities by several times running very forward and being placed in the Northern Junior Cross-Country Championship," The Sporting Chronicle reported.

Alfred Wyatt was a member of Radcliffe Harriers. Radcliffe was a small village approximately half-way between Bolton and Bury. Little is known about Wyatt but *The Athletic News* reported of his second place in the Northern "Junior" Cross-Country Championships, *"Wyatt, for a youngster, ran splendidly and he had the satisfaction of winning the gold medal for the first home from an unplaced team, the winner excepted. ... ... Lord was a trifle outclassed for he finished 70 yards behind Wyatt."*

The third placed finisher H S Perkin of Salford Harriers, was their fifth man in the 1907 National Cross-Country team which came fifth. In 1908, he was third in his Club's ten mile track Championship in January. He was their first counter in the Northern (3rd) and National (32nd) Cross-Country Championship, the team finishing 7th overall in the latter. He does not appear to have taken part in any of the further marathon trials.

Fourth placer William H Day of Birchfield Harriers had some good form in cross-country finishing in the National Cross-Country Championships: 3rd in 1902, 7th in 1904, 9th in 1907, and in the International Cross-Country Championships: 7th in 1904 and 7th again in Scotstoun, Glasgow, 1907, the last member of England's winning team of six! His performance over the country was poorer prior to the Manchester Marathon Trial as he finished 14th in the National, qualifying as a reserve to run in the International where he finished 26th out of 49 runners.

Prior to the race he was *"a man much fancied,"* and had *"the set idea of the race being done in about two hours and running accordingly."*

Alexander Duncan, fifth place finisher, was born in Kendal, Cumbria on 24th February 1884, making him 24 years old on race day. He was described as *"a fine athlete of six foot."* His first club was Kendal Welcome Harriers, and he probably worked as plantsman in his father's market garden as when he joined Salford Harriers on 27th May 1906 he retained his address as Mintsfeet Nurseries, Kendal. We have no record of Duncan competing over the country, but he showed good form on the track. In 1907, on 13th April he finished second to International Cross-Country Champion, Adam Underwood

9

(Birchfield Harriers) in the Amateur Athletic Association (AAA) 10 mile Championship at Fallowfield, Manchester in a time of 54:06 to the winner's 54:03. Then at Headingley, Leeds on 25th May he took the Northern 4 miles title in a time of 20:01.2, and on 6th July returned to Fallowfield to take the AAA 4 mile Championship, recording 19:51.4.

Alexander Duncan, Salford Harriers

A week after the trial *The Sporting Chronicle* commented:

"that the greatest surprise of all was gleaned from inquiries from amongst the competitors, including the placed men, who declared they had done little, if any, special training, and never in their lives had they run twenty miles.

Can we win the Marathon?

Surprise must be occasioned when the fact is revealed that so far we have not found a winner of the Marathon race. In 1896 S Louis (Greece) won; M Théato (France) claimed the honour in 1900; Thomas J Hicks (America) was the hero of 1904, while the neighbouring country, Canada, was enabled to have a share in the importance by providing the winner - W J Sherring in 1906. We have always claimed the reputation of having the finest long-distance runners in the world, and having men who possess the greatest stamina. Circumstances have prevailed in the past owing to venue of race or inability of men to leave business, and explains much. This time these difficulties should not exist.

What is Required

If we enter into the fray with determination, and studiously prepare our men, we ought to prove without doubt that our past reputation has not been a false one. We have commenced early with trial races, and therein clubs are showing a practical interest, but that is only a small item. Between now and July is a long space of time, and enthusiasm may wane, if not properly encouraged in each individual. Steady training for a long period, starting at once, will be a sure means of getting fit. A hurried preparation will be useless for such an event. The idea of sports promoters providing races for these candidates is out of the question. The one method of keeping fit and training on will be by the practice of once-a-week long-distance runs. This will mean the sacrifice of a lot of other pleasures, and possibly withdrawal from races of short distance, but it will be the only way will shall find the best men to represent us in the greatest distance race in the world. The honour is a great one, and worth striving for."

A total of eight "trials" have been identified, three of these being "closed" races. The second trial, a week after Manchester, 28th March, was one of these "closed" trials and was open to members of Ranelagh Harriers, one of the oldest cross-country clubs in the country, only. Their headquarters was at Richmond Park, London, south of the river Thames.

The road race was over a distance of 20 miles and the course was described as a tough, three lap, figure of eight. All 13 starters finished and the results were:

1	F B Thompson	2:08:30.2
2	F Church	2:14:44.2
3	T C Davis	2:21:47

Frederick Bertie Thompson, aged 27, was an excellent walker but had decided to compete in the Olympics as a runner. Ranelagh Harriers Centenary History records: *"It was a brave venture to institute a members' race over this distance at a time when long-distance road running was in its infancy, but entries and standards were maintained up to 1914."* F B Thompson won the race again in 1909 in 2:10:17.

On 4th April a trial was held in Liverpool which was "only open to those who are members of clubs affiliated to the Liverpool and District Cross-Country Association and were first claim by 1st February 1908." The object of this race, over 18 miles from the Sefton Arms, Aintree to the Richmond Hotel, Zoo Park, Southport, via Ormskirk was *"to ascertain the speediest and best stayers among members of their clubs, and further to recommend to the Olympic Committee the most likely competitors of the Marathon contest next July."*

Twenty athletes of 23 starters completed the course with three finishing under 2 hours. Result:

1	W T Clarke	Sefton H	1:46:08
2	W H Herbert	Liverpool Boundary H	1:53:44
3	J Edge	Sefton H	1:54:18

The same day, 4th April, Blackheath Harriers ran a trial for its own club members over 24 miles 670 yards. The route from "The Green Man" went through Eltham, Sidcup and Foot's Cray to Dartford returning via Welling and Shooter's Hill. Each runner was accompanied by a cyclist. The first mile was covered in 5:46 with H B Knapp forcing the pace. Ten miles was covered in 1:01:15. A hailstorm lasted from 12 to 17 miles and "softened the roads which was a relief to the runners." E R Small was least affected by the rain and led, but had a bad time around Shooter's Hill around 23 miles. He lost the lead to Knapp, but recovered later to win by 22 secs taking exactly 8 minutes for the last mile. Of the 11 entrants seven started and five finished. The first three to finish were:

1	E R Small	2:51:02.2
2	H B Knapp	2:52:24.8
3	E V Norman	2:53:52.1

The winner and second placed man "had shown capital judgement."

A week later, 11th April, another club, Derby and County had a closed trial race over 22 miles 1380 yards. Result:

1	R Eglington	2:37:40
2	H Ellis	2:46:50
3	T Turner	2:52:35
4	E Barnes	3:02:40

It was reported that Barnes walked the last seven miles.

Soon after the Liverpool trial concern was expressed that officials were unable to say exactly how candidates would be selected for the Olympic Marathon on 24th July, and it was feared that the various marathon trials to date *"would go for nought."* It began to become obvious that the Polytechnic Harriers Trial on 25th April, an open race of just under 23 miles, would be the official trial.

With less than three weeks to go before this trial further concern was felt that entries to the "Poly" would close and that the Olympic "team would not be representative of all parts of the country." In the event the entry deadline was extended and the Northern Counties Athletic Association resolved to send four northern runners at the expense, if required, of the Association. The four chosen were:

Frank Melville - Northern "Junior" Cross-Country Champion

and Morpeth to Newcastle, 14 miles winner,

Fred Lord and A Wyatt - first and second in the Manchester "Marathon,"

W T Clarke - Northern Cross-Country Champion

and winner of the Liverpool "Marathon."

However, later newspaper reports reveal: "credit does not belong after all to the Northern Counties Athletic Association. That estimable body, it appears, could not find its way to pay any of the expenses of the competitors. The Association has no funds to draw upon for such a purpose."

Melville did not travel and many athletes including Lord, Wyatt and Clarke had to endure a second trial.

The Manchester Guardian report (Monday 27th April 1908) cannot be bettered in its thoroughness:

A MARATHON TRIAL RACE - SALFORD HARRIER'S SUCCESS

"Over the course that will be used later in the year for the great Marathon contest the official trial race was decided on Saturday. By permission of the King the start took place in Windsor Great Park, and the race was by way of High street past Eton College, through Slough, Uxbridge, Ickenham, Ruislip, Pinner, Harrow and Sudbury to Wembley Park, a total distance of 22 miles 1420 yards. The event was under the auspices of the Polytechnic Harriers and it proved a great success. The weather was unfavourable, rain falling heavily when the men were sent on their journey, and snow fell later. The entries numbered 82, and were representative of the best long-distance runners in the country. They were constituted as follows:- South 66 names, North 9, Midlands 5, and Scotland and Ireland one each. Their were 16 absentees. After going half a mile G Pearce, the Southern Cross-Country Champion, went to the front, and the rear was brought up by A R Edwards, Lancashire Walking Club. Five miles were covered in 27 mins 12 sec. when the following five Northerners were in close company at the head of the others:- F Lord (Wibsey Park AC), G W Colcroft and G C Rhodes (Bradford AC), A Duncan (Salford Harriers) and A Wyatt (Radcliffe Harriers). At the end of ten miles (55 min 19 sec) J G Beale (Polytechnic Harriers) was just ahead of Lord and Duncan. A dozen yards behind the trio came F Appleby (the holder of the 15 mile record), followed by Colcroft, A Williams (Kent AC) and A H Pearson (Cambridge University). Soon afterwards Wyatt complained of headache and retired from the race. Fifteen miles were reached in 1 hour 24 min 35 sec, Lord, Beale and Appleby being in close company. In the next three miles Beale had established a lead of 50 yards from Duncan, Lord and Appleby, and the latter, dropping in the rear, retired before the twentieth mile. In the last mile or so Duncan (four and ten miles AAA champion) drew level with the leader, and, making his effort, soon began to leave Beale. The Salford Harrier entered Wembley Park amidst loud cheering, and, finishing the last half mile on the track, won by about 400 yards. Forty-nine runners completed the distance."

The first 12 competitors finished as follows:

1	A Duncan	Salford H	2:15:45
2	J G Beale	Polytechnic H	2:17:00
3	F Lord	Wibsey Park AC	2:18:04
4	T Jack	Edinburgh S H	2:18:42

5	H F Barrett	Polytechnic H	2:18:46
6	F B Thompson	Ranelagh H	2:20:05
7	J J Burgess	Shaftesbury H	2:21:34
8	C S Silsby	Hampstead H	2:22:37
9	E Barnes	Derby and County H	2:26:15
10	G Pearce	Highgate H	2:27:40
11	G W Colcroft	Bradford AC	2:27:57
12	A E Wooller	Brighton & County	2:28:20.

Others of note include:

16	J B Powell	South London H	2:31:26
22	W T Clarke	Sefton H	2:33:30
24	R Eglington	Derby & County	2:35:02
36	E R Small	Blackheath H	2:45:32

On the 9th of May two weeks after the Polytechnic Harriers trial, Birchfield Harriers organised a Midland Counties trial over a distance of 25 miles. Twenty four runners contested this race and fourteen finished. The results:

1	J T Price	Small Heath H	2:37:13
2	W H Day	Birchfield H	2:54:30
3	J Edwards	Small Heath	2:56:45

A final open trial was held on 23rd May, organised by South London Harriers. Run over most of the "Poly" route and the same distance of 22 miles 1420 yards, but this time from Eton to Wembley, it was held with the "laudable idea of giving some of the runners who were beaten by the weather in the Polytechnic Trial a chance of showing what they could do under the weather conditions they could reasonably expect in July."

The result:

1	J B Powell	South London H	2:28:23
2	R S Bugg	Salford H	2:30:33
3	A E Wooller	Brighton and C	2:32:13

Powell ran three minutes faster than he had in the Polytechnic Trial, where he placed 16th, but it was not enough to impress members of the AAA Selection Committee who were present. "Ex-Champ" wrote in The Athletic News that the Selection Committee "could not have seen any likely candidate for a place on Great Britain's chosen dozen."

The Olympic team of twelve was announced on 10th June. Naturally the greatest importance had been placed on the Polytechnic Trial and the first six from this race were selected:

A Duncan	Salford H

J G Beale	Polytechnic H
F T Lord	Wibsey Park AC
T Jack	Edinburgh Southern H
H F Barrett	Polytechnic H
F B Thompson	Ranelagh H

For some unknown reason seventh and eighth placers Burgess and Silsby were not selected.

E Barnes	Derby and County AC

Ernest Barnes had finished ninth in the "Poly" trial and was picked even though he had only finished fourth in his club trial on 11th April.

W T Clarke	Sefton H

William Clarke had had a bad run in the "Poly" trial finishing a lowly 22nd and it is likely that an emphatic win in the Liverpool Marathon plus his 1908 form at cross-country, winning the Northern Counties and finishing fifth in the International, clinched his selection.

A Wyatt	Radcliffe H

Alfred Wyatt had dropped out of the "Poly" trial soon after 10 miles with a headache. Placing a close second to Lord in the Manchester Marathon must have secured his place in the Olympic team.

J T Price	Small Heath H

Jack Price did not feature in the "Poly" trial and his win in the Midlands trial two weeks later plus excellent cross-country form in the previous two years probably ensured his nomination.

F Appleby	Herne Hill H

Fred Appleby had been prominent in the "Poly" trial, a close-up fourth until he dropped out before the 20th mile. He declined to run in the Midlands trial and, although invited to run in the South London Harriers trial, was advised by his doctor not to run due to injury. What may have influenced the selectors was that in 1902 Appleby beat the great Alf Shrubb over 15 miles on the track to set a World Record of 1:20:04.4. This record stood until 31st August 1937 when the Finn Erkki Tamila set a new time of 1:19:48.5.

S Stevenson	Clydesdale H

We have no indication as to why Sam Stevenson was selected for the marathon event. He appeared in none of the marathon trials in England, but had some previous form at 4 miles and 10 miles on the track. He was also picked for the team in the Olympic 5 miles track race.

Twelve men were the maximum permitted in any sport and Great Britain and Ireland had their full complement for the marathon. Canada was the only other nation to field a full team.

Marathon Distance

The Olympic Marathon of 1908 is significant for one important reason. It established the exact distance of the marathon as we know it today: 26 miles 385 yards or 42 kilometres 195 metres. This came about by accident.

The race started in the grounds of Windsor Castle and proceeded via Slough, Uxbridge, Ruislip and Harrow to the White City stadium, Shepherd's Bush, London. Originally the start line was in the street outside Windsor Castle, but the Princess of Wales wanted her children to witness the occasion and the start was moved to the castle grounds near to a nursery window. Queen Alexandra would attend the Games on that day, sitting in the royal box, which was opposite the entrance where the marathon runners would emerge on to the track. It is probable that the distance aimed at by the organisers was 26 miles, but the 26 miles brought the athletes only to the entrance of the stadium and extra distance was needed to take the marathon runners to the finish in front of the royal box. That extra distance was found to be 385 yards and thus the official distance was established and has remained.

Preparation for the Race

Britain wanted her athletes to do well in this race, and it appears that funds were made available if any marathon runner wanted to undertake special preparation. Three runners we know took advantage of this. Alec Duncan, the Kendal man went to Brighton and Hove for three weeks with his trainer Bob Ramsden. He was Britain's favourite for the Olympic title.

Fred Lord left Wibsey to spend three weeks in London training for the big day where he put on five pounds in weight. The 29-year-old worked as a stoker in a chemical works and when asked if he could stand the heat, he replied, "If I can stand t' heat o' t' stoke hole, I can stand all t' heat o' t' sun."

The Radcliffe Harrier, Alf Wyatt went to Blackpool to prepare at the seaside.

The 1908 Olympic Marathon

The Times reported the conditions as a *"glorious hot July afternoon with hardly a breath of wind."* The temperature would reach almost 80° F (27° C), not good for a marathon race.

We will endeavour to narrate the race from the British point of view. Of our dozen runners, Sam Stevenson was a non-starter. He contested the Olympic 5 mile track race but ended up in the fastest heat, finishing third. With only two proceeding to the final, that was his Olympics over.

At just after 2:30 the starter's pistol fired and there was a mad dash by 55 athletes for the castle gates with W T Clarke first out. The opening mile was downhill, but even so the pace was fast with Thomas Jack passing the first mile in 5:01.4, with the last Briton, Thompson in around 20th position. The pace can only be described as suicidal as Jack passed 2 miles in 10:11.4 with Price, Duncan and Lord just behind. Our runners threw caution to the wind and totally ignored any thoughts of pacing the distance in pursuit of the leaders. Jack passed 3 miles in 15:42 with the sturdy little collier, Wyatt, Duncan, Lord and the Italian Pietri Dorando just behind. Four miles was reached in 21:15 and by now Jack was pulling away, leading Price and Duncan by 40 yards with Beale about a quarter of a mile behind. But the effort was beginning to tell and whereas Jack's 4th mile took 5:33, his 5th mile was 5:46.

At 5 miles Jack lead Lord, Price, Duncan and the South African Charles Hefferon, with Dorando at his heels. All had been sucked into this reckless pace, and suddenly Jack dropped to a walk, presumably to take some refreshment. It was at the 5 mile point that runners' helpers were allowed to join the race, each athlete being allowed two cyclists to provide sponging and drinks. Jack was quickly running again and, although in the second group for a while, was never in contention again and dropped out at the half-way point.

You can imagine the scene now with in addition to the 55 runners, up to 100 cyclists on the road making their way through huge crowds which lined the course on almost all of the route.

Fred Lord now took the lead along with Jack Price and at 6 miles they were over 20 seconds ahead of a group containing Dorando, Hefferon and William Clarke. In the 7th mile Alec Duncan, suffering from stitch, began to walk. He continued, but a report in the *Westmorland Gazette* states, and we estimate this to be at around the 11 mile point, "*At 4 o'clock Duncan dropped to a walk and, after a pause and a pull at a shoe, turned into a cottage. He was out within a minute, and began to walk uphill, his trainer sponging him. He walked without distress, with his head up, and shook his head to the renewed cheer. Price, the leader had passed 23 minutes earlier. Duncan was clearly among the stragglers. An omnibus passes and Duncan might almost as well have been in the omnibus.*"

Duncan walked on and finally dropped out at Ruislip after covering about half the distance. He told the *Westmorland Gazette* he had never built himself up on winning the race, simply because he knew it all depended on the weather. He added, "*It was the heat that killed me. If it had been a proper wet day the result would have been different. It was about 80 degrees when we set off and only those who took part in the race could have any idea of what we went through. I don't think I should be tempted to run another marathon in summer. I felt in fairly good trim when I started but when I had done about 8 miles I began to feel the effects of the heat.*" He also felt he would have done better if he had gone to the race straight from home rather than training in Brighton and Hove.

Price and Lord were really racing each other now and 7 miles was reached in 38:58. They were followed by Dorando, Hefferon and Tom Longboat, the Onondaga Indian representing Canada. At 9 miles Price and Lord were still together but shortly before 10 miles Price began to draw away. reaching that mark in 56:53 just 2 seconds ahead, with Hefferon and Dorando close behind. By 11 miles Price's lead had stretched to 29 seconds and Lord was in trouble being passed by Hefferon in the 12th mile.

At 12 miles, Price now held a lead of 41 seconds, ahead of Hefferon, Lord, Dorando, Longboat, Appleby, and Beale, but Barrett, Thompson, Barnes and Clarke were still racing. It is probable that Wyatt had retired before this point, and Barrett is not mentioned in any further race reports and most likely gave up somewhere between here and 20 miles.

At 13 miles, just before half-way, Price passed in 1:15:13, 38 seconds ahead of Hefferon with Lord a further 29 seconds behind. 14 miles went by in 1:22:03, but now Hefferon was only 7 seconds behind, and Lord fading fast was now 1 minute 10 seconds behind the South African.

Lord's helper was a famous athletics journalist of the time, Fred Hatton, who wrote for "*The Athletic News.*" Of Lord's condition just after 13 miles he wrote, "*Near Ruislip School he held out signals of distress. He wanted tea; he wanted something to quench his terrible thirst. That was procured, and with plenty of encouragement he set about his task once more.*"
Suddenly, whilst still in the lead Jack Price dropped out. Price "*stopped in the 15th mile, quite run out, and sat down, leaving Hefferon with the lead.*" Hatton says, "*(Price) was complaining of being done up. A sudden collapse, the terrific heat of the sun, an equally strong pace were all joining forces that betokened the early retirement of the Birmingham man; spent by his own folly and lack of forethought.*"

At 15 miles Hefferon went through in 1:28:22 with Lord exactly 2 minutes behind, and Dorando a further 6 seconds back with the Canadian Longboat fourth. Thompson, probably our 6th man here, was suffering from heat and an injured foot, and took no further part in the race.

Eventually, after having decided to retire, Lord recovered somewhat, Hatton reporting, "*He was induced to rise and try to walk. His back was bad; his feet were sore; but the pace he had helped to set and the effects of the sun's rays, which penetrated the white-veiled hat he wore, had done their deadly work. From a walk he tried to trot, but it seemed obvious he could never recover to take a leading place in the race. The man's own pluck, and the magnificent way the ladies on the wayside tried to encourage him and others to go on were one of the happy features of the day's toil.*"

Early in the 16th mile Lord faltered. Hatton writes, "*Without going much further, and whilst taking a gradient in an easy style, Lord whispered that he felt done. His gait altered, and there was all the evidence of a man cracking up. A mile further Lord staggered, and quickly dismounting from my cycle I just broke his fall as he tumbled into a bed of nettles by the roadside.*" Another report states: "*At about the half distance Lord collapsed into a bed of nettles with feet so skinned by leather shoes that they must have caused him agony. He had departed from the schedule Harry Andrews had planned for him and in trying to race Price ... ... had brought about his own downfall.*"

Thus in the 16th mile our first Manchester Marathon winner was out of the medal contention, but bravely continuing.

By 17 miles, Longboat had had enough and dropped to a walk, supposedly having downed a bottle of champagne carried by his handler. He walked and ran to 21 miles then quit the race.

Hefferon continued to build his lead, but there was a glimmer of hope for Britain as Fred Appleby had somehow got up to third place at the 18th and 19th mile points. Unfortunately, just after 19 miles he stopped and his race was over.

By 20 miles Hefferon had a massive lead of 3 minutes 30 seconds over Dorando, and it was still almost that at 21 miles with J J Hayes, USA, third. The surviving British contestants with 5 miles to go were Clarke 13th, Beale 14th, Barrett 15th and Lord 17th.

Hefferon's lead began to diminish rapidly, but even so it was still around 2 minutes at 24 miles. One hundred yards further on he slowed to a walk and at 25 miles had been passed by Dorando and not long after by the American, Hayes.

The Italian's efforts had taken their toll. Twenty yards from the doorway to the stadium he was reeling. On reaching the track he made a right turn instead of left and had to be directed in the opposite direction. Five times he fell onto the cinders and at least once was helped to his feet. Both Hayes and Hefferon had now come into the stadium. Finally, Dorando struggled through the tape, assisted by an official, in a time of 2:54:46.4. John Hayes finished in 2:55:18.4 followed by Hefferon 2:56:06.0 and another American, Joseph Forshaw 2:57:10.4.

The Americans protested that the Italian had received illegal help and Dorando was disqualified leaving Hayes with the gold medal. For Pietri Dorando's brave effort, the Queen presented him with a specially engraved trophy the next day. It read, "*For P Dorando, In Remembrance of the Marathon Race from Windsor to the Stadium, July 24 1908. From Queen Alexandra.*"

Twenty-eight men finished the race, one runner, Dorando being disqualified. Of the Britons W T Clarke finished "*comfortably*" in 12th position, 3:16:18.4; E Barnes ran in *"strongly,"* 13th in 3:17:30.8; F Lord *"slow but very sure"* recorded 3:19:08.8 for 15th place, and finally J G Beale. *The Manchester Guardian* reported, *"Then Beale tried to run in after Lord, but Goldsthorp, a sturdy smiling Canadian entering some way behind sprinted after him. Beale did not accept the challenge. He was beat at the post for 17th and so lost the cheer .... he did not seem to care."* Beale's 17th place was in a time of 3:20:14.

Of the British starters in the 1908 Olympic Marathon, many continued their athletic careers in some form or another. Starting with the finishers, the Sefton Harrier William T Clarke won a 25 mile race in Hastings, on 16th December, a truly winter "marathon," in a very respectable time of 2:37:16.8. He later turned professional and recorded his best marathon time of 2:51:55 finishing third in a track race at Salisbury on Wednesday 29th June 1910.

Ernest Barnes carried on running for his club, Derby and County where he was their vice-captain. On 20th March 1909, he competed in the International Cross-Country held on Derby Racecourse and although in 10th place did not count in England's scoring six.

The Yorkshireman Fred Lord, our first Manchester Marathon winner continued to run well. He was second in a 22$^1/_2$ mile race in Bristol on 31st October in 2:38:13. In 1909 his cross-country prowess gained him a place on the International team when he finished 7th, three places ahead of Barnes, and part of England's successful team. He ran a personal best of 2:44:43.0 in the 1909 Polytechnic Marathon, 9th May for second place. Three years later he was fifth in the Polytechnic Marathon, the third Briton, qualifying for his second Olympics in Stockholm where he clocked 3:01:39.2 for 21st place and the third place for Britain behind Harry Green, 14th in 2:52:11.4 and Arthur Townsend, 19th in 3:00:05.0. He was the only Briton to finish both the 1908 and 1912 Games.

Lord was the first Briton to finish the 1913 Polytechnic Marathon, fifth in 2:49:07.8. The Manchester Guardian reported that *"Lord got in front at Southall Town Hall, about 13 miles, and was soon beaten off."* Alex Alhgren, a Swede led four Scandinavians home winning in a new World Best of 2:36:06.6.

After the Great War he returned to compete with Wibsey and in 1921 won their 'Rowland Muff' Cup for the fastest in a sealed handicap.

Even in 1932 his feats were still celebrated in the Wibsey AC Club card.

An extract from the Wibsey Park members' Rule Book is shown:

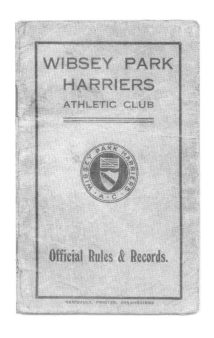

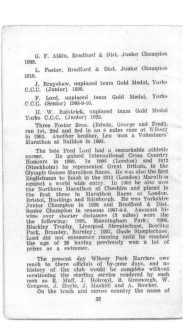

Wibsey Park Harriers Rule Book 1932 (Courtesy H Hardaker)

James G Beale, the Polytechnic Harrier continued running until 1912 at least. His marathon best was set in the Windsor to Stamford Bridge trial for the Olympic Games that year, finishing 8th in a time of 2:45:35.0, but the course was 360 yards short. Eight Britons were selected and he was one of the four who did not finish in Stockholm. His club-mate H F Barrett was another who did not complete the distance.

Thomas Jack, Edinburgh Southern Harriers became a headmaster in Scotland and was President of the Scottish AAA in 1912.

Jack Price, the Midlander from Small Heath Harriers, won the Bristol 22½ miler in October with 2:20:22.8 and was fifth in the 25 mile at Hastings in December, 2:40:33. Like Clarke and Appleby, he turned professional, after finishing 9th in the 1909 International Cross-Country Championships on Derby Racecourse, being England's last counter. In 1910 he ran a 2:40:07.5 marathon on the track at Powderhall, Edinburgh, winning on his pro debut.

Herne Hill Harrier Fred Appleby turned professional in 1909 and travelled to the USA to race three full marathons plus a 15 miler in the space of twenty-four days, after which he came home to resume his career as a dentist.

"Harry" Barrett, Polytechnic Harriers won the first Polytechnic Marathon over the full distance on 8th May 1909. The 28-year-old did not join the leaders until 20 mile and then drew up to Lord with 2 miles to go. His time was 2:42:31, and he finished 2 minutes 2 seconds ahead of Fred Lord. He died in December 1927 at Wandsworth.

Alec Duncan continued to pay his subscription to Salford Harriers until 1910. The outbreak of the First World War ended his running career. From nurseryman he became a policeman, working first in Kendal and then Stoke-on-Trent. After 30 years service he retired to tend his rock garden at The Mount, Hale, Lancaster passing away in 1959 at the age of 75.

F B "Bertie" Thompson continued to run in Club events for Ranelagh Harriers up to the Great War. After the Second World War he was President of both Ranelagh Harriers (1948-50) and London AC (1951). He died in Surrey in 1956 aged 76.

Alf Wyatt left Radcliffe Harriers and joined Bolton United Harriers and by 1910 his cross-country capabilities saw him being selected as an England reserve. He was still running cross-country in 1914.

Chapter 2

The Second Manchester Marathon
Sandbach to Fallowfield - 1st May 1909

NEW AMATEUR WORLD RECORD

The 1908 Olympic Marathon spawned a whole series of long-distance events, professional and amateur, both in Europe and across the Atlantic.

On the 10th of October that same year a professional marathon race was held over the London Olympic route promoted by the Evening News. The winner was 20-year-old J Henri Siret, a famous French pedestrian who paced himself well, taking the lead at 23 miles. Many newspapers noted that the winning time was far superior to that of the Olympic competition, but the weather had been much less trying than in July. Result:

1	J Henri Siret	France	2:37:23
2	Pat White	Ireland	2:40:15.4
3	J Keywood	Bromley	2:41:19.8

The prizes were rather disproportionate, with the winner taking £100, but second, third and fourth were £15, £10 and £5 respectively. The first "veteran" (over 40 years) was recognised and A Turner of West Ham won £10 having finished in a time of 3:02:38.4.

On Saturday 28th December 1908 *The Athletic News* announced,

A GREAT MARATHON EVENT

"Broughton have little to learn in sports promotion. For some years they have with growing success carried out open sports meetings. This year they intend to launch forth with something that will make them known in a much wider sphere than the North of England. With several objects in view, the main one, however, being the promotion and cultivation of long-distance running in England, they intend to open the summer season of athletics by holding a mammoth sports meeting at Fallowfield.

The means they are relying on for reaching fame is an open Marathon of twenty-six miles, which will start somewhere in Cheshire on a main road and finish on the track at Fallowfield. So far this has been kept somewhat of a secret, for they recognise such an event and such an afternoons programme will be costly. However, the secret is out, and so is the promise of financial support.

A trophy will be presented by a well-known person, but not connected with the borough of Salford.

To secure entrants of prominence is the next move and there is reason to believe this will not be a great task in view of the importance of the event and the tone that will generally be lent to the meeting. The date is important May 1st and coming as it does betwixt winter and summer, it should be an opportune time to hope for success."

But a week later and 4th January 1909, the same newspaper followed up with,

"Marathon race"

"Several communications are to hand in reply to the statement in this column last week regarding Broughton Harriers Marathon race, the date of which was given as May 1. The Broughton Harriers and AC Committee may or may not have known that the London Polytechnic Harriers had already fixed their marathon race on the Olympic course for the same date. If aware of that fact they may believe there is room for two such important races on the same day. I do not agree.

If aware then they will be wise in reconsidering the matter. This will answer my Wibsey Park friends. The interview I have had with one or two Broughton men, quite unofficially, gives me the opinion they may decide to adhere to the date of May 1, for, as they observed the Marathon Race is but part of a huge sports programme which will be in progress at Fallowfield simultaneously with the Road race."

In the end the "Poly" Marathon organisers moved their date a week later. Quite what the Wibsey Park members' comments about the Manchester date were we will never know, but in the end their best athlete, Fred Lord contested the "Poly" race.

The decision to move the date of the "Poly" gave Manchester the honour of hosting the very first amateur marathon race in Great Britain over the new official distance of 26 miles 385 yards, after the 1908 Olympic race, of course.

There was much interest leading up to the marathon which would start in Sandbach and finish at the Fallowfield Stadium in Manchester. On Good Friday, 9th April, a 15 mile race was promoted by "Chronicle" AC, running over the latter part of the marathon route, in fact from Chelford to Fallowfield.

Salford Harriers had a trial run over 12 miles of this course the week before, *The Manchester Guardian* reporting, *"W H Whittingslow (Northern 4 mile Champion) and G Rowbottom finished together with E Grantham next in order, the latter showing good form. H S Perkin had to ease up due to an injured toe. A Sucksmith and J A Johnson also ran."*

The Manchester Guardian described the 15 mile race thus:

"Soon after the start the leaders were J Murphy, F H Reay, F Melville, James Roberts, W H Whittingslow, and the two Coxons. The changes in the placings were unimportant until Handforth was reached. There Roberts, who had been content to allow others to make the pace, made his effort and with such good purpose that at Cheadle Asylum he had a lead of quite 50 yards. After that he gradually increased his advantage and won easily. J T Rimmer, who ran near tenth for over half the distance, made up a lot of ground towards the end and secured second."

The result of the race where there was a large attendance in the Fallowfield Stadium was:

1	J Roberts	Sefton H	1:24:00.4
2	J T Rimmer	Sefton H	1:25:22
3	F H Reay	Elswick	1:25:55
4	W H Whittingslow	Salford H	1:26:51
5	F Melville	Elswick	1:27:33
6	A Aldous	Hallamshire	1:28:40

Runners had travelled from afar as evidenced by the team results: 1 Sefton H 1, 2, 15 = 18; 2 Elswick 3, 5, 17 = 25; 3 Hallamshire H 6, 8, 13 = 27; 4 Sutton H 9, 12, 14 = 35; 5 Birchfield H 10, 11, 18 = 39; 6 Heaton 7, 20, 26 = 53; 7 Salford H 4, 23, 28 = 55; 8 Moss Side 21, 29, 34 = 84. "Crewe only finished one man 25th and North Manchester H only two - 30th and 33rd."

The prime award for what was described as the Great Northern Marathon on 1st May was a silver cup and a gold medal, and it was an international event thanks to the presence of Emile Bonheure of the Sporting Club de Vaugirard, Paris, France. Bonheure had finished second to Pietri Dorando in a "marathon" in Paris in 1905, but had dropped out of the "Interim" Olympic Games Marathon in Athens in 1906 when only 15 of the 52 starters finished.

The Paris "marathon" result was interesting. The story from *The Manchester Guardian* (18th October 1905) was:

MARATHON ROAD RACE

"The victorious Birchfield Harriers arrived in London from France last night brought with them the bronze statuette which formed the challenge trophy in Sunday's 18.75 mile amateur Marathon road race. Wigginton had been placed 2nd owing to an objection to the amateur status of the first man home, the Italian Pietri Dorando. H Hulford was 3rd, W H Day 8th and J Taylor 9th.

Seeing that the Birchfield men had not undergone any preparations for the distance run, their performances were distinctly good, especially those of Wigginton (2:02:35) and Hulford (2:04:10) for the 18.75 mile. Colley and Lewis were in prominent positions after going about 5 miles when they were knocked down by bicycles, of which there were many pacing the French competitors."

So Dorando had been disqualified from this 30 kilometre competition as a professional and yet appeared in the 1908 Olympics as an amateur.

Bonheure was a *"well-built athlete with a particularly graceful action."* He was one of the favourites along with James Roberts of Sefton, winner of the 15 mile road race earlier, plus the second placer in their race, John ("Jack") Thomas Rimmer, also of Sefton. Rimmer had some pedigree having won the 4,000 metre steeplechase in the 1900 Paris Olympics, and taking a gold medal in the 5,000 metre team race when he was in second place overall.

The Sporting Chronicle previewed the race,

"Today (1 May) we shall see the first Marathon race in the Manchester district. The Broughton Harriers and AC have left nothing to chance in their endeavour to make a good entry. The total makes up to 36, and amongst the names are some familiar to those who follow the pastime of distance running. W T Clarke is the most prominent and his club-mate is a worthy colleague. France sends a couple of men and although not known on this side of the Channel, Messrs. V Millerot and E Bonheure have sufficient form to support their nomination, as to hope they will make a brave show in the contest."

The headline in *The Athletic News* for the May 1st event was

MANCHESTER MARATHON
BROUGHTON HARRIERS AMBITIOUS MEETING

It was bleak, showery weather at the Fallowfield Stadium. The 28 competitors were taken by motor bus to the starting point "15 yards on the Sandbach side of Mr Merrill's Park House Farm, Congleton road, Sandbach." The official start time was 2:30pm. W T Clarke, the Sefton club-mate of Roberts and Rimmer, and Britain's first finisher in the previous year's Olympic arrived with the rest of the runners. However, the *Crewe Chronicle* reports *".. .. .. before taking the mark each competitor had to be certified as fit by Dr E Moir, the official medical officer, and Clarke, who was one of the favourites, did not succeed in this respect, and consequently did not turn out."*

The Manchester Guardian gives the fullest account of the race, in its 3rd May 1909 edition:

ATHLETICS
BROUGHTON HARRIERS SPORTS
FINE LONG-DISTANCE FEAT

"The first of two athletic gatherings of the season promoted by the Broughton Harriers and AC was decided on Saturday at Manchester Athletic Ground, Fallowfield. The programme was more than usually attractive, the chief event being a race over 26 miles 385 yards, starting at Sandbach and finishing on the track at the athletic enclosure. The entries totalled 720, of which 36 were down for the big race. In the latter all but nine went to the starting point, the principal absentee being W T Clarke, the first British competitor in the Olympic Marathon and V Millerot of the French international cross-country team.

The competition included the two ex-champion runners J Roberts and J T Rimmer (who were first and second in the 15 mile race on Good Friday) and E Bonheure, the French representative who came with a good reputation as a good stayer, having finished second to Dorando in the Paris Marathon four years ago. When a start was made 38 minutes after the advertised time A E Twist (Broughton H & AC) dashed to the front, with J Morris (Sutton) and A Wyatt (Whitefield) in close attendance. At Holmes Chapel (4$\frac{1}{2}$ miles) Bonheure, Wyatt, J Bolt (Chester) and Morris were at the head of the others of whom Roberts and Rimmer were next fifty yards behind. There was little alteration by the time Chelford (9$\frac{1}{2}$ miles) was reached, but Roberts then began to draw nearer to the leaders. Hereabouts a heavy hailstorm had to be faced, and before arriving at Alderley (14 miles) the Sefton man was in front, followed by Morris, Bonheure and Bolt. Afterwards the Frenchman took second place and at Cheadle (21 miles) was a minute in the rear, Morris being next, whilst J McCracken, the captain of Moss Side Harriers, had taken fourth place. When Didsbury (23 miles) was reached Roberts was quite half a mile ahead, and continuing to increase his advantage eventually won remarkably easily by nearly twelve and a half minutes, the order and times of the first eight being as follows: -

1 J Roberts..............(Sefton H)............................... 2:40:28.8
2 E Bonheure.........(S C Vaugirard)...................... 2:52:56
3 J McCracken........(Moss Side H)........................ 2:59:34.2
4 J Morris...............(Sutton)................................... 3:08:56
5 J Parsonage.........(Warrington)........................... 3:09:28
6 A Gardner...........(Lancaster Friends)................. 3:13:10
7 E Godfrey............(Sutton, Notts)....................... 3:14:09
8 E Grantham.........(Salford H)............................. 3:16:07.4

Roberts was cheered loudly at the finish of his fine performance, whilst Bonheure came in for an equal share of the applause. It is interesting to note that the time of Dorando Pietri (Italy), disqualified in the Olympic Marathon, was 2 hours 54 minutes 46.4 seconds and that of the winners time J J Hayes (USA) was 2 hours 55 minutes 18.4 seconds. Whilst the race was in progress the sports had been watched by 3,500 spectators."

James Roberts, Sefton Harriers, at Fallowfield, 1909.
(Picture: Manchester Courier.)

MANCHESTER

SALFORD

FALLOWFIELD   FINISH

1909
MANCHESTER
MARATHON

DIDSBURY

STOCKPORT

CHEADLE
HULME

WILMSLOW

ALDERLEY EDGE

KNUTSFORD

MACCLESFIELD

HOLMES CHAPEL

CONGLETON

N

SANDBACH
START

0   5   10
miles

Route map for 1909 Marathon (Prepared by Tony Duffy).

It seems that Bonheure put in a great effort and overtook Roberts at 19 miles, but in the end the Sefton Harrier pulled away to establish an enormous lead and set a new amateur record, a World Best, for the full marathon distance of 2:40:28.8.

Gynn and Martin in their book *"The Marathon Footrace"* states, *"It is very doubtful if this particular course had been measured correctly, although it was advertised as 26 miles."*

Based on the World Record track times, amateur or professional, at 20 miles (1:51:54) and 25 miles (2:33:42) it is obvious that athletes were capable of around 2:40 for the marathon, indeed Henri Siret had recorded 2:37:23 on the Olympic Windsor to White City course in a professional race on the 10th of October 1908.

In fact the Sandbach to Fallowfield race was advertised as "26 miles 385 yards" and the precise starting point "15 yards on the Sandbach side of Mr Merill's Park House Farm," plus the newspaper statement, "making the distance 26 miles 385 yards, the exact distance of the old time Marathon," suggest that the course had been carefully measured.

The intermediate distances at the various points described in the race report seem accurate, except for Chelford which in fact was 10½ not 9½ miles, and although we do not know the exact way for the end of the marathon in the Fallowfield area, measuring the route on the map gives us a distance of around 42 kilometres.

The course contained no real hills and on the day of the race one newspaper described "a gentle breeze, direction very variable between N and SW." If between 3:30 and 6:30 pm the breeze had been SW it would certainly have been in favour of the runners.

Based on this evidence we feel that the time of 2:40:28.8 was genuine and an amateur World Best for the distance.

The following weekend 67 athletes started the "Poly" Marathon. Ten miles was passed in 56:57, 15 miles in 1:28:04 and 20 miles in 1:58:57 where Fred Lord was leading but pressed by Harry Green of Sutton Harriers, (Surrey). Harry Barrett drew up to Lord and at the 24 mile point Lord faltered allowing Barrett to win. The Athletic News said of their finish, *"At 5:37 pm Barrett, who had stayed grandly, entered the enclosure amid magnificent enthusiasm of his fellow club members. After trotting twice round he finished up quite fresh the winner by 500 yards. Lord, who had arrived just before Barrett had completed his last lap, had obviously had enough of it and was 2 minutes 2 seconds to the bad."*

Results:

1	H F Barrett	Polytechnic H	2:42:31
2	F Lord	Wibsey Park	2:44:33
3	H Green	Sutton, Surrey	2:49:00.8

The Athletic News commented that *"I think few will disagree with me that his performance was quite as good as that of the Sefton Harrier (James Roberts), the week before."*

Marathons were not to return to Manchester for another fourteen years.

Chapter 3

The Third Manchester Marathon
Saturday 2nd June 1923

THE MARATHON RETURNS TO MANCHESTER

On Saturday 2nd June 1923 a festival of sport was organised at Fallowfield Stadium, Manchester. According to *The Sporting Chronicle* the objectives of this festival were threefold:
1 the propagation of the best form in athletes;
2 the staging of a carnival of instruction for Northern enthusiasts; and
3 aiding of a desperate club (Manchester Athletic Club).

A wide range of events in athletics and cycling were on the programme including scratch and handicap events. A young sprinter, Harold Abrahams was attracted to the event and was described as "a rare type of athlete ready to give his talents to the forthcoming festival at Fallowfield." Abrahams was Cambridge University President.

The Northern Marathon was the full distance of 26 miles 385 yards and would start and finish on the track. The following is a quote from *The Sporting Chronicle* 12th May:

An Ideal Marathon Course

"When measurements have been checked and any necessary changes made, I am convinced that an ideal marathon course will be found to result. The start will be on the Fallowfield track, with four laps of the track (1 mile) and the outward journey will be past the University Ground to Moseley road, and so on to Kingsway (the new arterial road which leads direct to Parr's Wood). This road has a very slight gradient and has a good surface which should be conducive to good running. From Parr's Wood the route is onto Cheadle Village and thence to Gatley. This stretch of road is also good, and the Police authorities have undertaken specially to assist in regard to traffic control at important points.

Continuing on a nice surface and being spared any abnormal gradients, runners proceed up through Sharston, Baguley, Timperley, where a turn to the left, probably at the Hare and Hounds, to strike the main road at Hale Barns and Ringway. Then, in order, to avoid a steep dip and stiff climb, a sharp turn to the left will be taken in making for Styal. Thus, the competitors will be well on the homeward journey.

There now arose the problem of Schools Hill, which is not always very healthy, but it has been felt that this could be avoided nicely by a slight detour through Moss Nook and Heald Green, and emerging onto the Stockport road at Gatley. From this point the return would be along the road as taken on the outward journey - Cheadle, Parr's Wood, Kingsway and Moseley Road to finish on the track."

The Sporting Chronicle also reported that there would be *"plenty of attendants on route to prevent any possible interference."*

The marathon route was *"designed to avoid all stiff gradients and to give a fast running surface while at the same time leaving behind at the first opportunity all stretches likely to bear considerable motor traffic."*

The Fallowfield Stadium was famous throughout the country and before the Great War had hosted:

The AAA Championships in 1897 and 1907;

The Football Association Cup Final in 1893,
> Wolverhampton Wanderers beat Everton 1-0;

The 1897 International Rugby Union Match,
> England beat Scotland 12-3; and

Two Northern Union (now Rugby League) Challenge Cup Finals.
> 1899 - Oldham beat Hunslet 19-9 and
> 1900 - Swinton beat Salford 16-8.

The runners were competing for a magnificent trophy. *The Sporting Chronicle reports that "the winner will receive a solid silver cup of the full value by the AAA and hold for one year the handsome 75 guinea trophy presented by Sir Edward Hulton, Bart. This cup, which is to be known as the Sporting Chronicle Marathon trophy, can be secured outright by two wins in succession or three in all."* The trophy was also described as *"a massive silver cup surmounted by the figure of Mercury"* and *"a handsome specimen of the silversmith's art."*

Sir Edward Hulton, Bart was the son of Neddy Hulton, a very successful newspaper publisher who began in the mid 19th century by publishing *The Sporting Chronicle* at Manchester's Withy Grove, today the home of 'The Printworks.'

The *Sporting Chronicle* race day report describes the favourites:

"The long run will start with one mile (four laps) on the track and finish with another span to complete the distance after the Cheshire roads have been negotiated.

Now of course, we are particularly interested in the respective merits of the 21 men who have entered for this classic event. I must confess I was surprised not a little at the entries of Walter Freeman and Bruce Hall. Exceedingly capable distance men. I did not know they had marathon ambitions, but knowing their great qualities I am prepared to see them put up big performances. E Leatherland, who runs in the colours of the Polytechnic club and will wear "No 11," however, proved by his success in the Brighton Marathon that he can get the distance at a good pace, and C J Bryant, of Preston and Bolton, got fourth in the Windsor Marathon two years ago and fifth last year. The South looks with confidence to Leatherland, but the Midlands and North have dour contenders.

The race is timed to start at 2:45, and any event not completed towards the end of the programme will be held suspended when the return of the leaders is signalled.

Special tramcars are being put on and intending spectators are asked to be in their places early so that the marathon men may be got away from the ground without delay."

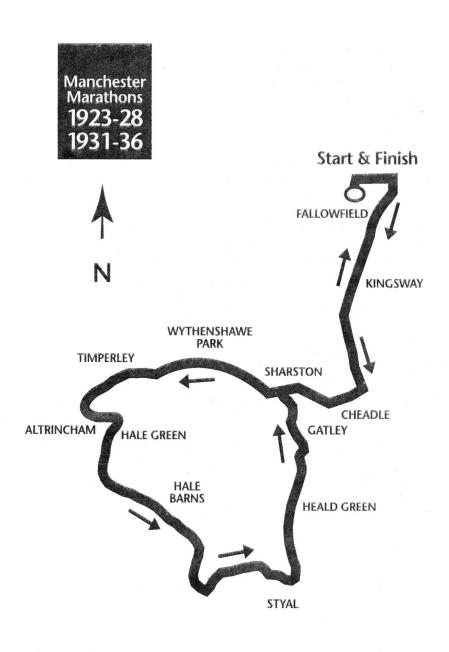

Route map for 1923-28 and 1931-36 Marathons. (Prepared by Tony Duffy)
[Note: the 1931 and 1932 races started and finished at Belle Vue.]

33

Birchfield's Freeman had been winner of both the National and International Cross-Country Championships in 1921. Bruce Hall, Salford Harriers' Club Captain, was the current Northern Counties A A 4 mile Champion and had been Salford's 10 mile club champion in 1920, 1921 and 1922, each time under 57 minutes. Ernie Leatherland's 1922 Brighton Marathon win had been in a time of 3:16:04. Chris Bryant's times in the Windsor "Poly" marathons had been 1921, 3:11:31.6 and in 1922, 2:59:22.4. This time for fifth place had been to Leatherland's fourth, 2:59:09. Another fancied runner was J E Wilson of Chesterfield C and AC who had been third in the 1921 Windsor ("Poly") Marathon in 3:07:27, one place in front of Bryant.

One newspaper reported "ideal cricketing weather," the maximum temperature that day being 65° F whereas another described the day as "sultry." We will leave the race description to the complete story in *The Sporting Chronicle,* not least for the quaintness of the reporting style.

Magnificent Running by Londoner

"Let us deal with the great Marathon race first.

The first time the full classic course has been undertaken here, [3] there was a splendid entry of 21, and the following faced the starter: - W Freeman (ex-International and ex-National Cross-Country Champion and National Business Houses Champion), Birchfield H; C J Bryant (fourth in the Windsor Marathon, 1921), Bolton UH; Bruce Hall (NCAA four miles champion), Salford H; F A Peace, Sparkhill H; A Farrimond, Leigh H; E Sykes, Broad Oak C and AC; H S Salt, Wallsend H; A G Wall, Derby and County C and AC; J E Wilson, (3rd in Windsor Marathon, 1921), Chesterfield C and AC; M Ward, Morley H, Leeds; E Leatherland, (Brighton Marathon winner, 1922), Polytechnic H; J F Kermode, Sefton H; E J Morris, Sutton H; R T Norton, Bolton UH; J Thompson, Bolton UH; R L Topping, Salford H; and W Gittins, Old Trafford.

All passed the medical test made by Dr E Moir, and they looked quite fit as they toed the mark. Bryant, it should be added, recently had been confined to bed with illness.

They had a rousing send-off from the great crowd, and they at once settled down to their own pre-arranged plans for getting the distance. First running four laps of the cinder track, Ward, Hall, Freeman and Wilson were inclined to force the pace. Leatherland lay handily, Bryant started at an easy gait, and Kermode, Norton and Thompson plodded along in company to whip up the pace on leaving the ground.

Taking to the fine arterial road, Kingsway, leading out to Parr's Wood, Ward was heading Hall and Freeman by about ten yards. Along the Wilmslow Road to Cheadle, and then turning right in the direction of Gatley, Ward still led, but near Cheadle Church, Ward was confused by the crowd and was inclined to take the wrong route. He was soon put right, and this was the only fault, but no real damage was done.

[3] This is not true. The 1909 Manchester Marathon was over the full "classic distance."

The First Check

At Cheadle Church, where the first official check was made, the times of the leaders were: - Freeman, 28 mins 15 secs; Hall, 28:16; Ward, 28:17; Leatherland, 28:50; Peace, 29:40; Farrimond 29:42; Morris, 29:56; Wall, 30:16; Topping, 30:25; Gittins, 31:10; Wilson, 31:26; Bryant, 31:50.

The fast-topped Stockport Road being struck for Sharston, Baguley and Timperley, some speed running was indulged in. At Sharston Hall, Freeman and Ward were running together well ahead of Leatherland, but near Baguley the last-named piled on the speed and joined the leading trio.

Just before going into Timperley, Hall showed some signs of distress, and fell away. Leatherland forged to the front, and entering Timperley Freeman dropped behind. Ward, too, appeared to be having trouble, but Farrimond was creeping up nicely.

At the 10 mile check Mr F Beresford, the official watch-holder, reported the following times:- Leatherland, 59 min 45 secs; Ward, 59:56; Freeman, 60:05; Hall, 60:53; Farrimond, 61:36; Morris, 63:30.

Freeman, it subsequently transpired, suffered foot trouble, he was wearing new shoes, and retired after covering about 12 miles.

At Timperley, as at many other parts on the route, there were large crowds of spectators and big bunches of cyclists. The Cheshire police helped greatly to keep the course clear, but quite forceful measures had to be adopted at times to prevent obstruction by cyclists, whose intentions - to provide the runners with company - no doubt were quite good.

Many Early Casualties

Turning along Green-lane and carrying on to the Wilmslow-Hale road Hale Barns and Ringway were passed, but of the 17 starters only nine remained in action at the half distance, the Chronicle car bringing up the rear being in much demand. The ambulance men and the Oxo attendants did excellent service.

The next check was on the road to Styal, after turning left at the Styal-Altrincham-Wilmslow signpost, the positions then being:- Leatherland, 1 hr 30 min 20 sec; Farrimond, 1:33:56; Ward, 1:34:05; Morris, 1:36:35; Hall, 1:43:50; Bryant, 1:45:15; and Salt and Wilson together at 1:47:30.

Bruce Hall retired on the stretch leading through Styal, but the positions of the others remained unchanged. At the next check, on the Stockport-road just before reaching Gatley again, Leatherland was timed at 2 hr 6 mins 59 secs.

The crowd on the ground was notified of the progress at the half-way stage, and also when the leaders struck Cheadle on the home journey.

Leatherland, at this point, was about 9 min. ahead of Farrimond, and both appeared quite strong, but Ward now began to show signs of leg strain, and along Ringway was compelled to progress at a walk.

The Concluding Stages

A great ovation was given Leatherland when he reappeared on the ground to run a portion of a lap and one to complete the finish. At the Gatley return check Ward was third, Morris fourth, Bryant fifth, Salt sixth and Wilson seventh.

Morris was now overhauled by Bryant and Wilson, and before reaching Fallowfield Salt retired. Leatherland and Farrimond finished the course quite strongly, but Ward frequently had to stop running to massage his right leg. Bryant looked well enough to cover another mile or so, and Wilson amused the spectators running sprightly to the dressing tent after finishing, but Morris had to call upon reserves of pluck to complete the distance.

Six finished, the times being:-

1 E Leatherland......(Polytechnic)........... 2:51:25
2 A Farrimond........(Leigh H)................ 3:05:45
3 M Ward...............(Morley H, Leeds)... 3:21:05
4 C J Bryant............(Bolton United)....... 3:21:55
5 J E Wilson...........(Chesterfield)..........3:30:45
6 E J Morris............(Sutton)................. 3:38:22

In addition to the first prize of the maximum value allowed by the AAA Leatherland now holds for one year the massive silver cup - the Sporting Chronicle Great Northern Marathon trophy - presented by Sir Edward Hulton; this can be secured outright by two successive wins or three in all.

Leatherland lives in the Nottinghamshire district. His business takes him a cycle ride of 50 miles per day, and it is a remarkable circumstance that he is still suffering from frost-bitten toes, a legacy of the war.

There had been some doubt as to whether he would be able to start, and his performance must be writ down as a magnificent one.

Farrimond is 29 years of age, and never previously had attempted such a distance, "his previous longest run being in a 12 miles trial with Bryant seven days before."

Other reports describe how Leatherland *"had a tremendous reception on entering the ground minutes after 5 o'clock,"* and *"Each of the runners was cheered in and Leatherland carried shoulder high at the end."*

Harold Abrahams did not have a perfect day. Winner of the long jump with 21 feet 7 inches he could only manage 3rd in the 100 yards sprint, the distance at which he was to strike Olympic Gold in Paris a year later.

Ernest Edward Leatherland was born at Bulwell, Basford, Nottinghamshire on 23rd June 1894. How he came to be a Polytechnic Harrier we do not know, but he later belonged to Mansfield Harriers, then Sutton-in-Ashfield Harriers. He served in the Great War as an officers' 'bat man' and suffered from frost-bitten toes. He convalesced first in Walsall, then Port Errol, a small village in Perthshire, Scotland. His occupation was a paper bag manufacturer in Hawsworth, Nottinghamshire, a job which took him on a cycle ride of 50 miles per day. Is this the first evidence of cross-training having an extremely beneficial effect?

Arthur Farrimond was born in Hindley, Wigan in 1893. He joined Leigh Harriers and became an excellent cross-country runner. In 1914 Leigh Harriers won the East Lancs Junior Cross-Country Championships with Arthur third overall. This race was a qualifier for the Northern Cross-Country Championships two weeks later where he was fourth and took a medal for first home of an unplaced club. Before the Great War Farrimond was a commercial traveller for a wine and spirit merchants.

The Daily Dispatch cartoonist, GITTS', view of the marathon race.

*Leatherland at Cheadle pursued by a posse of cyclists
(Picture: Daily Dispatch.)*

Leatherland with the Sporting Chronicle Trophy
(Picture: Daily Dispatch.)

When hostilities broke out, he enlisted with the Ninth Royal Scots (the "Dandy Ninth"). He saw active service on the Western Front, but eventually he was wounded twice, the second time through a bayonet charge. Immediately after the War he had recovered from his wounds and competed with success in athletic sports meetings and fell races.

In the early 1920s he was part of the successful Leigh Harriers Cross-Country team finishing 4th in the East Lancs Championships in 1921, 7th in 1922 and 3rd in 1923. After having won a few handicap miles, he moved up to the marathon distance in 1923.

The fourth man Charlton J Bryant also began his career as a cross-country runner, first with Preston Harriers, and was 22nd in the 1908 Northern 'Junior' Cross-Country Championships. He was the inaugural West Lancs Junior Cross-Country Championship in 1911, but the same year must have joined Bolton United Harriers as he travelled with them to Glasgow and was part of their successful team in a "marathon," actually a 16 mile road race. It was reported in the *Bolton Journal* that "the team trained under Mr J W Foster." J W Foster was a maker of running shoes of all types. His grandsons' Joe and Jeff were later to found the brand *"Reebok."*

After the Great War he resumed his running career. In the 1924 Northern Cross-Country Championships Bolton United Harriers won bronze medals and Bryant was their fourth man in 30th place. His staying-power did not go unnoticed because the Bolton newspaper, *"Cricket and Football Field"* said, *"he picked up ten places on the third lap and five on the last lap. Goodness knows what he would have finished if the race had been double the distance."*

We know nothing of third placed man, M Ward, Morley Harriers, Leeds. E J Morris of Sutton Harriers, we believe, hails from the Doncaster area of South Yorkshire since he ran in the 1930 *"Sheffield Independent"* Marathon under 'Sutton and Doncaster LNER,' the latter being the regional railway company.

On the third objective of the sports carnival, Manchester Athletic Club's History published in 1934 states, *"The net profit amounted to £309, and once more the club seemed to be again launched on the high road to sports promotion eminence."*

Chapter 4

The Fourth Manchester Marathon
Saturday 31st May 1924

NORTHERN OLYMPIC TRIAL

The first of the two Manchester Marathons in 1924 was held on 31st May, at a meeting named the "Four Club Carnival." This meeting was again underwritten by Sir Edward Hulton, Bart, but the clubs to benefit, in addition to Manchester Athletic Club, were Broughton Harriers and AC, Manchester Harriers and Salford Harriers.

This was to be one of the two trials to select a team for the Olympic Games in Paris. Two would be selected from the Manchester Marathon, the Northern Trial and four from the Polytechnic Marathon, or the Southern Trial. Both were on the same day.

To give Northern competitors an opportunity to familiarise themselves with the route, an 18 mile run was held over the last part of the marathon course three weeks before the big race. Such was the interest in running in those days that this run itself merited a full report in *The Sporting Chronicle*. This is the journalistic description with some interesting comments on footwear:

18 Mile Training Run before the Race
MARATHON TEST
Novice's Good Form
Derby and Leigh Runners' Experiences

"A E Swales, of Derby, is a novice so far as marathon running is concerned. When he ran some 18 miles in the marathon training spin to the MAC ground, Fallowfield on Saturday, it was the first time he had travelled over ten miles. He is small, but stockily built, and when he had completed the distance he assured me that he had enjoyed the outing, found the course quite comfortable, and escaped every possible disability except a blister on the tread of one foot.

The main body of the runners who participated in the outing, to the number of eleven, were conveyed in a Chronicle covered motor van to Baguley, where they started the long jaunt to the track.

Mr E Owen, who, of the NCAA standing, motored in front to show the way, took checks at various points. Swales ran with A Farrimond, of Leigh, who finished second in the marathon race won by E Leatherland, practically throughout the journey, and the two finished together. Farrimond, too is on the small side, but is rather more sturdily built, and, while Swales had a rather troublesome time in the reaction, the Leigh Harrier was quite merry and bright at a subsequent little repast in town.

To trace the run, however - Albert Hall of Rochdale was in front of Charlton J Bryant, of Bolton Harriers (the veteran marathon performer is 39 years of age); Farrimond and Swales; Joe Chappell (Broughton H), S Moseley, W Hand (Broughton H), H Burgess (Cheadle), C B Barlow (Broughton H), A Shaw (Broughton H), and J G Thornton (Rochdale) in the early stages.

A mile or two further on Bryant led Farrimond, Swales, Chappell and Moseley. Striking the Stockport-road at Gatley practically the same order was maintained, but hereabouts, Bryant not feeling too well dropped out.

Farrimond and Swales together, followed by Burgess, Hall and Hands, now started the long run in from Gatley, the other six having retired. The five named completed the spin, and all had a cheer as they finished, from the spectators assembled for the Lancashire County track championships. They had been cheered, too, by the onlookers assembled at various points on the route, and I believe everybody will agree that the outing was a big success in every way.

Where the Strain Came

Bruce Hall (Salford H, captain) and R L Topping started on foot from the athletic ground with a view to covering the full distance, but retired at Cheadle.

The weather remained favourable for the event, and every athlete who finished agreed that the roads were in excellent condition. Bryant, Farrimond, and Swales, in subsequent conversations, declared the slight rise at Styal the most testing piece, coming when more than half the course had been covered. One or two men had a tendency to cramp, but all to finish declared they felt well bodily.

Bruce Hall ran very upright, but the others inclined nicely forward, Burgess and Hands adopted a distinct roll, but both Farrimond and Swales ran with a kind of measured stride as though competing in a mere ten mile race. Bruce Hall told me afterwards that his legs felt the strain after twelve miles, but after a rub and a rest he said he felt ready almost for another outing.

Most of the runners wore socks and rubber pumps. The socks idea is an excellent one, but whether runners will be more suitable than heeled running pumps (with the spikes removed, of course) on a hot day is a decided question. Bruce Hall ran in ordinary running pumps (spikeless) without heels!

One now looks forward with enhanced interest to the last Saturday in this month, when the thirteen athletes named and others will compete in the great race over the full distance, for the Sporting Chronicle Marathon trophy and other awards. Performances in this race are to be given consideration when the British team for the Olympia Marathon is being selected. Saturday's training spin suggest that Mr T M Abraham, of Crewe, who has been deputed to watch the running, is going to have a very impressive report to make. Arthur Farrimond is going to make one of the finest of Marathon runners, if not so already, and a standard through him must command the greatest respect.

Intending competitors are urged to send along their entries, accompanied by a doctor's certificate as to fitness, at once, in order that details may be communicated to them in good time."

The morning of the marathon The Sporting Chronicle advised, *"The intending competitors are urged to report at the MAC pavilion at one o'clock for medical examination and final instructions. The race will be started at 2:15 prompt, and it is hoped that intending spectators will keep clear of the footpath leading to Moseley-road about this time."*

Heavy rains in the morning and early afternoon affected the gate, nevertheless almost 10,000 spectators attended the event. The Olympic Marathon Trial was the showpiece and the Daily Dispatch states, "Not only were those on the ground roused to a wild state of enthusiasm as the various men finished, but along the whole of the 26 mile 385 yards of the course intense interest was apparent." The route was the same as that in 1923.

The Sporting Chronicle report follows:

A THRILLING MARATHON
'Sporting Chronicle' Trophy Won
by Leatherland

"Saturday's Marathon race, over Lancashire and Cheshire roads, from and to the MAC Grounds, Fallowfield, for British Olympic favour and the Sporting Chronicle Marathon Challenge Trophy and other handsome prizes, provided as thrilling a spectacle as surely only such an event could do.

Since last year, when, with some thought directed to the Olympic Games of 1924, the first race of its kind was staged in the North, great interest, active and popular, in Marathon running has been developed. For Saturday's race the entries more than doubled those of last year, the athletes with some experience have been encouraged to train for the race, and new men, of distinct promise, have taken up the sport.

E E Leatherland, the paper bag manufacturer of Hawsworth, a village seven miles from Nottingham, last year came straight from a victory in a Southern Marathon to beat the next best by 14 mins. 20 secs. This time it was felt that he would have a sterner test.

That he actually was given a gruelling race of it he himself can testify, while the fact that the second man was only 3 mins. 35.8 secs. behind him, the third but 37.4 secs. further away, two others within a reasonable reach and six men inside three hours, is further testimony.

Representatives of the AAA Olympic Committee were to watch the races specially with a view to considering the team to be selected to represent Great Britain in the Olympic Marathon race next month. Had they taken advantage of the facilities offered to them they would have witnessed some magnificent running out in the country. Still, Mr A Fattorini noted the comparative freshness and good style of the leaders as they finished with a lap and a bit of the track, however. Also, Mr W Wilkinson, secretary of the NCAA, who followed the race throughout as official timekeeper, and exercised the closest possible observation of the men, can only present a very convincing report, I am sure.

Lines taken either through C J Bryant - sixth home - or the winner, indicate the really classy nature of the performance by all the prize-winners. Let us review the great contest from gun to tape.

Setting a Fast Pace

Of the 46 athletes whose names appeared on the programme, 40 lined up for the start. They were: - E E Leatherland, Polytechnic H; A Northcliffe, Slaithwaite UH & AC; A Farrimond, Leigh HAC; A E Swales, Derby C & AC; M Ward, Morley H; Bruce Hall, Salford H; R L Topping, Salford H; M Lopez, Buxton; J Chappell, Sale H; D Smith, Wibsey Park AC; H Battle, Salford H; J E Wilson, Chesterfield C & AC; M, Sutton H; S Mounsey, Manchester YMCA; H Wood, Makerfield H; R Edwards, Sutton HAC; T B Bowley, Nottingham H; J E Sharman, Sheffield; H G Minnett, York H; E Cox, Rochdale H; H Burgess, Cheadle; G K Carr, East Cheshire H; L T Davies, Sutton HAC; P S Needham, Sutton H & AC; G G Gough, Birchfield H; W Bennett, Sheffield UH; J G Thornton, J F Kermode, Sefton H; A Brown, Sheffield UH; J H Bolt, Wirral AC; C K Hissett, Sheffield UH; E J Morris, Sutton H; A Hall,

Rochdale H; E Sykes, Broad Oak C & AC; C J Bryant, Bolton UH; W Maleedy, St Helens Sacred Heart H; J C Birtles, Salford H; A Pownall, Wirral AC; and J Thompson, Bolton UH.

They were given a great send-off by crowd of spectators as they ran 3_ laps of the track and departed on their long trail.

Farrimond, Bowley, Brown, and Maleedy were the first to show in front, and the order of the leaders as Moseley-road was struck read: Farrimond, Maleedy, Wood, Swales, Sharman, Brown, Bryant, Bowley and Carr.

Turning into Kingsway Sharman raced in front of Farrimond, and started to force the pace. Maleedy, went after and passed him, and at Parr's Wood had set up a lead of 8 secs, Sharman being in front of Brown, with the youngster Wood lying fourth. Farrimond, keeping up an even gait, fifth and Swales next. Maleedy, running in rubbers, looked exceptionally well trained, though he ran rather heavily. Sharman was moving much more freely, and the styles of Swales and Farrimond impressed hereabouts.

At Cheadle Church, which was the first check, the men who eventually were to constitute the prize-winning six, were in the first ten, two minutes covering the lot of them. The pace had been a little slower than last year, when W Freeman led in 28 min 15 sec and Leatherland was 1 min 56 sec behind his own time. They made up for it later. The times of the first dozen here were:- Maleedy, 28 min 45 sec; Sharman, 30 min 11 sec; Brown, 30 min 20 sec; Wood, 30 min 20 sec; Swales, 30 min 31 sec; Farrimond, 30 min 31 sec; Edwards, 30 min 31 sec; Leatherland, 30 min 45 sec; Bruce Hall, 30 min 45 sec; Bryant, 30 min 45 sec; Hissett, 30 min 55 sec; Bowley, 31 min.

How the Race Developed

Passing the Royal Oak, Timperley, Maleedy was holding his own with Sharman, but Bryant, Leatherland, and Bruce Hall had moved up. The last-named was running very smoothly, and appeared to be timed to a useful schedule. I thought him of great promise hereabouts. Brown and Wood now fell away a little, Swales, Farrimond, and Edwards passing them.

At the second official check - Ellisland, Timperley:- Maleedy was two and a half minutes ahead of Leatherland's time of last year, the latter being fifteen seconds slower and ten seconds behind Bryant, who seemed inclined to go after the leader. The first two dozen now were:- Maleedy, 57 min 15 sec, 1; Bryant 59 min 50 sec, 2; Leatherland, 60 min, 3; Sharman, 60 min 15 sec, 4; Farrimond, 60 min 27 sec, 5; Northcliffe, 60 min 42 sec, 6; Edwards, 60 min 50 sec, 7; Swales, 60 min 58 sec, 8; Wood, 9; Brown, 10; Chappell, 11; Carr, 12; Hall, 13; Bolt, 14; Bennett, 15; Hissett, 16; Wilson, 17; E J Morris, 18; M Morris, 19; Bowley, 20; Wall, 21; Mounsey, 22; Smith, 23, and Pownall, 24.

From this point quite a thrilling race developed. Maleedy seemed to find the incline leading to Hale road a very testy proposition, but he turned in the direction of Hale Barns and Ringway holding a lead of 2 min 10 sec over Leatherland, with Bryant ten yards behind the Polytechnic Harrier, and Sharman some 150 yards further away, inclined to move in snatches. Maleedy signalled that he was feeling all right, and his action changed very little; but at the next check, on the road to Styal, just beyond the "Styal-Altrincham-Wilmslow" sign post, he was coming back to Leatherland very fast.

The official positions here were:- 1, Maleedy, 1 hr 27 min 20 sec; 2, Leatherland, 1 hr 28 min 23 sec; 3, Bryant, 1 hr 28 min 26 sec; 4, Sharman, 1 hr 29 min 53 sec; 5, Farrimond, 1 hr 30 min 55sec; 6, Northcliffe, 1 hr 30 min 55 sec; 7, Wood; 8, Edwards; 9, Chappell; 10, B Hall; 11, M Morris; 12, Bennett; 13, Wilson; 14, Smith; 15, Hissett; 16, Carr; 17, Needham; 18, Wall; 19, Burgess; 20, Pownall; 21, A Hall; 22, Minnett; 23, Mounsey; 24, Ward; 25, Lopez.

A Series of Challenges

Bryant very soon after this actually called upon Leatherland for another effort and went past him. A desperate struggle ensued, and the two of them overhauled Maleedy up the incline leading into Styal. Bryant, 39 years of age, had not the resources of Leatherland, however, and the latter went out to force the pace. All the leaders were well inside last year's times at this stage.

Leatherland, swinging his arms freely, put in a lot of running through Moss Nook and Heald Green; occasionally taking a glance over his shoulder to see how Bryant was progressing.

Eighteen out of the 40 starters were registered at the next official check - the "Northenden - Cheadle" finger post on the Stockport road above Gatley - and it will be noted that all of these finished. They were:- 1, Leatherland, 2 hr 4 min 54 sec; 2, Farrimond, 2 hr 9 min 7 sec; 3, Maleedy, 2 hr 7 min 36 sec; 4, Sharman, 2 hr 7 min 42 sec; 5, Bryant, 2 hr 6 min 46 sec; 6, Wood; 7, B Hall; 8, Chappell; 9, Wilson; 10, Smith; 11, Bennett; 12, Needham; 13, Carr; 14, Edwards; 15, Wall; 16, Hissett; 17, Mounsey; 18, A Hall.

Leatherland really won the race on this stretch from just before Styal, and it will be noted, that by comparing the times with the finish, that Farrimond ran the concluding six miles or so at a much faster speed than the Polytechnic Harrier.

On the stretch from Gatley to Cheadle Sharman passed Maleedy and Bryant, and went after Leatherland, gradually gaining along Kingsway. Farrimond now came along very fast, and there was every prospect of a great finish. Sharman, however, had a mishap just before turning into Moseley road for the Athletic Grounds, and was passed by Maleedy, who, however, could not hold Farrimond.

The Leigh Harrier, indeed, never altered his one pace, and if he could have speeded up between 15 and 20 miles might have had an even greater say in the matter than he did.

Leatherland had a tremendous reception as he entered the ground to complete his task with a lap and a portion on the cinder track. He never altered his action, and he was quite comfortable at the finish. He looked a happy young man as Mr E W Parry placed the laurel wreath over his shoulders, and I communicated to him the warmest congratulations of all who had witnessed his performance. Representing the Sporting Chronicle and deputed by the Editor, I had the privilege of handing him the Sporting Chronicle challenge trophy, which he made his own by two successive victories. But he would value most of all, I know, the greeting given to him by his wife and which called forth another demonstration of acclaim from the crowd.

Farrimond finished wonderfully fresh, and he, too, had a tremendous reception. After last year and this, he knows now that he can get the distance very soundly, and he tells me he is going to try and develop his speed a little more during the next week or so. Harry Clarke, of Leigh has undertaken to help him, and other athletes who are ready to lend assistance on the Leigh track are invited to get in touch with Clarke. The performances by Maleedy and Sharman, too were exceptionally sound, and the next time they are likely to do even better after their experiences. Bryant's show also was a pleasure; Wood is young, and has years to develop; whilst Bruce Hall must have been still further forward had he not felt it necessary to change his footgear during the race.

Eighteen starters finished some of them with a lively sprint and one of them minus his pumps, which he had discarded just before reaching the track. All had a cheer from the spectators - and deserved it.

THE ORDER OF MERIT

The order of finish was as follows:-

1 E Leatherland......(Poly H)................. 2:48:43.8
2 A Farrimond........(Leigh H)................. 2:52:19.6
3 W Maleedy..........(Sacred Heart)......... 2:52:57
4 J E Sharman........(Sheffield)................ 2:53:52.2
5 C J Bryant............(Bolton U H)........... 2:55:56.6

6 H Wood..............(Makerfield H).........2:59:59.2

7, Bruce Hall; 8 G K Carr, East Cheshire H; 9 W Bennett, Sheffield UH; 10, D Smith, Wibsey Park AC; 11, J Chappell, Sale H; 12, J E Wilson, Chesterfield C & AC; 13, P S Needham, Sutton H & AC; 14, C K Hissett, Sheffield UH; 15, A G Wall, Derby County C & AC; 16, R Edwards, Sutton H & AC; 17, S Mounsey, Manchester YMCA; 18, A Hall, Rochdale H.

Mrs Leatherland gave me a few details of her husband's career. It is only two years ago that he first found that he could race the marathon distance. In pursuit of his business he pushes a cycle very many miles a day, but gets a run in when he can. He has found plain, wholesome food to agree best with him, and during late weeks has found benefit from a drop of sherry. She added that when returning the cup a week or so ago he wrote to the sports secretary asking him "to take care of the box as he would need it to take the cup back with him." He had travelled up by train, but a party of them were returning to Hawsworth by motor 'bus.

Now then for a word as to the arrangements. I can testify to the thoroughness with which Mr J Foster as chief marshal, Mr George Hitchins as chief steward, Stockport harriers as stewards on the course, and Mr W Wilkinson as official checker, carried out their duties. Two Sporting Chronicle vehicles and several motor cars were placed at the disposal and my responsibility for making all arrangements was made very easy indeed by the readiness of all to help. The carnival secretary, Mr T E Wilkinson, did his share well, and the police and spectators along the route were helpful.

Be it added rain made the roads cool to the feet, but the atmosphere was damp and hot, though the weather conditions also favoured the event."

Thus Leatherland and Farrimond were selected for the Olympics, with Maleedy desperately unlucky less than 40 seconds behind Farrimond.

The results of the "Poly" trial were:

1	D McL Wright	Shettleston H	2:53:17.4
2	S Ferris	RAF, Uxbridge	2:54:03
3	A R Mills	Polytechnic H	3:02:46.6
4	R Morton	Surrey AC	3:04:31.2
5	G H Mumford	Brighton & County H	3:05:20
6	M J Morgan	Metrogas AC	3:07:42

Wright, Ferris and Mills were selected as of right. Jack McKenna (Small Heath H) collapsed at 25 miles whilst in third position. He had run such a good race up to that point that he along with the first three joined Leatherland and Farrimond in Paris.

The six Britons joined 52 others from 19 nations for the marathon race from the Paris stadium by the Seine on a warm, breezy day, the last day of the athletics. We reproduce the excellent account from the 19th July 1924 edition of *Cricket and Football Journal,* a national sports paper printed in Bolton, relating how our men progressed.

The Daily Dispatch cartoonist, GITTS impressions of the 1924 Northern Olympic marathon trial.

How Farrimond Fared in The Olympic Marathon

"Arthur Farrimond, of Leigh, was a very unfortunate young man at Colombes. I had considered him one of Great Britain's most promising entrants for the Olympic Marathon, and I had observed the wind up of his training with great interest and hope.

He had made many friends among the other aspirants, and had been out over the course with the South African, Phillips, and others. He had made himself well acquainted with the roads and gradients, and had got in some practice, both on the route and on the training track alongside the Stadium.

When I saw him on the morning of the race he looked well enough, and I fully expected him to put up a very good account of himself as the only real Northerner in the race.

He was dogged by ill-luck, however, for a drunken spectator, in one of the villages along the route persisted in running alongside him and bumping into him, and in contending with this man and eventually knocking him down, Farrimond suffered a twist which, although slight, was sufficient to slow him down and prevent him from speeding up just at the critical stage of the race.

Farrimond had been taking his pace from Leatherland, the winner of the Northern Marathon, but after this mishap he could not get travelling freely again.

He did persevere to the end of a gruelling race, however, and actually proved the second Britisher to finish, running quite strongly over the concluding half lap of the Stadium track.

He appeared to be as fresh as anyone over the last kilometre, and in the dressing room afterwards was soon knocking about as though he had only been for a quiet stroll.

STORY OF THE RACE

I had a good view of the race throughout and so am able to give a somewhat detailed account of the running by the British representatives.

The first three or four kilometres of the road were very rough surfaced and dusty and in addition were a steady climb.

At about four kilometres out Farrimond was running 12th, 4 places behind J McKenna, one of the surprise Southern representatives. Leatherland, moving nicely, was behind a group which included McLeod Wright, the Scotsman who won the Polytechnic Marathon, while S. Ferris and Mills were in close attendance. Little divided the British contingent here, but I thought they might have done better to have packed up together in the very early stages.

At 8 kilometres Farrimond had gone out to 22nd position, running with J McKenna,, whereas Mills had gone forward to 17th position, Leatherland being 34th, Wright 35th and Ferris 41st.

Every Britisher looked quite comfortable here and, while hopeful that they would show up more prominently in the later stages, I considered they might with advantage have moved up a little nearer the pace-makers.

The actual winner of the race, Albin O Stenroos, the Finn, as a matter of fact was running in 11th place here and taking all the pace that a group of competitors could give him.

There was a very testy incline hereabouts and some took it better than Farrimond who was some 40 yards behind Mills now and apparently running stronger.

The Britishers were grouping better now and, though appearing well down the list on the checking sheet, were very little behind the actual leader Alexandros Kranis (Greece) or Stenroos on time calculations.

WHERE WINNER MADE HIS EFFORT

Nearing the half-way stage, the first Britisher would be about 200 yards behind Stenroos, who now had started in earnest pursuit of the leader, now Georges Verger of France. McLeod

Wright, now was 11th, while McKenna was 15th, Mills 16th, Leatherland and Farrimond running together just behind, and Ferris moving up nicely.

It was on the stretch comprising the actual turn that the race was won and lost for, whereas the Britishers preferred to maintain a nice, regular gait, Stenroos now put in some very fast running and actually went into a quarter mile lead inside three miles! It was an extra-ordinary performance and Stenroos's tactics were very much on a line with those adopted by Leatherland when twice winning the Northern Marathon.

Wright now was ninth, Mills 15th, McKenna 16th, Leatherland 20th, Farrimond 25th and Ferris 27th. This was at 23 kilometres.

It is interesting here to note that Ferris eventually finished 5th and Farrimond 17th.

At 27 kilometres, Wright began to flatter exceedingly being fifth, only some three minutes behind the leader, Stenroos, the winning Finn, the next Britisher being Leatherland another three minutes away.

Very soon afterwards, however, he fell to pieces and retired, Mills also giving up the struggle. McKenna too disappeared somewhere about here and, as a matter of fact did not again reach the dressing rooms until a very late hour.

Round about 35 kilometres, Ferris, Farrimond and Leatherland were still moving soundly, however, the first-named having improved his position to ninth.

BRITISHERS GOOD FINISH

Farrimond now was beginning to overcome the shaking he had had, and over the concluding seven kilometres he began to pick up places rapidly. So did Ferris, who was moving forward very fast.

With four kilometres to go Ferris had become sixth and Farrimond 20th and, although Leatherland, in endeavouring to race down one of the inclines, developed cramp and been forced to stop. I got back to the Stadium to await the finish full of hope.

Ferris eventually came romping in fifth, smiling all over his face and obviously having plenty of running left in him. Farrimond improved his position, too, and, considering his mishap, he did very well to finish in 17th position - there were 58 entrants.

Farrimond who had maintained quite a short stride throughout had quite a cheer to himself as he sprinted the concluding half lap and then finished with a run across the field to the dressing rooms.

I saw him half an hour later with Ferris, both looking fit and well, and his only expression of regret was that he had been involved in that mix-up with a spectator. I believe, like him, that it imposed a big handicap on him, and that his actual performance in finishing so comparatively well forward was all the more meritorious."

Thirty finished, an attrition rate of 51.7%.

R S E in *The Sporting Chronicle* concluded his **"Marathon Reflections"**:

"D McL Wright, the Southern winner, J McKenna and A R Mills were very disappointed young men and it is a thousand pities that the Northerner Maleedy was not preferred, but they will have an opportunity on August 16 to prove that their running was all wrong.

I gave a detailed account of the running in Tuesday's *Sporting Chronicle*, but there are one or two points that I would like to add. A fairly upright carriage, with the arms nicely bent and carried with a nice easy swing half across the body, and the Finn roll on the feet, seemed to be the most effective mode of progression. Thick rubber-soled shoes were the best footgear for Sunday's race, while a linen head-dress helped keep off the full effects of the sun far better than brimmed hats.

Sponges were found very useful indeed by those who carried them, and another useful idea was the use of waterproof pouches.

Very often it is the little things that count in the long run."

Arthur Farrimond, Leigh Harriers,
in his 1924 Olympic kit.

Chapter 5

The Fifth Manchester Marathon
Saturday 16th August 1924

"AIRMAN'S MISFORTUNE"

The venue for the second of the 1924 Manchester Marathons was Fallowfield again and the occasion a second *"Sporting Chronicle* Four Clubs Carnival,"* which welcomed many of our Olympic competitors, and which had been planned early in the year.

As Ernie Leatherland had won the cup outright in May, a new trophy, a "handsome 75 guinea bowl - *The Sporting Chronicle* Marathon Challenge Trophy" was presented by the directors of Allied Newspapers Limited.

Thirty-three men had entered and *The Athletic News* summed up the contenders in the race, *".......... at least half a dozen men with somewhat equal hope of winning. The favourite was undoubtedly S Ferris, RAF, the first Britisher home in the last Olympic Marathon. There are others like E E Leatherland, who had covered the course twice to win The Sporting Chronicle trophy outright. There was a man like W Maleedy, Sacred Heart Harriers, who was suffering a grievance because he had not been selected to run for Great Britain in Paris."* Not mentioned was Arthur Farrimond, our second finisher in Paris.

The weather for the race was described as, *"Very trying .... heavy and frequent rainstorms fell throughout the afternoon,"* and the course the familiar one over the roads of Cheshire.

The race did not proceed smoothly and *The Sporting Chronicle* gives the best account of what happened.

A TESTY MARATHON
Handsome trophy goes to Scotland

"Immediately afterwards followed the marathon race, to which we had all been looking forward so eagerly. Now, in seeking fairly to record the happenings in this event, a preliminary statement is necessary.

For the previous two marathons which had been held the task of acting as pointsmen along the route had been undertaken almost entirely by Stockport Harriers. This time their services were not available, and the four clubs concerned were asked to supply three men each to assist the chief steward, Mr H Harland. Manchester H supplied their full complement and Salford H one.

With only four men available at a late hour, it was decided they should be placed at the most exacting turnings, and the chief steward was taken round the whole course on the motor vehicle which he would use during the race; later another steward was posted. In addition there would be other cars on the route with the runners, so that provision was made for checking to

50

be made by the official timekeeper at 5, 10, 15 and 20 miles, and checks by the four men at six other points along the road. I have before me the whole of the cards made out at these checks, and I have heard the story of the race from the pointsmen and other officials.

At Styal village S Ferris, (the first Britisher home in the Olympic race) was directed to the right instead of left, and before he could regain the right direction, D McL Wright (Polytechnic Marathon winner) and W Maleedy (Sacred Heart H) had passed along the right route.

Then at a turning towards Gatley, just before reaching Stockport road, where a right turn towards Gatley was to be made, it is contended that Wright and Maleedy went along a shorter and incorrect route, whereas Ferris and others were directed along the correct and longer road.

The check card of the pointsman appointed for this turning has crosses against the numbers of Wright and Maleedy, and his marking then shows E E Leatherland and Ferris third and fourth respectively. Wright and Maleedy eventually were adjudged to have finished first and second respectively, and, an objection later being lodged, the checking cards were referred to on the arrival of the checkers.

The checker concerned explained the meaning of the special marks. He explained that when he went to his checking point he was informed that numbers 5 and 3 had taken the wrong turn, and so he put them on his card in order to report the fact, then proceeding to record the numbers in order of the other runners. Numbers 5 and 3, he added, had not passed him.

Long consideration was given to the matter by the judges who finally held that as the checker had not happened to be at the troublesome point the moment Wright and Maleedy passed, the two men should not be made to suffer, and the placings at the finishing post must stand.

Ferris was a very unfortunate young man indeed.

The Race by Stages

Owing to the late completion of the championship walk there was some delay in starting the race. Twenty-one men paraded and when they had covered three-quarters of a lap A Northcliffe (Slaithwaite UH) ran down to the scratch mark and raced after them.

Leaving the ground (one mile) the order was: S Mounsey (Manchester YMCA), P S Needham (Sutton H), E E Leatherland (Polytechnic H); H Wood (Makerfield H), S Ferris (RAF), C J Bryant (Bolton UH), A Farrimond (Leigh H), W Maleedy (Sacred Heart H), H Burgess (Cheadle), D McL Wright (Shettleston H), A Hall (Rochdale H), J Chappell (Sale H), C Gould (Wibsey Park AC), D Smith (Wibsey Park AC), M Cusack (Makerfield H), D Clancey (NMH), G H Carr (East Cheshire H), A Northcliffe (Slaithwaite UH), S Taylor (British Legion, Lancashire Branch), W Fairburn (Salford H), and H Barnes (Royton H).

At Parr's Wood, Leatherland forced the pace from Farrimond. Six men, however, were bunched in front at five miles (Cheadle Church), viz., Leatherland, Maleedy, Ferris, Farrimond, Chappell, and Wood. They were timed at 30 min 11 sec. The official timekeeper was Mr E Lever, and he performed his duties throughout in a praiseworthy style. Then came Northcliffe, 30 min 26 sec; Wright, 31 min 5 sec; Bryant, 31 min 39 sec; Needham, 31 min 52 sec; Gould, 32 min 9 sec; Carr, 32 min 18 sec; Cusack, 32 min 44 sec; Burgess, 33 min 11 sec; Mounsey, 33 min 26 sec; Hall and Smith, 34 min; Mason and Barnes, 34 min 56 sec; Taylor, 35 min 9 sec.

The only real change among those at Baguley was that Needham had dropped back. At 10 mile Leatherland led in 59 min 26 sec being followed by Ferris and Maleedy in 59-33; Northcliffe 59-55; Wright and Wood 60-5; Farrimond 60-33; Chappell 61-9; Bryant 62-39; Gould, 64-7; Carr, 64-21.

No change in this order was recorded at Timperley Cricket Ground, where Carr was followed by Cusack, Needham, Mounsey, Smith, Hall, Burgess, Mason, Barnes, Taylor, Clancy, and Fairburn. Thus all the competitors were still in running.

The order and times at 15 miles were: Ferris and Leatherland 1 hr 27 min 10 sec; Wright 1 hr 27 min 35 sec; Maleedy 1 hr 27 min 40 sec; Wood 1 hr 30 min 7 sec; Farrimond 1 hr 30 min 52 sec; Chappell, 1 hr 33 min 47 sec;. Northcliffe, 1 hr 34 min 50 sec; and Gould 1 hr 36 min. Also checked were Cusack, Bryant, Needham, Smith, Hall, Mounsey, Taylor, and Mason. A mile further on Northcliffe retired.

On the Homeward Stretch

Ferris now set up a decided lead from Leatherland, but at Styal was wrongly directed to the right as stated and had to return a considerable distance.

Then came the short cut also referred to - just before the 20 miles mark. The checker's cards bear special marks against the numbers of Wright and Maleedy. Officially checked past by him were Leatherland, Ferris, Wood, Chappell, Farrimond, Cusack, Bryant, Gould, Smith, Hall and Needham. At 20 miles Leatherland was timed in 2 hr 6 min 20 sec, with Ferris second. Almost immediately afterwards the winner of the last two Northern Marathons slowed down to a walk and retired.

At Cheadle Green the official return was as follows:- Wright, Maleedy, Ferris, Wood, Farrimond, Cusack, Chappell, Bryant, Smith, Hall, Gould, and Needham. On this last home stretch Chappell and Gould retired, while Bryant and Cusack exchanged places, the order and times at the finish, and as they were declared to stand after consideration of the objection, being:-

1 D McL Wright......(Shettleston)............ 2:36:25
2 W Maleedy..........(Sacred Heart)......... 2:37:40
3 S Ferris................(RAF)...................... 2:47:44
4 H Wood...............(Makerfield)............2:51:33
5 A Farrimond........(Leigh H)................. 3:02:52
6 C J Bryant............(Bolton UH)............ 3:09:45
7 M Cusack.............(Makerfield H)........ 3:12:31
8 D Smith...............(Wibsey Park H)..... 3:22:44
9 A Hall..................(Rochdale H)...........3:24:18
10 P S Needham......(Sutton H)................3:39:15

Thus Wright becomes the first holder of the handsome 75 guineas bowl-the *Sporting Chronicle* Marathon Challenge Trophy- presented by the directors of Allied Newspapers Limited. The marathon stewards were H Harland (in charge), J Parr, B Smith, L Smith, W F Adshead, and A Foden."

The Sporting Chronicle noted that Sam Ferris *"covered extra distance variously estimated from half a mile to two miles."*

We estimate that Wright and Maleedy cut the course by about 500 - 600 metres equating to around two to two and a half minutes. It is possible without the short cut McLeod Wright would have run sub-2:40 and probably Maleedy too. Ferris was 11 minutes 19 seconds down at the end, equating to a deficit of around nine minutes if the first two had run the full course. He had been leading when misdirected, we do not know by how much but it is probable that he ran more than an extra mile and a half.

Duncan McLeod Wright, of Shettleston Harriers, affectionately known as "Dunky," was born in Glasgow in September 1896. His running included cross-country and his win in the 1924 "Poly" was his marathon debut.

William Maleedy, of Sacred Heart Harriers, St Helens, must have been even more frustrated finishing so close behind someone who had been selected for the Paris Olympics and did not finish.

Sam Ferris, the RAF man, was born in Dromore, Co Down, Northern Ireland in August 1900. He enlisted in the RAF in 1918 and began running during service in India. His second place in the 1924 "Poly," fifth place in the Paris Olympics and third place, after being misdirected in the fifth Manchester Marathon was the prelude to a distinguished marathon career.

Chapter 6

The Sixth Manchester Marathon
Saturday 8th August 1925

McLEOD WRIGHT SUCCEEDS AGAIN

The *"Sporting Chronicle* and Four Clubs Carnival" moved to an August date, emulating the second of the 1924 carnivals. Of the 23 entrants, 20 started and only nine finished.

Again The *Sporting Chronicle* gives a complete account of the race:

GREAT FINISH TO A GRUELLING MARATHON
'Sporting Chronicle' and Four Clubs Carnival Success

"This year's race for the *Sporting Chronicle* Marathon trophy - constituted the chief feature of the Sporting Chronicle and Four-Clubs Carnival on behalf of Broughton H and AC, Manchester H, Manchester AC, and Salford H at Fallowfield on Saturday was a thrilling affair indeed.

Starting with a run of four laps (one mile) on the cinder track, the twenty competitors, out of the twenty-three entrants, provided a magnificent struggle over Lancashire and Cheshire roads, which culminated in a gruelling finish and a desperate last lap (to complete the 26 miles 385 yards) between Duncan McLeod Wright (who had one share in the trophy) and E E Leatherland (who won the first cup given by the *Sporting Chronicle*).

As joint secretary to the Carnival Committee I knew a fine programme of track and field events was designed for the spectators on the sports ground, but, as this was in good hands, I was fortunate in being able to provide for and accommodate the marathon men and get my details of the racing in what proved a magnificent contest at first hand.

Below I relate the actual progress of the race, but I must deal with it also as a whole. It was a fine spectacle and such a splendid competition.

In the first place was the challenge to the past winners from the Irish champion J O'Reilly, and others of note, all being passed as very fit by Dr E Moir, who kindly officiated as hon medical officer. He, by the way, specially connoted the ages of the competitors, and drew my attention to the fact that, taking them as a whole, they were a younger lot than had competed previously.

One or two of them, notably H Wood of Makerfield H and who is 22 years of age, impressed me considerably as to their possibilities.

The race began to thrill in the very first mile, for Maleedy and O'Reilly went off at a great pace, and at the half distance Maleedy was actually 4 min 43.8 sec and O'Reilly 3 min 24.4 sec ahead of Wright, who eventually won.

It was observed that these times were nothing like so fast as were returned last year when Wright won in 2 hr 36 min 25 sec, but on Saturday the atmosphere was oppressive, being damp and warm, and there was quite a troublesome wind at a critical stage of the journey.

The roads were in fine condition 'tis true, but the atmosphere was against distance record breaking.

The actual racing was great to watch. I have prepared a chart based on the official checks, and this shows that Wright really won the event after the half-way stage had been entered. He started slowly, improved his position shortly after five miles had been run, hung on up to ten miles, and then, doing a lot of racing up to fifteen miles, secured what proved a winning advantage between fifteen and twenty miles.

Leatherland Loses Ground

Leatherland, by comparison, ran more consistently, but sacrificing some ground between fifteen and twenty miles tried to give too much away over the past six miles. Apparently he left his effort too late, for in a tremendous finish he just failed to overhaul the Scottish champion.

Maleedy and O'Reilly did all their racing in the early stages. O'Reilly fell away on the Hale road and alternately ran and walked, but Maleedy, although having beaten himself by his misjudgement, never stopped, and he finished well. Maleedy obviously has both the pace and stamina required, but was faulty in judgement.

Wood ran consistently after he had settled down, always being third, fourth, or fifth, and he was not distressed at the finish.

Charlie Bryant, the veteran of the party, put up another good showing, but was out of the prizes.

The marathon men were allowed the use of the dressing-rooms at the University pavilion where they could obtain baths, and this consideration was highly appreciated.

As I have remarked, a tremendous finish between Wright and Leatherland resulted, and the whole struggle will remain vividly in the memory of those fortunate enough to watch it.

The Carnival with which it was associated was a great sporting success throughout. Cecil Griffiths' fine half mile; Gaby's delightful hurdling; frequent displays of good sportsmanship; young Cozens' success in the National Cycling Union (NCU) (Manchester Centre) quarter-mile cycle championship; the good understanding between the competitors and the AAA and the NCU officials; and the happiness of the big crowd, will long be remembered.

The starters in the great Marathon were:- D McLeod Wright, Shettleston H and Caledonia AC (holder), (Scottish 10-mile and 4-mile champion and Olympic competitor); E E Leatherland, Mansfield H (winner outright of the first Sporting Chronicle Marathon trophy); Jack O'Reilly, Galway City HC (Irish Marathon champion); W Maleedy, Sacred Heart H and AC, (second in 1924 Marathon); J Lally, Galway City HC; W Bennett, Sheffield UH and AC; J Chappell, Salford H; J Clarke, Manchester and Salford Lads' Clubs; M Cusack, Makerfield H; P Entwistle, Bury AC; A H Gould, Bradford (Yorkshire); L Gould, Wibsey Park AC; M Lopez, Heaton Chapel; W Mather, Oldham; E J Morris, Sutton H and AC; M Morris, Sutton H and AC; S Mounsey, YMCA, Manchester; J E Wilson, Chesterfield C and AC; H Wood, Makerfield H; C J Bryant, Bolton United H and AC.

THE MARATHON STORY
Where McLeod Wright Made His Winning Effort

Leaving the sports ground and proceeding via the footpath alongside the University Athletic Grounds, Maleedy was the first to strike Birchfields-road, O'Reilly and Wood being in close attendance. M Morris was fourth, forty yards away, and then followed Chappell, E J Morris, Mounsey, Bennett, Leatherland, Bryant, Entwistle and Wilson, with Wright running easy.

Turning into Kingsway Maleedy just showed the way to Wood and O'Reilly, but Maleedy and

O'Reilly immediately piled on pace and a mile further on had drawn well away from Wood, who was accompanied by M Morris. Chappell, running steadily, was fifth. Leatherland had advanced to sixth, Bennett was seventh, E J Morris eighth, Wilson ninth, Mounsey tenth,

Entwistle eleventh, and Wright twelfth.

At Parr's Wood, where was struck the road to Cheadle, O'Reilly had taken over the lead from Maleedy. Wood was third, Morris fourth, Chappell fifth, Bennett sixth, Leatherland seventh, E J Morris eighth, Bryant ninth, Mounsey tenth, Gould eleventh, Wright twelfth, Wilson thirteenth, Entwistle fourteenth, Lopez fifteenth, Cusack sixteenth, Lally seventeenth, Gould eighteenth, Mather nineteenth, and Clarke twentieth.

Maleedy had regained the lead at Cheadle Green, O'Reilly being a close second. Wood was running behind Morris, Leatherland had advanced to fifth. Chappell having eased a little, while Wright had moved up to tenth place.

First Time Check

The latter did not seem any too happy here and he had gone back to twelfth position at Cheadle Church, where, including the mile run on the track, was the first time check (5 miles). The order was :-

1 Maleedy.............. 29 min 11.6 sec	4 M Morris............. 30 min 55.6 sec
2 O'Reilly.............. 29 min 19.6 sec	5 Leatherland......... 30 min 55.8 sec
3 Wood................. 30 min 6.4 sec	6 Bennett.............. 30 min 55.8 sec

7, Chappell; 8, E J Morris; 9, Bryant; 10, Gould; 11, Mounsey; 12, Wright; 13, Wilson; 14, Lopez; 15, Entwistle; 16, Cusack; 17, Lally; 18, Mather; 19, Clarke.

Maleedy hereabouts was running splendidly, with nice lift of the arms, low foot action and leaning well. O'Reilly kicks up his heels rather high but has a good balance. Wood, appearing very happy, has a strange action with the left arm, but did not appear to have suffered from the early racing.

Wright began to improve his position along the stretch to Timperley and, while there was little change in the first half dozen, he had advanced to seventh place, just behind Leatherland, who was running very steadily. Maleedy was running strongly here, and had completely shaken off O'Reilly, who now began to fall away rapidly.

At ten miles the official check was as follows:-

1 Maleedy.............. 58 min 41.2 sec	4 M Morris............. 61 min 50.2 sec
2 O'Reilly.............. 60 min 0.6 sec	5 Chappell............. 62 min 36.6 sec
3 Wood................. 60 min 44.6 sec	6 Leatherland......... 63 m 4.6 sec

7, Wright, 63 min 25 sec; 8 E J Morris; 9, Bryant; 10, Mounsey; 12, Gould; 13, Entwistle; 14, Wilson; 15, Cusack; 16, Lally; 17, Clarke.

Then came the stretch which always seems a strenuous contest, the winding roads, the sharp turnings, and the testing gradient to Hale road, and so on to the fifteen mile check.

Wright began his effort round about ten miles, for at Timperley Cricket Ground he had become sixth, at Green-lane he was fifth, at Hale-road fourth, and the finger post pointing to Styal, just before the fifteen mile check, he was second.

O'Reilly still fell away, and on the Hale road he was passed by both Wright and Leatherland, while Wood gained upon him rapidly. He had found the gradient to the Hale road somewhat exacting for his long striding, and he started to settle down to a shorter step.

Entwistle gained places, but this was largely because several men retired on this stretch

Maleedy Still Leading

Official times and placings at 15 miles were:-

1 Maleedy..............1 hr 31 min 39.8 sec	4 Wood................. 1 hr 35 min 56 sec
2 Wright.................1 hr 34 min 32.6 sec	5 O'Reilly.............. 1 hr 36 min 10.4 sec
3 Leatherland......... 1 hr 34 m 33.2 s	6 Chappell............. 1 hr 38 min 10 sec

7, E J Morris; 8, Bryant; 9, Mounsey; 10, Entwistle.

Here Maleedy was seen to be tiring rapidly: he was paying for his early pace-making, like O'Reilly, and though he still led at Styal turning to Hollins-lane he was overhauled rapidly by Wright and Leatherland. They passed him before Moss Nook was reached, Wright putting a lot of devil into his work whereas Leatherland, though moving fast, seemed to be preferring to keep something in reserve.

Wright really won his race hereabouts, and Leatherland must regret having stopped at Heald Green for a refresher for he must have lost half-a-minute as a result.

The positions at the finger post, just before reaching the 20 miles point, and where Wright was supposed to have taken a wrong turning last year, proved to be the same as were occupied at the finish. Leatherland here was in running again, and apparently stronger than Wright, who seemed suddenly to have become leg-weary. Still, at 20 miles Wright had obtained a very useful lead, the official placings being:-

1, Wright, 2 hr 4 min 58 sec; 2, Leatherland, 2 hr 7 min 7.4 sec; 3, Maleedy, 2 hr 7 min 56.2 sec; 4, Wood, 2 hr 12 min 21.6 sec; 5, Chappell; 7, O'Reilly; 7, Bryant; 8 Mounsey; 9, Entwistle.

A Desperate Finish

Then came the desperate effort by Leatherland to overhaul the leader. Gaining gradually at every mile, Leatherland got to within a hundred yards of his rival at the 25 miles mark. Then ensued a thrilling finish.

Wright, spurred on by his Scottish followers, re-entered the sports ground about fifty yards ahead of Leatherland. They had a lap and a third to travel to complete the journey, and Leatherland appearing the stronger of the two, made a determined bid to overhaul the leader.

Wright struggled on gamely, however, and, all out, he won by 14 yards. The crowd gave both men a great reception, their tremendous struggle over the last lap being to the accompaniment of constant cheering. Both men are to be congratulated on an accomplished and game display, their fine finish being an appropriate conclusion to a great Marathon.

The order of the finish was as follows:-

1 D McLeod Wright	(Shettleston)	2:44:07.8
2 E E Leatherland	(Mansfield H)	2:44:14.6
3 W Maleedy	(Sacred Heart)	2:58:46.2
4 H Wood	(Makerfield)	2:59:43
5 J Chappell	(Salford H)	3:08:52.8
6 J O'Reilly	(IRE & Galway City H)	3:12:18
7 C J Bryant	(Bolton U H)	3:16:58.4
8 S Mounsey	(Manchester YMCA)	3:42:47.4
9 P Entwistle	(Bury AC)	4:12:38

Thus McL Wright made the second *Sporting Chronicle* Marathon trophy his own property, by his two wins in succession. It will be remembered that Leatherland was the winner outright of the first trophy offered.

It was announced that the *Sporting Chronicle* were prepared to offer another valuable trophy for another marathon next year, this announcement being received with great delight by the crowd and the athletes.

Be it added that the official times were taken on the chronograph which was used by Polytechnic Marathon, and it is expected now that a formal application will be made to the AAA to recognise next year's Marathon race in the North as the AAA championship.

In conclusion I must place on record the good work done by Mr J W Foster, of Bolton, as the chief marshal, and by the stewards on the course, who were:- L Ingles, H Wilson, F Brown,

T H Michelson, J Jarvis, T Shawcross, W Burgess, L Downes, R Smith, L Smith, C E Kershaw, F Knott, S Ingram, H Fitzgerald, M F Clark, R L Topping, and C E Bolton - members of Broughton H, Manchester H and Salford H.

Every precaution was taken to give the competitors as clear a run as was possible, the convenience of the runners being the first consideration throughout, and it was impossible for any competitor to take a wrong turning unless, of course, wilfully and against the direction of the stewards and marshals.

I earnestly commend the event to immediate AAA recognition."

McLeod Wright enters the MAC ground for his second win.
(Picture: Manchester Guardian.)

Sixth placer Jack O'Reilly, a member of Galway City Harriers, was Irish Marathon Champion in 1925, 1926 and 1927. He never returned to the Manchester Marathon, but was to represent Ireland at the marathon in the first British Empire Games in Hamilton, Ontario, Canada arriving 9th out of 10 finishers. He had emigrated to Canada marrying a Canadian judge's daughter. He died in Canada in 1983 at the age of 84.

Most interesting in *The Sporting Chronicle's* report at the end was the proposal to apply for the 1926 Manchester Marathon to be the official AAA Championship.

58

Chapter 7

The Seventh Manchester Marathon
Saturday 12th June 1926

FIRST WIN FOR HAROLD WOOD

Although Championships for track and field athletics had been organised by the Amateur Athletic Association (AAA) since 1880, and indeed these had been held at the Fallowfield Stadium in 1897 and 1907, the Marathon event was only introduced in 1925. It was awarded to the Polytechnic Harriers Marathon, and Sam Ferris became the first AAA Marathon Champion on 30th May 1925, winning the race in an excellent time of 2:35:58.2.

In the winter of 1925/6, Manchester, having made a formal application to stage the 1926 AAA Marathon Championships, was told that "arrangements for the Polytechnic Marathon had been advanced so greatly" that it would be staged in the South once more. Naturally, the Northern committee was aggrieved at being overlooked in this manner.

Sam Ferris won his second AAA title, held at the "Poly" on 29th May, in a time of 2:42:24.2. William Maleedy, now of Pilkington Recs., travelled south for this race. Despite being only 15 seconds behind Ferris at 15 miles, he finished third in 2:51:50 having run the last five miles in bare feet. Polytechnic Harriers Arthur Robert ("Bobby") Mills, a Paris Olympian, had been second in a time of 2:46:11.2.

The Sporting Chronicle speculated on the favourites for this Manchester Marathon in the race day edition:

"J O'Reilly, the Irish champion told me last year that he enjoyed himself so much that all being well he would enter again. He was one of the first to do so, and I hope there will be travel facilities to enable him to be with us. He is of more than average ability.

E E Leatherland and Duncan McLeod Wright are entered again - a handsome new trophy being provided by the *Sporting Chronicle* - and W Maleedy, of St Helens, and J E Wilson of Chesterfield, are always likely to produce something great.

Great interest will be directed, however, to the reappearance of S Ferris, who is the AAA champion. He ran in the corresponding marathon two years ago, but left the course and only finished third. If he keeps up today he will be a likely winner, but Maleedy may yet spring a surprise if he uses better judgement than he has shown hitherto, and if he is properly shod - he ran bare-footed over the last mile or two of the recent Polytechnic Marathon.

As is commented in the souvenir programme, it had been hoped that Ernest Harper would have entered, but this he has not done. Harper is likely to make a great marathon runner, and if he has any ambitions in this direction he would have been wise to have tackled the distance this season.

Certainly he ran in a 15 miles event in Scotland the other day - losing the road and then only just being beaten into second place - but he should be running marathons as regularly as possible now if he aspires to Olympic distinction in 1928.

Ferris would provide him with all the test that was necessary, for the airman is possessed of a fine turn of speed for a distance runner and uses good judgement."

Neither Sam Ferris nor Jack O'Reilly made it to the start. Mid June was the seventh week of the general strike and coal miners had joined the dole queue doubling the number unemployed to 1.6 million. It is possible that the strike had made distance travel nigh on impossible.

We will let The *Sporting Chronicle* tell the story of the race again, even if the format is rather peculiar where the finishers are discussed first and the details of how the competition progressed follows:

BRILLIANT VICTORY IN MARATHON RACE
MANY THRILLS AT FALLOWFIELD
Sporting Chronicle and Four-Carnival
Successful Event

"Although rain fell heavily during the morning and the sky was leaden at the time arranged for the start of the *Sporting Chronicle* and Four-Club Sports Carnival (under AAA and NCU rules) at Fallowfield, Manchester, on Saturday, a capital crowd assembled, and, I believe thoroughly enjoyed the many good things, sporting and spectacular, which the promoting committee had done their very best to provide. ... ...

Desperate Speed Display

Now let me tell the story of this year's marathon. The event was a thrilling one indeed for all who took part in it. There was desperate racing from start to finish, and the best man won after a display of great speed and endurance and after one of the gamest efforts ever seen in the series of "*Sporting Chronicle*" and Four Club marathons.

It will be remembered how the event ought to have been constituted the AAA championships this year. After another successful promotion we look confidently to the future, as there has been a promise of "next time, perhaps."

S Ferris, the AAA champion, was entered. His programme, linen number, and tickets were dispatched on Thursday night, but he did not arrive. J O'Reilly, the Irish champion, I understand, ran at a meeting in Ireland. D McLeod Wright, the Scottish champion, however, turned out, and finished second after having a gruelling time. E E Leatherland, also competed and showed up very prominently for three-parts of the journey, where he had a bad time and retired. Another noteworthy competitor was H Wickington of Woodford Green AC. He travelled north overnight, and eventually finished third. Considerable interest also attached to the appearance of G C White, of the Wolverton AAC, but he retired about 23 miles.

I have not mentioned the winner. He calls for very special reference indeed. This was H Wood, of Makerfield H. He has run in previous marathons, and all along has been showing considerable promise, but his success on Saturday, and more so the outstanding character of it, was in the nature of a huge surprise.

He had intended entering for the Southern Marathon, but six weeks ago he suffered an attack of influenza, and he decided to concentrate on Saturday's event. A collier - asked how he trained, he said he had done so "on strike pay." His training runs had been about twelve miles, fairly frequently, but he had done very little walking.

Twenty-three years of age, single, he is of sturdy physique. His build is of complete contrast to Leatherland's. He is almost thick-set, with powerful looking legs and shoulders. In running he inclines well forward, never raises his heels much, while he swings outwards with the arms, particularly with the left one. He put in a tremendous amount of running after 20 miles, but was quite fresh at the finish. Let us follow him through the race.

Early Struggles

There were 21 starters. Wood was first on the roadway after the preliminary mile on the MAC track, the start and finish being in the Fallowfield grounds. In close attendance were P Entwistle (Bury AC), Leatherland, J Chappell (Salford H), H G Wickington, W Maleedy (Pilkington Recs), P Houghton (Pilkington Recs), G White, and S Johnson (Broughton H & AC), Wright was twelfth.

On the fine stretch of roadway, Kingsway, Wood, Entwistle, Leatherland, and Chappell led alternately, Wright, Maleedy, Houghton, and Johnson being bunched close behind.

At the first official check, Cheadle Church, five miles, including the mile on the track, Wood just led Leatherland, Chappell, and Entwistle in 31 min 44 sec. There were not three yards in any of the four. Thirty seconds later came Wright, Maleedy, Houghton, White, and Wickington in a group, C E Mitchell (Chesterfield C & AC) being tenth in 32 26 sec, and Johnson eleventh in 32 min 30 sec.

Wood, Leatherland, and Chappell now started to force the pace, and Entwistle dropped away. Chappell was surprising greatly, and for a long stretch had a discussion with a cycling policeman. Wood and Leatherland also chatted freely. Going through Timperley Chappell took the lead for a time. Wood and Leatherland, however, went to his shoulder again very soon after, and the three were in a dead line together at ten miles. The placings and times at ten miles were:-

1 H Wood (Makerfield)............ 1:02:40	11 S Taylor (Lancaster H).............. 1:04:40
1 J Chappell (Salford H)............ 1:02:40	12 A Shaw (Broughton H)............. 1:07:25
1 E Leatherland (Mansfield)......1:02:40	13 S Moseley (Manchester H).......: 1:07:30
4 D M Wright (Caledonian)....... 1:03:28	14 D Smith (Wibsey Park AC)....... 1:08:30
4 W Maleedy(Pilkington Recs).... 1:03:28	14 B Brady (Wibsey Park AC)........1:08:30
6 G C White (Wolverton)............1:03:28.2	16 J E Wilson (Chesterfield).........1:09:05
7 P Houghton (Broughton)......... 1:03:28.2	17 A E Rumney (N Manch.)......... 1:09:15
8 HG Wickington (Woodford...... 1:03:41.6	18 A S Jones
9 C E Mitchell (Chesterfield)......1:04:05.2	(Loughborough Colleges)............. 1:09:55
10 S Johnson (Broughton)......... 1:04:35	19 A Appell (Bolton UH).............. 1:10:00

EFFORT BY WRIGHT
Scottish Champion's
Great Promise

The roads, otherwise in splendid condition, had been greasy up to this point following the rain, but they were easier for running over the next stretch, and there was welcome sunshine.

The three leaders continued to test one another, Leatherland once attempting a special spurt, but not being able to get away. In Green-lane leading to Hale-road, Wood and Leatherland drew away, and Chappell dropped rapidly away. At Hale Barns, after eighty minutes racing, Wood and Leatherland were still together, but Wright and Maleedy were gaining slowly.

At Ringway, Wood and Maleedy had gone in front of Chappell, and they were within a hundred yards of Wood and Leatherland. The last named couple again speeded up, however, and at fifteen miles the order was:

1 Leatherland.......1:34:26.2	7 Houghton........1:38:58	13 Wilson...........1:46:04
2 Wood................1:34:26.2	8 Mitchell............1:39:36	14 Shaw.............1:49:14
3 Wright..............1:34:40.2	9 White...............1:40:02	15 Jones.............1:49:16
4 Maleedy............1:35:07.6	10 Taylor............1:41:56	16 Moseley.........1:50:02
5 Chappell...........1:35:58.2	11 Smith.............1:46:01	17 Appell............1:50:03
6 Wickington.......1:36:01.2	12 Brady.............1:46:02	18 Johnson.........1:51:00

A desperate effort to get on terms with the leaders was now made by Wright. At Styal Wright was within twenty yards of Leatherland, who had been dropped by Wood. Half a mile further Wright went into second place, and after two hours the Scottish champion went to Wood's shoulder.

Leatherland was in difficulties, and at this point had lost 100 yards. Wright, who still runs upright, evidently was feeling the effect of his exertions, whereas Wood appeared very confident. The Makerfield harrier had a look at his rival, and then started to pile on the pace again.

Several men dropped out on this stretch, where the roads were greasy again, and the order at 20 miles was as follows:-

1 Wood................ 2:05:40.2	5 Maleedy............2:11:33	9 Brady............... 2:24:18.4
2 Wright...............2:05:41.6	6 Chappell...........2:13:07.8	10 Wilson............ 2:30:00
3 Leatherland...... 2:07:05.6	7 Mitchell............2:18:09	11 Shaw................2:36:02
4 Wickington.......2:09:50.2	8 Smith................ 2:24:12	12 Appell.............2:37:00

Where Great Strain Told

On the return road to Cheadle, Leatherland started walking and was passed by Wickington. Wright could not hold Wood at all, and after passing Cheadle Green he, too, stopped to a walk. Wood, however, continued to forge ahead, and by the time Kingsway was reached again he had opened up an astonishingly big gap.

Leatherland retired, and Mitchell went in front of Maleedy and Chappell just after passing Parr's Wood. The thrilling race for premier honours was now all over, of course, for Wood never stopped running, and he was as fresh as anybody over the last stretch.

The approach of the leader was awaited with keen interest on the ground, and there was much excitement when to signal the fact that he was half a mile away, between 200 and 300 racing pigeons, provided by distinguished Lancashire fanciers, were released simultaneously on the ground. This was a pretty spectacle, and I must say it is hoped to develop the idea considerably on some future occasion.

Of the 21 starters eleven finished, and each had a great reception. Wood was not in the least distressed, and Wright had recovered from his bad time. Wickington moved smoothly, and will do better if he perseveres. Mitchell finished quite sprightly. It should be explained that he was the only one about whom Dr Moir had any doubt about. Before racing, probably excited, he was advised to rest awhile. He did so, and then was promptly given permission to run. Maleedy sprinted the last 100 yards. The order of finish was:-

1 H Wood................(Makerfield H)........ 2:43:51.8
2 D McL Wright.......(Caledonian AC)......2:51:12.4
3 HG Wickington....(Woodford Gn)........2:57:06.2
4 C E Mitchell..........(Chesterfield AC).....2:57:30.2
5 W Maleedy............(Pilkington Recs).....3:04:51.8

7 D Smith...............(Wibsey Park AC)......... 3:10:32.6
8 B Brady...............(Wibsey Park AC)......... 3:17:28
9 J E Wilson............(Chesterfield C&AC)..... 3:20:12.6
10 A Shaw...............(Broughton H & AC).... 3:26:01.2
11 A Appell.............(Bolton UH & AC)........ 3:31:56.2
    The handsome new trophy provided by the directors of Allied Newspapers Ltd was
presented to the winner by Mr W H Clarke, Editor of the *Sporting Chronicle*."

Harold Wood of Makerfield Harriers was born on 28th November 1902 in
Wigan. He joined the Harriers in December 1922 and was 20 years of age
before he ran a race of any kind. His first race would be at cross-country in
a club match versus Bolton United Harriers where he finished third and later
took 12th place in the West Lancs Cross-Country Championships, signs that
good results would come with some training.

After two fourth places in Manchester he now had a win and an excellent
time to his credit.

Harold Wood at Birchfields Road nearing the end of his journey.

63

McLeod Wright did not compete in any more Manchester marathons.
His 1930 Empire Games win, which saw a defeat for Sam Ferris, was followed up by a bronze medal four years later in London. He closed his Olympic account in 1932 with fourth and a personal best of 2:32:41.0.

Winner of Manchester Marathons (1924 and 1925), two AAA titles (1928 and 1932) and two "Polys" (1924 and 1934), his ability to come good spanned well over a decade.

A member of various clubs in Scotland - Maryhill H, Clydesdale H, Caledonian AC, it is likely that he was influential in Sam Ferris joining Shettleston, another club with which he was affiliated. Wright was third in the 1936 "Poly," one of two selection races for the Berlin Olympics. He was not selected and did not contest the second trial held over the "Poly" course a month later, a race won by his Maryhill club-mate Donald McNab Robertson.

He continued running into his fifties and died in Glasgow on 21st August 1976, a month short of his eightieth birthday.

Significant marathons by 'Dunky' Wright

Year	Marathon	Position	Time
1924	"Poly"	1	2:53:17.4
1924	Olympics	dnf	
1924	Manchester	1	2:36:25 **short route taken**
1925	Manchester	1	2:44:07.8
1926	Manchester	2	2:51:12.4
1928	AAA	2	2:38:09
1928	Olympics	20	2:45:30
1930	AAA	1	2:38:29.4
1930	British Empire Games	1	2:43:43
1931	AAA	1	2:49:54.2
1932	AAA	2	2:34:34
1932	Olympics	4	2:32:41 **personal best**
1934	British Empire Games	3	2:56:20
1936	"Poly"	3	2:37:25

Chapter 8

The Eighth Manchester Marathon
Saturday 30th July 1927

AAA HAT TRICK FOR FERRIS

At last Manchester got to stage the Amateur Athletic Association Marathon Championship. A crowd of 5,000 at the Fallowfield witnessed the start and finish of the race over the now familiar course of Lancashire and Cheshire roads. The sun came out in the afternoon which may have given difficulty to some of the runners.

The favourites were stated to be Sam Ferris (RAF Uxbridge), AAA Champion in 1925 and 1926, and Polytechnic Marathon winner in 1925, 1926 and 1927; Harold Wood (Makerfield Harriers), holder of *The Sporting Chronicle* trophy; Ernie Leatherland (Mansfield Harriers), the winner outright of the first *Sporting Chronicle* trophy; J J O'Reilly, the Irish Marathon Champion; and T Heeley, Sparkhill Harriers, Birmingham. Of the 44 entrants, 40 started. As last year O'Reilly did not show up.

Again *The Sporting Chronicle* takes up the story:

"A trim figure with a Number 1 on his sky blue costume led the parade of competitors before the Amateur AA Marathon at Fallowfield on Saturday. Over two and three quarter hours later (writes T C) he was still Number 1, so much so that when he re-entered the Fallowfield sports ground to complete the Marathon distance of 26 miles 385 yards by running once round the cinder track before breaking the tape amid a storm of cheering, he was two miles ahead of the next in a field of 40, of whom 16 finished.

He was Sam Ferris, a storekeeper in the Royal Air Force at Uxbridge, and for the second time this year he completed a hat trick in Marathon successes. The rosy-cheeked native of County Down, who will be 27 next month, thus won his eighth Marathon as in the last three years he has also won races of this kind in Italy and Denmark.

Of the 44 starters (there were four non-starters including J O'Reilly, Tyrone, Army Marathon champion), many ran splendidly up to 15 miles, but after that the race became a procession. Even so, Ferris, who took the lead in the 16th mile, had the hardest race of his career - all through an error of tactics.

He was very tired at the finish, but by no means distressed, and this was entirely due to the pre-arranged plan for him to keep up with the fastest men for 15 miles and endeavour to maintain the same pace to the finish.

This was not intended as a record-breaking attempt so much as an experiment, but he will never repeat it. He and his trainer, "Bill" Thomas, Herne Hill Harriers' trainer, both frankly confessed this had been a lesson to them, and Thomas added "never again!" By that he meant that Ferris would in future run in the manner he had hitherto adopted - lying a little behind the leaders, and allowing them to make their own pace until he was ready to spurt in the last 10 miles.

Wood's Failure

The surprise of the race was the failure of H Wood, last year's winner of the Sporting Chronicle Trophy. He started finely, but soon faded passing the third check, and retired on account of stomach trouble at 21 miles.

Wood and Ferris ran abreast as leaders of a group of ten competitors approaching the first five mile check at Cheadle Church, but C E Mitchell, a sturdily built Chesterfield runner, led all the way there passing the time-keeper 120 yards ahead of the others in 32 min 36.2 sec.

Mitchell lost the lead in the eighth mile, and Leatherland and Ferris passed the ten miles mark at Ellisland House 25 yards ahead of Wood, and their time was 1 hr 2 min 9.6 sec.

Mitchell was fourth and E Rawlinson, (Leigh), next well ahead of the rest.

At Ringway Mitchell was 200 yards behind Wood, who was 300 yards behind Ferris, and Leatherland led by 80 yards, which he increased to 120.

But when the third check loomed near Ferris began to draw out, and he was only yards behind the older man at the 15 miles mark near Styal. Leatherland's time was 1 hr 33 min 22 sec - two minutes behind the time of the leader in the 1925 race, but as the runners now had their backs to the strong southerly wind there were hopes of an improvement in the times.

We got it in the shape of wonderful running by Ferris, who in spite of the heat of the sunshine which a few minutes before had succeeded a dull sky, romped away, and was perfectly fresh and comfortable. T Heeley, (Sparkhill), I had seen travelling much better than anybody else in the wake of the champion, at 18 miles, and passing Heald Green he overtook Leatherland, who was in bad shape and walking, as well as Mitchell and Wood.

Ferris reached the 20 mile check with a half-mile lead, and in 16 sec under the time for the leader at that point two years ago, and recorded 2 hr 4 min 41.6 sec.

Ferris Miles Away

Leatherland refreshed himself with a drink at Gatley, and then ran strongly. Here two young Londoners, H W Fisher and his club-mate, C H Thiroff, were going finely - two youngsters, who should be heard of again in long-distance events. Ferris was "miles away," and he finished in 2 hr 48 min 46.4 sec - 12 min 48.2 sec outside his own record in his first National Marathon, Windsor - London, two years ago. Heeley, who had struggled on valiantly and alone in the "desert" of Kingsway's great stretch of macadam - one of the most difficult parts of the run, because its straight length seemed endless - was just completing his final lap of the Fallowfield track when Mitchell ran on. Heeley's was all the finer performance because this is his first year as a marathon runner. Hitherto his distance has been the half-mile and mile.

Ferris received the Fattorini trophy, presented by the Amateur AA, and the *Sporting Chronicle* challenge trophy.

Heeley also received a cup and an AAA medal.

All the competitors spoke in terms of high appreciation of the arrangements for the race."

The 16 competitors who finished were: -

1	S Ferris	(RAF Uxbridge)	2:48:46.4
2	T Heeley	(Sparkhill H)	3:00:22.4
3	C E Mitchell	(Chesterfield C & AC)	3:02:13.6
4	E E Leatherland	(Mansfield H)	3:06:31.6
5	H W Fisher	(Mary Ward AC, Ldn)	3:08:28.2
6	C W Thiroff	(Mary Ward AC, Ldn)	3:12:52.2
7	J E Wilson	(Chesterfield C & AC)	3:18:00

8	A Farrimond	(Leigh H)	3:18:56.6
9	E Rawlinson	(Leigh H)	3:21:02.6
10	C J Bryant	(Bolton UH)	3:21:14.2
11	W H Ashton	(Pilkington Recs H)	3:25:11.6
12	G E Hubert	(Polytechnic H, Ldn)	3:27:31.8
13	J Spiby	(Preston H & AC)	3:28:24.8
14	F J Murphy	(Manchester H)	3:48: —
15	H Mumford	(Royton H)	3:50: —
16	E G Whant	(Lyons AC, London)	3:55: —

Standard time 3 hr 15 min.

Sam Ferris wins the 1927
Manchester Marathon
(Picture: Daily Dispatch.)

Sam Ferris holding two cups - the AAA Trophy and Sporting Chronicle Trophy (Picture: Daily Dispatch.)

Another column offered some advice to Ferris:

"Ferris stood in a class by himself, and he will be England's first choice for the Olympic Marathon next year. But he learnt on Saturday something that neither he nor his two advisers and trainers knew before - that it is a mistake from his natural style, especially when he can win easily enough without an experiment such as that which caused him to finish much more fatigued than some of the more experienced runners.

The simple point is that he took too much out of himself in the first 15 miles or so in the fulfilment of his desire to keep among the leaders, instead of quickening his pace later on as is his custom.

Those people who have never seen long-distance races, and wonder what manner of men are those who take part in Marathons, will be interested to know that Ferris, who has two hat tricks in Marathons - the National Amateur event and the London Polytechnic Club's Marathon - is a store-keeper in the Royal Air Force. He weighs 9st 11lbs, but in a race like Saturday's he loses five or six pounds.

SIX MILE SPURT!

Heeley, of Birmingham, who finished second through grand running in the last six miles, is an oxy-acetylene moulder. Mitchell, third home, aged 24, is a turner in an engineering shop. Wilson, the 41-year-old runner who finished seventh and sprinted at the finish, is an iron moulder, and a week before this Marathon, had his first long run of the year - a little effort of 13 miles!

Thiroff, a 21-year-old Londoner, a slip of a lad who was as pleased as a dog with two tails when he finished sixth and thus qualified for a silver cup, is a plumber and has been a long-distance runner two years. He gave the praise of his good work to his chum, Fisher, a big lad of

Sam Ferris never returned to run a Manchester Marathon.

Two months after his Manchester victory, he won the inaugural Liverpool Marathon, on Wednesday 28th September, in 2:35:27, breaking his own British record (2:35:58.2) set when winning the inaugural AAA title, over the "Poly" course two years earlier. Harold Wood had recovered from his Manchester difficulties and finished second in Liverpool, but his 2:45:13 was almost 10 minutes down.

Sam Ferris was a member of several clubs over the years: Shettleston Harriers, Ulsterville, Uxbridge Harriers, Herne Hill Harriers, Polytechnic Harriers and the Road Runners Club, of which he was President in 1954.

He had an illustrious career, some of which is mentioned later and ran in three Olympic Marathons: 1924, 5th; 1928 8th; and 1932 2nd. He was second in the 1930 British Empire Games in Hamilton, Canada.

Of Ferris's training F A M Webster wrote in *"Athletics of Today – History, Development and Training (1929)"*: 'Ferriş is a non-smoker, but does not favour dieting, and holds definite views as to the value of massage, sun-baths and time schedules. He builds up the intensity of his training over six to eight weeks - in the sixth week he runs ten to twelve miles on Wednesday and twenty-four on Saturday. Three times during the seventh week he travels fast on the track at eight to twelve miles and finishes off his training to the end of the eighth week with long strolls.'

Sam Ferris's marathons

1924	"Poly"	2	2:54:03
1924	Olympics	5	2:52:26
1924	Manchester	3	2:47:44 **misdirected**
1925	"Poly"/ AAA	1	2:35:58.2
1926	"Poly"/AAA	1	2:42:24.2
1926	Turin	1	2:46:18
1927	"Poly"	1	2:40:32.2
1927	Manchester /AAA	1	2:48:46.4
1927	Liverpool	1	2:35:27
1928	"Poly"	1	2:41:02.2
1928	Olympics	8	2:37:41
1928	Liverpool	1	2:33:00

1928	Turin	2	2:48:24	
1929	"Poly"	1	2:40:47.4	
1929	AAA	2	2:39:12	
1930	AAA	2	2:41:46.4	
1930	British Empire Games	2	2:47:13	**estimated**
1931	"Poly"	1	2:35:31.8	
1932	"Poly"	1	2:36:32.4	
1932	Olympics	2	2:31:55	**personal best**
1933	"Poly"	1	2:42:42.2	

After his eighth success in the "Poly" 1933, he was posted to Iraq and then on to Karachi where he served from 1936 to 1939. This, and the outbreak of war effectively ended his competitive career. He turned to coaching, was Assistant Honorary Secretary of the Polytechnic Marathon for many years and reported road races in *Athletics Weekly* and the *Road Runners Club Newsletter*. With the rank of Warrant Officer he left the RAF in 1950.

He was a much-loved man and died at Torbay in Devon on the 29th of March 1980 after a nineteen years struggle with Parkinson's Disease. He was survived by his wife Marjorie, and daughters Rosemary and Kathie.

Ninth placer in Manchester, one behind Arthur Farrimond, Teddy Rawlinson of Leigh Harriers was quite a character. He had finished ninth the year before in 3:21:02.6. He too ran the 1927 Liverpool Marathon finishing fifth. On the previous Thursday he was second in a race across the sands of Morecambe Bay from Silverdale to Morecambe, a distance of 6 to 7 miles, and at the weekend came fourth in a 20 mile race from Preston to Cleveleys, 2:11:37, won by Duncan McLeod Wright in 2:00:38. This gave him three races in seven days, a feat described by his club scribe as "a remarkable performance."

This was C J Bryant's last appearance in a Manchester. Later in the year at age 42 he took the veterans prize in the Preston to Cleveleys race, seventh in 2:19:48.

Teddy Rawlinson, Leigh Harriers.

Chapter 9

The Ninth Manchester Marathon
Saturday 19th May 1928

WOOD'S WONDERFUL WIN

1928 was another Olympic year, the venue this time being Amsterdam. Manchester was not nominated as an official trial, and the "Poly" was held the next weekend, but *The Sporting Chronicle* stated, *"The 36 competitors will start with the knowledge that the event will be closely watched on behalf of the British Olympic authorities, in view of the approach of the Olympiad in Amsterdam."* Once more it was the *"Sporting Chronicle"* and Four Clubs Festival.

There was a slight change of course:

"The course is one that has been used for all the marathons at this carnival, and its measurement, 26 miles 385 yards, is in complete accordance with Olympic requirements.

Competitors run one mile (four laps) on the Fallowfield track and leave by the main gate to Whitworth-lane, turning to the right into Old Hall-lane, and right again into Birchfields-road to Moseley-road, under the railway bridge to Kingsway. Thence the usual route to the south. The course then turns sharply left at Timperley Cricket ground, and the new road is taken to Green-lane on the right and its continuation (Delahey's-road) where the runners pass through Hale Barns and Ringway."

The first half dozen home would receive a solid silver cup.

A downpour commenced one hour before the meeting was due to begin, but this did not deter the 4,000 spectators at the Fallowfield Stadium. The conditions underfoot were difficult on parts of the course, but weather-wise it proved good for a marathon.

Again *The Sporting Chronicle* gives us the full story:

WOOD'S WONDERFUL WIN
Marathon Victor Chips Nine minutes
From AAA Title Time: By WANDERER
YOUTH SCORES

"In some respects the great marathon race was unique. Never before have the younger competitors shown up so prominently and the winner's time - 2:39:29.2 - represents a magnificent performance well worthy of the attention of the British Olympic Marathon selectors.

The race furnished the favourite Harold Wood, the 25- year-old Makerfield Harrier, with the finest performance of his career. He was never headed, and after the tenth mile seemed a certain winner, though the supporters of J T Slaney (Sutton-in-Ashfield) had great hopes of the latter's ability to overtake him after the 15th mile.

READY AGAIN
Leatherland to Run in Poly

Wood's time was over nine minutes better than that returned by Sam Ferris, the RAF runner, in winning the AAA championship in this race last year, and Wood, who is a miner, finished so fresh that one of the officials exclaimed when he passed the winning post, "Why he looks as if he could run it again now!'"

Wood afterwards said to me: "The conditions were champion, though the roads have been better. Last years race took place on a very hot day, and my only regret is that Ferris was not running today. I was never pushed, or I could have done better time. I think I am out to make the cup my own."

While the cold and rain were conducive to good times not all the competitors found the conditions to their liking: a few of the younger ones were very cold when they finished. But E E Leatherland, the diminutive Mansfield Harrier, winner outright of the *Sporting Chronicle* trophy, was so fit at the end that he declared he will compete in the London Polytechnic Marathon this weekend.

At one part of the race I thought Leatherland, who was fourth last year to Duncan Wright (who won by 6 sec) in this race in 1925, could not possibly make up the leeway to enable him to be one of the first six men home, who each qualified for a special silver cup, but he strode out with remarkable dash after the tenth mile, and was beaten by less than half a minute for second·place by J T Slaney (Sutton-in-Ashfield, winner of the British Games 14 miles at Stamford Bridge last year, and who was making his first Marathon attempt.)

NO CHALLENGERS

The rest of the story of Saturday's race is soon told. Wood, L Lomas, (Chesterfield C & AC), and a youngster W Fish (Royton H), ran from Fallowfield together beyond the first five miles check at Cheadle Church. Then Wood, Slaney, W Maleedy (St Helens), and Lomas, one of the tallest and sturdiest men in the race, at the ten-mile check at Timperley - with W Maleedy and Slaney further behind and Leatherland lying eighth.

The leader had no one to challenge him afterwards. At 15 miles - Styal - he was a good quarter of a mile in front of Slaney, with Northcliffe (Slaithwaite) and Lomas running together third, and Bryant, C Brace (Burbage) and Fish coming on. Wood's time at that stage was 1 hr 29 min 14.8 sec, and Slaney's 1-29-46.8 (just inside his own estimate). Five miles further on at Heald Green - Wood was nearly a mile ahead of Slaney, and the respective times of the first four were:-

Wood...................... 1:58:21.8;
Slaney..................... 2:03:17.4;
Leatherland.............. 2:09:15.4;
Bryant..................... 2:09:15.6.

Mr F A Fattorini, the timekeeper could not reach the 25 mile check in time to secure the leaders' figures and he had to hurry on to Fallowfield for the finish. Wood won by about a mile and a half, and received a great ovation as he ran smiling past the post.

THE PLACINGS
The Stamina of a Veteran

No one finished so fresh as he and Leatherland, but there was an unprecedented incident

73

(for a marathon) when the fourth and fifth runners returned to the track to complete the course by running one lap. Bryant was exactly half a lap in front of Wroe, also a new entrant, but before the last bend Wroe passed him. The pair sprinted along the straight, and were level a few yards from the post, but Bryant could not hold out and was beaten for fourth place by three yards. Both runners were warmly cheered.

The first six runners home each received special silver cups, and the Sporting Chronicle trophy, valued at 75 guineas, was presented to Wood by Mr W H Clarke, chairman of the Carnival Committee.

As last year, when he was seventh, J E Wilson (Chesterfield C & AC), the veteran of the race - he is 42 - showed wonderful stamina. He finished tenth.

22 FINISH

Of the 33 starters 22 finished and all but four of those who failed to finish (to) complete the course dropped out in the last stages.

No one was seriously distressed."

The final placings were:-

1	H Wood	(Makerfield H)	2:39:29.2
2	J Tom Slaney	(Sutton-in-Ashfield)	2:51:07
3	E E Leatherland	(Mansfield H)	2:51:34.6
4	A Wroe	(Small Heath H)	2:58:41.6
5	E T Bryant	(Portsmouth RC)	2:58:42.2
6	S Widdop	(Bingley H)	3:00:10.4
7	E J Morris	(Sutton H)	3:02:18
8	A Northcliffe	(Slaithwaite)	3:02:44.4
9	M Cusack	(Makerfield H)	3:07:37
10	J E Wilson	(Chesterfield C & AC)	3:08:44
11	G E Ross	(Sutton H)	3:10:59
12	W Fish	(Royton H)	3:12:06.4
13	G P Birchall	(St Helens)	3:13:25.2
14	L Lomas	(Chesterfield C & AC)	———
15	F J Murphy	(Manchester H)	———
16	A Farrimond	(Leigh H)	———
17	H Ashmore	(Leicester H)	———
18	G H Westcott	(Burbage AC)	———
19	G Sutton	(Winton H)	———
20	A Hughes	(Manchester H)	———
21	A Johnson	(Ravenhead H)	———
22	W Maleedy	(St Helens)	———

Sporting Chronicle cartoonist, Gannon's, impression of Harold Wood and Trainer

Later information revealed that Wood *"trains by running nine or ten miles on Tuesday and Thursdays. Leatherland was asked how he trains. "On my bicycle, and on Woodbines and tea,"* he replied."

This was the last Manchester Marathon sponsored by *Sporting Chronicle*.

A week after Manchester, Saturday 26th May, Sam Ferris won the Polytechnic, Windsor to London race for the fourth successive year. The first four home were:

1	S Ferris	(Royal Air Force)	2:41:02.2
2	S S Jones	(Cambridge H)	2:50:59.4
3	H Bignall	(Highgate H)	2:53:04.6
4	H W Payne	(Woodford Green)	2:54:50.8

Six weeks later, on Friday 6th July, the AAA Championships were contested over this same course, and this must have been the main trial for the Olympic team for Amsterdam in August. Sam Ferris did not start due to injury. Harold Wood led through 5 miles in 28:19, 10 in 58:37, but got in trouble around 12 miles and retired. The winner was Harry Payne, Woodford Green, in a new British Record of 2:34:34, and the first six were:

1	H W Payne	(Woodford Green)	2:34:34
2	D McL Wright	(Maryhill H)	2:38:09
3	E Harper	(Hallamshire H)	2:39:09
4	H Bignall	(Highgate H)	2:45:10
5	A W Adams	(Maryhill H)	2:46:40
6	E T Bryant	(Portsmouth R & RC)	2:48:48

The Great Britain team selected for the Olympic Marathon in Amsterdam, just four weeks later, was Payne, McLeod Wright, Harper, Bignall, Ferris and Wood. *"Athletic News"* observing Payne's win in the "Poly" trial noted, *"Payne for such a trial of strength finished quite fresh. Our chances of winning the Olympic Marathon at last seem to be quite good."* The Sporting Chronicle commented, *"Payne finished very strongly and his time is only two minutes outside the Olympic record."*

The British Olympic Marathon team in Amsterdam:
(lt to rt) Harold Wood, Ernie Harper, Sam Ferris. Herbert Bignall,
'Dunky' McLeod Wright with Marthinus Steytler (South Africa).

But a medal was not to be.

On Sunday 5th August, on a cool windy day over a flat course, the race was won by the French Algerian, Boughera El Ouafi in the excellent time of 2:32:57. Second was a Chilean runner Manuel Plaza Reyes, 2:33:32, and third Martti Marttelin, Finland, 2:35:02.

All of the British team finished and best was Sam Ferris, running conservatively due to a slight leg injury, in eighth place with 2:37:41. He admitted that he could have done better if he had been more aggressive. All of our team finished as follows: Harold Wood, 11th, 2:41:15; Harry Payne, 13th, 2:42:29; Duncan McLeod Wright, 20th, 2:45:30; Herbert Bignall, 21st, 2:45:44; Ernest Harper, 22nd, 2:45:44.

The Sporting Chronicle headlined: **"BRITISH RUNNERS FAIL IN LONG-DISTANCE EVENT,"** but the British Olympic Team Captain, the sprinter Harold Abrahams, was more kind when he reported in The Athletic News "In the Marathon followers of athletics may have been disappointed that none of our men were placed, yet I unhesitatingly say that they all ran to their best form, and for the whole six to finish inside 2 hours 46 minutes and in the first 22 is a performance of which we may well be proud."

The Daily Dispatch was less sympathetic stating, **"ENGLISHMEN'S BAD TACTICS.** The Englishmen had the mistake of running too slowly at the start with the result that they found themselves in a very backward position. In the last mile Ferris moved up from 27th to 8th. ... ..."

Harold Wood in Olympic kit with the Sporting Chronicle trophy

Sam Ferris might have done better in the Olympics. Just under eight weeks later he returned to the Liverpool Civic Week Marathon on Wednesday, 26th September, and in winning for the second time in succession not only made

77

the gold cup his own property, but set a new British Record of 2:33:00. Harold Wood, as in 1927, was second, but this time was almost 15 minutes behind in 2:47:52. Third was M Gooch, Cheltenham and County H, in 2:56:52.

In fourth place in Liverpool was an interesting character, John Duncan (Jock) Semple, Clydesdale H, Glasgow, 2:57:42. He had finished ninth (2:52:37) in the July Polytechnic Marathon and went on to complete ninety marathons in his career. He was famous as being "Mr Boston Marathon," race director from 1952 to 1982. I remember him well, taking care of me and cheering me from the press bus when I set a Boston record of 2:10:30 in April 1970. He did a similar favour for me in July 1970, when he returned to his native Scotland and encouraged me in my personal best performance of 2:09:28, set in the Edinburgh Commonwealth Games, where I took the gold medal. He passed away on Wednesday 9th March 1988 in Massachusetts at the age of 84.

Chapter 10

The Tenth Manchester Marathon
Saturday 25th July 1931

WOOD WINS AGAIN

We do not know the reasons, but no Manchester Marathons were held in 1929 or 1930. But marathons did not disappear from the north. In 1929, Liverpool successfully hosted their Civic Week Marathon and shortly after that a marathon was held for the first time in Bolton.

The Liverpool Marathon appeared to be going from strength to strength. In the first edition, 1927 there had been 47 starters and 25 finishers; in 1928, 96 started and 77 finished, and "a quarter of a million cheered them round a circular route in the city."

The 1929 event was even bigger and on Wednesday 18th September 1929, 132 athletes started in front of St Georges Hall. The race was won by Harold Wood in 2:45:22 with his Olympic team-mate Herbert Bignall of Highgate Harriers second in 2:45:58. Third was Ernie Leatherland in 2:49:59. William Maleedy (Sutton Harriers), who at one stage held a lead of one mile, finished sixth in 3:03:22.

Eleven days later the Bolton Civic Week Marathon took place. There was the suggestion that the *"Sporting Chronicle"* people be approached to put up their 75-guinea trophy to be run for in this race, in the absence of a Manchester event, but it was also felt that this might be unfair for the present holder of the trophy, Harold Wood, to be asked *"to stake his hold on the trophy so soon after such a gruelling race as that at Liverpool."*

The trophy did not appear at Bolton, and Maleedy ran a far more sensible race to win in 2:53:18.6, over half a mile ahead of Harold Wood (2:57:50), with S H Smith, Birchfield Harriers third (3:02:31.4) and E J Morris (Sutton H) fourth (3:03:19). The race had attracted 51 entrants of whom 45 started and 36 finished. The marathon did not take place again..

Sheffield, Blackpool and Liverpool were the venues for northern marathons in 1930. Wood contested two of them and succeeded in both of them. The first at Blackpool was organised by the recently re-formed Blackpool and Fylde Harriers and Athletic Club. Harry Clarke, whose brother Jack had been at Leigh advising Arthur Farrimond in 1924, had moved to Blackpool to establish a business and was a founder member of the new club.

He may have been instrumental in ensuring that the *Sporting Chronicle* trophy won by Harold Wood in Manchester in 1928 was contested for in the 1930 Blackpool Marathon. Certainly Clarke made a tremendous effort to weaken Wood's grip on it. He led Wood by half a mile with three miles to go, but on drinking a glass of water cramped up and collapsed. This allowed Wood to cross the line first in 2:46:44.8 and win the *Sporting Chronicle* trophy outright. Of the 30 starters two others were regulars at Manchester: Ernie Leatherland, fourth in 3:05:46 and George Birchall, seventh in 3:16:34.

By winning the 1930 Liverpool Marathon in 2:41:28 for the second time in a row Wood also made the trophy his own property. This gave rise to the headline at the time: "HOUSE LIKE A JEWELLER'S SHOP"

The Manchester Marathon was revived in 1931 by the *Daily Dispatch* which along with the previous title organiser, *The Sporting Chronicle,* was part of the Allied Newspapers empire and printed on presses at Withy Grove, Manchester. It was part of a charity athletics meeting, organised on behalf of the Manchester Royal Infirmary, and held at the Belle Vue Speedway track.

The course was essentially the same as that of 1928 and previous years when it started at Fallowfield, but we have no details of exactly how athletes reached Kingsway or whether some distance had to be deleted from the far reaches of the course, but it was stated to be 26 miles 385 yards, and commenced with two laps of the track.

Of the 24 entrants, Harold Wood was far and away the favourite. By now he was 28 years old, married and lived at Stubshaw Cross, Ashton-in-Makerfield, near Wigan. He had left the coal-mines and worked as a labourer at the Vulcan Locomotive Works, Earlestown. One month before Manchester he won the second Blackpool Marathon in a time of 2:43:15, finishing *"the course strongly and surprisingly fresh."*

The start of the revived race in 1931 (Picture: Daily Dispatch.)

The *Daily Dispatch* gives us the story of our Manchester Marathon held on a showery day and starting and finishing in front of a very small crowd:

RUN AWAY WIN IN 26-MILE MARATHON
Roadside Cheers by Motorists
"DAILY DISPATCH" TROPHY

"H Wood of the Makerfield Harriers, the winner of many other marathons, scored a runaway win in the marathon race for the *Daily Dispatch* Cup, which was held on Saturday, his time for the distance of 26 miles 385 yards being 2 hr. 42 min. 18 2-5 sec.

Eighteen competitors out of the 26 entered, had covered the preliminary two laps of the track at Belle Vue Speedway and were leaving the track for the road when a man in shorts, and without a running number, burst on the track and was urged to catch up the others. He continued to run strongly, as a complete mystery man, and without a chance of winning a prize even if he finished, until at the 20-mile check, when he was lying fourth, he had to retire owing to cramp.

Cyril Gartlon, of the Sutton H and AC, acted as pace-maker for the first ten miles, which he covered in 59 min 45 sec. At the 15 mile check, however, Wood and G Malcolmson, a young Liverpool harrier had the lead, running alongside each other as they had done since the start, their time being 1 hr 31 min 5 sec. H R Clarke, of the Liverpool Harriers was 15 seconds behind them here on time, and Gartlon, who retired shortly afterwards, fourth.

SHOULDER TO SHOULDER

The field was spreading out at this point, and the three leaders were well out in front. Just before reaching the 20-mile Clarke went in front, with Wood and Malcolmson a few yards behind, but at the check in Cheadle, Wood and Clarke passed running shoulder to shoulder at a fine pace, their time being 2 hr. 2 min. 15 sec. Malcolmson, after a very plucky effort, was tiring, and arrived two and a half minutes later, and was compelled to retire at 21 miles.

Immediately after leaving Cheadle, Wood literally ran away from Clarke and had a lead of one and a half miles when Clarke retired within two miles of the finish. On arriving at the track, where the Manchester Royal Infirmary Charity Athletic Festival was being held, Wood finished with wonderful vigour and received the *Daily Dispatch* Cup from the hands of the Lord Mayor of Manchester (Alderman G F Titt) amid the cheers of the spectators.

SECOND HOME

With the retirement of Clarke and Malcolmson, R Forshaw of Broughton H and AC ran into second place in 2 hr. 50 min. 55 sec., and G P Birchall, of the Warrington AC, was third in 2 her. 52 min. 4 sec. G Sutton of Winton H and AC was fourth in 3 hr. 4 min. 20 sec. Other finishers were J Horne, Makerfield Harriers, A Hughes, Manchester Harriers, E D Sullivan, Leamington C and AC, and J Peers, Makerfield Harriers.

In spite of the heavy traffic on the roads the runners were given a clear run in a very sporting manner by motorists, who stopped to cheer them on their way. The police, both in the Manchester City and Cheshire areas, did everything possible to assist the runners and deserve special thanks. Wood won the *Sporting Chronicle* Trophy outright in 1926-28-1930, the Liverpool and Blackpool Marathon outright in 1930, and the *Sheffield Independent* and Blackpool Marathons this year. His time yesterday was only six minutes outside the record."

Harold Wood wins the 1931 marathon
(Picture: Daily Dispatch.)

Daily Dispatch Cup Marathon Race (26 miles 385 yards)

1	H Wood	Makerfield H	2:43:18.4
2	R Forshaw	Broughton H and AC	2:50:55
3	G P Birchall	Warrington AC	2:52:04
4	G Sutton	Winton H and AC	3:04:20
5	J Horne	Makerfield H	3:04:58
6	A Hughes	Manchester H	3:11:22
7	E D Sullivan	Leamington C & AC	3:13:10
8	J Peers	Makerfield H	3:20:40

It is a pity that Harry Clarke of Leigh Harriers (the *Daily Dispatch* erroneously has him as Liverpool Harriers) had to drop out as he had been showing fine long-distance form in 1931. Perhaps his schedule of the "Poly" Marathon on 30th May, from Windsor to Stamford Bridge, 3rd in 2:45:55.6; the Blackpool Marathon, on 20th June, 3rd in a time of 2:47:43, and then competing in this Manchester Marathon, had taken its toll. He recovered from Manchester quickly and thirteen days later, 3rd July, took third place in the AAA Marathon on a scorching day on the Windsor to Stamford Bridge course in 2:45:55.6.

However, Harold Wood had been successfully busy as well, for in addition to his Blackpool Marathon win he had scored a victory in the *Sheffield Independent* Marathon on Easter Monday, 6th April in a time of 2:49:26, beating Harry Payne, who had been ill for a month with influenza, by 3¹/₂ minutes.

Some snippets from the *Sheffield Independent* newspaper give us some insight in to the running scene at that time. About Harold Wood: *"He is a likeable fellow and very popular with his colleagues and supporters of his club, a motor-coach party of whom had made the journey from Makerfield to follow his fortunes, and who made their presence known both en route and at the end."* Of Wood's running action: *"Without in any way detracting from the meritorious performance of Wood, it can scarcely be said that he possesses the same beautiful style as does Payne, who moves with an ease and a grace that stamps him as the perfect athlete. Anyway, no doubt style will come to Wood as he gains in experience. One thing is certain, however, that Wood is one of England's best long-distance men and many future honours should be his."* Of the race: *"Runners were accompanied by an escort of cyclists, the Vulcan Cycling Club generously provided the travelling marshals,"* and *"scores of thousands of people watched the Marathon."*

The newspaper also described Payne's long journey to Sheffield: *"Rising at five o'clock, Payne walked about a mile from his home at Woodford Green to Higham's Park, caught a suburban train to Liverpool Street, then walked to King's Cross in a downpour of rain to catch the train to Sheffield, which was late in arrival and which gave little respite after a long and tiring journey before setting out on the gruelling marathon course."*

Harry W Payne set a British Marathon Best of 2:30:57.6 when he took the AAA title in the 1929 race on 5th July over the Windsor to Stamford Bridge course. This lasted for nearly 22 years until Jim Peters won the 1951 "Poly" race on the 16th of June with a time of 2:29:42.

Chapter 11

The Eleventh Manchester Marathon
Saturday 16th July 1932

ANOTHER GREAT WIN BY WOOD

1932 was another Olympic year and this time the games would be held in Los Angeles.

A newcomer to the marathon scene was Harold Doggett, the Captain of Salford Harriers. He was born in Moston, Manchester in 1901 and worked in the family business delivering coal. This was heavy work as each bag of coal weighed one hundredweight (112 lbs / 51 kilograms). Initially a member of Hugh Oldham Lads Club in Collyhurst, Harold joined Salford Harriers in 1923, at the age of 22. He became Club Captain in 1927, and won the Club 10 miles Championships in 1929 in a time of 55:29.

It seems there was some doubt over which races were considered to be trials for selection and Doggett, Harold Wood and Ernie Leatherland of Sutton-in-Ashfield entered the Blackpool Marathon on the 11th June in the belief that this race was the "Northern Selection Trial." As a first timer Doggett ran extremely well, not only winning in 2:42:20, but breaking the course record by 55 seconds and beating third placer Wood, who was obviously not running to form, by more than five minutes (2:47:25).

Harold Doggett, Salford Harriers, second in Manchester, here after winning the Blackpool Marathon, 1932. (Courtesy Geoff Doggett.)

84

Thirty-eight-year-old Leatherland was second in a lifetime's best (2:44:10) and A C Chamberlain, Sheffield United Harriers, fourth (2:49:00), also a lifetime's best.

Sam Ferris had set a time of 2:36:32.4 in winning the Polytechnic Marathon on the 28th May. Harold Doggett argued through his club secretary Mr Harry Hardwick, then a top name in the sport, that he should be picked for the Olympics on the strength of this excellent performance against a field of very experienced men. Mr Hardwick was over-ruled by the selectors who said that in view of the fact that it was his first marathon he should run the AAA Trial in three weeks time!

In fact this is what he did, catching the train to London and then on to Windsor. He later recalled that there were discreet royal notices advising the runners not to use the bushes for their last call of nature. On Friday 1st July his bid for an Olympic place did not succeed in this race, and although leading through 15 miles in 1:29:01 he began to falter at 17 miles and faded to seventh

Several Manchester Marathoners are seen here at the start of a race from Talbot Square, Blackpool in 1929: right of centre is Harold Doggett (Salford), to his left Harry Clarke (Blackpool & Fylde), then in Leigh's banded shirts and black shorts are Dick Sutton and Teddy Simms. Far right is Harry Hardwick. Behind Doggett and Clarke is John W Grainey (Leigh H).

place. The race was won in an exciting finish by Donald McNab Robertson (2:34:32.6) just 1.4 seconds ahead of his Maryhill Harriers club-mate, Duncan McLeod Wright (2:34:34), 1925 Manchester Marathon winner. Third was Harry Payne (Woodford Green AC) with 2:40:30. The race had been run on the 1908 Olympic course, finishing at the White City.

Sam Ferris opted not to run the AAA Trial, and Harold Wood, at the time unemployed, could not afford to go to the race. Whether Doggett and Wood thought there was still a chance of selection is unclear. Donald McNab Robertson would not accept selection as he could not get time off from his work as a coach painter in Glasgow, therefore theoretically there was still a place spare. The Olympic rules had changed so that each nation could only send three runners, whereas in 1928 it had been six.

Whatever, these two lined up, along with Ernie Leatherland, who had also run the AAA Trial finishing sixth in 2:47:14.6, for the eleventh Manchester Marathon. *The Sporting Chronicle and Athletic News* gives us the story, but perhaps the esteem and public interest in the marathon was summed up by the brevity of the report compared to those in the 1920s:

GREAT WIN BY WOOD
"Daily Dispatch" Cup Retained
By W R S

"Even the prospect of witnessing the finish of such a spectacular event as a Marathon race failed to attract the public to Belle Vue Speedway on Saturday afternoon for the sports festival organised on behalf of the Manchester Royal Infirmary.

The attendance was very sparse, and one can only conclude that the venue is not popular with patrons of track sport. Possibly Fallowfield might have provided a more suitable setting.

Apart from a few blemishes in the organisation - notably lack of facilities for permitting ticket holders to enter the stadium - the meeting was quite a good one, though curiously enough the tit-bits were crowded into the second half of the programme, which coincided with the arrival of the Marathon men.

Twenty three of these long-distance exponents set off at two o'clock on their arduous journey round the neighbouring Cheshire roads. A little over 2½ hours later H Wood had breasted the tape to carry off the *Daily Dispatch* Cup for the second year in succession. Another victory and the trophy will be his own.

As Wood completed the final circuit of the speedway, H Doggett who had fought against the more experienced Makerfield man until about five miles from home, appeared on the scene, and the Salford Harrier finished a good second, so that in three essays at the full Marathon distance he had finished first, seventh, and second in turn - no mean feat for a newcomer to the game.

LEG-WEARY LEATHERLAND

Leatherland, the Sutton stalwart, contested the issue dourly with Wood and Doggett for two-thirds of the journey, but then fell back, and though finishing third was a tired man. I fear he is suffering from a surfeit of distance running. Birchall and Murphy, fourth and fifth, were much fresher, but then a long interval elapsed before Cowin of North Liverpool Gymnasium, appeared and painfully plodded round the final circuit."

Results:

1	H Wood	(Makerfield H)	2:36:12	
			course record and lifetime's best	
2	H Doggett	(Salford H)	2:37:59	**lifetime's best**
3	E Leatherland	(Sutton-in-Ashfield)	2:50:33	
4	G P Birchall	(Warrington AC)	2:52:55	
5	P Murphy	(Makerfield H)	2:53:15	
6	W E Cowin	(N Liverpool Gym H)	3:14:32	

Wood's outstanding time was a course record and a personal best. His time ranked him fourth best in the country and after the withdrawal of McNab Robertson, he should have been our third man at the Olympics.

It was the end of Harold Doggett's marathon career. His son Geoff said, "Although my father competed until 46 years of age, his marathon career was over in 36 days!"

This was the last time Ernie Leatherland ran Manchester. He was in the 1933 Blackpool Marathon, but did not finish after being sent off course, and retired from marathons at the age of 39, probably to concentrate on a hardware business he had started with his father in 1928.

In a career of 27 marathons he won two Manchesters, was second in one, third in two, fourth in one, and twice did not finish making a total of eight starts. His lifetime's best, 2:44:10, came in Blackpool, 1932.

Ernie Leatherland's marathons

1922	Brighton	1	3:16:04
1922	"Poly"	4	2:59:09
1923	Manchester	1	2:51:25
1924	Manchester	1	2:48:43.8
1924	Olympics	dnf	
1924	Manchester	dnf	
1925	Manchester	2	2:44:14.6
1925	"Poly"	4	2:46:07.4
1926	AAA	5	2:56:02
1927	Manchester / AAA	4	3:06:31.6
1927	Liverpool	4	2:58:14
1928	Manchester	3	2:51:34.6
1928	Liverpool	competed - dnf?	

1929	Sheffield	3	2:59:11
1929	AAA	3	2:49:22
1929	Liverpool	3	2:49:59
1929	Bolton	competed.	
1930	AAA	8	2:52:20
1930	Liverpool	5	2:54:32
1931	Sheffield	10	3:04:43
1931	Blackpool	competed - dnf?	
1932	Blackpool	2	2:44:10 **personal best**
1932	AAA	6	2:47:14.6
1932	Manchester	3	2:50:33
1933	"Poly"	4	2:53:54.6
1933	Blackpool	dnf	

He built his own house in Sutton-in-Ashfield giving more room to display his numerous cups and medals. Attached to this house was an aviary in which he kept budgerigars. During the Second World War he was in the Home Guard and cycled to and from a munitions factory near Nottingham, where he worked. He died in 1947 leaving a wife and daughter who eventually sold up and moved to Devon.

Our two Olympic representatives did superbly well in Los Angeles. The marathon was held on 7th August and a fast finishing Sam Ferris just failed to catch Juan Zabala of Argentina (2:31:36) and took silver, just 19 seconds behind (2:31:55) in a lifetime's best. "Dunky" Wright was leading at 22 miles and although he faded, he was on the track as the winner crossed the line, and got home fourth in 2:32:41, also a lifetime's best. Third was Armas Toivonen, Finland, in 2:32:12.

Chapter 12

The Twelfth Manchester Marathon
Saturday 5th August 1933

WOOD'S DRAMATIC COLLAPSE IN MARATHON

In 1933 the *Daily Dispatch* Marathon race was held in conjunction with an athletics meeting in aid of the Manchester Royal Infirmary and the Chronicle Cinderella Fund. The venue returned to Fallowfield and the marathon route was the familiar one of 1928 and before: one mile on the track, Whitworth Lane, Old Hall Lane to Birchfields Road, Kingsway, Cheadle Green, Gatley Station, Sharston, Timperley, Green Lane to Hale Road, and thence through Styal village, Heald Green to Gatley and back by the course followed outward.

Favourite for the race was Harold Wood (Makerfield H) who had been victorious in 1931 and 1932, and if he performed the hat trick would win the *Daily Dispatch* Cup outright. Other runners of note were Robert Forshaw (Broughton H and AC) and George Birchall (Warrington AC) who had been second and third respectively in the 1931 race, and S J Brooks (Chesterfield C & AC), the Midlands Champion.

The weather was awful for marathon running. It was the hottest weekend for 38 years. By 10 am it was 78° F (26° C) in the shade and by noon had risen to 83° F (28° C). Newspapers reported that there were 20 bathing tragedies, bathing pools were so full that no one could swim, 18 were killed on the road and three died on account of the heat. Thirty-two athletes had entered the race which commenced at 2:00 pm.

Twenty-seven starters left the track and in addition to the heat they had to contend with the dust and noise of main roads crowded with holiday traffic as Monday was a bank holiday. The pace was not slow and at 5 miles, Cheadle Church, the field was led by Joseph G Halsey (Manchester AC) followed closely by Wood, A C Chamberlain (Sheffield United H), and Brooks. The time of 31:03, sub-2:43 pace, was somewhat incautious and several competitors had given up at this early stage.

More retired before 10 miles where Chamberlain had a slight lead over Wood with Brooks third. There was little change at 15 miles, but not long after, Brooks, after a busy season, dropped out and Wood began to forge ahead. By 21 miles he was half a mile ahead of Chamberlain, but suddenly the conditions got to him and he collapsed suffering from sunstroke. Chamberlain

The start of the 1933 Marathon. No 16 is the eventual winner A C Chamberlain. No 19 is Charlie Bourne, (See Chapter 16). (Picture: Daily Dispatch.)

Cyril Chamberlain being presented with the Daily Dispatch cup by Walter P Cobbett, CBE., the Chairman of Manchester Royal Infirmary. (Picture: Daily Dispatch.)

had a two mile lead over the next man, Birchall, and was able to conserve his resources reaching the finish exhausted but elated in a time of 2:56:37, almost 20 minutes ahead of second man Birchall.

Only eight men finished. Wood, who was in a bad way, was taken by car back to Fallowfield Stadium, and thence, suffering a temperature of 102° F (39° C) to Manchester Royal Infirmary, where he remained until Monday.

Results:

1	A C Chamberlain	(Sheffield U)	2:56:37
2	G P Birchall	(Warrington)	3:15:16
3	E J Simms	(Leigh H)	3:21:55
4	R Forshaw	(Broughton H)	3:25:05
5	E D Sullivan	(Leamington C & AC)	3:25:37
6	W Maleedy	U G B M (St Helens)	3:41:05
7	J Horne	(Birchfield)	3:43:08
8	E Lawson	(Winton H)	3:45:41

Arthur Cyril Chamberlain's slight build favoured him under these extreme conditions with a large body surface area compared to body weight. He was born in Sheffield on 22nd April 1897, and had a tough start to life being one of six surviving children whose father left home when Cyril was young. At one stage he was going to school in bare feet enabling the youngest brother the privilege of wearing shoes. He did not marry and it fell to him to look after his mother until she died in 1948.

He had wanted to be a jockey, and had the build for it, but this did not work out and he became interested in marathon running at a relatively late age. We know he entered the *Sheffield Independent* Marathon in 1931 as he is mentioned in the start list, but he was not in the results and probably did not start. Self trained, he was described as being of a quiet nature and reserved. At the age of 35 he finished fourth in the 1932 Blackpool Marathon in a personal best time of 2:49:00. That same year, in the AAA Marathon, from Windsor Castle to the White City, he ran sub-3:15 to win a "standard medal," but we do not know his time or position. In addition to Manchester 1933, he had another victory, this time in the Blackpool Marathon of 1934 (2:52:28). His ability to withstand heat stood him in good stead in the 1935 AAA Marathon, where the temperature was so high that out of forty-one starters, only five finished. *The Manchester Guardian* headlined the race **"Marathon Massacre."** It was the slowest AAA Marathon on record and was won by Bertie Norris (Polytechnic H) in 3:02:57.4 with the reigning Balkan Champion, Stylianos

Kyriakides of Cyprus second in 3:03:20. Cyril Chamberlain was third in 3:20:15. The race is mentioned again in Chapter 14.

Of the nine marathon starts he failed to finish only one and this was the 1933 Blackpool when he went off course. His marathon career spanned a mere five years, and he died in Sheffield in 1977 at the age of 80.

Arthur Cyril Chamberlain's Marathons

1932	Blackpool	4	2:49:00	**personal best**
1932	AAA	?	under 3:15	wins a standard medal
1933	Manchester	1	2:56:37	
1933	Blackpool	dnf		
1934	Blackpool	1	2:52:28	
1934	AAA	8	3:06:00	wins a standard medal
1935	Blackpool	7	2:54:30	
1935	AAA	3	3:20:15	
1936	Polytechnic	?	2:57:35	not in first 20

Chapter 13

The Thirteenth Manchester Marathon
Saturday 30th June 1934

WOOD'S EASY CONQUEST

For the 1934 Manchester Marathon the course was the usual one, commencing at the Fallowfield Stadium and run over the Cheshire roads. Although a glorious afternoon, the sports carnival attracted a poor crowd, for those days, of around 3,000. The marathon race for the *Daily Dispatch* Cup looked set to be a scorcher with Harold Wood not necessarily the outright favourite. The high temperatures of the day would not suit an athlete of Wood's stocky build. He had collapsed the previous year at the 21 mile point and only a month before the present race, on 2nd June, could muster only fourth place in the Blackpool Marathon under heat wave conditions where it was reported that Wood had *'turned out with a cabbage leaf on his head, kept in place by a knotted handkerchief.'* The winner in Blackpool had been 1933 Manchester Marathon winner, A C Chamberlain of Sheffield United Harriers (2:52:28), almost six minutes ahead of Wood (2:58:26); however, Chamberlain did not contest Manchester because he had been selected by the Northern Counties to run in the AAA Marathon in July.

However, the second man at Blackpool, J E Brockbank of Askam-in-Furness, who had actually led Chamberlain by three minutes at the 20 mile point in that race, would be on the start line. Also there was the third placer from Blackpool, George Birchall of Warrington AC. Thirty were entered in the programme which noted the prize for the winner was a "Gent's Waltham Watch (Hunter) and Solid Gold Albert" whilst the runner-up received an "Oak Grand-daughter Clock - 14 days' strike."

At the half-way point in the race, Brockbank was forcing the pace, disputing the lead with F M Kean Jr (Slaithwaite), R Fish (Royton) and of course Harold Wood. Gradually the Makerfield man's rivals fell away with Brockbank lasting longest. The 21 mile point must have been a psychological barrier for Wood, but he had run at a far more sensible pace and in the end was almost nine minutes ahead of second man, Sydney Brooks, formerly of Chesterfield C & AC and now with Sutton-in-Ashfield. This third victory gave Wood the *Daily Dispatch* Cup outright.

OFFICIAL PROGRAMME

COMPETITOR

Manchester Royal Infirm

The Fourth Annual Charity

ATHLETIC
FESTIVAL

(Under A.A.A., N.C.U. and W.A.A.A.)

MANCHESTER ATHLETIC CLUB
GROUND - - - FALLOWFIELD

Saturday, June 30th
1934

MARATHON AT 2-0 P.M.
TRACK EVENTS AT 2-30 P.M.

Under the distinguished patronage of
THE LORD MAYOR AND LADY MAYORESS OF MANCHESTER

WALTER P. COBBETT, Esq., C.B.E.,
Chairman, Manchester Royal Infirmary
JAMES WATTS, Esq.,
Deputy Chairman, Manchester Royal Infirmary
C. M. SKINNER, Esq., *Treas., Manchester Royal Infirmary*

SPORTS COMMITTEE :
Chairman :
FRED BERESFORD, Esq., President, N.C.A.A.
Committee :
H. M. McKECHNIE, Esq., M.A.   F. K. ASHWORTH, Esq., M.B., Ch.
(President, University Union) J. ALLCOCK, Esq., N.C.A.A.
J. ADAMS, Esq., N.C.A.A.   R. THOMAS, Esq., N.C.A.A.
W. WRAY, Esq., N.C.A.A.
Hon. Secretary :
EDWARD W. ROBINSON, Esq. (M.R.I.).

The cover of the 1934 programme (Courtesy Roy Wood

94

Results:

1	H Wood	(Makerfield H)	2:56:11
2	S Brooks	(Sutton-in-Ashfield)	3:04:59
3	J Grainey	(Leigh H)	3:05:48
4	G P Birchall	(Warrington)	3:07:23
5	J Simms	(Leigh H)	3:08:12
6	R Forshaw	(Broughton H)	3:14:16
7	E J Morris	(Railway Houses)	3:15:36
8	E D Sullivan	(Leamington C & AC)	3:21:21
9	A Lee	(Warrington AC)	3:22:37

On the strength of this victory Harold Wood was selected to run for England in the British Empire Games Marathon, London, six weeks later. England and Scotland used the "Poly" and AAA Marathons as their primary selection races. The "Poly" Marathon, which was the same day as the Blackpool Marathon, was won under warm conditions by Scotland's Duncan McLeod Wright in 2:56:30 from R F J Nicholls of Reading AC in 3:00:44 and Laurie Weatherill of South London Harriers, 3:01:30. Scotsman Donald McNab Robertson of Maryhill took the AAA title for the third year in succession in 2:41:55, the race taking place on 13th June over a circular route from the White City. Bertie Norris, of the Polytechnic Harriers was the runner-up recording 2:55:05. The two Scotsman were selected and England chose Nicholls, Weatherill, Norris and Wood.

The second Empire Games Marathon on Saturday 7th August 1934 was held on a circular route from the White City Stadium in London. Of the twelve starters there were seven finishers with Wood a creditable fourth.

Results:

1	Harold Webster	(CANADA)	2:40:36
2	Donald McNab Robertson	(SCOTLAND)	2:45:08
3	Duncan McLeod Wright	(SCOTLAND)	2:56:20
4	Harold Wood	(ENGLAND)	2:58:41
5	Percy Wyer	(CANADA)	3:00:40
6	Wilf Short	(WALES)	3:02:56
7	Reg Nicholls	(ENGLAND)	3:05:23

Chapter 14

The Fourteenth Manchester Marathon
Saturday 29th June 1935

A WIN FOR WARRINGTON'S G P BIRCHALL

The popularity of marathon running seemed to be on the wane by 1935. The Manchester Marathon for the *Daily Dispatch* Cup was held as usual with the Manchester Royal Infirmary Charity Sports Festival. A mere 22 runners entered and only 18 started.

The most notable absentee was the holder, Harold Wood. He had his eye on the AAA title, in a race to take place two weeks further on, 13th July, on a route from the White City into the Middlesex countryside and back to the stadium. He had already won the Blackpool Marathon on 18th May in a new course record time of 2:37:20 and must have fancied his chances. A Wirral AC man, Sam Dodd, winner of both Northern and National Cross-Country titles in 1934, had been second in Blackpool, (2:39:32), with J E Brockbank (Lancaster Primrose H) running 2:39:45 in third place. Fourth man home was George Birchall of Warrington AC in the very respectable time of 2:44:52. This would make him favourite as he had finished second in the 1933 Manchester Marathon.

Again, the crowd was disappointing as the weather was ideal. For spectating that is. The intense heat was of no help at all to the marathon racers. That day the shade temperature would reach 80° F (27 °C) and 14 hours of sunshine were recorded.

Some runners did not sufficiently take the adverse conditions into account and paid the penalty for too rapid a start as only eight finished, some of them in desperately slow times. The leader at 10 miles was Northcliffe of Slaithwaite United Harriers, but G P Birchall kept his head and by the finish was over 17 minutes ahead of his club-mate, Arthur Lee. He crossed the line tired but happy at his first ever success over the marathon distance.

Results:

1	G P Birchall	(Warrington AC)	3:01:20
2	A Lee	(Warrington AC)	3:18:55
3	R Forshaw	(Broughton H & AC)	3:26:42
4	E D Sullivan	(Leamington C & AC)	3:30:45
5	R T Bailey	(Liverpool H & AC)	3:45:00
6	F Poole	(Sale H)	3:49:05

We have no details of finishers 7 and 8.

Left, George P Birchall winning the 1935 Marathon, and right, receiving the Trophy. (Picture: Daily Dispatch.)

Born in 1900 George Peter Birchall was a stalwart of Warrington AC. His marathon career spanned 19 years with 22 finishes. Eighteen of his races were in Lancashire including eight Manchesters and the rest in Liverpool, Blackpool and Warrington. He had two forays over the Pennines in to Yorkshire for the 1931 Sheffield Marathon and the 1946 Doncaster to Sheffield where he placed third in the Northern Counties Championships. He got better with age, smashing his personal best by over ten minutes in securing only his second victory at the distance recording 2:35:45 in the 1939 Warrington race.

The war put paid to any further progress. Twelve years after his Manchester victory he returned in 1947 to finish 12th in 3:18:03.

Long distance race walking became part of the Warrington man's training and competitive programme, a move which resulted in considerable success. Joining the Lancashire Walking Club in 1933, he soon made his mark: in 1936 he became Centurion number 101 by walking 100 miles within 24 hours (19:40:35). Team and individual medals and prizes in the Race Walkers Association Championships, Liverpool to Manchester and Manchester to Blackpool events came George's way over the next twenty years. His son

George Joseph followed his father's example and after the Second World War was the first novice in the 1948 Liverpool to Manchester walk won by his father! According to his son, his father's best achievement was to finish third in the 1936 Manchester Marathon on Easter Saturday and then on Easter Monday then help the Lancashire Walking Club win the team for the Sunderland to Darlington, a walk of over 40 miles.

George P Birchall (1900-1986). (Courtesy George J Birchall)

In 1954 soaked by a stormy sea father and son set off from Blackpool, walked to Manchester, then back to Blackpool, a distance of 100 miles, all within 24 hours, a feat unique in the annals of the Centurions. They were given the same time: in fact the time by Mr Birchall senior was not only another first class time, but eight minutes faster than he took 18 years previously! His last competition was at the age of 71 when he finished the Manchester to Blackpool walking race, and he was reportedly still running 50 miles a week at the age of 81. He suffered a stroke whilst out running and died in 1986.

George P Birchall (Warrington AC) Significant Marathons

1928	Manchester	13	3:13:25.2	
1928	Liverpool	16	3:23:47	
1929	Liverpool	14	3:18:21	
1930	Sheffield	11	3:00:36	
1930	Blackpool	7	3:16:34	
1931	Sheffield	5	2:57:25	
1931	Blackpool	5	2:52:10	
1931	Manchester	3	2:52:04	
1932	Blackpool	5	2:50:10	
1932	Manchester	4	2:52:55	
1933	Manchester	2	3:15:16	
1933	Blackpool	3	2:51:37	
1934	Blackpool	3	2:56:08	
1934	Manchester	4	3:07:23	
1935	Blackpool	4	2:44:52	
1935	Manchester	1	3:01:20	
1936	Manchester	3	2:50:28	
1938	Warrington	1	2:46:29	
1938	Blackpool	5	2:46:20	
1939	Warrington	1	2:35:45	**lifetime's best**
1946	Doncaster to Sheffield	5?	3:05:15	3rd NCAA
1947	Manchester	12	3:18:03	

Harold Wood picked a bad day to challenge for the AAA title. As described in Chapter 12, A C Chamberlain, the 1933 Manchester winner, went on to finish third in the 1935 AAA's race the *Manchester Guardian* deemed "Marathon Massacre." Wood was second at 5 miles, but in the end did not finish. Only five completed the race. *The Manchester Guardian* noted that the first two finished *"reasonably fresh, but the other three were sorry cases."* Behind Norris (3:02:57.4), Kyriakides (3:03:20), and Chamberlain (3:20:15) were J McShane of Saltwell H (3:22:45) and E D Sullivan of Leamington C & AC (no time available). Sullivan recalled 36 years later that this was "his most noteworthy race."

Chapter 15

The Fifteenth Manchester Marathon
Saturday 11th April 1936

WOOD AGAIN WINS MARATHON

The annual marathon race for the *Daily Dispatch* Cup, held in conjunction with the Manchester Royal Infirmary Charity Sports at the Manchester Athletic Club ground at Fallowfield, was considerably earlier than previously. It was an Olympic year once more, and perhaps Harold Wood (Makerfield H) was secretly hoping for cooler weather and a chance to set a fast time which would catch the eyes of the selectors.

These gentlemen would almost certainly have their attention focussed in marathons in the south, namely the Polytechnic Marathon on 13th June and the AAA Marathon Windsor to the White City on 11th July. It is not surprising then that the Manchester race was contested almost entirely by runners from the North West. Wood's main opposition would come from the holder, George P Birchall (Warrington AC) and a first time marathoner, George Bailey (Salford H). Just short of 30-years-old, Bailey was at the height of his career. He had the British steeplechase records for 2 miles (10:14.8) and

The start of the 1936 Marathon at Fallowfield (Picture: Daily Dispatch.)

3,000 metres (9:16.0), and won the first ever British Empire Games steeplechase title in 1930. He was twice the Northern Cross-Country Champion over 9 miles (1931 and 1935), and held his club's record for 10 miles on the track at 51:45.2. He was obviously fast, but could he last the distance?

The course was the normal one and as this was Wood's 11th foray over the course he certainly had the advantage of course knowledge.

Twenty-nine starters left the stadium and headed out on to the Cheshire roads. Wood was content to occupy third position at the five, ten and fifteen mile check-points behind Bailey and his club-mate Harold Crowther, but easily in contact. The time at 15 miles was 1:28:20. By 20 miles (2:01) Wood had joined Bailey and from then on they kept close company, entering the ground almost together, for a final lap of the track. Bailey made a tremendous effort and took the lead at the first bend but the stronger and more experienced Wood came again with a fine burst of speed and took the race by forty yards. Such was the pace of these two men over the final ten miles that the third man home, holder, George Birchall was almost two miles behind at the end. There were 19 finishers in all.

The winner Harold Wood, left, with George W Bailey on the right.
(Picture: Daily Dispatch.)

Results:

1	H Wood	(Makerfield H)	2:40:02
2	G Bailey	(Salford H)	2:40:14
3	G P Birchall	(Warrington)	2:50:28
4	J F Howarth	(Buxton)	2:52:43
5	A Lee	(Warrington)	2:53:02
6	W Richards	(Sale H)	2:54:18
7	C Morgan	(Sale H)	2:56:25
8	H Crowther	(Salford H)	2:56:59
9	S T Bailey	(Liverpool H)	3:00:25
10	S H Leigh	(Warrington)	3:04:08
11	R Forshaw	(Broughton H)	3:05:55
12	D Fish	(Middleton Junction)	3:12:27
13	D G Edgar	(Sefton H)	3:13:18
14	J T Fidler	(Salford H)	3:13:32

No results are available for the last five.

The "Poly" Marathon on 13th June was won by Bertie Norris of the host Club in a time of 2:35:20. He was selected for the Olympics in Berlin. A month later, in the AAA Championship, Ernie Harper (Hallamshire H), who had finished fourth in the "Poly," had a tremendous battle with Donald McNab Robertson, losing out by a mere 1.2 seconds, 2:35:02.4 to 2:35:03.6. These two took the remaining Olympic berths. Wood was a worthy fifth in this AAA race, 2:41:45, and therefore did not make the Olympics.

In the Berlin Olympic Marathon Ernie Harper ran a fantastic race to take a silver medal (2:31:32.2) behind Kitei Son (Japan) (2:29:19.2). Third was the Japanese, Shoryu Nan (2:31:42.0), whilst McNab Robertson was an excellent 7th (2:37:06.2). Norris did not finish.

Second man home in Manchester, George Bailey did not run another marathon. He was still turning out for his club after the War, most notable running a leg of the Manchester to Blackpool relay. He was born in Buxton, Derbyshire in 1906. For many years he worked in a quarry and would run and walk the ten miles there, in heavy boots, and return home in the same manner. Reputed to be as strong as an ox, one story has it that he won a long-case clock in Scotland. Returning by rail, he walked from the station to his home with the clock strapped to his back! He retired to Suffolk where he died in the year 2000 aged 94.

The Sporting Chronicle / Daily Dispatch series of Manchester Marathons ended here. This period 1923-1936 was certainly hailed as the "Harold Wood era." Of the 13 Manchester Marathons of this period Harold Wood started in eleven, finished nine and won six.

He had one more marathon victory, that being at Blackpool, 1938, in a time of 2:41:58, and the following year he got third in Warrington with 2:42:04, another highly respectable time.

Harold Wood and his array of silverware won over the years.
(Courtesy Roy Wood).

The beginning of the war signalled the end of Harold Wood's running career. He was in the coal delivery business and was exempt from military service. He said, "The war went on too long." (for him to get back in to running.) He died in 1975 at the age of 72. His son, Roy, who represented the victorious Lancashire Cross-Country team in the Inter-counties race of 1964, inaugurated a "Harold Wood 8" (7³/₄ miles actually) road race in 1976, which lasted for 15 editions.

The Marathon career of Harold Wood (Makerfield H)

Date	Venue	Pos	Time
31 May 1924	Manchester	6	2:59:59.2
18 Aug 1924	Manchester	4	2:51:33
8 Aug 1925	Manchester	4	2:59:43
12 Jun 1926	Manchester	1	2:43:51.8
30 Jul 1927	Manchester /AAA	dnf	
28 Sep 1927	Liverpool	2	2:45:13
19 May 1928	Manchester	1	2:39:29.2
6 Jul 1928	London / AAA	dnf	
5 Aug 1928	Olympics	11	2:41:15
26 Sep 1928	Liverpool	2	2:47:52
18 Sep 1929	Liverpool	1	2:45:22
29 Sep1929	Bolton	2	2:57:50
7 Jun 1930	Blackpool	1	2:46:44.8
17 Sep1930	Liverpool	1	2:41:28
6 Apr 1931	Sheffield	1	2:49:26
20 Jun 1931	Blackpool	1	2:43:15
25 Jul 1931	Manchester	1	2:43:18.4
11 Jun 1932	Blackpool	3	2:47:25
16 Jul 1932	Manchester	1	2:36:12 **lifetime's best**
5 Aug 1933	Manchester	dnf	
2 Jun 1934	Blackpool	4	2:58:26
30 Jun 1934	Manchester	1	2:56:11
7 Aug 1934	Empire Games	4	2:58:41
18 May 1935	Blackpool	1	2:37:20
13 Jul 1935	London /AAA	dnf	
11 Apr 1936	Manchester	1	2:40:02
11 Jul 1936	London /AAA	5	2:41:45
7 May 1938	Blackpool	1	2:41:58
7 Aug 1939	Warrington	3	2:42:04

Sporting Chronicle and Daily Dispatch Marathons
RANKING OF TOP 50 TIMES - 1923-36

Rank	Name	Club	Year	Place	Time
1	Harold Wood	(Makerfield H)	1932	1	2:36:12
2	Harold Doggett	(Salford H)	1932	2	2:37:59
3	H Wood	(Makerfield H)	1928	1	2:39:29.2
4	H Wood	(Makerfield H)	1936	1	2:40:02
5	George Bailey	(Salford H)	1936	2	2:40:14
6	H Wood	(Makerfield H)	1931	1	2:43:18.4
7	H Wood	(Makerfield H)	1926	1	2:43:51.8
8	D McLeod Wright	(Shettleston H)	1925	1	2:44:07.8
9	Ernie Leatherland	(Mansfield H)	1925	2	2:44:14.6
10	Sam Ferris	(RAF)	8/1924	3	2:47:44 *
11	E Leatherland	(Polytechnic H)	5/1924	1	2:48:43.8
12	S Ferris	(RAF)	1927	1	2:48:46.4
13	G P Birchall	(Warrington AC)	1936	3	2:50:02
14	E Leatherland	(Sutton-in-Ashfield)	1932	3	2:50:33
15	Robert Forshaw	(Broughton H)	1931	2	2:50:55
16	J Tom Slaney	(Sutton-in-Ashfield)	1928	2	2:51:07
17	D McL Wright	(Caledonian AC)	1926	2	2:51:12.4
18	E Leatherland	(Polytechnic H)	1923	1	2:51:25
19	H Wood	(Makerfield H)	8/1924	4	2:51:33
20	E Leatherland	(Mansfield H)	1928	3	2:51:34.6
21	G P Birchall	(Warrington AC)	1931	3	2:52:04
22	Arthur Farrimond	(Leigh H)	5/1924	2	2:52:19.6
23	J F Howarth	(Buxton AC)	1936	4	2:52:43
24	G P Birchall	(Warrington AC)	1932	4	2:52:55
25	William Maleedy	(Sacred Hearts)	5/1924	3	2:52:57
26	Arthur Lee	(Warrington AC)	1936	5	2:53:02
27	P Murphy	(Makerfield H)	1932	5	2:53:15
28	J E Sharman	(Sheffield UH)	5/1924	4	2:53:52.2
29	W Richards	(Sale H)	1936	6	2:54:18
30	C J Bryant	(Bolton U)	5/1924	5	2:55:56.6
31	H Wood	(Makerfield H)	1934	1	2:56:11
32	C Morgan	(Sale H)	1936	7	2:56:25
33	A C Chamberlain	(Sheffield UH)	1933	1	2:56:37
34	Harold Crowther	(Salford H)	1936	8	2:56:50
35	H G Wickington	(Woodford Green AC)	1926	3	2:57:06.2
36	A Wroe	(Small Heath H)	1928	4	2:58:41.6
37	E T Bryant	(Portsmouth H)	1928	5	2:58:42.2
38	W Maleedy	(Sacred Hearts)	1925	3	2:58:46.2
39	C E Mitchell	(Chesterfield C & AC)	1926	4	2:59:30.8
40	H Wood	(Makerfield H)	1925	4	2:59:43
41	H Wood	(Makerfield H)	5/1924	6	2:59:59.2
42	S Widdop	(Bingley H)	1928	6	3:00:10.4
43	T H Heeley	(Sparkhill H)	1927	2	3:00:22.4
44	S T Bailey	(Liverpool H)	1936	9	3:00:25
45	G P Birchall	(Warrington AC)	1935	1	3:01:20
46	A Farrimond	(Leigh H)	8/1924	5	3:02:52
47	S H Leigh	(Warrington AC)	1936	10	3:04:08
48	G Sutton	(Winton H)	1931	4	3:04:10
49	Arthur Farrimond	(Leigh H)	1923	2	3:04:45
50	W Maleedy	(Pilkington Recs)	1926	5	3:04:51.8

* denotes the longer route taken in the August 1924 race by Ferris.
The first two finishers in this race are not ranked due to taking a shorter route.
(See Chapter 5)

Chapter 16

The 16th Manchester Marathon
Saturday 3rd May 1947

HENNING'S WIN CONSOLIDATES HIS LEGEND

This Manchester Marathon was a one-off event, part of the celebrations to mark the Golden Jubilee (fifty years) of the *Manchester Evening Chronicle*. It was again part of an athletics festival with the English Secondary Schools holding their annual championships at Fallowfield with an entry of between 800 and 900 athletes.

The 26 miles 385 yards course was only similar to the 1920s and 30s series, starting with one lap of the track and using Cheshire roads to the south. The route was: Birchfields Road, Moseley Road, Wilmslow Road, Princess Road, Princess Parkway, Sale Road, Northenden Road, Marsden Road, Brooklands Road, Altrincham Road, Hare and Hounds, Green Lane, Delaheys Road, Ringway Golf Links, past Ringway Airport, past Fairey's Works in the direction of Styal, Hollin Lane, Styal Road, Moss Nook, Heald Green, Peel Hall Road, Altrincham Road, Longley Lane, Forum Cinema, over Mersey Bridge, Palatine Road, La Scala Cinema into Moseley Road, Whitworth Lane and back to the Manchester Athletic Club ground to finish with a lap of the track.

There were 49 entrants drawn from all over the country. Favourite for the race was 38-year-old John Henning (Duncairn Nomads), who had travelled from Belfast. After trying fly-weight boxing, becoming Ulster Champion at 18, and then soccer, he took up running and was advised by Sam Ferris. His first marathon was the North of Ireland Championships in 1944 when he was second to Tom Orr (Willowfield Temperance H) 2:53:50 to 2:48:00. He then became Northern Ireland Champion in 1945 and 1946, and All-Ireland Champion in 1946. A decade earlier he had run cross-country for Ireland, 1935, 1936 and 1937.

Another leading contender was 42-year-old Leslie Griffiths (Reading AC), who was the Polytechnic Marathon Champion in the War years (1940, 1942 and 1943), whilst Arthur Tyrer (Sutton Harriers) had retained his Northern Marathon title a month before (9th April) when he was second (2:46:49) to Jack Holden (2:41:55.8) in the Doncaster to Sheffield Marathon. Interestingly Henning had been only fifth in that race, over 11 minutes behind Tyrer in a time of 2:58:21.

106

Of the 49 entrants, 36 lined up for the starter's pistol at 2:30pm. They faced rain and a gale-force wind; not much fun for a marathon.

A Sale Harrier, Alf Toon, set a fast pace and had a slight lead as the runners left the track and emerged on to the road. Toon reached 5 miles in 28:55, a fast time for those days, with Griffiths and Tyrer on his heels, followed by Frank Grattan, a promising Manchester runner and Francis Stainforth, from Hull. Toon actually ran his next five miles faster still, taking to the pavement at seven and a half miles, whilst his followers kept to the rough macadam of the road. His second 5 miles took 28:40, as he reached the 10 mile marker in 57:35. Despite this he was only 50 yards ahead of his chasers. Approaching the 15 mile point, Toon was still in front, but the rapid early pace finally took its toll, and he cramped up and had to retire at 16 miles.

Griffiths and Henning then fought for the lead and were practically together at 20 miles, reached in 2:01:35. Soon after this Henning piled on the pace and Griffiths had to let him go. From then on there was only one man in it, and Henning powered away, entering the track in excellent style to win by nearly twelve minutes in 2:45:37.

The 1948 "Poly" field being presented to the Queen Elizabeth, the late Queen Mother. No 137 is John Henning. (Courtesy Roy Henning.)

Over the last four miles Griffiths ran with his Reading AC club-mate W H Kelly and the two men lapped the Manchester AC track together, finishing within one second of each other. Alf Tyrer, the Northern Champion had had a lot of hard racing in the previous four weeks and was disappointing in ninth place, whilst Mike Porter of Sale Harriers had an excellent debut finishing fifth.

Results:

1	J A Henning	(Duncairn Nomads)	2:45:37
2	L H Griffiths	(Reading AC)	2:57:22
3	W H Kelly	(Reading AC)	2:57:22
4	F Stainforth	(Hull H)	3:07:38
5	M F Porter	(Sale H)	3:08:34
6	G H Houghton	(Wirral AC)	3:10:00
7	G E Haslam	(Bolton U H)	3:12:10
8	R Forshaw	(Manchester & D Lads)	3:13:23
9	A E Tyrer	(Sutton H & AC)	3:14:55
10	G Sutton	(East Cheshire H)	3:15:00
11	A Ellis	(Harborne H)	3:16:15
12	G P Birchall	(Warrington AC)	3:18:03
13	G F Stewart	(Liverpool H & AC)	———
14	J L Coomber	(East Cheshire H)	———
15	C A Bourne	(Liverpool Pembroke)	———
16	L Flynne	(M and D Lads' Club)	———
17	E Whitehurst	(Sheffield U and AC)	———
18	W E Cousins	(Sheffield U and AC)	———
19	J Gorman	(M and D Lads Club)	———
20	H Barraclough	(Wibsey Pk & Centurions)	———

John Henning was described *"as a man with good long-distance action and at 38 years of age is capable of improvement."* A training programme devised by Sam Ferris consisted of three runs a week: 10, 15 and 20 miles with an occasional marathon. The following year he was an obvious contender for the British Olympic team for the Games to be held in London; however, in the "Poly," the sole trial for the Olympics, he suffered from blisters and took two wrong turns following a cyclist who was not an official. Despite this he finished a mere ten seconds behind the third placer, Stan Jones of Polytechnic Harriers. He was not selected and must have been mightily annoyed and frustrated.

That year, the British team was the first three in the "Poly," Jack Holden (Tipton H), Tommy Richards (South London H) and Stan Jones. The Olympic race was won by Delfo Cabrera (2:34:51.6) with Tommy Richards just 16 seconds behind for a silver medal. Bronze medallist was the Belgian, Etienne Gailly, who had led in to the stadium, in a time of 2:35:33.6. Jack Holden did not finish, whilst Stan Jones was 30th in 3:09:16.

This disappointment over the Olympic selection did nothing to dent Henning's enthusiasm for running. In 1949 he won the Sheffield Marathon in 2:38:15, and in the AAA Championships the same year he finished second to the inimitable Jack Holden, running the last six miles in bare feet. From 1945 he was Northern Ireland Champion for nine consecutive years, and in the 50s was crowned Irish Champion six times. In 1958 he ran for Northern Ireland in the British Empire and Commonwealth Games in Cardiff and at almost 50 years old was the oldest athletics competitor, finishing 20th in the marathon.

Well before these, the sixth British Empire and Commonwealth Games, he had succeeded in ultra-distance running, in December 1952 setting world bests on the track for 40 miles (4:25:38) and 50 miles (5:35:19). In the late 50s he regularly ran in the Manx TT (40 miles) and the London to Brighton race (52 miles). In the 60s and 70s he competed in four World Veterans Championships in Canada, Sweden, New Zealand and Germany.

After the 1958 Commonwealth Games, he served as an official at the next four Games. He was a religious man who never raced or trained on a Sunday. In 1985 he was appointed MBE commenting, "What an honour for myself, but also for the road running fraternity which I have been involved with since 1927 as a competitor, administrator and organiser." He died in 1999.

Three athletes crossed the War years between the last Manchester Marathon of the "Harold Wood" era, 1931-1936, and the 1947 race: Robert Forshaw (Manchester and District Lads Club Harriers) whose best was second in 1931, 8th in 1947; George P Birchall (Warrington AC), winner of the 1935 Marathon, 12th in 1947; and Charlie Bourne (Liverpool Pembroke AC), did not finish 1933, 15th in 1947.

Charlie Bourne provides us with a link to the Maxol era, the next series of Manchester Marathons covering 1969 to 1973 where he was race secretary and referee.

Charles Arthur Bourne was born in March 1912 and was interviewed by Neil Shuttleworth. Here are some of the topics covered in their conversation.

"Harold Wood

Harold Wood, nicknamed "Checky" Wood, won the 1930 Liverpool Marathon. He was a dogged individual. Worked down the mines. His shoulders were hunched. Certainly not a classic runner, but a nice chap. They say a friend came into his house and asked what the trophy on the sideboard was for? Harold said, "Running," and the enquirer said, "Running whippets?" as they would be popular in the area then.

1930 Liverpool Marathon

I'd be 16th in a little over 3 hours. It started in St George's Square. I was 18 at the time and felt like a schoolboy as most of them were men in their thirties.

For this, my first one, I was an apprentice who took the afternoon off with a pal who paced me on a bicycle. He did a good job and when we got to the grounds of the Wavertree they would not let him in. He had all my money and so I had to walk the ten to twelve miles home to Litherland. It rained all the way. Next day it was work as usual. The race was on a Wednesday.

1933 Manchester Marathon

This was a really hot one and I dropped out. Chamberlain from Sheffield won it and he was a small guy. Their club colours were the same as ours - red hoops - and also my number 16 or 19 was similar too. So at a later stage I was told I was in the lead - the marshals had either got my number or club vest mixed up. The sun was beating down so hot that every time my feet hit the ground my head felt as if it was being thumped on top, so I stopped before the heat really got to me. "Checky" Wood ended up in hospital and came out on the Monday. One of the reasons Chamberlain succeeded may have been because he was small.

I only dropped out of two, that and a "Poly" Windsor to Chiswick Marathon, won by Jim Peters, some time in the early 50s. I had broken two ribs the day before and had been told not to start.

1947 Manchester Marathon

I ran that one too and must have done quite well because I won a Gold MAC Medal. Henning from Duncairn Nomads won it and I had only gone along to pace a club-mate. I got to 15 or 20 miles and hit the wall.

Training

I was advised by Arthur Newton who said when I was in Cairo on War Service to get out every day even if it's only for ten minutes. And the same went for when I was stationed in the East. Yes, he wrote to say keep up the running every day, even if it is five miles into the desert! His last letter apologised for not writing sooner as he had been on a 3,000 mile cycle tour around Britain.

Pembroke 20 mile Road Race

We organised the Pembroke 20 for the first time in 1953 over four laps in Huyton (Liverpool). Ron Hill did 1:36:28 in 1968 (Arthur recalled the time to the second). I had the course checked by surveyor's wheel from the surveyors on the council. (<u>Authors' note</u>: I'm glad the course was found to be accurate as it was a World's Best and stood for many many years. I was honoured to win the Pembroke 20 nine years in succession from 1962 to 1970).

Maxol Marathon

I was called upon to organise the Maxol Marathons 1969-1973, and there the course was measured by bicycle."

Chapter 17

The 17th Manchester Marathon
Sunday 20th July 1969

THE START OF THE MAXOL ERA

In the late 60s there were few International marathons around the world to which top British athletes were invited: Fukuoka (Japan), Enschede, now the Twente Marathon (Holland), Kosice (Czechoslovakia now Slovakia). Then, of course, there was the most famous of them all, the Boston Marathon in the USA, to which Britain occasionally sent a runner. But there were no invitational marathons in the United Kingdom.

In 1969 the Road Runners Club (RRC) decided to rectify this. A sponsor was found in W H Dean and Son Ltd, a Burnley, Lancashire, company which made industrial gas heaters. Their trade name for heaters used in the catering trade was "Maxol," and thus "The International Maxol Marathon" was born.

The race in Manchester on 20th July 1969 would include the AAA Championship, the Road Runners Championship, and it would be the selection trial for the upcoming European Championships in Athens in September. A good proportion of the £5,000 sponsorship put up by W H Dean was spent on bringing in top class foreign athletes.

By good fortune, fastest marathon runner of all-time, Derek Clayton was on a European tour. Clayton was born in Barrow-in-Furness, Lancashire, on 17th November 1942. Whilst still young, he and his family moved to Belfast for some years, finally emigrated to Australia in 1964. A tall, heavy runner renown for his high mileage, he set a World Best of 2:09:36.4 in Fukuoka on 3rd December 1967. His European tour began with the Ankara Marathon on 19th May when on a hot day he won in 2:17:26. On 30th May, having had little time to recover, he ran a marathon in Antwerp, Belgium, astounding the running world with another victory, but this time knocking over a minute from his own World's Best with 2:08:33.6. He arrived in Manchester owning the two fastest marathon times ever. This is what we believed at the time. However, this time is not accepted by some experts as the course was measured by a car odometer and could have been up to 800 metres short.

Britain's Bill Adcocks (Coventry Godiva Harriers), a 27-year-old self-employed gas fitter, was also having a fantastic season. He had been fifth in the 1968 Mexico City Olympic Marathon, but more significantly had recorded 2:10:47.8 in winning the Fukuoka Marathon on 8th December 1968. At the time this was the second fastest marathon ever recorded, and obviously the fastest ever by a Briton. To add to that, earlier in 1969, the 6th of March, he had clocked an amazing 2:11:07.2 to win the classic Marathon to Athens race, giving him at that time two of the three quickest times ever for a marathon. Clayton and Adcocks, between them owning the four fastest times ever, would line up in Manchester. You may wonder why with Adcocks' recent record, he had to run the trial at all, but at that time things did not always make sense and he feared that if he did not race he would be automatically excluded from the British team for Athens.

The Japanese had responded to their invitation with two world-class runners. The first was 28-year-old Kenji Kimihara, silver medallist at the Mexico Olympics. He had set a personal best when finishing second to Adcocks in the Marathon to Athens race with 2:13:25.8. Kimihara was no stranger to racing in Britain as he had won the 1968 "Poly" Marathon in 2:15:15. The second Japanese was 24-year-old Yoshiaki Unetani whose personal best was 2:12:40.6 set in the December 1968 Fukuoka race, where he was second to Bill Adcocks. Perhaps more significantly, Unetani had won the Boston Marathon in April and set a new course record of 2:13:49. The two Japanese runners spent a week in Manchester, with their coaches, acclimatising to the time change and the weather. Such was the interest of the Japanese media that a special press centre was set up at the finish of the race so that news of the results could be flashed to Tokyo without delay.

East Germany (German Democratic Republic) sent over their top runner, 26-year-old Jurgen Busch who was the national record holder with 2:13:45.2 set in finishing third to Bill Adcocks (2:12:16.8) in Karl Marx Stadt, 19th May 1968. He had finished 15th in the Mexico Olympics (2:30:42.6).

Other British runners in serious contention included Jim Alder, the 29-year-old Morpeth, Northumberland, brick-layer, who was the current British Empire and Commonwealth Champion (Kingston, Jamaica, 1966) and who ranked third Briton in 1968 with a time of 2:14:44.4 set in finishing fourth in the Karl Marx Stadt Marathon to Jurgen Busch's third. Alder had run the Mexico Olympic Marathon, but collapsed twice in the race and had to be stretchered off at around the half-way point.

The current European Champion from Budapest, 1966, Jim Hogan (Walton AC) would also be on the start line, anxious for a chance to defend his European title in Athens. Hogan had contested the Mexico Olympic 10,000m with myself, so obviously he had speed as well as stamina.

From my own point of view, my ambition was to make the GB team for Athens. Arraigned against this talent, on paper, my chances of doing well in this race were far from certain. My personal best was 2:14:12 set five years previously when finishing second to Basil Heatley's World Best of 2:13:55 in the 1964 "Poly" Marathon. In 1968 I ranked only fourth in Britain with a 2:17:11, fourth place in the Olympic trial at Cwmbran, Wales. That year, in my view, I had been let down by the selectors.

I felt I had learned the art (or science!) of peaking. I wanted to be at the top of my form at the Olympics in Mexico, but knew that the trials for the 10,000m and the marathon would be early on in my training cycle when I was not fully fit. It was a gamble I had to take, but I had planned to show the selectors my capabilities as a marathoner by a good performance in the Liverpool Pembroke 20 mile road race on 25th May. I had trained for that race and recorded 1:36:28. Did the selectors notice? I doubt it. Three weeks "rest" at 69, 75 and 70 miles and I began a long build up for Mexico. One hundred and five miles, 123 miles, a slight taper-off of 90 and 90 miles brought me to the AAA 6 mile championship where I finished fourth in 27:30.6 (equal to 28:30.6 10,000m) behind Tim Johnston (Portsmouth AC), Mike Tagg (Norfolk Olympiads) and Jim Alder. A training week of 113 miles, a taper week of 72 and it was the marathon trial where I placed fourth again behind Tim Johnston, Bill Adcocks, and Jim Alder.

I knew I could do well in the marathon at the high altitude of Mexico City, and that I was nowhere near my peak. After the race I said to Arthur Gold, one of the chief selectors, "Look, I'm interested only in the marathon in Mexico." He replied that I'd been fourth in both trials, many of the same people were involved, and I would get what was left over when the others had picked. I was left with the 10,000 metres! Weekly miles of 109, 125, 126, 121, 120, 116, 130, 122, 104, 101, 100, brought me to the Olympic 10,000 metres, and after only nineteen days at altitude I finished seventh, after leading with five laps to go. In front of me were four high altitude natives and two runners who had spent at least six months training at altitude. The next day I ran 20 miles feeling absolutely fine. I had obviously been in the wrong event!

But my performance showed me that my training was fully correct for me, and I had trained properly for a peak at the Maxol. Unfortunately there had been one setback. Nineteen days before the Maxol race, I had competed in a 10,000m track race at the "World Games" in Helsinki. The race almost turned into a fight and with six laps top go I was left sprawled on my back on a wet cinder track, looking up at the floodlights. I got back in contention and out sprinted three Ethiopians up the home straight to win in a personal best of 28:40.6. My right shoe felt very wet and when I looked down I discovered I had a four inch gash on the inside of my ankle and the shoe was full of blood. The wound was stitched and I was running in agony for a few days. The stitches went septic and I was on anti-biotics for a while, but I still kept up my schedule, albeit a bit more slowly than normal, and logged 129 miles, and 101 miles in the two weeks before the big race.

The course had been carefully designed to be as flat as possible and "ran" as follows:

After a lap of Albert Square, the competitors leave by Princess Street and kept straight on into Brook Street, Upper Brook Street and Birchfields Road, then turn right into Moseley Road. Continuing into Wilbraham Road, there is a left turn into Princess Road, a dual carriageway, and the 5 mile point is at the Cresta Service Station. At the Barlow Moor Road roundabout the lap is commenced, the competitors continuing straight on into Princess Parkway to the end of the dual carriageway, turning left into Altrincham Road and left again into Longley Lane.

The 10 mile point is at the Royle Green Garage. There is a right turn into Palatine Road and a left turn into Barlow Moor Road, which leads back to Princess Road, the completion of the lap. Turning left into Princess Road the lap is repeated. The 15 mile mark is at the footbridge, 100 yards beyond the Sharston Hotel in the Altrincham Road on this second lap. Having completed the lap twice, competitors then cross Princess Road at the roundabout, continuing along Barlow Moor Road, and pass Chorlton Park on its right. The 20 mile point is at Chorlton Police Station.

There is a left turn into Wilbraham Road, then a right turn into Edge Lane, and a right turn into Kings Road just before the ascent over the railway. A left turn (Great Stone Road), a right turn (Talbot Road) and past the county cricket ground and the Town Hall. A left turn (Warwick Road) up to Chester Road which is crossed, and the Manchester United Football Stadium is passed on the left at $23^{1}/_{2}$ miles.

The race continues into Old Trafford Trading Estate, turning left into Trafford Park Road, and continuing for over a mile to the turning point (24 miles 960 yards) at the Carborundum Works. The same route is retraced to the Stadium, which is entered by the gate adjacent to the Munich Memorial Plaque in the main stand. A tunnel leads into the ground and one lap of the track completes the race.

A separate route is planned for spectators who can see the race at the start, at a central point where the race passes three times and then at the end when the race passes on the crucial out-and-back course to Trafford Park.

The route map is on the next page.

One thing that could not be designed was the weather. In relation to the European Championships in Athens, the date was right, but it was mid-

115

summer and the UK was in the middle of a heatwave. Add to that the 2:00 pm start and it was highly possible that things were not going to be easy. The

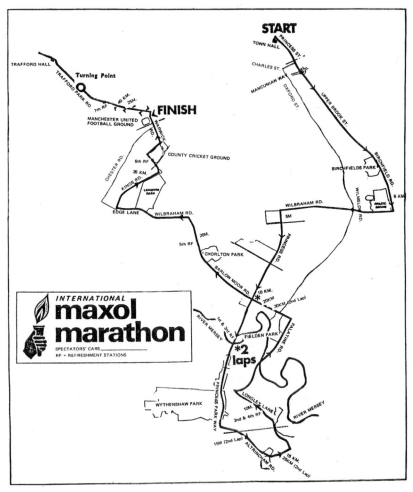

Route map for 1969-73 Marathons. (Courtesy RRC.)

[Note: the 1969–71 races started in Albert Square and the 1972 -73 started in St Peter's Square.]

maximum temperature recorded that day at Manchester Airport would be 74.5° F (23.6° C), the minimum being 60.4°F (15.8° C).

Because of the nature of the course and the standard of the field, the press were speculating on a new World Record, the *Daily Telegraph* suggesting that the two hour marathon barrier might be in danger, but Bill Adcocks was quoted, "If the weather is hot, an exceptional time is improbable and we're going to find it tough," whilst I suggested, "If people think Clayton likes the sun, they're going to be in for a surprise. It was scorching in Ankara, Turkey six weeks ago, and he ran one of his slowest times." I'd done my research.

Most of the race account is from my point of view, and taken from "*The Long Hard Road - Part 2.*" It was overcast with close, sticky conditions when Sir Matt Busby, chairman of Manchester United Football Club, fired the gun to send 167 long-distance specialists on their 26 mile 385 yard journey.

I immediately got up with the leading group and, climbing the gentle rise of Upper Brook Street, all that could be heard was the slap, slap of flat road shoes on black tarmac and the occasional shouts of encouragement from the few spectators on that early part of the course. It was a big group and I could see Adcocks, Unetani, Busch, but Clayton, Ron Grove (Leicester Coritanians), Alder, Hogan, Kimihara, Dave Holt (Hercules-Wimbledon AC), Don Macgregor (Edinburgh Southern), and John Fewery (Blackpool and Fylde AC) were all there. There was no talking. This was a serious race. After three miles at Birchfields Park, Clayton showed up right at the front.

At 4½ miles as I strode out along Wilbraham Road, following close behind Unetani, I began to feel spots of moisture landing on me. The clouds had turned to rain. I glanced up at the clouds; it wasn't raining at all. I looked ahead and Unetani was throwing off a shower of sweat as he ran along. I quickly switched positions in the group! Five miles was reached in 25:16.

After 5 miles, Adcocks (65) and Clayton (200) lead Hill, Kirkham, Hogan (hidden), Unetani, Alder, Busch and Fewery. Holt (71), Macgregor (33) and Grove are dropped. (Picture: B Butterworth.)

As the field headed south along Princess Road and Princess Parkway, Clayton began putting in short bursts, as if he were testing the field; moving ahead with me following right behind him, then dropping back to the bunch. I hoped that this would give the impression that I was going well, but I was thinking at that time that both he and Bill were running better than I was as they were slightly faster on the downhill stretches. By $7^1/_2$ miles, Grove and Holt were off the back, and half a mile later Busch was dropped, as some clown ran into the road and baulked him, and Fewery was following behind, him.

Approaching ten miles, on Altrincham Road in Wythenshawe, Clayton's efforts had whittled the leaders down to three, himself, myself and Bill. The sun had finally destroyed the clouds, and our bodies cast short shadows on the tarmac. By ten miles, Clayton had a seven or eight yard lead, and he passed in 50:07, three seconds ahead. He grabbed a drink, Bill and I ignored the refreshments, and we were quickly up to him. At ten miles, unknown to me, Kimihara was right behind in 50:13, with fifth Hogan (50:24), sixth Alder (50:28), seventh Unetani and Busch together (50:30), ninth Fewery (50:37), tenth Holt (50:39), 11th Macgregor (50:57), 12th Grove (51:09), 13th Juan Taylor (Coventry Godiva) (51:35), 14th Ian MacIntosh (Ranelagh H) (51:42) and 15th George Brockbank (Manchester and District LCH) (51:51).

Dodging the traffic, which was accompanying the race, and by now stretched back for miles, I passed Clayton, but was quickly caught by the pair. Along Barlow Moor Road, approaching the start of the second loop, Clayton again applied the pressure a couple of times and we dropped Bill; but each time he slowed and Bill made contact again. Up Princess Parkway, approaching the Mersey Hotel, after another of Clayton's efforts, I sensed Bill drop again by five or six yards. I took the lead with a sharpish burst to drop Bill once and for all, taking Clayton with me, alongside and finally ahead of me. I was happy to tuck in behind and slip-stream the big Australian. I was feeling quite comfortable.

At 15 miles, Clayton and I were together in 74:57, with Bill still only 13 seconds behind. Clayton grabbed for his drink once more, and once more I ignored it. I sensed I had a break and just picked up the pace slightly to worry him and make it more difficult to get back. Down the hill at tree-shaded Longley Lane, I was more or less waiting for him to rush back up to me immediately; but he didn't come. Spectators were shouting to me, "50 yards," then "60 yards," I couldn't believe it. "100 yards." Could I hang on?

Before 15 miles Jim Hogan had dropped out with leg trouble, and Ron Grove retired at the 15 mile point. Here Kimihara was fourth (75:55) and the order after that was Alder (76:07), Busch (76:15), Unetani and Fewery (77:04).

The heat had now strung the field right out and the next to pass were Juan Taylor, (77:39), Macgregor (78:00), MacIntosh (78:30), Holt (78:54), Eric Austin (Worcester YMCA H) (78:59), and Brockbank (79:06). Holt dropped out not long after 15 miles.

I was now wondering whether I could hang on, but told myself to relax, stride out and hope for the best. I knew I had to finish. As I left the loop for the second time and headed down Barlow Moor Road, with an escort of dozens of cyclists, I suddenly had a bad patch. My legs went tired, my whole body felt fatigued and I panicked thinking about the eight miles to go. The sun was shining; it was hot. I wiped my face with my hand and my chin felt rough; I looked at my hand; it was covered with salt that had crusted on my face.

At 20 miles I passed in 1:40:27, with no idea how far Clayton was behind. In fact he had not dropped that much and was only 28 seconds in arrears (1:40:55). Adcocks was still in third position, 45 seconds behind Clayton (1:41:40), but was beginning to have a bad time and Alder had moved into fourth place (1:41:59) cutting his deficit over Adcocks from 57 seconds at 15 miles to just 19 seconds. Busch passed fifth in 1:43:55 and Kimihara had blown up dropping to seventh place (1:44:01) one second behind his team-mate Unetani who had stormed through to sixth place. After Kimihara, in eighth place was Fewery (1:44:28) followed by Juan Taylor (1:45:02), Austin (1:45:04), MacIntosh (1:45:05), Macgregor (1:46:21), then a big gap to Brockbank (1:47:31), Mel Edwards (Thames Valley H) (1:47:44) and Martin Craven (Kendal AC) (1:48:02).

At 20 miles I grabbed a wet sponge, squeezed it over my head, wiped my neck and arms then threw it away. I was refreshed for about one mile, then the heat hit me again after that. I worked out that there should be another sponge station at 22^1/$_2$ miles. There was none there. I was running in a dream-state, tired, anxious, thinking that Clayton must be catching me. I passed Old Trafford Football Ground, at 23^1/$_4$ miles worrying about being caught and wanting to stop. Left into Trafford Park, and into a strong head-wind heading away from the finish. A long straight road, and I could not see the turn-around point and thought I would never make it. I thought about walking, letting Clayton catch me, then going with him and trying to beat him on the sprint. The turn came and I didn't want to look; I was sure Clayton would be right there.

He wasn't; my spirits lifted; I got a sponge at 25 miles and a bit further on, Frank Morris, my Bolton United club secretary handed me a pink sponge. I was holding off cramp, but managed to climb the short hill to Old Trafford then run down the hill for one rectangular lap, anti-clockwise, of the football

Ron Hill two miles away from victory (Picture: Daily Mirror.)

pitch. There were roars and cheers, from the 6,000 strong crowd. I thought it was Clayton catching me and turned, but I was alone as I wobbled the last few metres to the finish. I'd won in a personal best time of 2:13:42.

Derek Clayton pushed on bravely. It could not have been easy for a 6' 2" man weighing 160 lbs (11 stone 6 lbs) in those hot and humid conditions, especially in view of his previous marathon races in 1969. But he never gave up. Although I thought I was dying, I still ran the last "10 Km" faster than anyone else (33:15). Actually it was 10 Km less about eight metres which is equivalent to 6 miles 385 yards. Derek was second fastest (34:45) to finish the race completely exhausted in 2:15:40. He was to tell me twelve days later at the AAA 10,000m Championships at the White City Stadium in London that it was the only time in his life he had "run his backside off in a race."

Jim Alder passed Bill Adcocks shortly after 20 miles and ran in a comfortable third (2:18:18), while Unetani also passed Bill to claim fourth place. Bill gamely hung on to fifth, despite having to walk at 23 miles and taking a painful 38:33 for the last 10 Km. Revelation of the race was John Fewery taking sixth place, the Blackpool and Fylde runner taking multiple scalps including those of the Olympic silver medallist, Kimihara who was 1:42 behind.

Both Juan Taylor and Mel Edwards had abandoned the struggle over this final stage, whilst Don Macgregor took a staggering 45:48 for the final "10 Km" dropping from 12th to 28th place.

Results:

1	Ron Hill	(Bolton U H)	2:13:42
2	Derek Clayton	(AUSTRALIA)	2:15:40
3	Jim Alder	(Morpeth H)	2:18:18
4	Yoshiaki Unetani	(JAPAN)	2:19:37
5	Bill Adcocks	(Coventry G)	2:20:13
6	John Fewery	(Blackpool & F)	2:21:43
7	Kenji Kimihara	(JAPAN)	2:23:25
8	Jurgen Busch	(GERMAN DR)	2:23:37
9	Ian MacIntosh	(Ranelagh H)	2:23:37
10	Martin Craven	(Kendal)	2:24:51

11, A Domleo (Derby & C) 2:25:30; 12, A Grant (Coventry G) 2:25:31; 13, B Allen (Windsor, Eton & Slough) 2:25:50; 14, R Cressy (Hillingdon) 2:25:50; 15, E Austin (Worcester YMCA) 2:26:34; 16, J Roberts (Cambridge & C) 2:26:36; 17, G Brockbank (Manchester & D LCH) 2:27:03; 18, J Clare (RNAC South) 2:27:51; 19, J Wight (Edinburgh AC) 2:28:11; 20, P Hampton (RNAC South) 2:28:49; 21, J Newcombe (Stafford) 2:29:09; 22, W Stoddart (Greenock Wellpark) 2:29:16; 23, T Hart (Belgrave) 2:30:13; 24, R Ellis (Thames V) 2:30:20; 25, D Nunn (Maidenhead) 2:30:38; 26, D Davies (Thames V) 2:30:59; 27, D Makin (Bingley) 2:31:50; 28, D Macgregor (Scottish AAA) 2:32:09; 29, K Lee (Notts) 2:32:47;

30, A Walsham (Salford) 2:32:48; 31, T Honeychurch (Paignton) 2:33:58; 32, B Hercock (Boro of Enfield) 2:34:47; 33, R Raymen (Herc Wimbledon) 2:35:08; 34, R Franklin (Thames V) 2:35:26; 35, R Moore (Notts) 2:35:58; 36, M Thorpe (Coventry G) 2:36:48; 37, M Frost (Rotherham) 2:37:52; 38, C Haines (Blackheath) 2:38:41; 39, A Joutenlahti (Finland) 2:39:12; 40, P Kilbey (Manchester AC) 2:39:30; 41, C Johnson (Sutton, St Helens) 2:39:30; 42, A Matheson (Morpeth) 2:39:34; 43, J Comber (Hamilton AC, New Zealand) 2:40:30; 44, A Matson (Edinburgh Southern) 2:42:00; 45, P Birks (City of Stoke) 2:42:35; 46, G Taylor (Cambridge) 2:43:11; 47, G Johnson (Tipton) 2:43:31; 48, J Sawyer (Longwood) 2:43:46; 49, K Jones (Orion) 2:44:06;

50, G Gough (Portsmouth) 2:45:00; 51, H Gray (Hull) 2:46:02; 52, N Shuttleworth (Bolton) 2:46:32; 53, G Astill (Notts) 2:46:41; 54, F Gilson (South London) 2:46:42; 55, N Jones (Warrington) 2:46:44; 56, M Teer (N Belfast) 2:46:45; 57, M Smith (Manchester & D LCH) 2:47:18; 58, T

Townsend (Portsmouth) 2:47:24; 59, A Swindlehurst (Liverpool) 2:47:57; 60, M Prosser (Ilford) 2:49:35; 61, J Haslam (Bolton) 2:49:47; 62, B Flanagan (City of Plymouth) 2:49:55; 63, R Thompson (Gosforth) 2:50:01; 64, W Carr (Tipton) 2:50:05; 65, J Masselink (AV, Holland) 2:50:10; 66, D Morgan (Port Talbot) 2:50:25; 67, W Preston (RNAC South) 2:50:36; 68, L Nicholson (Liverpool Pembroke) 2:50:42; 69, K Haith (Cambridge) 2:51:06;

70, F Lucop (Hull) 2:51:17; 71, C Hosken (Sale) 2:51:53; 72, T Buckingham (Leamington) 2:51:54; 73, I Syred (Worthing) 2:51:54; 74, P Chaplin (Cambridge) 2:52:21; 75, J Lawton (Leeds City) 2:53:03; 76, D O'Leary (Manchester YMCA) 2:53:03; 77, B Simms (Leigh) 2:53:38; 78, B Harbach (Tipton) 2:54:15; 79, D Lee (Bolton) 2:54:27; 80, K Fozard (Harrogate) 2:54:34; 71, P Edwards (3rd Bat Lt Inf) 2:54:47; 82, A Lawton (Leeds City) 2:55:34; 83, C Lucas (Newport) 2:55:39; 84, G Dixon (Sunderland) 2:55:39; 85, J Offley (Thames V) 2:56:30; 86, D Gray (Morpeth) 2:56:59; 87, R Annis (Coventry) 2:57:18; 88, G Chase (Paignton) 2:57:19; 89, P Hart (Northampton) 2:57:20;

90, D Woodruf (Allestree) 2:59:01; 91, B Woolford (Sutton, St Helens) 2:59:17; 92, R Bond (Orion) 3:01:22; 93, J Hall (Belgrave) 3:02:23; 94, R Meadowcroft (Bolton) 3:02:31; 95, K Mackay (Preston) 3:04:44; 96, D Deegan (Portsmouth) 3:05:14; 97, M O'Neill (Leigh) 3:06:19; 98, J Hartland (Plymouth) 3:06:59; 99, H Smith (Manchester YMCA) 3:07:09; 100, G Moan (Altrincham) 3:08:41; 101, W McGlenaghan (RNAC South) 3:09:30; 102, W Boland (Bury & Radcliffe) 3:10:00; 103, A Byers (Border) 3:13:17; 104, D Brown (Port Talbot) 3:14:27; 105, M Porter (Stretford) 3:15:06; 106, A Hardman (Altrincham) 3:15:42; 107, D Bonsar (Belgrave) 3:16:27; 108, B Roberts (Birchfield) 3:17:32; 109, M Bromley (Hallamshire) 3:19:04; 110, J Loftus (Manchester AC) 3:19:41; 111, L Durant (Orion) 3:26:28; 112, M Canham (Orion) 3:26:28; 113, D Rosenfield (Manchester YMCA) 3:28:43. 206 entered; 167 started; 113 finished.

In addition to a medal for winning the RRC Championships and a plaque for victory in the AAA Championships, all I received as a prize was a stainless steel tankard engraved "Maxol Marathon." How times have changed!

Positions in the RRC Team Championships were:

1	Thames Valley Harriers	34 points	(Ellis,Davies, Franklin);
2	Royal Navy AC	41 points	(Clare, Hampton, Preston);
3	Coventry Godiva H	41 points	(Adcocks, Grant, Annis)
4	Bolton United Harriers	44 points.	

That fourth team included myself, co-author Neil Shuttleworth (52nd in the race in 2:46:32) and Jack Haslam (61st, 2:49:47).

I went straight in to running to work and back and totalled 113 miles, including the marathon that week. I ran my normal 20$\frac{1}{2}$ miles Sunday run a week later preparing for the AAA 10,000m Championship on the following Friday night. In that race I finished third in a personal best time of 28:39.2 to Dick Taylor (Coventry Godiva) 28:27.6 and Mike Tagg (Norfolk Olympiads) (28:36.4). Theoretically I had qualified for the 10,000m in Athens, but then I made probably the most important decision of my athletics career. I opted solely for the marathon event.

The European Marathon over the original course from Marathon to Athens was held nine weeks later. I passed Jim Alder at about 32 Km to get in silver medal position, then overtook Gaston Roelants of Belgium with only one kilometre remaining to win the gold and achieve one of the proudest victories of my life. Jim Alder hung on to bronze. Sadly, Bill Adcocks had been struggling with an injured foot all year. Well behind at 25 Km, and mindful of the remaining climb to 32 Km, he decided to call it a day.

The results were:

1	R Hill	(GREAT BRITAIN)	2:16:47.8
2	G Roelants	(BELGIUM)	2:17:22.2
3	J Alder	(GREAT BRITAIN)	2:19:05.8
4	J Busch	(GERMAN DR)	2:19:34.8

Chapter 18

The 18th Manchester Marathon
Sunday 23rd August 1970

JAPANESE DOMINATE THE MAXOL

The second Maxol Marathon was held later in the year than the first, on Sunday 23rd August. There were three further important changes.

Firstly, at the request of the police, the start was moved to 10:00 am, so that all the competitors had finished the race before a traffic build-up occurred. This worked, and the congestion of the inaugural race when hundreds of spectators attempted to follow the race, did not happen. The runners too must have been happy with this change, as the possibility of mid-afternoon sun, as was the case in 1969, could lead to tough conditions for racing. It was still the norm in those days for races to be held on Saturday afternoons, so this was a significant departure from the norm. Actually, Saturday races were better for long-distance runners as everyone worked in those days, and they could get in the traditional and necessary long run on Sunday mornings. Traffic was not so bad thirty-odd years ago so Saturday races were practical.

The second departure from the common practice was that intermediate timing points were every 5 kilometres rather than 5 miles. This brought the Maxol in to line with the other major International marathons, but called for many more volunteers. The local clubs rose to this challenge resulting in a first class organisation.

The third change was to comply with international rules for the provision of drinks and sponges. Previously the first drinking and sponging station was at 10 miles with three more, 15, 20 and 25 miles. The IAAF rule stated that drink stations would be at 10 Km and every 5 Km thereafter, with sponging stations half-way between these points. To keep it "Imperial," drink stations in this race were at 7 miles and then every 3 miles up to 25 miles. The Maxol Marathon was not the first in Britain to comply with the IAAF rule: this honour went to the Commonwealth Games Marathon in July, 1970.

There was excellent overseas representation, but the response of the top British runners was disappointing to the organisers. The reason for this was that the Commonwealth Games Marathon had been held in Edinburgh on 23rd July and all the best of our runners had been there.

The selection for the England team had been a bit more relaxed than for Great Britain teams. Bill Adcocks had run a 2:13:46 in Otsu, Japan on 12th April. I was going through a purple patch and had run 2:11:54.4, 7th December 1969, finishing second to Jerome Drayton, Canada, 2:11:12.8 in the Fukuoka Marathhon; then I became the first Briton to win the Boston Marathon on 20th April, with 2:10:30, taking over three minutes off Yoshiaki Unetani's 1969 course record of 2:13:49. Despite this time I was still not definitely selected, but was told to be reasonably confident that three runners would not beat that time in the trial. A newcomer, Don Faircloth (Croydon AC) won the AAA Championships trial held in conjunction with the "Poly" Marathon on 13th June in a time of 2:18:15. Bill and I were selected.

Scotland had had a trial on 16th May over the Commonwealth Games course in Edinburgh, resulting in excellent times: - Jim Alder, 2:17:11; Don Macgregor, 2:17:14; and Fergus Murray, who had been my team-mate in the 1964, Tokyo Olympic 10,000m, 2:18:25.

The results of the Edinburgh Commonwealth Games Marathon were:

1	Ron Hill	(ENGLAND)	2:09:28
2	Jim Alder	(SCOTLAND)	2:12:04
3	Don Faircloth	(ENGLAND)	2:12:19
4	Jack Foster	(NEW ZEALAND)	2:14:44
5	John Stephen	(TANZANIA)	2:15:05
6	Bill Adcocks	(ENGLAND)	2:15:10

None of us wanted a marathon a month later.

My time was a World Best, but not recognised then because of Derek Clayton's 2:08:33.6, on the short course in Antwerp, 1969.

Ten of the countries invited to send a team to the Maxol declined "owing to other commitments." Nevertheless there was an excellent field of overseas runners, Japan sending three of their top men. Yoshiaki Unetani had been fourth in the 1969 Maxol and had placed second to Bill Adcocks in the Otsu Marathon in April with 2:14:19. In the same race, Tsugumichi Suzuki had clocked 2:18:01. The third Japanese, 27-year-old Akio Usami, had been ninth in the Mexico Olympic Marathon.

Jurgen Busch, eighth in the 1969 race, was back with GDR team-mate, Paul Krebs. These two had raced the Karl Marx Stadt Marathon on 10th May with Busch leading all the way for victory in 2:14:41.2 and Krebs second in 2:18:34.2. Sweden entered an official team of three, Chris Wade (also of Ranelagh Harriers), K Bjoernfor and B Rostrum. Chris Wade, the brother of

Virginia Wade, the 1977 Wimbledon Tennis Champion, had finished second to Don Faircloth in the "Poly" trial, in 2:19:15 and had taken the Swedish national title in 1969 with a 2:17:42. Other countries represented were: Australia, F Claxton and Neil Ryan; Canada, R Evans; and New Zealand, T Little. However, these runners happened to be resident in the UK at that time. Even so, the Road Runners Club estimated that ten nations in all were represented.

One runner who would have featured prominently but for an unfortunate accident was the Turkish athlete Ismail Ackay, fourth placer in the Mexico Olympic Marathon. He had set the Turkish record of 2:13:43.6 finishing fourth behind Bill Adcocks' unbelievable 2:11:07.2 in the April 1969 Marathon to Athens classic. Ten days before the Maxol he had been knocked down by a car in the Balkan Games Marathon in Bucharest, Romania. X-Rays in Manchester showed no broken ribs, but he started the race heavily strapped and got only as far as 20 Km before dropping out.

The British hopes rested on Colin Kirkham (Coventry Godiva) with a best of 2:20:06, set in 1968; John Fewery, sixth in the 1969 Maxol; Martin Craven, tenth in 1969; Alan Grant, 12th in 1969; Bernie Allen, 13th in 1969; and the consistent Eric Austin, 15th in 1969.

The course was the same as in 1969 commencing with a lap of Albert Square in front of the Town Hall, and finishing inside Old Trafford, Manchester United Football Club's ground.

The temperature at 10:00am, the start of the race, was 57° F (14° C) with the sun breaking through in the latter stages to give a finish temperature of 67° F (19° C), better conditions than in the previous year's race. Once more, Sir Matt Busby acted as starter for the assembled 115 runners.

From the start the Japanese runners made their intentions clear and went straight into the lead. A large group passed 5 Km, just before the right turn in to Wilbraham Road, in a time of 15:30. Usami, Suzuki, Busch, and Krebs, were towing along George Brockbank, Lionel Mann (Belgrave H), Chris Wade, John Fewery, Tony Byrne (Blackpool and Fylde AC), the Australian Ryan, and Barry Watson (Cambridge H). Surprisingly Colin Kirkham was 22 seconds behind at this point, but by 10 Km, after what must have been a tremendous effort (5 Km in 15:23) he was up with the leaders. One second behind Kirkham came Martin Craven, with Joe Clare (Blackheath H) and Bernie Allen (Windsor and Eton AC) passing in 15:57.

At 10 Km, 31:15, (a second 5 Km split of 15:45) as they commenced the first of the two 10 Km laps, the group was still twelve strong, having gained

Kirkham, but lost Brockbank who passed in 32:06, accompanied by Craven, Clare and Allen. The leaders kept up the pace (a second 5 Km of 15:45) with a third 5 Km of 15:49 up the slight rise of Princess Parkway. Wade fell away shortly after 10 Km, then in succession Byrne, Krebs, Ryan and Mann drifted

Soon after the start and already the Japanese lead. (Picture: RRC Newsletter.)

off the back leaving a group of seven holding the pace: Usami, Unetani, Busch, Kirkham, Fewery, Suzuki and Watson. That third 5 Km of 15:49 showed 47:04 at 15 Km.

As they headed down to the start of the second lap Busch began to test the others with short sharp bursts, but each time easing and returning to the bunch. The fourth 5 Km in 16:03 resulted in Fewery beginning to struggle badly and by 20 Km he was 11 seconds adrift, 63:18 to 63:07.

At the half-way point, the leaders were suddenly down to five as Watson succumbed to stomach cramps and had to stop temporarily. He was still sixth at 25 Km, but then dropped out. Up Princess Parkway for the second time Kirkham was dropped briefly, but with an effort was able to join Usami, Unetani, Suzuki and Busch at 25 Km in 79:00. Krebs was now over one minute behind (80:34), but still in seventh position. Mann and Ryan (81:00) plus Tony Byrne (81:25) made up the top ten at this stage.

Busch again put in a burst, gained a short lead, but was pulled back as they ran down to the river Mersey bridge on Palatine Road. This effort finally put paid to Kirkham's hopes and he was dropped by 28 Km. Suzuki too, was in trouble, his legs almost seizing, and he fell behind rapidly.

The leading group at about 10 Km (lt to rt): Kirkham, (88), Mann, Ryan (13), Busch (5), Usami, Suzuki, Krebs, Watson, Unetani (2), Leeming (98).
(Picture: RRC Newsletter.)

Commencing the run for home only Usami and Busch remained at the head of the field at 30 Km (94:40). Unetani was only three seconds away but was losing contact. Kirkham had lost 46 seconds over that 5 Km segment, and Suzuki 1 minute 39 seconds. Krebs was still sixth (96:54), but Allen had moved up to seventh alongside Mann (98:36) and Byrne had just overtaken Ryan to move in to ninth place.

At 35 Km (1:50:50), approaching the Lancashire County Cricket Ground Usami had finally broken Busch and had a 15 second lead, while Unetani still had the first two in sight a further 32 seconds back. Although almost 1¹/₂ minutes behind Unetani, Kirkham was hanging on well and now himself had a 1¹/₂ minute buffer over Krebs (1:53:06 to 1:54:37). Producing a storming finish was Martin Craven passing five people to move in to sixth place (1:56:50). Allen was seventh (1:57:00), Byrne now eighth (1:57:08), but beginning to really suffer, Mann ninth (1:57:59) and Brockbank moving up to tenth (1:58:08).

Busch's hard work had taken its toll and over the next 5 Km Unetani gained 52 seconds to overtake him and to enter runner-up position behind a flying Usami. This is how the first three remained at the finish with Usami breasting the tape in 2:13:45 (just three seconds outside my time of 1969). Kirkham held his position and recorded a personal best of 2:18:59. Almost all the other positions remained the same in the top ten, except for Byrne who fell from 11th to 14th in the last 2 Km, having been overtaken by Chris Wade before 40 Km.

Results:

1	Akio Usami	(JAPAN)	2:13:45
2	Yoshiaki Unetani	(JAPAN)	2:16:00
3	Jurgen Busch	(GERMAN DR)	2:16:57
4	Colin Kirkham	(Coventry G)	2:18:59
5	Paul Krebs	(GERMAN DR)	2:20:45
6	Martin Craven	(Kendal AC)	2:21:05
7	Bernie Allen	(Windsor & Eton)	2:22:35
8	George Brockbank	(Manchester & D L)	2:23:25
9	Lionel Mann	(Belgrave H)	2:24:07
10	Chris Wade	(Ranelagh H)	2:24:41

11, E Austin (Worcester YMCA) 2:24:50; 12, M Cranny (Wirral) 2:24:59; 13, A Grant (Coventry G) 2:25:50; 14, A Byrne (Blackpool) 2:26:09; 15, J Lunn (Leeds City) 2:26:26; 16, J Fewery (Blackpool) 2:26:47; 17, J Clare (Blackheath) 2:29:05; 18, D Gray (Morpeth) 2:29:31; 19, D Case (Ealing & Southall) 2:29:45; 20, T Little (New Zealand) 2:30:54; 21, K Bjoernfor (Sweden) 2:31:35; 22, N Ryan (Australia) 2:31:59; 23, D Horsup (Thurrock H) 2:32:41; 24, T Suzuki (Japan) 2:32:41; 25, J Offley (Thames V) 2:34:36; 26, D Locke (Ranelagh) 2:34:52; 27, K Mayor (Bolton) 2:36:27; 28, M Whiteside (Wallasey) 2:38:22; 29, H Blenkinsop (Sale) 2:38:36;

30, D Weir (Sale) 2:39:23; 31, J Egerton (City of Stoke) 2:40:01; 32, B Woolford (Sutton) 2:41:15; 33, C Jackson (Birchfield) 2:41:27; 34, T Buckingham (Leamington) 2:41:35; 35, B Shaw (Blackpool) 2:42:02; 36, G Williams (Wirral) 2:24:08; 37, P Lever (Bolton) 2:43:03; 38, M O'Neill (Leigh) 2:43:19; 39, R Goodyear (Manchester YMCA) 2:44:54; 40, H Smith (Manchester YMCA) 2:45:24; 41, M Chapman (Bolton) 2:46:23; 42, A Byers (Border) 2:46:46; 43, G Spink (Bingley) 2:47:30; 44, W Boland (Bury & Radcliffe) 2:47:46; 45, C Groom (Small Heath) 2:48:08; 46, E Johnson (City of Stoke) 2:48:17; 47, I Blakey (H Wimbledon) 2:49:30; 48, D O'Leary (Manchester YMCA) 2:49:50; 49, M Flynn (Waterloo H, Liverpool) 2:50:42;

50, D Cooper (Havering) 2:50:53; 51, J Tunnacliffe (Holmfirth) 2:51:31; 52, R Blois (Basildon) 2:51:34; 53, B Hicks (Metropolitan Police) 2:54:13; 54, I Syred (Worthing) 2:54:29; 55, M Newell (Morpeth) 2:54:59; 56, P Jagan

(Hereford) 2:55:10; 57, R Thompson (Gosforth) 2:56:12; 58, A Walker (Horwich RMI) 2:56:27; 59, J Lawton (Leeds City) 2:56:37; 60, G Sargeant (Essex B) 2:56:37; 61, P Jones (Pembroke, Liverpool) 2:57:05; 62, G Lovell (Small Heath) 2:57:41; 63, P Hant (Northampton P) 2:58:38: 64, W Pehla (West Germany) 2:58:50; 65, B Cordes (Gosforth) 2:58:52; 66, E Andreos (Havering) 2:59:53; 67, A Lawton (Leeds City) 2:59:57; 68, S Cottier (Waterloo H, Liverpool) 3:00:08; 69, D Bonser (Belgrave) 3:00:54;

70, D Lee (Bolton) 3:00:56; 71, B Roberts (Birchfield) 3:03:27; 72, R Mann (Hereford) 3:05:24; 73, S Quennell (Warrington) 3:05:41; 74, R Bond (Orion) 3:06:08; 75, M Porter (Stretford) 3:06:19; 76, C Whiteside (Pembroke, Liverpool) 3:09:16; 77, J Insoll (Bridgend YMCA) 3:12:04; 78, J Orton (Gateshead) 3:13:44; 79, J Loftus (Manchester AC) 3:14:42; 80, A Knowles (Waterloo H, Liverpool) 3:17:07; 81, C Brothers (RAF & Hereford) 3:17:38; 82, A Hardman (Altrincham) 3:17:47; 83, J Preston (Jarrow) 3:18:54; 84, F Claxton (Australia) 3:18:55; 85, J Grimshaw (Salford) 3:22:50; 86, J Osborn (Blackburn) 3:24:25; 87, J Hedley (Jarrow) 3:26:36; 88, C Nuttall (Sparkhill) 3:27:05; 89, M Armstrong (Kendal) 3:27:26; 90, J Teesdale (Saltwell) 3:35:53; 91, H Down (Thames V) 3:38:48. 163 entered; 115 started; 91 finished.

The RRC Team Championships the results reflected the strength of the northern entry:

1	Blackpool & Fylde AC	12
	(Tony Byrne, John Fewery, Barry Shaw)	
2	Bolton United Harriers	22
	(Kenny Mayor, Peter Lever, Mike Chapman)	
3	Manchester YMCA H	28
	(Ralph Goodyear, Harold Smith, Dave O'Leary)	
4	Leeds City	28
	(John Lunn, J Lawton, A Lawton)	

Akio Usami continued to enjoy good form and later in the year won the prestigious Fukuoka Marathon in a new Asian and Japanese record of 2:10:37.8. Early in 1971 he won the Marathon to Athens classic in 2:19:25 and at the end of the year got second place in the Fukuoka Marathon with 2:13:22.8. He never returned to Manchester, but did return to England to win the 1974 "Poly" Marathon in a time of 2:15:16. He was to be Japanese Marathon champion five times in all and raced in two further Olympics: 1972, Munich (12th), and 1976, Montreal (32nd).

Unetani improved later in 1970 to finish third in the Fukuoka Marathon and record a personal best of 2:12:12. He was selected for the 1972 Olympics, and finished 36th in 2:25:39.

Bernie Allen and Lionel Mann both set personal bests.

Chapter 19

The 19th Manchester Marathon
Sunday 13th June 1971

THIRD MAXOL - 63 RUNNERS INSIDE 2 $^1/_2$ HOURS

The third Maxol Marathon, 13th June 1971, was a trial for the European Championships to be held in Helsinki, the marathon being on 15th August, eight weeks away. This did not fit my peaking plans. How could I be at my peak for a trial and be in the best form for the target race of the year eight weeks later? I had requested that I be allowed to miss the trial and be pre-selected for Helsinki on my previous record. Winner of the first Maxol in 1969, European Champion 1969, Boston Marathon winner with a record 2:10:30 in 1970, Commonwealth Champion 1970 with a personal best of 2:09:28. My verbal request met with the reply, "Percentage-wise your time in Edinburgh (2:09:28) was not that much better than the second best runner (2:12:04)." How could you argue with that? Plus, my last race of 1970 had been a poor ninth place in the Fukuoka Marathon in a time of 2:15:27. I had experimented with higher mileage than normal with weeks of 95, 113, 126, 131, 132, 152, 164 and 75 before the race. It hadn't worked and I would go back to my tried and tested regime.

The British Amateur Athletic Board decreed that all aspirants to the European Championships would have to run the Maxol. Incorporated in the race was an International Match between Great Britain and West Germany, and the latter country sent across a team of eight athletes. Apart from that no other countries accepted the invitation except the German D R who nominated Jurgen Busch once more for his third outing in Manchester. No Japanese athletes competed this year.

New Zealand was represented in the person of 35-year-old Jeff Julian who on the programme appeared as "Cambridge Harriers and New Zealand." Julian had competed in the 1960, Rome Olympics, where he was 18th. In 1963 he won Fukuoka Marathon (2:18:00.6), and went on to race in the 1964 Tokyo Olympics (29th). Six years later, he contested the Commonwealth Games in Edinburgh, placing 18th.

The Great Britain team was Jim Alder (Morpeth H), myself, Ron Hill (Bolton United H), Don Macgregor (Edinburgh Southern H) and Alastair Wood (Aberdeen AAC). Wood had been fourth in the 1962 European Championships in Belgrade, and the Scotsman set a British and

Commonwealth Marathon record of 2:13:45 on 9th July 1966 in the Forres to Inverness Marathon, a record which stood until 1968 when Bill Adcocks demolished it.

One athlete, untried at the marathon was 25-year-old Hallamshire Harrier Trevor Wright. Trevor had been improving for sometime and in 1970 had won the Northern and National Cross-Country championships. He also relieved me of my AAA 10 mile track title which I had won five times in succession, 1965 - 1969. This year he had retained the title in a superb 46:51.6, the third fastest time ever recorded at this distance. However, he had never raced further than 10 miles.

The course was identical to the 1969 and 1970, the start time was as in 1970, 10:00am and the starter was L F Hiles, Esq., Chairman of the sponsors, W H Dean and Son Ltd.

This year the weather was cool, 54° F (12° C) throughout the race, and we were treated to some rain; ideal conditions for marathoning.

Although I had not wanted to run this race, I had trained diligently: a rest of 56, 42 and 60 mileage weeks, followed by weeks of 88, 110, 119, 133, 130, 141 and a taper week of 90 miles. Two of these weeks had been hot weather training in Majorca where I covered 275 miles in 14 days. Mentally, I ignored this test until about five minutes before the start. With 210 starters, it was one of the biggest, if not the biggest marathon ever held in the United Kingdom. Again most of the account is from the second part of my autobiography: *"The Long Hard Road - To the Peak and Beyond."*

When the gun went I got immediately near the front to keep an eye on the field. I seemed to be moving pretty well. Don Faircloth took the early lead, and John Newsome, the Wakefield runner, chased him. By two miles, the pair had been pulled back and by 5 Km (15:36) a huge group was at the head of the field. At this point I began to think, "Why take it easy and use up energy running slowly, when I can relax at a faster pace?" I side-stepped the leaders, clicked into gear, and strode to the front. Down Wilbraham Road, John Newsome was the only taker and after a couple of miles I relaxed a bit and Jim Alder pulled a big group through to join us up Princess Parkway.

The second 5 Km took 15:31 and at 10 Km (31:07) I was leading with Trevor Wright, Bernie Plain (Cardiff AC), Busch, Alder, Steve Badgery (Hercules Wimbledon AC) and Newsome. Timed at 31:08, but obviously still in contact were Julian, Eric Austin, Jeff Norman (Altrincham AC), Jim Craven (Rowntree AC), and Brian Popel (Westbury AC). But I was feeling great and on all the short uphill sections kept putting in bursts to break the field up and

The leading group at about 2 miles: Macgregor (12), Preston (196), Hill (17), Busch (in white cap),Jackson (138), J Craven (84), Faircloth (101), Newsome (179). (Picture: RRC Newsletter.)

upset the other runners. Each time they came back to me. At the top of the Parkway, turning left towards Sharston, it came on pouring down; cooling rain, making running that more efficient, that much easier.

The faster bursts had worked, and at 15 Km (46:47) the lead group was down to six, myself, Wright, Plain, Alder, Badgery and Newsome with Busch seven seconds down, Julian 12 seconds, Norman 24 seconds, and Eric Austin 28 seconds behind. I dropped to the back of our group to let Jim Alder make the pace for a while. He seemed confident. I went up front again, pushing the pace, and listening to the footsteps on the wet road behind me; hearing footfalls matching my own, stride for stride. That would be Trevor Wright, like me wearing a string vest; quieter, quicker footsteps, that was Bernie Plain in the red vest of Wales.

Left onto Barlow Moor Road, just before 20 Km, someone called, "Jim Alder's ten yards down." I turned the screws and speeded up the pace, hitting him where it was hurting. Wright and Plain stayed with me through 20 Km in 62:02, after what proved to be the fastest 5 Km of the race, 15:15. Alder had fallen back four seconds, Busch and Badgery followed in 62:55, Newsome in 62:43, Julian 62:45, Norman 63:11 and tenth Eric Austin, 63:12. A group of three, Kirkham, Harry Leeming (Derby and County) and Craven clocked 63:37, with Alastair Wood 14th (64:40). It continued to rain, and my paper race number "17" became sodden and dropped off.

Right up to just before 25 Km I towed Wright and Plain round until suddenly the quicker footsteps began to die away. I didn't look round. Plain had gone. At the 25 Km he had dropped by three seconds as we clocked 77:30, for an intermediate 15:20, 5 Km. Alder was now 25 seconds back in fourth place, Badgery (78:09) had left Busch (78:21), Newsome had faded out of the picture leaving Julian seventh (78:50) followed by a group of four (79:27): Kirkham, Leeming having pulled up around 25 seconds to catch Norman and Austin.

At about 16 miles Trevor Wright and Ron Hill battle it out for first
and second place.
(Picture: Daily Express.)

At around 27 Km we hit Palatine Road for the second time, and Trevor was beginning to move alongside. A spectator called, "Plain's 50 yards down." There were just the two of us now. I saw Trevor touch his side. "How are you?" I asked. "Great," he replied, "Just my vest is a bit tight." I thought, "Well, if you feel that good, you can do some leading." I slowed fractionally so that he could get ahead. I wanted to put some pressure on him; I knew how pressure could hurt in a marathon, and this was his debut.

With 28 Km gone a man came alongside on a bike and to my astonishment handed Trevor a note. "From Joe," the cyclist said, then dropped back. Trevor read the note, half handed it to me, thought better of it, and threw it away. "Joe" was Joe Lancaster, a brilliant journalist, a friend of mine and coach to Trevor. In his time the Salford Harrier had been a great long-distance runner himself, in 1955 breaking the World Record for 20 miles and 2 hours on the track and beating the famous Gordon Pirie into second place.

The note incident did not rattle me, and I ran with and behind Trevor through 30 Km (93:04), with him keeping up the pace for a 15:34, 5 Km split. Plain (93:36) was losing ground rapidly, whilst Alder was hanging on to fourth place. Busch (94:12) with a 15:51, 5 Km had overtaken Badgery (94:39) who had run 16:30 for that 5 Km segment. Leeming had sprinted away from his group of four to catch Julian (95:23), leaving Kirkham (95:21), Austin (95:47) and Norman (96:16) well strung out.

We were still together at 20 miles (32 Km), and although I wasn't moving too badly, just a bit of stiffness creeping in, I was getting a little bit worried. Trevor was showing no signs of slowing up. Although I had started the race solely wanting to make the team for Helsinki, my competitive instincts came to the fore and now I wanted to win the race. However, although I wanted to win, Trevor and I were still mates and I was talking to him, giving him directions, as I knew the course, telling him to bear left, then right, to cut the corners and save distance where we could.

In the next 5 Km, leaving the loop and heading down Barlow Moor Road, then Wilbraham Road and Edge Lane, with a right turn in Kings Road to Longford Park and the 35 Km marker, the pace increased slightly for the second fastest split of the whole race, 15:26. Our lead over the third man had extended from 32 seconds to exactly two minutes, as Plain (1:50:58) slipped painfully to fifth place and Alder (1:50:32) took third place. Busch (1:50:38) was now fourth, Badgery (1:51:10) sixth, Kirkham (1:51:37) had moved up quickly from tenth to seventh, with Leeming (1:51:44) eighth, Julian (1:51:46) ninth and Austin (1:51:56) tenth.

Suddenly, at about 36 Km (22 miles), Trevor said, "Go on, Ron." "What's up?" I asked. "My legs have gone," he gasped. "What the hell do you think mine are like?" I retorted. On a short, sharp, hump-backed bridge over a railway, I got ahead, but decided to wait for him and run together. Past Old Trafford cricket ground, I talked to him; the slightly slower pace had allowed me to recover well and I encouraged him and told him how much further there was to go. Not far. We could see the tall gantries and floodlights of Manchester United's football ground. As we passed the entrance to the ground for the 3 kilometres (2 miles) two miles out and back loop into Trafford Park I just said to him, "O.K.?"

"Yes, go on, Ron," he replied, and I strode away.

I found it easy for the end of a marathon, just a slight cramp in my arms near the end. I finished smiling, with plenty left, 2:12:39. Trevor ran the fastest marathon debut of all-time, 2:13:27.

By 39 Km Jurgen Busch (2:03:04) had overtaken a struggling Alder (2:04:00) and Kirkham (2:04:19) was on his heels, with Badgery (2:04:27) slipping back, and Julian (2:04:35) on a charge. Austin (2:04:59) was now eighth, Wood (2:05:12), having a storming finish was ninth and Leeming (2:05:19) tenth.

Over the last 3 Km (2 miles) there were some dramatic changes though Busch remained secure in third place. Julian roared through to take fourth place (2:15:19) just two seconds ahead of Kirkham (2:15:21). Both of these had overtaken the fading Alder (2:15:43) who managed to hold off Badgery by one second. Wood (2:16:06) passed Austin (2:16:24) to take eighth place, whilst Norman (2:16:45) overtook Leeming for tenth spot. My Bolton United team-mate Mike Freary (2:17:10) also passed the desperately tired Leeming (2:17:44) (12th) for 11th place. Bernie Plain went from fifth to 21st in the last 7 Km.

Results:

1	Ron Hill	(Bolton U)	2:12:39
2	Trevor Wright	(Hallamshire H)	2:13:27
3	Jurgen Busch	(GERMAN DR)	2:14:03
4	Jeff Julian	(Cambridge H & NZ)	2:15:19
5	Colin Kirkham	(Coventry G)	2:15:21
6	Jim Alder	(Morpeth H)	2:15:43
7	Steve Badgery	(Hercules W AC)	2:15:44
8	Alastair J Wood	(Aberdeen)	2:16:06
9	Eric J Austin	(Worcester)	2:16:24
10	Jeff Norman	(Altrincham)	2:16:45

11, M Freary (Bolton) 2:17:10; 12, H Leeming (Derby) 2:17:44; 13, J

Craven (Rowntree) 2:17:48; 14, L Austin (Stoke) 2:17:56; 15, G Brockbank (Manchester & D) 2:18:51; 16, P Angenvoorth (West Germany) 2:18:57; 17, S Taylor (Aberdeen) 2:19:28; 18, R Richardson (Blackheath) 2:19:31; 19, D Macgregor (Edinburgh S) 2:19:34; 20, C Leigh (Salford) 2:19:38; 21, B Plain (Cardiff) 2:19:49; 22, M Steffny (West Germany) 2:20:33; 23, H Hellbach (West Germany) 2:20:53; 24, A Byrne (Bolton) 2:21:32; 25, K Boyden (Tipton) 2:21:37; 26, A Walsham (Salford) 2:21:38; 27, T Godolphin (Harrogate) 2:21:51; 28, J Myatt (Wirral) 2:21:57; 29, A Reavley (Tipton) 2:22:00;

30, M Craven (Kendal) 2:22:11; 31, L Carroll (Wirral) 2:22:15; 32, S Edmunds (Sale) 2:22:30; 33, T Hart (Belgrave) 2:22:50; 34, J Lunn (Leeds City) 2:23:30; 35, B Popel (Westbury) 2:23:35; 36, R Profitt (Salford) 2:23:42; 37, J Newsome (Wakefield) 2:23:50; 38, P Reiher (West Germany) 2:24:01; 39, M Child (Wakefield) 2:24:09; 40, R Cressy (Hillingdon) 2:24:20; 41, J Clare (Blackheath) 2:24:31; 42, C Johnson (Sutton, St Helens) 2:24:40; 43, C Haines (Blackheath) 2:24:55; 44, D Davies (TVH) 2:25:37; 45, A Hudson (Blackpool) 2:25:38; 46, K Mayor (Bolton) 2:25:39; 47, R Atkinson (Barry) 2:26:11; 48, D Horsup (Thurrock) 2:26:20; 49, B Hercock (Enfield) 2:26:31;

50, G Lawson (Manchester & D) 2:27:16; 51, K-H Sievers (West Germany) 2:27:25; 52, D Jones (Blackpool) 2:27:38; 53, W Weba (West Germany) 2:27:43; 54, F McGuire (Blackpool) 2:27:49; 55, D Cockburn (Morpeth) 2:28:10; 56, J Wilson (Blackheath) 2:28:16; 57, 57 D Prior (Woodford G) 2:28:28; 58, D Nunn (Windsor) 2:28:47; 59, G Gough (Portsmouth) 2:28:57; 60, J Berry (Wakefield) 2:29:11; 61, J Brandon (Thames VH) 2:29:29; 62, D Morgan (Vale of Glam) 2:29:39; 63, K Peers (Leigh) 2:29:55; 64, A White (Longwood) 2:30:16; 65, C Jackson (Birchfield) 2:30:18; 66, P Kilbey (Manchester AC) 2:30:22; 67, J Walsh (Derby) 2:30:54; 68, I Wainwright (Sheffield) 2:30:55; 69, A Burkitt (Tipton) 2:30:57;

70, K Hodkinson (Sale) 2:31:13; 71, R Franklin (Thames VH) 2:31:17; 72, C Woodward (Leamington) 2:31:18; 73, G Harrold (Enfield) 2:32:58: 74, K Fozard (Harrogate) 2:33:11; 75, B Kemp (Ealing) 2:33:12; 76, S Allen (Herne Hill) 2:33:33; 77, H Artiss (Verlea) 2:33:35; 78, J Prater (Sheffield) 2:33:45; 79, J P Egerton (Stoke) 2:33:49; 80, M Letzerich (West Germany) 2:34:19; 81, B Woolford (Sutton, St Helens) 2:34:20; 82, J Offley (Thames VH) 2:34:42; 83, M Flynn (Waterloo) 2:34:44; 84, J Sawyer (Longwood) 2:34:58; 85, J Slater (Wycombe) 2:35:02; 86, N Shuttleworth (Bolton) 2:35:07; 87, P Edwards (Wakefield) 2:35:42; 88, C Woodcock (Blackheath) 2:36:01; 89, M Chandler (Westbury) 2:36:09; 90, J MacDonald (Victoria Park AAC) 2:36:34; 91, P Jones (Liverpool P) 2:36:42; 92, S Hardicker (Manchester AC) 2:36:43; 93, R Meadowcroft (Bolton) 2:36:46; 94, K Werther (West Germany) 2:37:06; 95, K Northard (Derby) 2:37:27; 96, M Chapman (Bolton) 2:37:35; 97, G Williams

(Wirral) 2:37:38; 98, A Matson (Wycombe) 2:37:45; 99, D Turner (Epsom) 2:38:01; 100, M Case (Wycombe) 2:38:27. 244 entered; 210 started; 181 finished.

Great Britain easily won the International Team Race, scored on aggregate time:

| 1 | Great Britain | Hill, Alder, Wood | 6:44:28 |
| 2 | West Germany | Angenvoorth, Hellbach, Sievers | 7:07:15 |

The result of the RRC Team Race was:

1	Bolton UH	Hill, Byrne, Mayor	15 points
2	Blackheath H	Richardson, Clare, Haines	41 points
3	Tipton H	Boyden, Reavley, Burkitt	47 points.

In depth, this was the finest marathon ever seen in Britain, and would not be matched until the early London marathons. One hundred and eighty one runners finished, 180 of them inside $3^1/_2$ hours. Sixty three athletes, 55 of them Britons, finished within $2^1/_2$ hours, and 21 runners, 18 from Britain, broke 2:20.

First veteran home, nine days short of his 41st birthday, was Arthur Walsham of Salford Harriers. He was my regular Sunday morning, long run, training partner in those days and recorded a magnificent 2:21:38 for 26th place. This time would give him victory in many of today's marathons.

This quality field throws up a few more connections. In 1965 I had broken the last of Emil Zatopek's World Records, 15 miles and 25 kilometres on the track at Leverhulme Park, Bolton. Second in that race had been John Lunn of Leeds City AC. In the 1971 Maxol Marathon he was 34th, almost three minutes faster than 1970, yet 19 positions worse!

Similarly, third in that World Record track race had been Tony Byrne, then Blackpool and Fylde AC, now with my own club, Bolton United Harriers. In the 1971 Maxol Marathon he was 24th, 2:21:32; in 1970 he had been 14th, but in 2:26:09, almost five minutes slower. In 1976, Tony won the Barnsley Marathon in 2:22:10, and in 1980 was victorious in the *Goldenlay* Polytechnic Marathon in 2:22:23.

Another runner worthy of mention is Mike Porter of Stretford AC. He just failed to beat three hours, recording 3:00:08, in 157th place. 1970 saw him finishing in a time of 3:06:19. Incredibly, Mike had run in the 1947, Manchester Marathon as a Sale Harrier. He was a founder member of the Northern Veterans Athletic Club, sadly dying in 1994.

The selectors had a problem. Two places on the Helsinki team were obvious, myself and Trevor Wright, but the third was not quite so clear cut. Colin Kirkham had set a personal best, 2:15:21, and finished one place ahead of the experienced Jim Alder, 2:15:43, indeed European silver medallist two years earlier. In the end experience counted for nothing and Kirkham was selected.

I had a problem. There was little time to rest, as I would normally have done, as the Helsinki Games were only eight weeks away. I allowed myself two weeks easy, 76 and 43 miles, but continued to race. Two weeks after the Maxol Marathon, I contested the Manchester YMCA 20 Km race. Such was the standard of local competition this was never going to be an easy race. We passed 5 miles in 23:18, then ran the second 5 miles in 23:07 for 10 miles in 46:25. There was only myself and Mike Freary left at the front, and eventually I prevailed in 58:07.

But I had done too much. The next morning, I stepped out of the door for my morning run, and my right leg collapsed and I fell. My hamstring had torn, right at the origin where it attaches to the pelvis. I got up, ran my 5 miles, and continued my training as planned. But it did not recover, and I ran the European Marathon injured. My training mileage per week was 103, 124, 129, 123, 146, 125 with 96 miles taper. Added to this injury, all three of us got some kind of food poisoning in Helsinki, and diarrhoea on the day of a marathon is not the best of condition to be in.

The result in Helsinki was:

1	Karel Lismont	(BELGIUM)	2:13:09.0
2	Trevor Wright	(GB)	2:13:59.6
3	Ron Hill	(GB)	2:14:34.8
4	Colin Kirkham	(GB)	2:16:22.0

I was devastated. Knowing that but for a trial and a leg injury I could have easily won the race. I told the selectors, there and then, "If you want a gold medal in the Munich Olympic Marathon next year, you had better select me now!"

Chapter 20

The 20th Manchester Marathon
Sunday 4th June 1972

FOURTH MAXOL - THE BEST OF THEM ALL

The 1971 Maxol Marathon had been a great race in terms of depth of performance, but the 1972 edition proved to be even better. As in 1969 the race included both the AAA and RRC Championships, plus this year it was the selection race for the Munich Olympics.

A strong overseas entry was not expected, but things turned out otherwise as West Germany and Spain designated the Maxol as their trial for Munich. The Germans nominated eight athletes officially, but a further eleven runners made their way to Manchester hoping to make the national team selection. Other countries represented were Austria, Canada, Finland, Greece, Netherlands, New Zealand, Portugal South Africa and Sweden.

Initially the date of the race was announced as 2nd July, but Bill Adcocks and I objected strongly to this and eventually the 4th June was accepted giving the possibility of four weeks "rest" after the trial, followed by ten weeks build-up to the Olympics. This change of date necessitated a slight alteration to the course as a veteran car rally had already booked Albert Square for their start, well before the Maxol change of date. We therefore started in St Peter's Square, at the other side of Manchester Central Library, but the route, *via* Moseley Street, soon joined the original course at Princess Street.

I had been watching the build-up to the race carefully and my most feared opposition would come from the British. Bill Adcocks had returned to form six weeks before the Maxol with a victory in the Inter Counties 20 mile road race, held in conjunction with the Finchley 20, in the remarkable time of 1:39:01, over three minutes ahead of second man Barry Watson (Cambridge H). Unfortunately for Bill, he sustained a leg injury after this race, but still decided to chance his arm.

Trevor Wright had been running well finishing fifth in the International Cross-Country Championships, but he himself picked up a foot injury and would not start. Jim Alder was determined to make his second Olympics, but was getting so wound up about the trial that he was reported to be on tranquillisers. Don Faircloth, with a 2:12:19 performance in the Commonwealth Games would line up as would Colin Kirkham fourth in the European Championships in 1971. Bernie Plain would have to be watched as he had run well for most of the way in last year's Maxol, and had shown form this year winning the AAA 10 mile track championships in 48:28.8.

The foreign entry was somewhat unknown. Lutz Philipp of West Germany had been seventh in the Helsinki European Championships, his time of 2:18:18.6 did not signify danger. The Spaniard Mariano Haro had been second in the International Cross-Country Championships, 25 seconds ahead of Wright, so he could be in contention as could the Finn, Ristimaki, with a 28:45 10,000m to his name.

All the pundits had me down as favourite. Why could not the British selectors think the same way? I had written a five page letter to them, outlining all the reasons for my being allowed to miss the trial, and offering to run a 30 Km trial to prove my fitness, without that debilitating last 12 Km (7½ miles) of a marathon; but it fell on deaf ears. "Race, or don't go to Munich was the message."

It was a good day for a marathon, the temperature 50° F (10° C) at 10:00 am start rising to only 54° F (12° C) by the finish, low humidity, little wind. Ideal.

Once more I report the race from my own perspective, again, mainly from *"The Long Hard Road - Part 2."* At ten o'clock, 272 starters from an entry of 326 surged forward. I set off down the field. The Spaniards went straight into the lead, but I was content to lope along in the 20s, feeling relaxed, keeping an eye on the front-runners. At 3 Km a runner with red shorts, a red vest trimmed with white and a white cap went to the front and gained five metres on the field. With these colours, I thought it must be Bernie Plain in his Welsh strip. This was potentially dangerous, and I increased my pace, rounding the other runners and caught him. It wasn't Plain; it was number 4, Ristimaki of Finland. The rest of the bunch had followed me up and we closed together, around forty athletes being led through 5 Km in 16:02.

Suddenly, just after 5 Km, Bernie Allen of the Windsor, Slough and Eton club, shot into the lead and increased the pace until it was uncomfortably fast. This broke the field up and at 8 Km, I was only aware of two Spaniards in their national vests of red with two yellow bands, a third Spaniard, Haro, in a turquoise singlet, Ricky Wilde (Manchester and District Lads Club H), in a red vest with "Nos Galan" on the front, Bernie Plain in an all-white vest and Ristimaki. Wilde was the current indoor 3,000m World Record holder, so obviously had some speed.

The leading group (lt to rt) Daniels (127), Ristimaki (4), Perez (15), Fewery (149), Le Grange (10), Macgregor (226), Donkin (134). (Picture: RRC Newsletter.)

Allen dropped back having contributed to a 14:40 second 5 Km, and at 10 Km (30:46) it was Ristimaki, myself, Juan Hidalgo (Spain), Haro, Plain, Wilde, Agustin Fernandez and Carlos Perez (Spain), Philipp, with his West German team-mate Manfred Steffny, and Keith Boyden (Tipton H).

Haro kept treading on my heels, so I dropped to the side of the bunch to avoid him and be in a position to cover any breaks. Ristimaki kept surging ahead, but it was nothing dangerous, and at 11 Km he grabbed for a drink and practically stopped. The sun was out and it was proving to be an uncomfortable day. I just snatched a sponge and squeezed it over my head. Pushing the pace and hoping to take advantage of the break in rhythm at this feed station, I took the lead. It was not decisive enough and the Finn soon caught me bringing Wilde and the rest of the group with him.

At 15 Km (45:56), after a 15:10 5 Km split, I was still leading, but at 16 Km Haro was treading on my heels again, through running too close. Annoyed, I pulled sharply to the side and waved him past. I saw the Finn was still with us as also was Wilde and Plain. I didn't notice that Hidalgo, Fernandez or Philipp were still in the group. Immediately the pace began to drop, and as I knew that I could run faster and still be comfortable, I swept into the lead again, striding along. Dave Makin, a friend of mine, came alongside on a bike, and said, quietly, "Bernie Plain's struggling." I speeded up a tiny bit. I heard Haro begin to drop back with the others struggling to maintain contact. The 5 Km split up to 20 Km took 15:12 and it was beginning to hurt my pursuers. At 61:08, only Wilde recorded the same time, and Haro and Plain were three seconds down. Philipp had lost 16 seconds (61:24) one second ahead of Ristimaki, whilst there was a big gap to the next runners: Kirkham, Angus, Fernandez, Adcocks, Perez, and the South African Ferdi Le Grange (62:07), Austin (62:14), Macgregor (62:20), Faircloth (62:25) and Philipp.

I turned up Princess Parkway, and could feel I had a slight lead, and had almost broken the contact. Suddenly Plain fell back; I could tell this as his footsteps disappeared from hearing. This made me push a little bit harder, until Ricky Wilde's footsteps too died away behind me. My spirits lifted, my stride lengthened even further; at the top of the Parkway, at the left turn onto Altrincham Road, people were shouting that I had 80 to 100 metres lead. I thought to myself, "I've won it, I've won it." I took stock of how I felt. I was good. Admittedly I'd had a worrying moment between 17 Km and 19 Km when my leg seemed to go dead, but it had recovered, and I now settled down to run as relaxed as I could. That 5 Km had taken me 15:31 and I passed 25 Km in 76:39, ten seconds up on Philipp, with Plain (76:53) having overtaken Wilde (76:55) to move into third position, Haro fifth (76:57), and Hidalgo (77:39) sixth. The next runner was the South African, Le Grange (77:57), just in front of Perez (77:58), Eric Austin, Colin Kirkham and Fernandez (78:04), Keith Angus (Sheffield), (78:07) 12th, Ristimaki (78:12) 13th, Bill Adcocks (78:18) 14th, Macgregor (78:26) 15th and Don Faircloth (78:31) 16th. Shortly after 25 Km, Adcocks had to give in to his leg problems and retired. Jim Alder had dropped out before 25 Km suffering with blisters.

Running down Palatine Road for the second time, Dave Makin cycled alongside again and said, "Lutz Philipp's coming through like a bomb." I had time to reflect. "Well, I'm going pretty fast," I thought, "If he's going faster than I am, he's going to pay for it later. He's got no known great marathon form and running fast in the middle of a race should be disastrous." Messages kept coming from spectators and sure enough at 26 Km, just after some traffic had got in my way, he caught me, and passed me. Not a word was spoken. I watched his back; string vest - people soon catch on - and I made no attempt to stay with him. My pace I knew from instinct was exactly right to get me through to the end in my best time. I thought he'd blow.

His lead over me stretched only to 20 metres, then the gap stayed. For 3 kilometres he ran his pace, I ran mine, and they were identical until 29 Km when I sensed that he was coming back. I got pretty close to him by 30 Km. His split for that 5 Km section had been 15:23 to my 15:34 as he passed in 1:32:12 with myself one second back. By now we were almost a minute ahead of the third man, who was still Plain (1:33:03), Wilde was clinging on to fourth (1:33:08), Haro was fifth but dropping fast (1:33:44) whilst Le Grange (1:34:06), Kirkham (1:34:07), and Austin (1:34:08) and Perez (1:34:08) were running together. Angus (1:34:25) was still hanging in there ahead of Macgregor (1:34:27), Cyril Leigh (Salford) (1:34:43) and Faircloth (1:34:45). Hidalgo had retired and Fernandez was slipping back down the field.

Philipp must have heard me closing at the 30 Km check-point, because he suddenly shot off again. Nevertheless, at 20 miles (32 Km), timed in under 1:39:00, his lead was only 10 metres. I took stock of myself; my left foot was hurting pretty badly from a blister on the side of my foot, but it was only surface pain; there was no hurting in my thighs and I felt still pretty relaxed. He ran 10 metres ahead for another two kilometres until suddenly I was upon him. I could have gone past, but this was only a trial, a selection race, the big one was still to come. In any case, he was a spent force now. We passed 35 Km in 1:47:50. That 5 Km had taken us 15:38.

We were oblivious to what was happening behind, but Haro had slipped from fifth to well outside the top ten and would retire soon after. Wilde (1:50:00) was also having a tough time dropping to ninth place from fourth, 5 Km earlier. Plain (1:48:55) hung on to third place, but was losing ground rapidly. Kirkham (1:48:55), having overtaken Haro, Wilde and Le Grange, was now in fourth place, but closely followed by Austin (1:49:16). Forty-five metres further back came Le Grange (1:48:28), then Macgregor (1:49:35), now seventh having passed four in this section. Perez (1:49:50), Wilde and Faircloth (1:50:14) now made up the top ten, Angus having gone out of the picture. Macgregor was on fire, and had run that 5 Km split in 15:08!

I decided to shadow Philipp, but this lasted only about 800 metres. On a very short, sharp hill, a bridge over a railway line, I dropped him; but holding myself in check, I waited for him and slowed down to run with him. Side by side we ran down past Old Trafford football ground for the aggravating 6 Km run, out and back in Trafford Park. As we ran along the grim, gloomy industrial estate, he said, "I think we run together." That was alright by me. A man stood at the turn-point, with a car beyond. Lutz thought the car was the turn and ran on. He was soon shouted back and I waited for him before we started off back together. I thought I had it in the bag.

According to the official results that 5 Km had been very slow (17:39) as we passed 40 Km in 2:05:30. We could now see the other runners coming towards us for their turn-around and the order at 40 Km was Kirkham

(2:07:20), Macgregor (2:07:28), Plain (2:07:40), Austin (2:07:46), Faircloth (2:08:01), Le Grange (2:08:07), Perez (2:08:14) and Angenvoorth (West Germany) (2:08:34).

My legs were beginning to hurt a little, and I turned to him and said, "O.K.?" He didn't reply. Having seen the following runners, I knew we were in no danger of being caught. Approaching the right turn to the short hill up to the football ground, about 600 metres to go, he spoke. I thought I heard him say, "First I want to be," which I took to be, "I want to be first," and whilst my reactions were scrambling, - "Why does he need to win - what cheek - I've been waiting for him," my sub-conscious corrected my first impression to what he actually said which was, "First I want a beer." I almost laughed.

Up the final hill our pace increased in unison. Twinges of cramp began grabbing the backs of my thighs. We turned right again on to the concrete paved area below the back of the stands. I didn't see the point of a sprint. I knew that whoever got into the narrow dark tunnel first, would win, and for some reason I let him go first. He carried the momentum of the downhill on to the cinder path around the green turf and sped away. I knew I wouldn't catch him, and held the gap at about 10 metres.

Lutz Philipp and Ron Hill finish the 1972 race. (Picture: RRC Newsletter.)

Just before the tape he stopped, waited until I had almost caught him, and stretched out his hand to shake mine before breaking through just ahead of me. A sporting gesture. He got 2:12:50 to my 2:12:51.

Don Macgregor overtook Colin Kirkham in the last 2ᵏ Km to clinch his Olympic place. Kirkham was selected too. Don Faircloth moved up two places over the final stretch to miss out on an Olympic berth by 35 seconds, with the remarkable Eric Austin setting a lifetime's best to also be so close to Olympic selection.

Results:

1	Lutz Philipp	(W GERMANY)	2:12:50
2	Ron Hill	(Bolton)	2:12:51
3	Don Macgregor	(Edinburgh S)	2:15:06
4	Colin Kirkham	(Coventry G)	2:15:17
5	Don Faircloth	(Croydon AC)	2:15:52
6	Eric Austin	(Worcester YMCA)	2:15:59
7	Bernie J Plain	(Cardiff AAC)	2:16:18
8	Ferdi Le Grange	(SOUTH AFRICA)	2:16:19
9	Carlos Perez	(SPAIN)	2:16:27
10	Paul Angenvoorth	(W GERMANY)	2:16:44

11, M Steffny (West Germany) 2:16:45; 12, D Holt (Herc Wimbledon) 2:16:53; 13, M Rowland (Thames V) 2:16:53; 14, A Moore (Hillingdon) 2:17:18; 15, N Deakin (Stoke) 2:17:20; 16, R Richardson (Blackheath) 2:17:51; 17, M Freary (Bolton) 2:17:54; 18, C Leigh (Salford) 2:18:08; 19, L Austin (Stoke) 2:18:38; 20, A Wood (Aberdeen) 2:19:00; 21, J Norman (Altrincham) 2:19:22; 22, M Critchley (Cardiff) 2:19:33; 23, A Fernandez (Spain) 2:19:56; 24, A Wight (Edinburgh AC) 2:19:59; 25, A Aldegalega (Portugal) 2:20:21; 26, M Craven (Kendal) 2:20:35; 27, K Angus (Sheffield) 2:21:12; 28, S Edmunds (Sale) 2:21:17; 29, I MacIntosh (Ranelagh) 2:21:30; 30, T Florey (Middlesborough & C) 2:21:43; 31, G Pringuer (Southgate) 2:22:06; 32, H Landskron (West Germany) 2:22:17; 33, H Leeming (Derby & C) 2:22:34; 34, C Woodward (Leamington) 2:22:38; 35, M Emms (West Germany) 2:23:02; 36, R Wilde (Manchester & D) 2:23:04; 37, J Pearson (Morpeth) 2:23:11; 38, G Brockbank (Manchester & D) 2:24:00; 39, C Haines (Blackheath) 2:24:00; 40, D Hensman (Leicester C) 2:24:07; 41, H Schu (West Germany) 2:24:16; 42, J Keating (Blaydon) 2:24:06; 43, D Hope (Worcester YMCA) 2:24:32; 44, J Newsome (Wakefield) 2:24:44; 45, R Raymen (Herc Wimbledon) 2:25:00; 46, A Ida (West Germany) 2:25:03; 47, C Jackson (Sutton, St Helens) 2:25:41; 48, P Chivers (Ealing & Southall) 2:26:09; 49, G Forster (Austria) 2:26:13;

50, B Allen (Windsor, Slough & Eton) 2:26:16; 51, P Kilbey (Manchester AC) 2:26:25; 52, K Addicks (West Germany) 2:26:33; 53, Graham Tuck (Cambridge & C) 2:26:41; 54, A Pryor (South London) 2:26:55; 55, R A

Donkin (Sunderland) 2:27:38; 56, W Henser (West Germany) 2:27:22; 57, D Case (Ealing & Southall) 2:27:32; 58, C Woodcock (Blackheath) 2:27:38; 59, J Jones (Windsor, Slough & Eton) 2:27:41; 60, P Parker (Gateshead) 2:27:53; 61, D Davies (Sale) 2:28:00; 62, E Haslam (Bolton) 2:28:12; 63, R Wallingford (Canada) 2:28:15; 64, T Coyle (Edinburgh Southern) 2:28:42; 65, J Daniels (Norfolk G) 2:28:47; 66, A Richards (Tipton) 2:28:51; 67, R Donkin (Sunderland) 2:28:51; 68, J Balmer (Liverpool Pembroke) 2:29:29; 69, B Ellis (Wakefield) 2:30:06;

70, K Mayor (Bolton) 2:30:16; 71, C Jackson (Birchfield) 2:30:32; 72, D Watts (Essex Beagles) 2:30:46; 73, D Cockburn (Sale) 2:30:48; 74, S Milas (Greece) 2:30:51; 75, D Wildman (Wolverhampton & B) 2:31:14; 76, D Slatter (Wycombe Phoenix) 2:31:55; 77, J Hubbard (Longwood) 2:32:10; 78, B Kemp (Ealing & Southall) 2:32:10; 79, N Shuttleworth (Bolton) 2:32:29; 80, D Farmer (Sale) 2:32:36; 81, G Newton (Luton) 2:32:45; 82, H Weiss (West Germany) 2:33:03; 83, W Pryce (Cardiff) 2:33:13; 84, R Churm (Luton) 2:33:23; 85, A Steylen (Netherlands) 2:33:25; 86, K Peers (Leigh) 2:33:33; 87, D Anderson (Bingley) 2:33:39; 88, R Moore (Notts) 2:33:40; 89, G Freeman (Sunderland) 2:33:48; 90, K Hodkinson (Sale) 2:34:04; 91, P Raidy (Clayton-le-Moors) 2:34:38; 92, D Morgan (Vale of Glamorgan) 2:34:42; 93, A Hudson (Blackpool) 2:34:47; 94, J Mills (Sparkhill) 2:35:00; 95, H Morrison (Dundee) 2:35:10; 96, R Franklin (Thames VH) 2:35:12; 97, D Muir (Grimsby) 2:35:16; 98, D Prior (Woodford Green) 2:35:16; 99, D Horsup (Thurrock) 2:35:42; 100, J Sawyer (Longwood) 2:36:09. 326 entered; 272 started; 229 finished.

The result of the RRC Team race was:

1	Bolton United	(1 Hill, 7 Freary, 28 E Haslam)	36;
2	Blackheath H	(6 Richardson, 18 Haines, 25 Woodcock)	49;
3	Cardiff AAC	(3 Plain, 10 Critchley, 36 Pryce)	49.

This had been the greatest depth of marathon running ever seen in the Great Britain, probably the world, slightly surpassing the 1971 Maxol. Of the 229 finishers, 24 athletes, 18 of them Britons, had broken 2:20 and 69 had broken 2:30.

I had my four weeks rest and trained hard for Munich. The trial had to have taken something out of me, but I made two big mistakes in my final preparations. I trained three weeks at altitude in St. Moritz, Switzerland. Despite getting more and more tired, I would not deviate from my planned training and covered 94, 132, and 101 miles there, before travelling to Munich eight days before the marathon. Also unfortunately it was cold up there whereas Munich was hot. My second mistake was to do the "glycogen loading" diet to destruction, with virtually no carbohydrate for four days. I'm convinced this left my body a wreck. After two laps of the track at the start of the race I knew it was not my day, but fought hard all the way.

The Munich Olympic result was:

1	Frank Shorter	(USA)	2:12:19.8
2	Karel Lismont	(BELGIUM)	2:14:31.8
3	Mamo Wolde	(ETHIOPIA)	2:15:08.4
4	Kenneth Moore	(USA)	2:15:39.8
5	Kenji Kimihara	(JAPAN)	2:16:27.0
6	Ron Hill	(GB)	2:16:30.6
7	Don Macgregor	(GB)	2:16:34.4
20	Colin Kirkham	(GB)	2:21:54.8

The German team, selected from the Maxol placed in the Olympics as follows:

Paul Angenvoorth	(10th Maxol, 2:16:44),	16th,	2:20:19.0
Manfred Steffny	(11th Maxol, 2:16:45),	31st,	2:24:25.4
Lutz Philipp	(1st Maxol, 2:12:50),	32nd,	2:24:25.4

And of the Spaniards:

Agustin Fernandez	(23rd Maxol, 2:19:56),	39th,	2:27:24.2
Carlos Perez	(9th Maxol, 2:16:27),	50th,	2:33:22.6

Portugal had one runner from the Maxol:

Armando Aldegalega	(25th Maxol, 2:20:21),	41st,	2:28:24.6

It is perhaps not surprising that our future Olympic Marathon runners would feature in the Maxol series, the next Olympics being in Montreal in 1976.

Jeff Norman, Altrincham and District AC, was born on 6th February 1945, in Leigh, Lancashire, and finished 21st in the 1972 edition of the Maxol, in 2:19:22. He had run far better the previous year to record 2:16:45 for tenth place. He was a pharmacist at Manchester Royal Infirmary, and achieved these results whilst competing in his first love, "fell running," which has now attained a more respectable international face as "mountain running." He accomplished an unprecedented six victories in the famous Three Peaks race, in the Yorkshire Dales. This classic of around 23 miles takes in Pen-y-ghent, Whernside and Ingleborough, and Jeff's first triumph was in 1970. He had five wins in the ten mile Skiddaw race in the Lake District, three successes in the Three Towers race in Lancashire, and two victories in the fast 3¼ mile Rivington Pike Fell race, from Horwich, near Bolton, Lancashire. In 1974 he was awarded the title "Fell Runner of the Year," effectively British Champion.

In 1975 he won the famous, Sierre to Zinal race in the Swiss Alps, 28 Km and 1,850 metres ascent.

Jeff's first marathon was as a 21-year-old when he recorded 2:40:21 in the *'Milk'* Marathon from Preston to Morecambe to rank him 99th in the UK in 1966. After his exploits in the Maxol Marathon he advanced to win the 1975 AAA Marathon Championships at Stoke-on-Trent on 1st June in a personal best of 2:15:50, only four weeks after winning his sixth consecutive Three Peaks. The following year he bettered his time with 2:15:17 in the AAA and Olympic Trial in Rotherham, South Yorkshire on 8th May, but this time he was second.

Keith Angus, Sheffield AC, was 27th in the 1972 Maxol, in 2:21:12. He too improved and in 1975 was second to Jeff Norman in the AAA's Marathon in a time of 2:16:14, bettering this with a 2:15:55 third place in the 1976, Rotherham trial.

Barry Watson, Cambridge Harriers, had to drop out of the 1970 Maxol, but placed 15th in 1973 in 2:19:42. In the 1975 AAA's Marathon he was ninth, 2:18:30, but surprised many people in the Rotherham trial, winning in 2:15:08, nine seconds ahead of Norman.

Watson, Norman and Angus were all selected for the 1976 Montreal Olympics. I myself had been fourth in the Rotherham trial, 2:16:59, and nominated first reserve, somewhat disappointed that the selectors would take three runners, all novices at international level. In the event our representatives did not fare well and in a race won by Waldemar Cierpinski (GDR), 2:09:55.0, Norman was our best, 26th in 2:20:04.8, with Angus 31st in 2:22:18.6 and Watson 45th in 2:28:32.2.

On 7th May 1978 Jeff Norman set a lifetime's best of 2:12:50 finishing second to Tony Simmons (Luton United) (2:12:33) in the AAA Marathon Championships at Sandbach, Cheshire. This qualified him for the Commonwealth Games in Edmonton, Canada. The marathon race was won by Gidamis Shahanga (Tanzania) with Jeff, unable to produce his home form, 12th in 2:22:22.7.

He did put his considerable talents to further use in 1980, setting World Best marks for 30 miles (2:42:00) and 50 Km (2:48:06) on the track at Timperley, Cheshire. He appears in the next series of Manchester Marathons as a veteran.

Chapter 21

The 21st Manchester Marathon
Sunday 3rd June 1973

FIFTH MAXOL - NEW COURSE RECORD

The fifth Maxol Marathon was held on Sunday 3rd June, over the now established course, starting in St Peter's Square and finishing at Old Trafford, Manchester United's football ground.

The next major championship for British runners was the Commonwealth Games in Christchurch, New Zealand, in January 1974. Marathon-wise, the trial for the home countries would be the AAA Championship to be held at Harlow on 27th October, and for this reason the British big names gave the Maxol a miss, even though the trial was five months away.

The Maxol had by now such exalted status that nine countries responded to the invitation to send runners.

The American Athletic Union sent Paul Talkington, an Ohio schoolmaster who arrived just two days before the race.

The Japanese team of three, with their usual thoroughness travelled one week before the race. Yoshinobu Kitayama, with a best of 2:13:24, Yoshiaki Morita, and Kenichi Otsuki, third in the previous December's Fukuoka (2:14:00.6), had plenty of time to adjust for this special competition.

West Germany sent 1972 Maxol winner Lutz Philipp, Paul Angenvoorth, 10th in 1972, plus two others, named in the race programme as Schneider Strittmatter and Will. Belgium sent their National Champion Walter van Renterghem who had been 46th in last year's Munich Olympic Marathon in 2:29:58.4. Canada sent Brian Armstrong who had two recent sub-2:20 performances to his credit. East Germany was represented by Eckhard Lesse, a 24-year-old motor mechanic from Magdeburg whose debut marathon had been victory in Karl Marx Stadt, 1972, in 2:13:19.6. He won this race again a month before the Maxol in 2:17:36.2 on a torrid day. He had good speed credentials too with bests of 7:59.6 for 3,000m and 28:14 for 10,000m. Greece sent no less than six athletes, and Holland again selected Ad Steylen. Ferdi Le Grange returned from South Africa and was accompanied by a track runner, Ovid Serekwane.

The conditions for the 1973 contest were ideal and at 10:00 am it was dull and overcast with a temperature of 54° F (12° C) and hardly a breath of wind. From an entry of 299, 241 started.

The race truly was a race of attrition as the pace at the beginning was moderate, 16:17 at the 5 Km point, with all the overseas runners, except for the Greeks, up there, and the timekeepers noted 37 within 30 seconds, a massive group. The next 5 Km was a little faster, 15:39, and this had the effect of whittling down the leading bunch to around 14 athletes, spearheaded by the tall South African medical student, Ferdi Le Grange. Six Britons had stayed with the pace: Don Faircloth (Croydon AC), Alan Domleo (Derby and County), local runner Steve Edmunds (Sale H), John Newsome (Wakefield H), Mike Child (Wakefield H) and John Sheridan (Thames Valley H). These athletes were all now into their stride and little changed in the next 5 Km, slightly faster at 15:31, to pass 15 Km in 47:27. Steve Edmunds had slipped just slightly and was running with Bob Sercombe (Newport H).

Suddenly the heavens opened and there was a downpour lasting fully 15 minutes, the runners' paper numbers became sodden and fell off making the timekeepers' job very very difficult. But the cooling rain had the effect of refreshing the runners and Le Grange began to turn the screws with a 15:09, 5 Km up to 20 Km (62:36), almost the half-way point. The leading group was down to nine, Le Grange, Lesse, Morita, Kitayama, Philipp, Armstrong, van Renterghem, Talkington and Sheridan hanging on by the skin of his teeth. Faircloth and Domleo (63:02) followed, then Otsuki (63:10), Newsome and Child (63:27) and Edmunds (63:39) drifting even further back. The top 15 were all within 63 seconds.

Into the second 10 Km loop, and up Princess Parkway, splashing through the puddles Le Grange continued to force the pace. Lesse, Kitayama, Armstrong and Morita stuck right behind him, but by 25 Km (78:04) Philipp had had to let go and was five seconds behind, with Talkington and Sheridan a further five seconds down. Van Renterghem was fading in ninth (78:37), and Faircloth was tenth (79:13). Edmunds appeared to be taking a breather and was 15th (79:59).

Lesse took control and speeded up affairs with a 5 Km split of 15:12 reaching 30 Km, (93:16), just before the runners left the second loop and headed for home. Armstrong, Le Grange, and Morita were a stride behind (93:17) and Kitayama a couple of metres further back (93:19). Philipp (94:00) was now 44 seconds down on the leader, with Talkington (94:48) a further 48 seconds behind running with Sheridan. Van Renterghem was eighth (95:02), Faircloth ninth (95:23) and Domleo tenth (96:02). Eight seconds behind, Edmunds had recovered to 11th and was now running with Child (96:08).

At around 15 miles: left to right – Morita, Le Grange, Armstrong, Lesse, Kitayama. (Picture: RRC Newslettter.)

Another excellent 5 Km split (15:16) saw Lesse gradually dropping his pursuers and by 35 Km (1:48:32) he had a 12 second lead over Le Grange (1:48:44) just ahead of Kitayama and Armstrong (1:48:46). Morita was now losing ground (1:48:58) and the sixth man, Philipp was over two minutes behind the leader (1:50:38). Faircloth had moved past van Renterghem and Talkington and was now seventh (1:51:44). Both Edmunds and Angenvoorth were having storming finishes and were running together in tenth place (1:52:22).

From the 35 Km to the end, Lesse increased his lead to over a minute, winning the race in a course record 2:12:24 (taking 15 seconds off my record!) and setting an East German National Record. Armstrong entered the Manchester United football ground ahead of Kitayama, but in a desperate sprint finish the Japanese beat the Canadian by just one second, 2:13:29 to 2:13:30, the latter breaking his personal best by over five minutes. Le Grange held fourth, Morita fifth, and Philipp sixth. Revelation of the race was Steve Edmunds who at the half-way point was 15th. He ran the last 2.195 Km faster than anyone in the race (7:19) to clinch seventh place in 2:16:24. From the 40

152

Km point, where two seconds separated Edmunds, Angenvoorth and Faircloth, there had been a battle royal, these three running this last stretch faster than anyone else, 7:19, 7:23, 7:26. In fact, Edmunds probably has the fastest finish of any Maxol as the next fastest I can find are Lutz Philipp and myself in 1972, 7:20 to 7:21.

1973 Maxol winner Eckhard Lesse setting a course record.
(Picture: Jack Hickes.)

Results:

1	Eckhard Lesse	(GERMAN DR)	2:12:24
2	Yoshinobu Kitayama	(JAPAN)	2:13:29
3	Brian Armstrong	(CANADA)	2:13:30
4	Ferdi Le Grange	(S AFRICA)	2:13:58
5	Yoshiaki Morita	(JAPAN)	2:14:06
6	Lutz Philipp	(W GERMANY)	2:16:07
7	Steve Edmunds	(Sale H)	2:16:24
8	Paul Angenvoorth	(W GERMANY)	2:16:27
9	Don Faircloth	(Croydon AC)	2:16:32
10	Mike A Child	(Wakefield H)	2:17:18

11, A Domleo (Derby & County) 2:17:33; 12, W v Renterghem (BELGIUM) 2:18:15; 13, R G Sercombe (Newport) 2:19:04; 14, J Newsome (Wakefield) 2:19:30; 15, B Watson (Cambridge) 2:19:42; 16, C Woodward (Leamington) 2:19:50; 17, P Talkington (USA) 2:20:12; 18, S Curran (Salford)

2:20:13; 19, L Carroll (Wirral) 2:20:47; 20, Schneider Strittmatter (West Germany) 2:21:34; 21, E Austin (Worcester YMCA) 2:21:56; 22, D Cockburn (Sale) 2:22:00; 23, I Burgess (Southampton) 2:22:34; 24, E Vagianos (Greece) 2:22:36; 25, J Sheridan (Thames V) 2:23:13; 26, Will (West Germany) 2:23:15; 27, M Coleby (Darlington) 2:23:35; 28, T O'Reilly (Small Heath) 2:23:37; 29, R Belk (Airedale & Spen V) 2:23:59;

30, D Watson (Wirral) 2:24:20; 31, A Steylen (Holland) 2:24:33; 32, J Keating (Ealing & Southall) 2:25:25; 33, J Alcock (Wirral) 2:25:41; 34, I Viavilis (Greece) 2:25:43; 35, J Bryant (Thames H & H) 2:26:06; 36, D Lee (Bolton) 2:26:15; 37, P Chivers (Ealing & Southall) 2:26:41; 38, C Mitsikas (Greece) 2:26:50; 39, D Farmer (Sale) 2:26:59; 40, M Emms (Woodford Green) 2:27:39; 41, K Binks (Manchester & D LCH) 2:27:44; 42, C Woodcock (Blackheath) 2:27:57; 43, R Donkin (Sunderland) 2:28:31; 44, K Otsuki (Japan) 2:28:50; 45, D Bendy (Leamington) 2:28:54; 46, D Collier (Luton) 2:29:19; 47, P Kilbey (Manchester AC) 2:29:27; 48, G Newton (Luton) 2:29:48; 49, N Shuttleworth (Bolton) 2:29:49;

50, D Blakeley (Manchester & D LCH) 2:29:52; 51, D Wildman (Wolverhampton & Bilston) 2:29:53; 52, H Murphy (Salford) 2:30:14; 53, D Bagshaw (Sheffield) 2:30:25; 54, F Day (East Cheshire) 2:30:27; 55, A Horne (Ranelagh) 2:30:34; 56, N Argyropoulos (Greece) 2:30:40; 57, D Case (Ealing & Southall) 2:30:43; 58, J Steed (Verlea) 2:30:46; 59, C Johnson (Sutton) 2:30:50; 60, P Livesey (Clayton-le-Moors) 2:31:04; 61, K Mayor (Bolton) 2:31:18; 62, J Calvert (Blackburn) 2:31:19; 63, R Calvert (Small Heath) 2:31:19; 64, I Wilson (Blackheath) 2:31:30; 65, E Himsworth (Kendal) 2:31:41; 66, J Daniels (Norfolk) 2:31:51; 67, S Beardsell (Holmfirth) 2:32:01; 68, H Rhys (Leeds City) 2:32:24; 69, C Haines (Blackheath) 2:32:26;

70, B Pickersgill (Wakefield) 2:32:28; 71, M Darcy (Bolton) 2:32:40; 72, C Hunt (Wolverhampton & Bilston) 2:32:50: 73, F Crosland (Holmfirth) 2:33:35; 74, I Sharp (Hull Spartans) 2:33:55; 75, J Forrest (Ranelagh) 2:34:16; 76, B Kemp (Ealing & Southall) 2:34:19; 77, R Knutzen (Capetown Univ) 2:34:21; 78, A Bradley (Holmfirth) 2:34:22; 79, G Bennison (Barnet) 2:34:32; 80, F Ashton (East Cheshire) 2:34:39; 81, S Milas (Greece) 2:34:57; 82, D Watts (Essex Beagles) 2:34:58; 83, P Humphreys (Wirral) 2:35:05; 84, C Jackson (Birchfield) 2:35:16; 85, G Dearlove (Harrogate) 2:35:37; 86, M Whiteside (Salford) 2:35:41; 87, J Tarrant (Salford) 2:35:45; 88, E Price (Brighton & H) 2:35:46; 89, J Walsh (Cardiff) 2:35:51; 90, G Riley (Bedford) 2:36:11; 91, B Fletcher (Wakefield) 2:36:18; 92, A Hudson (Blackpool) 2:36:39; 93, D Prior (Woodford Green) 2:36:40; 94, P Martin (Salford) 2:36:44; 95, B Woods (Sefton) 2:37:23; 96, M Flynn (Waterloo, Liverpool) 2:37:37; 97, L Salter (Folkestone) 2:37:37; 98, J Brandon (Thames V) 2:38:15;

99, B Woolford (Sutton) 2:38:19; 100, J Wilkins (Cambridge) 2:38:50; 101, G Spink (Bingley) 2:38:54. 299 entered; 241 started; 221 finished.

The RRC Team Championship, scored on the lowest aggregate of three runners' times was a close-run affair:

Sale H	Edmunds, Cockburn, Farmer,	7:05:23;
Wakefield H	Child, Newsome, Pickersgill,	7:09:16;
Wirral AC	Carroll, Watson, Alcock,	7:10:48.

All the invited overseas runners finished, except for one Greek runner, P Sarafis, who looked set for a 2:43, about half-way up the field, then blew up taking 27:04 for his last 5 Km to 35 Km where he retired. The South African Ovid Serekwane was 110th (2:40:10).

Although not quite the same depth as 1972, it was still a fabulous race with 16 runners (including eight Britons) under 2:20, and 51 under 2:30. This compares quite favourably with both the 2001 and 2002 Flora London Marathons. There were 22 men (of whom there were 7 Britons) under 2:20 and 54 under 2:30 in 2001, and 18 (4 Britons - including Paula Radcliffe) under 2:20 and 54 under 2:30 in 2002.

With 221 recorded finishers this was another Maxol record as less than one in ten (8.3%) did not finish.

Eckhard Lesse's time was a new East German record by 55 seconds. Later in the year he finished third (2:13:53.8) in the Fukuoka Marathon. He went on to take a silver medal in the 1974, Rome, European Championships (2:14:57.4) and was third in the Karl Marx Stadt Marathon in 1975 (2:14:49.6).

Brian Armstrong's 2:13:30 made him one of the favourites for the Commonwealth Games in Christchurch, New Zealand, January 1974. He ran the Fukuoka Marathon, early December of 1973, finishing second (2:13:43.4) to Frank Shorter (USA), (2:11:45.0), but turning the tables on Lesse. Perhaps this was too much of an effort and he could only finish 11th in Christchurch with 2:20:52.6.

Steve Edmunds, 2:16:24, seventh place, led to his being tipped for a place in the Commonwealth Games team for England. It was not to be. He finished ninth in the AAA at Harlow, the official trial for the Games, in 2:18:11.

An unknown runner, Ian Thompson of Luton United won in 2:12:40 with me (Ron Hill) second in 2:13:22.

The results for the first ten were:

1	I Thompson	(Luton U)	2:12:40
2	R Hill	(Bolton U)	2:13:22
3	C Kirkham	(Coventry G)	2:15:25

4	M Thomas	(Thames VH)	2:15:59
5	M Coleby	(Darlington)	2:16:18
6	M Critchley	(Cardiff)	2:17:02
7	A Domleo	(Derby & C)	2:17:24
8	J McLaughlin	(Achilles, NI)	2:17:40
9	S Edmunds	(Sale)	2:18:11
10	S Kenyon	(Bolton U)	2:18:29.

The first three were selected for England. Thomas for Wales, and McLaughlin for Northern Ireland.

The result of the Commonwealth Games Marathon on 31st January 1974 was:

1	Ian Thompson	(ENGLAND)	2:09:12.0
2	Jack Foster	(NEW ZEALAND)	2:11:18.6
3	Richard Mabuza	(SWAZILAND)	2:12:54.4
4	Terry Manners	(NEW ZEALAND)	2:12:58.6
5	John Farrington	(AUSTRALIA)	2:14:04.6
6	Don Macgregor	(SCOTLAND)	2:14:15.4
7	Bernie Plain	(WALES)	2:14:56.2
8	Colin Kirkham	(ENGLAND)	2:16:06.6
9	Malcolm Thomas	(WALES)	2:16:46.8
10	John Robinson	(NEW ZEALAND)	2:17:05.4

I had a terrible race suffering from plantar fasciitis, and limped home in 18th place, 2:30:24.2.

Ian Thompson went on to take the Rome European Championship gold in September 1974 with a time of 2:13:18.8. The other Britons were Bernie Plain, fourth, 2:18:02.2, and Bob Sercombe, 14th, 2:27:13.0.

Co-author Neil Shuttleworth set a personal best in this race finishing 49th in a time of 2:29:49. He recalls running in the middle of the race with Salford Harrier, John Tarrant, 87th (2:35:45), and being in awe at the man's steady concerted effort. John was known as "*The Ghost Runner*" because when he first applied to become an amateur athlete he admitted to having won a total of £17 in unlicensed boxing matches, and as a result was banned from amateur athletics. He took to appearing at races, with no number, and hence was never in the pre-race programme or results. After much campaigning, 1958, he was allowed into competition, but under IAAF rules could never compete for his country. He became a legendary ultra-distance runner, setting World Bests at 30, 40 and 100 miles, as well as achieving victories in the

London to Brighton 52, Liverpool to Blackpool 48 and the Isle of Man 40. Unbeknown to us he was suffering from stomach cancer. Four months after the Maxol, 13th October, he ran his last race, the Cardiff AAC's 'Lake 15', where he finished 11th and first veteran. Sadly he died on 19th January 1974.

Shuttleworth finished three other Maxols, and made steady progress: 1969, 52nd, 2:46:32; 1971, 86th, 2:35:07 and 1972, 79th, 2:32:39.

Two men finished every race of the Maxol series: Tom Buckingham (Leamington C & AC) and Dave O'Leary (Manchester YMCA H). Their times totalled: 13:44:56 for Buckingham and 13:57:46 for O'Leary. The probably unsuspected rivalry was at its height in the 1972 race when O'Leary turned the tables and finished one place ahead of Buckingham.

Buckingham, a bespectacled and much respected runner, set his marathon best of 2:25:37 when placing fourth in the 1961 "Poly" aged 43. His highest honour came in 1961 when he was chosen to captain the GB team in the 54 mile Comrades Marathon in South Africa, where he himself finished fourth. Three years after this Maxol he died of cancer at the age of 58.

O'Leary, a dedicated clubman, went on to compete in the Tour of Tameside, the six stage double marathon, and became one of a select group of only four athletes who completed all twenty races (1981-2000).

At the post-Maxol dinner a date for the sixth Maxol was announced, Sunday 2nd June 1974. This was even advertised in the January 1974 edition of the "*RRC Newsletter*." Unfortunately, some time later it was announced that the sponsor had withdrawn at short notice "owing to the worsening financial climate." The Maxol was no more.

The Maxol series of races, instigated by the Road Runners Club, had put Manchester and Great Britain on the world stage of marathon running, and the quality of races is emphasised by the number of sub-2:20 performances, listed below. Remember, the last race was 30 years before this book was published!

Maxol Marathons - 1969-1973
Ranking of sub-2:20 marathon runners

Rank	Athlete	Club	Year	Position	Time
1	E Lesse	(GDR)	1973	1	2:12:24
2	R Hill	(Bolton U)	1971	1	2:12:39
3	L Philipp	(W GER)	1972	1	2:12:50
4	R Hill	(Bolton U)	1972	2	2:12:51
5	T Wright	(Hallamshire H)	1971	2	2:13:27
6	Y Kitayama	(JAPAN)	1973	2	2:13:29
7	B Armstrong	(CANADA)	1973	3	2:13:30
8	R Hill	(Bolton U)	1969	1	2:13:42
9	A Usami	(JAPAN)	1970	1	2:13:45
10	F Le Grange	(S AFRICA)	1973	4	2:13:58
11	J Busch	(GDR)	1971	3	2:14:03
12	Y Morita	(JAPAN)	1973	5	2:14:06
13	D Macgregor	(Edinburgh S H)	1972	3	2:15:06
14	C Kirkham	(Coventry G)	1972	4	2:15:17
15	J Julian	(N ZEALAND)	1971	4	2:15:19
16	C Kirkham	(Coventry G)	1971	5	2:15:21
17	D Clayton	(AUSTRALIA)	1969	2	2:15:40
18	J Alder	(Morpeth H)	1971	6	2:15:43
19	S Badgery	(Herc Wimb AC)	1971	7	2:15:44
20	D Faircloth	(Croydon AC)	1972	5	2:15:52
21	E Austin	(Worcester YMCA)	1972	6	2:15:59
22	Y Unetani	(JAPAN)	1970	2	2:16:00
23	A J Wood	(Aberdeen AC)	1971	8	2:16:06
24	L Philipp	(W GER)	1973	6	2:16:07
25	B Plain	(Cardiff AC)	1972	7	2:16:18
26	F Le Grange	(S AFRICA)	1972	8	2:16:19
27	S Edmunds	(Sale H)	1973	7	2:16:24
27	E Austin	(Worcester YMCA)	1971	9	2:16:24
29	P Angenvoorth	(W GER)	1973	8	2:16:27
29	C Perez	(SPAIN)	1972	9	2:16:27
31	D Faircloth	(Croydon AC)	1973	9	2:16:32
32	P Angenvoorth	(W GER)	1972	10	2:16:44
33	M Steffny	(W GER)	1972	11	2:16:45
33	J Norman	(Altrincham & D)	1971	10	2:16:45
35	D Holt	(Herc Wimb AC)	1972	12	2:16:53

35	M Rowland	(Thames VH)	1972	13	2:16:53
37	J Busch	(GDR)	1970	3	2:16:57
38	M Freary	(Bolton U)	1971	11	2:17:10
39	A Moore	(Hillingdon AC)	1972	14	2:17:18
39	M A Child	(Wakefield H)	1973	10	2:17:18
41	N Deakin	(City of Stoke AC)	1972	15	2:17:20
42	A Domleo	(Derby & C)	1973	11	2:17:33
43	H Leeming	(Derby & C)	1971	12	2:17:44
44	J W Craven	(Rowntree AC)	1971	13	2:17:48
45	R Richardson	(Blackheath H)	1972	16	2:17:51
46	M Freary	(Bolton U)	1972	17	2:17:54
47	L Austin	(City of Stoke AC)	1971	14	2:17:56
48	C Leigh	(Salford H)	1972	18	2:18:08
49	WvRenterghem	(BELGIUM)	1973	12	2:18:15
50	J Alder	(Morpeth H)	1969	3	2:18:18
51	L Austin	(City of Stoke AC)	1972	19	2:18:38
52	G Brockbank	(Manchester & D)	1971	15	2:18:51
53	P Angenvoorth	(W GER)	1971	16	2:18:57
54	C Kirkham	(Coventry G)	1970	4	2:18:59
55	A Wood	(Aberdeen AC)	1972	20	2:19:00
56	R G Sercombe	(Newport H)	1973	13	2:19:04
57	J Norman	(Altrincham & D)	1972	21	2:19:22
58	S Taylor	(Aberdeen AC)	1971	17	2:19:28
59	J Newsome	(Wakefield H)	1973	14	2:19:30
60	R Richardson	(Blackheath H)	1971	18	2:19:31
61	M Critchley	(Cardiff AC)	1972	22	2:19:33
62	D Macgregor	(Edinburgh S H)	1971	19	2:19:34
63	Y Unetani	(JAPAN)	1969	4	2:19:37
64	C T Leigh	(Salford H)	1971	20	2:19:38
65	B Watson	(Cambridge H)	1973	15	2:19:42
66	B Plain	(Cardiff AC)	1971	21	2:19:49
67	C Woodward	(Leamington C& AC)	1973	16	2:19:50
68	A Fernandez	(SPAIN)	1972	23	2:19:56
69	A Wight	(Edinburgh AC)	1972	24	2:19:59

Chapter 22

The 22nd Manchester Marathon
Sunday 18th October 1981

THE MANCHESTER CHARITY MARATHON
FAST ONE BY STEVE KENYON

The next Manchester Marathon was at the beginning of the explosion in "people's" marathons. Back in 1970, I had been amazed by the field of around 1,000 in the Boston (USA) race. This had doubled to 2,000 by the time I returned in 1975. The marathon boom in the USA had been catalysed by Frank Shorter's victory in the 1972 Olympic race.

Although Boston was the premier US race, it was more traditional than commercial in its outlook and between 1976 and 1981 the field grew from around 2,000 to almost 7,000. On the other hand the forward-looking management of the New York City Marathon, under the direction of Fred Lebow, grew far more rapidly. I was invited in 1976, and in a field of just over 2,000 finished tenth, in 2:19:43. When I was invited back in 1977 the field had multiplied to almost 5,000, and I was 18th in 2:20:00.9. By 1981 there were around 14,500 runners.

In 1979, Chris Brasher, the 1956 Olympic steeplechase champion and the *Observer* sports columnist, had been part of the 11,000 plus throng who completed the New York course and was inspired. He asked, "I wonder whether London could stage such a festival?" It could, and did, and the rest is history as many other cities followed suit. 7,747 entries were accepted for the first London in 1981, and 6,418 finished with 144 under 2 hours 30 minutes. Amazingly this was surpassed by the Pony British Marathon, held in Bolton, Greater Manchester on 23rd August 1981, where there were 8,753 entries of whom over 7,000 finished inside seven hours, which made it the biggest marathon in Europe.

Even more amazing, just five weeks later there were 9,000 entrants to the Manchester Charity Marathon. The race co-ordinator was Paul Kelly of the Manchester Spastics Association (now renamed Scope) and was sponsored by Piccadilly Radio. Piccadilly were devoting 5% of their airtime and much of their administrative skills to promoting the marathon. More than 25,000 entry forms were sent out, and the feeling was that the *Pony* Marathon, five weeks earlier, rather than detracting from the Manchester race was firing the enthusiasm of potential runners. The *Daily Mirror* Blackpool Marathon was incorporated in to the Manchester event which probably helped to swell the numbers. I acted as honorary race advisor.

The race course was essentially flat and took the following route: start outside Manchester University's Whitworth Hall, Oxford Road, Oxford Street, Peter Street, Quay Street, Water Street, Hampson Street, Oldfield Road, Ordsall Lane, Trafford Road, Chester Road, Cross Street, Washway Road, Manchester Road, Church Street, Inner Relief Road, Stockport Road, Shaftesbury Avenue, Altrincham Road, Northenden Road, Gatley Road, Wilmslow Road, Cheadle Road, Victoria Avenue, Queens Road, Ladybridge Road, Bird Hall Lane, Edgeley Road, Castle Street, Greek Street, Wellington Road South, Wellington Road North, Stockport Road, Dickenson Road, Wilmslow Road, Platt Lane. Finish at Platt Fields.

In contrast to the Maxol series, no foreign runners were invited and the field was domestic and mainly local. Favourite for the title had to be Steve Kenyon, formerly with Bolton United Harriers, but now running for Salford. Steve was born in Farnworth, near Bolton in May 1951. He was a precocious talent even as a junior athlete, and the 30-year-old came to the Manchester race with good speed credentials: 8:01.3 for 3,000m, 13:45.6 for 5,000m and 28:20.29 for 10,000m. He was a good cross-country runner with Northern titles in 1978 and 1979 and two bronze medal performances in the National (1976 and 1980). His attempts at the marathon had been spasmodic, but he was certainly the quickest in the field with a 2:18:29 from 1973, a third place 2:13:29.1 in New York in 1979 and finally a 2:12:34 earlier this year, 18th February, for sixth place in the Tokyo Marathon. He probably had something to prove to himself as five weeks before Manchester he'd had to drop out of the Montreal Marathon at half-way because of diarrhoea.

Second favourite was Colin Taylor of Airedale and Spen Valley. In 1978 he had finished seventh in the AAA Championships, held in Sandbach, recording 2:15:47. (I was 24th in that race in 2:20:02.) As a result he was selected for the European Championships in Prague where he finished 25th in 2:18:44.5, one place behind A Ristimaki (Finland) who ran in the 1972 Maxol.

Third favourite was another Salford Harrier, Alan Sladen, a Manchester PE schoolteacher who in July this year had won the inaugural *Chesters* Tour of Tameside, a six stage race, covering a double marathon distance, held in the Metropolitan Borough of Tameside, part of Greater Manchester. Five weeks later he had finished third in the Pony British Marathon in Bolton (2:24:10) to winner Stan Curran, another Salford Harrier (2:19:32), and Manchester's Des Austin (2:23:34).

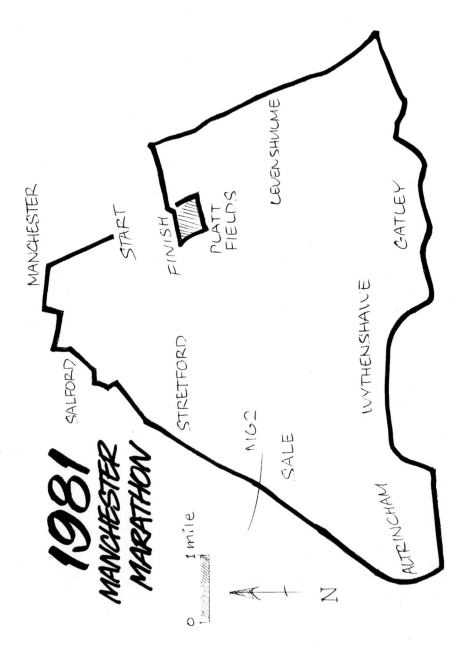

Route map for 1981 Marathon. (Prepared by Tony Duffy)

One major innovation was that for the first time in a Manchester Marathon, females were allowed to compete. The first prize for both man and woman was a trip to the 1982 Boston Marathon.

The weather for the race, beginning at 11am, was ideal; a temperature of 54° F (12° C), despite being a sunny day, and little or no wind. From around 7,500 starters a pack of four spearheaded the field down Manchester's Oxford Street, Alan Sladen, Kim McDonald (Bingley), Colin Taylor and Steve Kenyon. As they approached Sale at around the seven mile point Sladen fell away, with the other three together until around the ten mile point. It was there that Steve Kenyon took off and quickly left first McDonald, then Taylor behind. From then on it was a solo run of the highest quality and but for three stops he made in Levenshulme, about 22 miles, to alleviate a stitch, there might have been a sub 2:11:00 performance in Manchester. As it was, Steve stopped the clock in Platt Fields at 2:11:54. He reckoned he had lost around 40 seconds because of stitch, and elsewhere in the race he almost missed a subway resulting in a 50 metre, nine or ten seconds, extra run. Without these mishaps, and the big clock showing 2:11 in sight, a 2:10 performance might have been possible. As it was his time was the fastest time by a British runner in the UK for eleven years. McDonald must have had Taylor in sight throughout the last 16 miles, but could not catch him. Kevin Best of Bolton, moved up gradually, and finished fourth. Kenyon's brother-in-law Mike Wakefield was fifth.

First woman home was King's College, London student Katie Fitzgibbon in a time of 3:03:42, 273rd place overall. In fact she should not have been running as at 20 years old she was below the minimum age of 21. The second woman, Alice Rochester was not far behind with 3:05:57.

First veteran home, in eighth position, was 1966 Commonwealth gold medallist and 1970 silver medallist Jim Alder, from Morpeth.

Piccadilly Radio disc jockey Mike Sweeney finished in around 3:30.

Aside from the top few the race was about numbers and it was reckoned that over £1 million was raised for charity. One runner, Dave Hurst carried a dustbin all the way round on his back into which spectators threw money. Some weight to carry!

One example of successful charity work was a campaign by Neil Cliffe to raise £6,000 for an item of medical equipment, as a thank you to the surgeon who cured him of cancer of the colon. From not being able to run a step, Cliffe trained and completed this Piccadilly Marathon raising £10,000. He did not stop there and in later Piccadilly's a pipe band would lead an army of over 100 fund-raisers to the start in Platt Fields. This and other fund-raising ideas led to the foundation of the "Neil Cliffe" Cancer Centre at Wythenshawe Hospital, which celebrated its ten year anniversary in May 2002.

*The leading group of McDonald (3854), Kenyon (0261) and Taylor (4202).
Sladen is behind.
(261 is the radio station's wavelength.) (Picture: Piccadilly Radio.)*

Katie Fitzgibbon wins the 1981 Manchester Charity Marathon.
(Picture: Neil Shuttleworth.)

Results:

1	Steve Kenyon	(Salford H)	2:11:54
2	Colin Taylor	(Airedale & Spen)	2:17:56
3	Kim McDonald	(Bingley)	2:19:34
4	Kevin Best	(Bolton U)	2:21:43
5	Mike Wakefield	(Salford H)	2:23:09
6	Derek Blakeley	(Manchester & D)	2:23:39
7	Graham Huddleston	(Clayton-le-Moors)	2:23:49
8	Jim Alder	(Morpeth) V40	2:24:32
9	Alan Sladen	(Salford H)	2:26:28
10	Paul Kilbey	(Altrincham)	2:27:39

11, Steve Bullen 2:28:27; 12, Michael Lavelle 2:28:30; 13, David Helliwell 2:29:08; 14, Peter Lomas (Stockport) 2:29:50; 15, David Brennan (Warrington) 2:30:47; 16, David Evans 2:31:15; 17, Keith Shawcross (Manchester YMCA) 2:32:27; 18, David Lancaster 2:32:28; 19, A Houghton 2:33:20; 20, Barry Boxen (Manchester & DLCH) 2:34:02; 21, W Pearson 2:34:22; 22, A Merrifield 2:34:30; 23, G Bennison 2:34:41; 24, A Winterbottom 2:34:49; 25, R Davis 2:34:57; 26, A Balecke 2:35:02; 27, A Jessop 2:35:08; 28, P Curran 2:35:22; 29, B Morris 2:35:33;

30, M Cruickshank 2:35:42; 31, A Dunne 2:35:50; 32, D Rodgers 2:36:00; 33, D Jagger 2:36:23; 34, J Grant 2:36:57; 35, A Martin 2:37:06; 36, M Fern 2:37:44; 37, P Murray 2:37:55; 38, J Holden 2:39:29; 39, J Howe 2:39:34; 40, B Court 2:39:37; 41, D Mailer 2:39:57; 42, F Brooks 2:39:59; 43, G Thomason 2:40:07; 44, M Brooks 2:40:16; 45, P Hargate 2:40:28; 46, J Gibson 2:40:33; 47, G Lawson 2:40:38; 48, R Eccles 2:40:51; 49, A Verdie 2:40:54;

50, B Eden 2:41:22; 51, N Harney 2:41:26; 52, D Fish 2: 41:41; 53, F Sephton 2:41:55; 54, A Greenwood 2:42:11; 55, B Peers 2:42:23; 56, A Walsham 2:42:36; 57, G Smith 2:42:58; 58, J Grigson 2:43:17; 59, J Reid 2:43:25; 60, K Mackey 2:43:26; 61, M Harris 2:43:27; 62, R Crowley 2:43:36; 63, A Sidebottom 2:43:41; 64, – 2:44:03; 65, D George 2:44:10; 66, J Dwer 2:44:20; 67, S McGreevey 2:44:49; 68, D Holdship 2:44:52; 69, R Halenko 2:45:03;

70, R McElhaney 2:45:06; 71, D Addison 2:45:10; 72, J Jones 2:45:14; 73, J Soothill 2:45:18; 74, A Booking 2:46:04; 75, B Eckersley 2:46:05; 76, M Taylor 2:46:08; 77, L Duncalf 2:46:28; 78, J Cooper 2:46:32; 79, P Gibbons 2:46:49; 80, C Dobson 2:46:50; 81, G Howarth 2:46:50; 82, P Howcroft 2:47:03; 83, J Pendley 2:47:08; 84, A Parkinson 2:47:12; 85, J Lancaster 2:47:14; 86, B Sabini 2:47:15; 87, P Light 2:47:16; 88, M Neary 2:47:21; 89, B Robinson 2:47:26; 90, G Smith 2:47:26; 91, J Rowlinson 2:47:35; 92, D Shaw 2:47:38; 93, P Hartley 2:47:38; 94, R Keys 2:47:44; 95, P Garside 2:47:50; 96, W Halsall 2:48:09; 97, G Morson 2:48:16; 98, A Wynter 2:48:20; 99, D Todd 2:48:26; 100, T Glare 2:48:34.

Women:

| 1 | K Fitzgibbon | (London Olympiades) | 3:03:24 |
| 2 | A Rochester | (–?–) | 3:05:57 |

Steve Kenyon did not run Manchester again. He declined the trip to Boston as he wanted to compete in the European Championships. In 1982 the Manchester race coincided with the AAA Championships and the trial for the European Championships in Athens. Those AAA Championships were held in Gateshead and with another dominating run he pulled away at around 19 miles to win in a personal best of 2:11:40. Unfortunately, he was in trouble early in the Athens race and eventually pulled out.

Kim McDonald had been a sub 8 minute 3,000m and sub 14 minute 5,000m man before turning to the marathon. He ran a 2:21 marathon in Miami in 1982. Turning his hand to athletic management in 1984, he founded Kim McDonald International Management and became one of the most successful and respected managers in the world. Sadly, at the age of only 45, he died of a suspected heart attack in November 2001.

Seventh placer, Graham Huddleston, of my own club, Clayton-le-Moors Harriers, won the 1983 Windermere Marathon in 2:26:20. In 1992 he realised an ambition to run for England at fell running, and continues running to this day.

Katie Fitzgibbon improved to a respectable 2:46:40, finishing fourth in the Milan Marathon 1984.

STOCKPORT AND BOLTON

Stockport and Bolton were two of the ten constituent parts of Greater Manchester at the time of the Piccadilly series, and although not strictly "Manchester Marathons," as a courtesy to these races we are carrying brief stories and results.

STOCKPORT - 3rd May 1981

Following on from the success of the 1981 London Marathon, Stockport was one of the first to organise a "people's" marathon. Local government helped in several respects because of the scale of competitors involved, and liaison with two local clubs, Stockport and Manchester Harriers ensured the smooth running of a large event.

Springtime was chosen for the Stockport Marathon, a date which did not clash with the Manchester or Bolton marathons. The daffodils that are firmly established with spring became a feature in the race title: the Stockport Daffodil Marathon. For the next four years on a spring April Sunday thousands descended on Woodbank Park and, faced the serious challenge that gave this marathon the label "a tough one."

Results: 1, A Dunn (Stockport) V45 2:35:54; 2, D Atwell (Altrincham) V40 2:38:59; 3, D Curran (Altrincham) 2:39:20; 4, R Mills (Altrincham) 2:40:32; 5, A Shaw (Rochdale) V40 2:43:23; 6, G Entwistle (Manchester) V40 2:45:02; 7, W Armstrong (Bury) 2:46:32; 8, J Cooper 2:46:35; 9, T Markham 2:50:05; 10, T Burke V 2:52:10; 11, T Smith V55 2:52:18; 12, D Harrison 2:52:30.

BOLTON - 23rd August 1981

Salford Harrier, Stan Curran won the Pony British Marathon in Bolton in 2:19:32, from Manchester's Des Austin (2:23:34), and fellow Salford Harrier Alan Sladen, third in 2:24:10. For the record the following complete the top ten finishers: 4, W Domoney 2:24:39; 5, B Heath 2:24:55; 6, P Blakeney 2:25:37; 7, P Hayward 2:26:04; 8, K Best 2:26:55; 9, T Colton 2:27:11; 10, M Firth 2:27:22.

Women:

1, V Marot 2:51:52; 2, L Watson 2:56:25; 3, E Adams 3:03:27.

Chapter 23

The 23rd Manchester Marathon
Saturday 12th June 1982

THE PICCADILLY RADIO CHARITY MARATHON
KEVIN BEST IS BEST

In 1982 Piccadilly Radio became totally responsible for the marathon, its staff working long hours to organise the race. Tom Tyrrell was the race director with Paul Kelly as his deputy. The date of this race was rather surprising, a Saturday, but around 9,000 people entered and there would be just over 8,000 starters. Again it was a domestic, indeed local affair with the favourite being Kevin Best, a fireman at the Farnworth Fire Station, who had finished fourth in 1981. None of the first three from last year had entered. Alongside him was 1976 Montreal Olympian, Jeff Norman of Altrincham AC. Mike Critchley, the 35-year-old Welsh international with a sub 2:20 time from the 1972 Maxol and 2:17:02 achieved in the 1974 Harlow Marathon, had represented Wales in the 1978 Commonwealth Games, eighth in 2:19:50.9.

Favourite for the women's title was Leslie Watson of London Olympiades.

A new, more compact route, devised to take the athletes off the main roads, began and ended this year at Platt Fields. In essence the route went from Platt Fields into the city centre via Oxford Road and Oxford Street, then took in Salford, Eccles and Worsley to return via Trafford Park, Old Trafford, and Moss Side where the route proceeded within sight of the finish only to include a detour of several miles around Didsbury, Burnage and Rusholme: down Princess Road, Barlow Moor Road and Kingsway to get in the full distance.

The precise route was: Start on Wilmslow Road outside Platt Fields. Down Wilmslow Road, Oxford Road (B5117), Oxford Street, Peter Street, Quay Street, Water Street, Liverpool Street, Tootal Road, Lancaster Road (A5185), East Lancs Road (A580), Worsley Road (A572), Barton Road (B5211), Redclyffe Road, Barton Dock Road, Davyhulme Road, Chester Road (A56), Stretford Road, Rolls Crescent, Princess Road (A5103), Barlow Moor Road (A5145), School Lane, Kingsway (A34), Birchfields Road, Dickenson Road, Wilmslow Road to finish on Platt Fields.

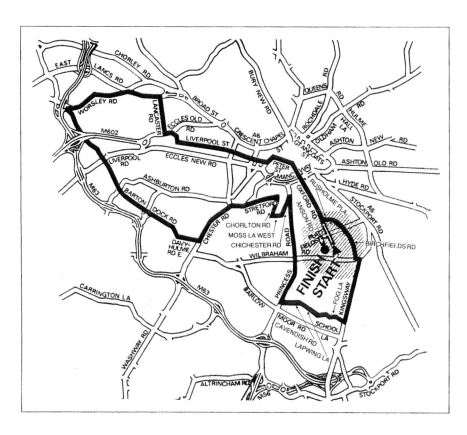

Route map for 1982-85 Marathons. (Courtesy Piccadilly Radio.)

The race, scheduled to start at 4 pm, went according to form and Bolton United Harrier Kevin Best powered away from Mike Critchley soon after the 20 mile point to record a convincing victory over his Bolton team-mate, 2:16:22 to 2:20:10. Welshman Critchley held off a late challenge from Jeff Norman.

Kevin Best en route to victory. (Picture: Piccadilly Radio.)

This was Best's first marathon win and he said at the finish, "I'm very pleased to have won. I ran a controlled race, and settled into a comfortable pace. It's a personal best time by three minutes 35 seconds. I wanted to win a race, and one in Manchester on my home ground has capped my athletics career."

Dave Hurst was back again. His efforts helped the Stockport Society for Mentally Handicapped and Stockport Spastics Society. He stopped four times to empty the money from his dustbin.

Two wheelchair veterans: Gerry Kinsella, 32, from Southport, Liverpool and Tim Marshall, 36, from Birmingham, completed the 26 mile route. First back in 3:30:13 was Kinsella who was training for the John O'Groats to Lands End.

The capabilities of veterans' running was demonstrated by fourth and fifth places when Peter Malcolmson battled with Brian Little, to forge a four second margin, 2:21:23 to 2:21:27, both excellent times.

Results:

1	Kevin R Best	(Bolton U)	2:16:22
2	Mike Critchley	(Bolton U)	2:20:10
3	Jeff Norman	(Altrincham)	2:20:23
4	Peter Malcolmson	(LiverpoolPemb) V40	2:21:23
5	Brian D Little	(Bolton U) V40	2:21:27
6	Ricky Gwilt	(Salford H)	2:22:31
7	Derek Blakeley	(Manchester & D)	2:24:00
8	Brian Aspden	(Salford H)	2:24:37
9	Adrian Williams	(Unatt Doncaster)	2:24:59
10	Godfrey Claff	(Salford)	2:25:35

11, M Dooling (Liverpool) 2:26:14; 12, I Corrin (Unatt) 2:26:40; 13, G Kerr (Stretford) 2:27:06; 14, P Morris (Wigan) 2:27:46; 15, E Furby (Warrington) 2:27:47; 16, F Day (E Cheshire) 2:27:55; 17, M Dunns (Sale) 2:27:57; 18, M Oldham (Manchester) 2:28:12; 19, Graham Bell (Halifax) 2:28:28; 20, C Hogarth (Spring) 2:28:34; 21, B C Eden (Manchester) 2:28:54; 22, T Martin (Halton AC) 2:28:57: 23, A Cole (Liverpool) 2:28:59; 24, S Baker (Wigan) 2:29:03; 25, D Brown (Salford) 2:29:23; 26, D Atwell (Altrincham) Vet 40 2:29:26; 27, G Woodburn (Stockport) 2:29:36; 28, I E Hamer (Hor) 2:29:45; 29, B J McKenna (Clayton-le-Moors) 2:29:58;

30, K Shawcross (Manchester YMCA) 2:30:17; 31, B R Wilkinson (RAF Sealand) 2:30:34; 32, I Holloway (Rochdale) 2:31:06; 33, P Adams (Sal) 2:31:25; 34, D J Wright (Ranelagh) 2:31:36; 35, K Lynch (Bingley) 2:31:41; 36, C Pooley (Lancaster & M) 2:32:09; 37, W Pearson (Wigan) 2:32:13; 38, D J Brennan (Warrington) 2:32:21; 39, R C Mills (Altrincham) 2:32:25; 40, M Cruickshank (E Cheshire) 2:32:27; 41, W N Hume (Southport Waterloo) 2:33:09; 42, I Clarkson (Rochdale) 2:33:32; 43, K Moss (Chorley) 2:33:34; 44, A P Greenwood (Blackburn) 2:33:43; 45, P J Robinson (Clayton-le-Moors) 2:33:50; 46, B J Feeney ((Notts) 2:33:57; 47, K J Darby (Wigan) 2:34:06; 48, R B Cooper (E Cheshire) 2:34:14; 49, D Townsend (??) 2:34:29;

50, P Lawton (Stretford) 2:34:36; 51, K Thornley (Sale) 2:34:44; 52, J P Finnegan (Unatt) 2:35:29; 53, B Furness (Unatt) 2:36:11; 54, C Britt (Unatt) 2:36:20; 55, R M Eccles (Bingley) 2:36:29; 56, T Rodgers (Longwood) 2:36:40; 57, P Matchett (Unatt) 2:36:40; 58, P R Wilkinson (Barr) 2:37:14; 59, C Aldred (Salford) Vet 50 2:37:28; 60, J S Calderbank (Oldham & Royton)

2:37:55; 61, M R Hopson (Bolton) 2:38:03; 62, B Court (Bolton) 2:38:10; 63, K Sharrock (Man) 2:38:16; 64, J A Kershaw (Macc) 2:38:19; 65, B Morris (Macc) 2:38:23; 66, G I Lawson (Man) 2:38:31; 67, P W Pickwell (Unatt) 2:38:32; 68, S Whittaker (Unatt) 2:38:41; 69, J Hampshire (Wake Hosp) 2:38:44;

70, S D Edmunds (Sale) 2:38:59; 71, I B Kippax (Shell) 2:39:04; 72, D M Flatley (Bolton) 2:39:18; 73, D Fossatti (E Cheshire) 2:39:26; 74, A Winterbottom (E Cheshire) 2:39:39; 75, S Peruzza (Kendal) 2:39:42; 76, I Hamilton (Leigh) 2:39:49; 77, M J Leeson (Unatt) 2:39:58; 78, P J Curran (Altr) 2:40:01; 79, H Clague (Plessey) 2:40:02; 80, B J Peers (Manchester YMCA) 2:40:15; 81, R G Profitt (Salford) 2:40:17; 82, R Crookes (Unatt) 2:40:21; 83, P Kilbey (Alt) 2:40:24; 84, J Horrie (Unatt) 2:40:32; 85, J E Thomas (Highgate) 2:40:37; 86, N V Smith (Unatt) 2:40:40; 87, D W Smith (Unatt) 2:40:56; 88, A N Campbell (Stret) 2:41:12; 89, I Brierley (Saddleworth) 2:41:20; 90, M Brooks (Alt) 2:41:22; 91, R Fowler (Horw) 2:41:24; 92, J A Gregson (Old & Roy) 2:41:30; 93, P C Abbott (Wins) 2:41:31; 94, C M Dobson (Old & Roy) 2:41:41; 95, G Jackson (Man YMCA) 2:41:46; 96, S Grace (Unatt) 2:41:58; 97, Gary Thomason (Salford) 2:42:04; 98, P N Waddington (Roch) 2:42:15; 99, G Morson (Buxton) 2:42:19; 100 A Sugden (Unatt) 2:42:20. 6,837 finished.

V40 Peter Malcolmson	(Liverpool Pembroke)	2:21:23
V50 Cyril Aldred	(Salford)	2:37:28
V60 James Strickland	(Brit Marathon)	3:30:42

Women:

1 L Watson	(London Olympiades)	2:45:07
2 B Robinson	(Bury AC)	3:03:53
3 S Exon	(Stretford)	3:06:57;

4, Y Dawber 3:16:51; 5, J O'Brien 3:18:51; 6, F Poland (Man YMCA) 3:20:17; 7, M Curran (Unatt - Gorton) 3:23:51; 8, S Brindley (Unatt - Sutton Coldfield) 3:28:17; 10, P Parr 3:28:34.

| **V35** B Robinson | (Bury AC) | 3:03:53 |
| **V40** P Parr | (Manchester H & AC) | 3:28:34 |

Leslie Watson, who ran a personal best, was the "glamour girl" of long-distance running and was to lower her personal best to 2:44:18 in New York that autumn. She was also a champion ultra-distance runner holding a World Best for 50 miles and winning the London to Brighton women's race when females were first allowed to enter in 1979 (6:55:11). Remarkably she won again in 1980 in a time just 59 seconds slower than her first attempt.

Leslie Watson

Brenda Robinson had been an Irish International in her younger days as Brenda Bailey. She married Rochdale Harrier Colin Robinson who was an International Cross-Country runner. Brenda had trained diligently for the Piccadilly, averaging 60 miles a week up to the race. Three hours had been her goal, but having passed Sue Exon at about 2 miles, she never saw another woman in the race and lost concentration in the last few miles.

STOCKPORT - 4th April 1982

On Sunday 4th April 1982 nearly 3,000 started (out of an entry of 3,400) and first back was American Steve Bolt (2:17:31) with Kevin Best third (2:20:59) exactly a minute behind runner-up John Skovbjer (Denmark). Three veterans filled the top ten: 4, P Hoffman (Denmark) 2:23:27; 5, D Blakeley (Manchester H) 2:29:30; 6, F Day (E Cheshire) 2:29:36; 7, R Turner (Rugby AC) 2:29:57; 8, B Little (Bolton) V40 2:30:33; 9, P Lomas (Stockport) V40 2:31:51; 10, S James (Southport Waterloo) V40 2:32:10. Vet 50 62nd, T Llewellyn (Lancaster & M) 2:50:19.

Bolton won the team from East Cheshire and Salford.

It was a close finish for the first three women: Coventry's Anne Kirkham, wife of Colin, our marathon Olympian in the 1972 Munich Games, was only ten seconds in front of Maureen Hurst (Blackburn H) (226th to 228th, 3:07:02 to 3:07:12). Dawn Harris from Chesterfield AC was the first veteran over 35 in 236th, 3:07:44.

Three runs stand out: Roger Bourbon, the Swiss waiter who ran with a bottle of water balanced on a tray. His time was 3:03:12. Wheelchair-bound Gerry Kinsella, a paraplegic athlete, went round in 3:56. Another note-worthy performance came from Dave Hurst who raised money for Stockport Spastics Society by running the marathon with a dustbin on his back again.

The carnival atmosphere continued with 156 under three hours, 1,270 under four hours and 2,464 registered finishers.

For me it was a "phantom" race, stopping just before the finish line in 2:46.

BOLTON - 22nd August 1982

Leslie Watson and Sue Exon were part of the cast of 8,000 who turned out for the Pony Marathon in Bolton ten weeks after Manchester. Watson won from Priscilla Welch, who was destined to compete in the first women's Olympic Marathon two years later. Women: 1, L Watson, 2:48:27; 2, P Welch 2:56:19; 3, A Pendlebury 3:06:41; 4, P Day 3:10:23; 5, S Exon 3:12:03.

The full result at Bolton was: 1, Brian Maxwell (Canada) 2:20:10; 2, Eric Ranicar 2:24:49; 3, Paul Campbell 2:25:24; 4, Gerry Helme 2:27:57; 5, Sean O'Callaghan 2:29:49; 6, M Dunne 2:29:54; 7, Eric Williams 2:30:04; 8, Brian Little 2:30:05; 9, B Lloyd 2:32:36; 10, G F Thomas 2:32:45.

Chapter 24

The 24th Manchester Marathon
Sunday 29th May 1983

THE SECOND PICCADILLY RADIO MARATHON
JIMMY ASHWORTH TRIUMPHS

This year, race director Tom Tyrrell of *Piccadilly Radio* had put a ceiling of 10,000 on the entries and a time limit of $6^1/_2$ hours. The course had gained a reputation for being fast as there were no significant hills on the route. The participants ran through many greatly populated areas of Greater Manchester and the large public interest generated by the constant radio promotion ensured this was one of the greatest local sporting events of the year. With organisation coming from outside the usual running club traditions new dimensions were added to the race promotion. Three days before the race Manchester United had beaten Brighton and Hove Albion to take the FA Cup. Not to be upstaged the race director, Tom Tyrrell, who happened to be United's pre-match commentator and also editor of their club magazine, was able to commandeer the trophy and it preceded the whole race in an open-top bus!

Also, this year, I was asked to be the official starter, setting the runners on their way from the cradle of a crane, high above the start line, and then lowered to ground level to join the race somewhere in the field.

One of the pre-race favourites was 1982 winner, Kevin Best, and he was given race number 261, the frequency of Piccadilly Radio. However, he was known not to be on the same form as 1982. Co-favourite was international Stan Curran from Salford Harriers. Stan had made a breakthrough in 1978 finishing sixth in the AAA Marathon at Sandbach in a time of 2:14:45. This gained him selection for the Commonwealth Games in Edmonton, Canada, where he placed tenth (2:21:17.6), one behind Trevor Wright (2:20:14.6), and one ahead of Canada's Brian Maxwell, (2:21:46.3), the 1982 Bolton victor. More recently he had won the inaugural 1981 *Pony* British Marathon (Bolton), not long after clocking a personal best of 2:14:08.8 for second place in Rotterdam. But he had had a disappointing 1983 London, 130th, with 2:22:05.

From across the Pennines came Yorkshireman Jimmy Ashworth (Bingley), who in 1982 had won a couple of 20 mile road races, but up until now the 25-year-old had only a weak marathon best of 2:29:53. One unknown Icelandic runner was Agust Thorstensson, who had been specially flown in from Texas, where he was at college, and where he had recently run a best of 2:21:53 in hot humid conditions.

On the women's side, Leslie Watson returned to defend her title.

It was estimated that 9,500 of the 10,000 entered started the race.

Curran made his intentions clear from the start at 3 o'clock and at five miles (25:55), he had an eight second gap over Ashworth. This soon changed and on the East Lancs road, where one lane had been completely coned off for the runners, Ashworth took off. By the time the ten mile point had been reached in Worsley, he was 64 seconds up on Curran, clocking 49:54. He had covered that second five miles in 23:51! A distant third at this point was Sale Harriers' Steve Edmunds ahead of Scottish veteran George Black (East Kilbride), and the Icelandic runner Thorstensson.

By 15 miles Ashworth's lead had extended, Curran was second, Edmunds third and Derek Blakeley (Swinton), winner of the 1983 Stockport Daffodil Marathon (2:30:43), was now fourth. Thorstensson was sixth and suffering from cramp eventually faded to 12th.

Jimmy Ashworth in his trademark baseball cap. (Picture: Ralph Goodyear.)

At 20 miles (1:42:45) Ashworth was over three and a half minutes clear of Curran, (1:46:24), who was himself now over a minute in front of Edmunds (1:47:36) and Blakeley (1:47:57). Over the last six miles and 385 yards, equating almost to 10 Km, Ashworth increased his lead even further, covering this final stretch in a respectable 32:45, to record 2:15:39, a personal best by nearly a quarter of an hour. The crowds were around eight deep in the finishing funnel and he arrived to a massive cheer. They had top wait for almost seven minutes for runner-up Stan Curran to appear. Derek Blakeley moved into fourth place and was followed home by Salford's Ricky Gwilt, then Kevin Best who had passed a fading Steve Edmunds in the last mile.

Second time winner Leslie Watson with her trophy. (Picture: Piccadilly Radio.)

The women's race was a much closer fought affair. At 15 miles Melanie Jones (Essex Ladies) (1:32:54) was leading Leslie Watson (1:34:32) with Gill Markwell (Leeds City) (1:37:05) third. Jones was leading right up to 24 miles when for some unknown reason she pulled out and disappeared. Watson was amazed when she arrived at the finish to find the tape unbroken. As it was she was a mere 19 seconds ahead of the second woman, Gill Markwell, 2:50:56 to 2:51:15, who herself was only 14 seconds in front of third placer, the local lady, Lynn Shingles of Middleton AC.

Ashworth chalked up his first marathon win. He had nothing but praise for the race stating, "If you can't do a good time in the Piccadilly, then you can't do a good time anywhere. The crowds are amazing, and that finish!" Leslie Watson commented, "It is the best in the world outside New York."

Tom Tyrrell, the race director, later made it clear that the 10,000 ceiling would be held for 1984, but the time limit would be six hours, half an hour less than 1983. With over 7,000 runners breaking the $6^{1}/_{2}$ hour limit, Tyrrell had a unique ambition looking for 10,000 sub four hour runners by 1988.

Results:

1	Jimmy Ashworth	(Bingley)	2:15:39 *
2	Stan Curran	(Salford)	2:22:56
3	Derek Blakeley	(Swinton)	2:24:24
4	Ricky Gwilt	(Salford)	2:26:25
5	Kevin Best	(Bolton U)	2:27:01
6	Steve Edmunds	(Sale)	2:27:18
7	Graham Bell	(Halifax)	2:27:32 *
8	Roy Gresty	(Sale)	2:27:41 *
9	Allen Jessop	(St Helens)	2:27:53 *
10	Michael J Lavelle	(Sale)	2:28:26 *

11, I Clarkson (Rochdale) 2:28:35; 12, A Thorstensson (Iceland) 2:29:07; 13, S O'Callaghan (W Yorks Police) 2:29:40; 14, D C Sykes (Holmfirth) 2:30:13; 15, P Haworth (Keswick) 2:30:20 *; 16, D J Nolan (Stretford) 2:30:26 *; 17, K R Peters (Springfield) 2:30:51; 18, K W Hesketh (Springfield) 2:30:59; 19, K Mayor (Bolton) 2:31:09; 20, P F McCormick (Sale) 2:31:29 *; 21, N Rose (Chorley AC) 2:32:13 *; 22, D Sutton (Verlea) 2:32:15; 23, M R Hopson (Valley Striders) 2:32:22 *; 24, B Lloyd (Wigan) 2:32:24 *; 25, A Hudson (Blackpool & F) 2:32:48; 26, K M Robinson (Kendal) 2:33:14; 27, T Lonergan (Bingley) 2:33:15; 28, D Townsend (Salford) 2:33:26 *; 29, N Shanley (Manchester YMCA) 2:33:38*;

30, D Mullins (Unatt) 2:33:49 *; 31, A Martin (Halton Sports) 2:34:32; 32, B Holden (Guernsey AA) 2:34:41 *; 33, I Newcombe (Worsley) 2:34:46 *; 34, P Wilkinson (Clayton-le-Moors) 2:35:04 *; 35, S Walker (Sale) 2:35:10; 36, S T Lonnen (Salford) 2:35:18; 37, R Hutchins (Unatt) 2:35:21 *; 38, A Shaw (Rochdale) Vet 45 2:35:27 *; 39, P Milroy (Salford) 2:35:37; 40, E McLaughlin (Stourport AC) 2:35:51; 41, B McKenna (Clayton-le-Moors) 2:35:54; 42, H Clague (St Helens) 2:35:54; 43, George Black (E Kilbride) Vet 40 2:36:03; 44, N Harney (Swinton Jog Fit) 2:36:03; 45, K Boyle (Clayton-le-Moors) 2:36:05 *; 46, M Lynch (Leigh) 2:36:15 *; 47, P Leviston (Barrow) 2:36:20; 48, A Greenwood (Blackburn) 2:36:21; 49, R Mills (Altrincham) 2:36:29;

50, K Shawcross (Manchester YMCA) Vet 40 2:36:35; 51, M Edge

(Salford) 2:36:38; 52, J Kershaw (Macclesfield) 2:36:40; 53, J Forte (Edinburgh S) 2:36:44; 54, D Roberts (Unatt) 2:36:53 *; 55, G Wheeler (Burnham Joggers) 2:35:53; 56, A Marchington (Buxton) 2:36:54 *; 57, R Drysdale (Elswick) 2:36:58 *; 58, B Scobie (Leeds City) 2:37:04; 59, G Kerr (Stretford) 2:37:08; 60, S Clegg (Salford) 2:37:12; 61, G Davis (Invicta) 2:37:12; 62, A Jackson (Saddleworth) 2:37:14 *; 63, M Poulton (Rochdale) Vet 40 2:37:14; 64, A J Llewellyn (Lancaster & M) Vet 50; 65, D Smith (Bolton) 2:37:19 *; 66, K Thornley (Salford) 2:37:23; 67, T Parr (Bolton) Vet 40 2:37:25; 68, D Carter (Chorley) 2:37:31 *; 69, B Heyes (Pilkington AC) 2:37:37 *;

70, K Smith (Darlington) 2:37:50 *; 71, L Stephenson (Kendal) 2:37:51 *; 72, M Woolrich (Halton) 2:38:05 *; 73, P Hargate (Middleton) 2:38:08 *; 74, D Helps (Leigh) 2:38:16 *; 75, B Wellings (Colwyn Bay) 2:38:25 *; 76, R Taylor (Stockport) 2:38:33; 77, J Purvis (Unatt) 2:38:36 *; 78, I Carter (Unatt) 2:38:39 *; 79, R Fowler (Horwich RMI) 2:38:46 *; 80, T Rodgers (Longwood) Vet 40 2:38:46 *; 81, P Matchett (Longwood) 2:38:50; 82, C Britt (Sale) 2:39:02; 83, K Appleyard (Skyrac) Vet 40 2:39:04 *; 84, P Smith (Brit Aerospace) 2:39:07 *; 85, G Owen (Wrexham) 2:39:07; 86, R A Lewellin (Rochdale) 2:39:09 *; 87, A Wood (Blackburn) 2:39:13; 88, H Purdy (Warrington) 2:39:16 *; 89, G Read (Rochdale) 2:39:21 *; 90, B Wilkinson (RAF) 2:39:26; 91, R Hand (Border) 2:39:28 *; 92, P Corless (Unatt) 2:39:33 *; 93, D Whaite (Sale) 2:39:35; 94, M Pinnington (Unatt) 2:39:39 *; 95, D Hughes (Clayton-le-Moors) 2:39:40 *; 96, M Harrison (Horwich RMI) 2:39:44 *; 97, S Marland (Manchester YMCA) 2:39:49 *; 98, C Bolton (Sale) 2:40:09 *; 99, M Hayhurst (YMCA) 2:40:20 *; 100, M Entwistle (Unatt) 2:40:30 *
* = personal best 7,363 finished.

Category winners
V40 A Shaw   (Rochdale)   2:35:27
V50 Tony Llewellyn (Lancaster & M)   2:37:15

Women:

1	L Watson	(London Olympiades)	2:50:56
2	Gill Markwell	(Leeds City)	2:51:15
3	Lynn Shingles	(Middleton)	2:51:29

4, V Wallace (Unatt) 2:57:16; 5, S Catterall (Unatt - Bolton) 3:01:34; 6, C Borrill (East Hull) V35 3:01:46; 7, R Cornu (Paris) 3:04:28; 8, L Hardley (Stockport) 3:07:37; 9, Z Hyde (Epsom & Ewell H) 3:08:04; 10, C Moorat (London RR) 3:10:39.

V35 C Borrill   (East Hull)   3:01:46
V40 K Krawczyk   (Bolton U)   3:14:45

V45 E Shepherd	(Unatt)	3:22:05
V50 B Timpson	(Unatt)	5:51:25
V55 R Scott	(Bolton U)	4:58:46

Jimmy Ashworth did not return to Manchester, but he did improve. In January 1984 he was second in the Orange Bowl Marathon in Miami in 2:14:06, won the Inter-counties 20 miles road race in 1:40:05, and in the London Marathon lowered his personal best to 2:13:49 in seventh place. In 1985 he won the Orange Bowl Marathon, 2:18:49, then followed this up in October with another international win, a 2:11:43 in Berlin. He was a member of Bingley Harriers, 1977 - 1987, then moved to Keighley Road Runners. In 1987 he won the Inter-counties 20 miles road race in 1:44:06 and finished fifth in the 1988 Great North Run, 68:08. High mileage led to injuries and retirement.

Stan Curran did not run another Piccadilly Marathon, but still continues to run and race today for Salford Harriers.

For me, it was another of several "phantom" marathons that I ran, getting to, but not crossing the finish line. In 1983 I got there in 2:47. My younger son Graham, not quite 18 years old, finished in 3:19:16. In 1999 he won the Leeds Marathon in 2:23:53.

The first veteran over 50, Tony Llewellyn, (Lancaster and Morecambe), had represented Britain at steeplechase in the early 1950s.

Leslie Watson continued to race marathons, but not Manchester. In 1984 she was runner-up at Rome (2:47:05) and by the end of 1985 had run in 131 marathons in many parts of the world. She has now retired from marathon running with a total of 206 finishes and a lifetime's best of 2:43:58.

STOCKPORT - 10th April 1983

Of the 2,000 entry list 1,500 started on a damp Sunday in a lack-lustre local affair. Enjoying his first win from 13 marathons was Derek Blakeley, now with Swinton. He won in 2:30:43 from Andy Merrifield (Liverpool H) 2:32:11 and top vet, Pete Lomas (Stockport) 2:34:29. The rest of the top ten were: 4, A Barlow (Altrincham AC) 2:35:21; 5, P Bates (Bury AC) 2:37:06; 6, P Haworth (Keswick) 2:38:29; 7, S Marland (Manchester YMCA) 2:38:45; 8, S Whittaker (Halton AC) 2:40:43; 9, D Mallings (Un / Holme) 2:41:23; 10, G Bennison (Bolton) 2:42:32. Vet 50 49th, B Forster (Winsford AC) 2:50:14.

The top three females were: 1, Carol Borrill (City of Hull) 3:06:42; 2, M Curran (Oldham & Royton) 3:17:39; 3, K Smith (Unatt / Barrow-in-Furness) 4:42:15. Vet Over 40 A Nally (Altrincham) 3:24:26.

Men's Teams: 1, Stockport, 10:49:11, 2 Bolton 11:06:17; 3, Manchester YMCA 11:06:47.

A key figure was Dave "Dustbin" Hurst who raised about £400 for charity.

BOLTON - 22nd August 1983

Now sponsored by adidas, the Bolton Marathon held on 22nd August, 12 weeks after the Piccadilly, saw 7,500 contestants line up on Beaumont Road. Race director Vince Regan had put together a star-studded line-up and Ron Clarke, the former Australian multi-world record holder acted as starter. The winners from 1981 Stan Curran and 1982 Brian Maxwell contested the race along with Ireland's Neil Cusack, the 1974 Boston Marathon winner (2:13:39) and many others inspired by the previous "people's" marathons.

The mercury nearly hit 80 Fahrenheit and yet a course record was set. Ian Thompson, then the fastest Briton, won in 2:18:09 from Birchfield's Ray Smedley (2:22:57), the former international miler who had been seventh the previous year in the AAA Championships at Gateshead (2:16:05). At the 1983 London Smedley improved to 2:14:45, a personal best and had run for England at the marathon in the previous Commonwealth Games being 11th in 2:15:50. The next ten at Bolton were: 3, Mike Neary (Leigh) 2:23:25; 4, Sa'Udor Szendrei (Hungary) 2:24:04; 5, David Clarke (Verlea) 2:24:17; 6, Nicky Lees (Derby) 2:24:44; 7, Tom Fleming (USA) 2:25:28; 8, John Offord (Leicester C) 2:26:43; 9, Jim Dingwall (Falkirk) 2:27:12; 10, Jeff Norman (Altrincham) 2:27:31; 11, H Clague (St Helens) 2:27:46; 12, Glyn Harvey (Staffs Moorlands) 2:31:21.

The international theme continued in the ladies section with Eileen Claugus, a Californian, breaking the course record with 2:39:08 in 27th place, just in front of John Whetton, the 1969 European 1500m Champion. Second lady was future British record holder Veronique Marot of Leeds City (2:49:51), and third was Lynne Shingles (Middleton) in 2:58:01.

Chapter 25

The 25th Manchester Marathon
Sunday 1st July 1984

THE THIRD PICCADILLY RADIO MARATHON
VICTORY FOR IAN THOMPSON

There were several estimates of the number of starters in the 1984 Piccadilly Marathon varying from 8,000 to 9,500, so it is probable that numbers were slightly down on 1983. One of Britain's best-ever marathon runners, Ian Thompson (Luton United AC) with a 2:09:12 from 1974 had been invited, in the hope of a star winner. Two weeks earlier he had won the Potteries Marathon in 2:20:54. Manchester's reputation for a fast course had got round and the runners had come from far afield, looking for a fast time.

The weather was ideal, 55° F (13° C) at mid-day and partly cloudy. Of the local runners, 26-year-old Paul Campbell of Bolton United Harriers, with a tenth place 2:14:04 marathon achieved three months earlier in Maassluis, Holland, and the 1982 winner of the *Chesters* Tour of Tameside double marathon stood out, along with 1982 Manchester winner Kevin Best, now with Stretford AC, and 1976 Olympian Jeff Norman (Altrincham AC).

The first prize was a Ford Escort XR-3 to be kept for a year.

The start of the 1984 Piccadilly Radio Marathon. (Picture: Piccadilly Radio.)

When the gun fired at 3:00 pm Paul Campbell was off like a rocket, hoping to get his hands on the car. He was operating at sub five minute mile pace and by five miles had a lead of over one minute on the chasing pack which contained Ian Thompson and the popular local man, Kevin Best. There was a slight head wind up to nine miles and into this, first Thompson just after five miles, then Best at $8^{1}/_{2}$ miles broke away from the chasing bunch. The pack in fourth place reached ten miles in 53:20, quite a sedentary pace for a top class marathon, with Colin Moxsom of Haringey leading and beginning to apply pressure. First Jeff Norman tried to break away, and then Sale's Eric Williams made a more determined effort and the bunch was broken up. Moxsom and Williams ran away and passed 15 miles together having clocked 69:10 at half-way. Campbell had passed three minutes earlier with Thompson two minutes and twenty seconds adrift, just ahead of Best.

Williams caught Best at the 18 mile mark, and passed 20 miles in 1:45 now in third place. Campbell was still leading at 20 miles, but his efforts in trying to win from the front were beginning to take their toll and he was starting to suffer from cramp. At 22 miles, Thompson passed and moved into the lead.

Williams was moving up nicely, and later said, "As I turned left on to Kingsway I saw a car with a clock on top, it didn't register as being the lead car; I hadn't seen it for 22 miles." He was now a mere 400 metres behind the leader, with less than three miles to go. But Thompson was not to be denied and although the gap closed to 48 seconds, a little over 200 metres, at the end, he broke the tape in 2:16:08.

Eric Williams recorded a personal best 2:16:56, and Campbell gamely continued with a buffer of over three minutes from fourth man Best, and was happy with his third place, 2:17:39.

In the women's race, by 15 miles Maureen Hurst (Clayton-le-Moors) was leading Londoner Libby Pfeiffer, with Welsh women's champion Jackie Hulbert third and Sue Catterall (Bolton) fourth. Hulbert was running with back problems and had been hit in that area early on, causing her to eventually withdraw.

Hurst was overtaken by Pfeiffer who went on to win by over five minutes whilst Hurst had run herself out and was pipped in the home straight by Catterall to lose second place by two seconds, 2:51:56 to 2:51:58.

Results:

1	Ian Thompson	(Luton)	2:16:08
2	Eric Williams	(Sale)	2:16:56
3	Paul Campbell	(Bolton)	2:17:39
4	Kevin Best	(Stretford)	2:20:43

```
 5  Colin Moxsom      (Haringey)      2:22:18
 6  Jeff Norman       (Altrincham)    2:22:19
 7  Steve Howcroft    (Unattached)    2:22:29
 8  Max Coleby        (Gateshead)     2:24:18
 9  Steve Brace       (Bridgend)      2:24:29
10  Graeme Birkett    (St Helens)     2:24:32
```

11, A Ritchie (Keswick) V40 2:25:53; 12, B Knappers (Netherlands) 2:26:31; 13, G Fairley (Kilbarchan) 2:27:25; 14, E Ranicar (Bolton) 2:27:30; 15, B Lee (Darlington) 2:27:38; 16, S Payne (Invicta) 2:27:45; 17, E Furby (Warrington) 2:27:53; 18, T Glare (Woodstock) 2:28:05; 19, W Greenhalgh (Leigh) 2:28:38; 20, D Mailer (St Helens) 2:28:57; 21, J Barker (Grims) 2:29:00; 22, T Rodgers (Long) V40 2:29:07; 23, W Keevil 2:29:41; 24, J Finegan (Sale) 2:30:07; 25, M Edge (Sal) V40 2:30:15; 26, A Robinson (Sale) 2:30:20; 27, R Taylor (Stock) 2:31:06; 28, M Woolrich (Liv) 2:31:09; 29, J Monks (Roch) 2:31:15; 30, C Bell (Hal) 2:31:18; 31, F McCormick (Sale) 2:31:21; 32, S Johnson (Les C) 2:31:23; 33, G Mason (Barr) 2:31:32; 34, I Carter (E Ches) 2:31:42; 35, S Walker (Macc) 2:31:45; 36, P Jones 2:32:07; 37, A Taylor (RR) 2:32:11; 38, C Haskett (Dund) 2:32:29; 39, K Smith (Darl) 2:33:53; 40, I Kippax 2:33:36; 41, K Thornley (Sal) 2:33:49; 42, R Winward (Barr) 2:33:52; 43, G Read (Roch) 2:33:59; 44, P Dent (Wig) 2:34:02; 45, D Thorpe (Leigh) 2:34:04; 46, C Heyes (Red Rose) 2:34:20; 47, V Meeson 2:34:20; 48, D Hankinson (Red Rose) 2:34:20; 49, P Gledhill (Barns) 2:34:22;

50, P Powell (Barns) 2:34:24; 51, M Wakefield (Sal) 2:34:25; 52, P Garside (Wors) 2:34:26; 53, P Bates (Bury) 2:34:29; 54, M Lavelle (Sale) 2:34:53; 55, G Gormley (Chelt) 2:34:50; 56, C Britt (Sale) 2:34:53; 57, W Platt (Chor) 2:34:54; 58, J Wycherley (St H) 2:34:57; 59, J Rogers (Sale) V40 2:35:05; 60, N Shanley (Man YMCA) 2:35:10; 61, C Hughes 2:35:21; 62, R Jones (Barr) 2:35:24; 63, A Gaffney (Blackburn) V40 2:35:25; 64, M Boyle (Ver) 2:35:41; 65, P Freeman (Grim) 2:35:49; 66, V Holman (Thet) 2:35:57; 67, S Edmunds (Sale) 2:35:59; 68, J Doig (Aberdeen) 2:36:09; 69, P Dale (Bolt) 2:36:13;

70, B Davies 2:36:26; 71, C White (Newton Aycliffe) 2:36:34; 72, I Barton (Roch) 2:36:34; 73, D Sutton (Ver) V40 2:36:44; 74, P Wilkinson (Clayton-le-Moors) 2:36:46; 75, J Forte 2:37:03; 76, J Meredith (Red Rose) 2:37:14; 77, P Turley (E & E) V40 2:37:18; 78, S Whittaker (Alt) 2:37:22; 79, A Parkinson (Man YMCA) 2:37:29; 80, T Burgess (St Helens) 2:37:30; 81, P Milligan 2:37:32; 82, R Fox (Sale) 2:37:34; 83, A Dunn (Stockport) V50 2:37:35; 84, J Warner (Stretford) 2:37:40; 85, B Heyes (Wigan) V40 2:37:45; 86, M Pinnington (Liverpool P) 2:37:58; 87, I Gordon (Cope) 2:38:37; 88, I Morris 2:38:39; 89, P Corless (Leigh) 2:38:43; 90, D Greenwood (Bingley) V45 2:38:48; 91, A Peet (Wigan) 2:38:49; 92, A Hesketh (Horwich RMI) 2:38:52;

93, A Barlow (Alt) 2:38:52; 94, R Fowler (Chorley) 2:39:00; 95, S Singh (Charn) 2:39:06; 96, D Parry (Midd) 2:39:09; 97, K O'Neill 2:39:20; 98, C Smith 2:39:21; 99, P Pickwell 2:39:24; 100, G Till (Eryri) V40 2:39:24. 6,337 finished.

V40 A Ritchie	(Keswick)	2:23:53
V50 A Dunn	(Stockport)	2:37:35

Women:

1	L Pfeiffer	(Barnet Ladies)	2:46:54
2	S Catterall	(Bolton)	2:51:56
3	M Hurst	(Clayton-le-Moors)	2:51:58;

4, V Hyland (Unatt) V40 2:55:44; 5, L Hardley (Altrincham) 3:04:49; 6, D Tsaktstansos V40 (Unatt) 3:05:12; 7, E Casteldine (Leigh H) 3:12:48; 8, K Krawczyk (Bolton U) 3:17:33; 9, P Turton (Unatt) 3:18:54; 10, M Platt Chorley AC) 3:19:15.

V35 K Cox	(Wirral AC)	3:23:52
V40 V Hyland	(Unatt)	2:55:44
V45 M Caldwell	(Bolton U)	4:17:38
V50 C Watson	(Swinton JC)	4:02:21
V55 R Scott	(Bolton U)	5:13:37
V60 -------	-----------	---------
V65 M Sharples	(Winchester)	5:05:51

Libby Pfeiffer and Ian Thompson.
(Picture: Neil Shuttleworth.)

Steve Brace (Bridgend AC), a week short of his 23rd birthday, had set a personal best of 2:24:29 in ninth place. He was only at the race because his girl-friend Jacqueline Hulbert was an invited athlete to the women's race. Three weeks later he returned to the Manchester area, with Jacqueline for the two of them to compete in the GMC Tour of Tameside. I remember this race well as I was competing, and on the last stage, the "Canal" race, I was alongside Steve when he was jostled and fell into the Huddersfield Narrow Canal. He got out and still beat me, finishing 13th overall. Jacqueline was third lady.

From these humble beginnings, he was still playing rugby as well as running, he was to rise to stardom. He returned to win the Tour of Tameside in 1986, and eventually ran for Britain in two Olympics: Barcelona, 1992, 27th, 2:17:49 and Atlanta, 1996, 60th, 2:23:28. He ended up with 52 marathon finishes, 26 of these under 2:20, and four under 2:12, his best being 2:10:35 in Houston Texas, January 1996. Nowadays he is the Director of Athletics at the Athletics Association of Wales.

First veteran in 11th place was Alan Ritchie (Keswick AC) in 2:25:53. I never realised that Alan, a modest man, had been such a good runner. Although he lives in Carlisle, he is still a member of Keswick AC and organises the annual Derwentwater '10', one of the most spectacular and beautiful courses in the country.

Maureen Hurst, later that year, on Sunday 30th September, ran 2:42:49 for third place in the Berlin Marathon.

Jacqueline Hulbert who did not finish is now married to Steve Brace. In April 1985 she won the Trinidad Marathon whilst five months pregnant, and later that year finished second in Malmo, Sweden, 2:49:57. She set her lifetime's best of 2:39:26 running for the Les Croupiers club and finishing ninth in the 1986 London, only 7^1/$_2$ months after giving birth to son, Ashley. Four weeks later she defended her title in Trinidad, running around three hours. The following day her "back packed up for good."

STOCKPORT - 8th April 1984

Footballer Bobby Charlton started them off and Steve Bolt from Alabama, the 29-year-old winner from 1982, returned first. He was the clear winner in 2:25:18 with Dave Turnbull of the host club runner-up in 2:26:11 and Ron McAndrew (Chorley AC) third, 2:27:53. Turnbull took 13 minutes off his personal best.

The first male veteran was Keith Shawcross (Manchester YMCA) in 2:38:39. Alec Dunn in 21st place (2:41:33) was the first over 45 and in 52nd was Malcolm Pittock, the first over 50, 2:47:20.

Four men broke 2:30 and Eleanor Adams (Sutton-in-Ashfield), the first lady, 2:56:21, was one of the 156 who broke three hours. From an entry of 2,148 1,576 finished.

The rest of the top ten were: 4, M Higginbottom (Salford H) 2:29:04; 5, R Taylor (Stockport) 2:32:54; 6, B Smith (Unattached / Bolton) 2:35:38; 7, P Kilbey (Altrincham) 2:35:40; 8, G Marrinan (Oldham & Royton) 2:36:31; 9, R Gresty (Sale H) 2:37:06; 10, D Wright (Hallamshire H) 2:37:28.

Stockport won the team race (10:26:07) from Leigh H (10:49:18) and Sale H (10:50:18).

The first three females to finish were: 1, Eleanor Adams; 2, Yvonne Miles V40 (Bournemouth AC) 3:04:49; 3, Liz Hardley (Altrincham) 3:12:08 (275th).

BOLTON - 2nd September 1984

Ian Thompson and Eric Williams renewed their rivalry six weeks after Manchester in the adidas Bolton Marathon on 2nd September. Williams, who headed the 6,000 plus entry, had bided his time, moved into the lead with eight miles remaining. Thompson, was off the leading group and drifting back, probably suffering from over-racing. The top ten were: 1, Eric Williams 2:21:33; 2, Peter Orton (Burton-on-Trent) 2:22:30; 3, Ian Thompson (Luton) 2:23:42; 4, Mike Neary 2:24:38; 5, John Offord (Leicester C) 2:25:18; 6, Petko Karpatchev (Bulgaria) 2:27:00; 7, Neil Cusack (Ireland) 2:27:43; 8, Tom Glare (Woodstock) 2:32:52; 9, Nigel Barlow (Horwich RMI) 2:32:55; 10, Michael P Harrison 2:33:48.

In the women's race Veronique Marot, who used the race as a training run for New York, finished together with Sally McDiarmid in 2:49:10. Christine Kennedy was third 2:53:08, fourth Sue Catterall, 2:56:09 and fifth Pauline Shore 3:13:47.

Chapter 26

The 26th Manchester Marathon
Sunday 30th June 1985

SWAN-SONG FOR THE PICCADILLY RADIO MARATHON
HARRY CLAGUE UNDER 2:20

Although Piccadilly Radio had found a commercial sponsor in the form of Puma, the sports shoe manufacturer, numbers were down in the 1985 race. Despite the fact that runners were fewer race organiser Tom Tyrrell claimed that this was the best organised race of the series, and that apart from London and Glasgow entries were falling in all other marathons. He went on to rue the fact that it in terms of quality up front it would cost so much to get the top runners.

No foreigners came and it looked as though the race would be between Harry Clague (St Helens) who had already won two marathons in June, the first, the Wirral Marathon, 1st June, with a 2:24, and the second on the 15th June, the Potteries Marathon, 2:19:05. Had he done too much? Had he recovered? Arraigned against him were 1972, Munich Olympian, Colin Kirkham, now a veteran, Kevin Best, winner in 1982, and Paul Campbell, third in 1984. On paper the fastest man in the field was John Offord of Leicester Coritanians with a 1984 best of 2:13:52.

Favourite for the women's title was 38-year-old Lorna Irving of Border Harriers. She had only started running in 1983, but later that year had won the Windermere Marathon in a course record of 2:52:08 on her debut. The following year she ran 2:44:15 in London (one place and two seconds behind Maureen Hurst) and followed that with an excellent 2:37:19 in Glasgow. Clayton-le-Moors' Maureen Hurst, having run a superb 2:41:30 Miami Marathon, January 1985, returned realistically hoping to improve on her bronze medal position of the year before.

It was a warm humid day when the race started at 3:00 pm. After less than three miles Offord, up with the leading group suddenly staggered to a halt suffering from severe pains at the bottom of his spine. "I couldn't run another step," he later reported. "The pain was frightening." I have never known anything like it."

At 5 miles Clague led from Best with Chris Woodhouse (Derby and County AC), Campbell and Nigel Barlow (Horwich RMI H) in hot pursuit.

Harry Clague winning the 1985 marathon (Picture: Piccadilly Radio.)

The leaders went through 10 miles in just over 53 minutes and at 15 miles, 1:19:10, Best was just ahead of Woodhouse, Clague and Campbell with Kirkham fifth.

Campbell began forcing the pace taking Woodhouse with him and at 20 miles these two were in front with a time of 1:46:10. Best and Clague followed alongside each other and the third group, only a minute down on the leaders comprised of Kirkham and Barlow, who had been joined by Steve Howcroft (St Helens AC). It was at this point that Campbell began to weaken.

Woodhouse made a break and it seemed victory was in his sights; but he had not reckoned with Harry Clague. Clague stepped up a gear just before 20 miles and soon caught the fading Campbell. Inspired by the rapidly closing gap, he strode by the dejected Woodhouse at 24 miles to finish a convincing winner in 2:19:31. Woodhouse hung on to second, but poor Campbell drifted back to fifth having been passed by the ever-popular Kevin Best, then Nigel Barlow of Horwich RMI. Colin Kirkham was a very creditable sixth and the first veteran home ahead of Sheffield's Malcolm Martin, ninth. The leading veteran over 50 was Peter Brennan, Manchester YMCA in an excellent 2:31:53.

Border Harrier Lorna Irving (Picture: Piccadilly Radio.)

The women's race was very close with Lorna Irving setting a course record of 2:44:13, 48 seconds ahead of Maureen Hurst. In third place came Jeannie Percival, of City of Hull, in 2:58:06.

I, myself, ran that marathon on a quest to reach 100 marathons in that year. Already I had finished ten marathons in the previous six months with a best of 2:29:27 in London. Manchester was my 95th marathon, the 2:36:36 placing me 38th overall. With Guernsey, Edinburgh, Ipswich, where I recorded my last ever marathon victory in 2:35:53, and Glasgow, my 99th was reached. On 13th October I raced the classic course from Marathon to Athens, scene of my European Games victory way back in 1969, to record 2:43:56 for my century of marathons. For good measure I ran another four that year: Bedford, Benidorm, Maryland and Barbados to give me 20 marathons in 1985.

Results:

1	Harry Clague	(St Helens)		2:19:31
2	Chris Woodhouse	(Derby & C)		2:20:14
3	Kevin Best	(Stretford)		2:22:22
4	Nigel Barlow	(Horwich RMI)		2:23:37
5	Paul Campbell	(Bolton U)		2:24:21
6	Colin Kirkham	(Coventry)	V 40	2:24:25

7	Steve Howcroft	(St Helens)		2:25:26
8	Guy Woolnough	(Kendal)		2:26:53
9	Malcolm Martin	(Sheffield)	V 40	2:27:10
10	Alan Robinson	(Sale)		2:27:17;

11, Tony Martin (Liverpool Pembroke) 2:28:31; 12, C Denet (Bury) 2:28:40; 13, J Eley (Derby & County) 2:29:36; 14, D Carter (Chorley H) 2:29:53; 15, M Hall (Potteries) 2:30:18; 16, R Jones (Liverpool Pembroke) 2:30:22; 17, G Dell (Vale of Aylesbury) 2:31:20; 18, M Church (Northampton) 2:31:32; 19, P Brennan (Manchester YMCA) V50 2:31:53; 20, G Bell (Rochdale) 2:32:22; 21, P Bailey (Unatt) 2:33:18 (Wheelchair); 22, D Grant (Wolverhampton & Bilston) 2:33:23; 23, P Hankinson (Blackpool & F) 2:33:28; 24, S Walton (Longwood H) 2:33:41; 25, R Robson (Prestatyn RC) 2:34:04; 26, J Marples (N Wales RR) 2:34:22; 27, R Moore (Unatt) 2:34:47; 28, J Monks (Rochdale H) 2:34:58; 29, P Edwards (Verlea AC) 2:35:03;

30, D Helps (Leigh H) 2:35:08; 31, B Gillespie (Wirral AC) 2:35:10; 32, B Hewitt (Leigh H) 2:35:40; 33, M Boyle (Invicta) 2:35:50; 34, D Oldfield (Sheffield AC) 2:35:54; 35, J Parr (Royal Navy) 2:36:08; 36, K Binney (Barnsley RR) 2:36:11; 37, M Cunningham (Manchester H) 2:36:18; 38, D Thorpe (Leigh H) 2:36:26; 39, R Hill (Clayton-le-Moors H) 2:36:36; 40, A Spilman (Riccall & Selby DAC) 2:36:42; 41, E Roberts (Eryri H) 2:37:02; 42, M Abbs (Unatt) 2:37:18; 43, D Mailer (St Helens AC) 2:37:29; 44, P Powell (Barnsley RR) 2:37:31; 45, C Manclark (Stockport H) 2:37:49; 46, A Simpson (Potteries MC) 2:37:52; 47, J Poston (Neath H) 2:37:59; 48, S Hunt (Askern DRC) 2:38:12; 49, S Marland (Manchester YMCA) 2:38:13;

50, A Mather (Sheffield AC) 2:38:19; 51, N Doherty (Clayton-le-Moors) 2:38:55; 52, P Gledhill (Barnsley RR) 2:39:01; 53, J Warner (Stretford AC) 2:39:04; 54, M Walker (Horwich RMI) 2:39:16; 55, B Crowney (Unatt) 2:39:19; 56, B Rigby (Rochdale) 2:39:20; 57, B Hayes (Wigan H) 2:39:24; 58, D Grayson (Staniforth) 2:39:26; 59, B Holden (Guernsey Island AC) 2:39:27; 60, M Pinnington (Pembroke AC) 2:38:37; 61, G Pinner (Preston AC) 2:39:42; 62, N Shanley (Manchester YMCA) 2:39:45; 63, A Winterbottom (E Cheshire) 2:40:00; 64, T Temple (Middleton RC) 2:40:13; 65, K McKeown (St Helens AC) 2:40:14; 66, S Humphries (Unatt) 2:40:17; 67, J Spillane (Wigan H) 2:40:22; 68, K Owens (E Cheshire) 2:40:24; 69, I Morris (Unatt) 2:40:28; 70, K Shawcross (Manchester YMCA) 2:40:29; 71, P Holsby (Dorridg Solihull) 2:40:33; 72, A Peacock (Unatt) 2:40:37; 73, R Harris (Kippax) 2:40:50; 74, M O'Sullival (Airedale & Spen V) 2:40:56; 75, M Banks (Airedale & Spen V) 2:41:18; 76, A Clegg (Stockport) 2:41:22; 77, G Savage (Unatt) 2:41:24; 78, I Gordon (Copeland) 2:41:34; 79, K Culshaw (AAA) 2:41:37; 80, K Swadkins (Unatt) 2:41:42; 81, J Davies (Les Croupiers) 2:41:46; 82, G Orritt (Preston

AC) 2:41:46; 83, R Ashby (Sale) 2:42:06; 84, C Walker (London RRC) 2:42:09; 85, M Valetine (Preston) 2:42:10; 86, C Jackson (Unatt) 2:42:18; 87, P King (Maidenhead AC) 2:42:26; 88, R Herring (Unatt) 2:42:34; 89, H McCarron (Manchester YMCA) 2:42:38; 90, M Davies (Sefton) 2:42:47; 91, R Derbyshire (Stockport) 2:43:06; 92, R Seddon (Kippax) 2:43:26; 93, T Pares (Royal Marines) 2:43:34; 94, A Boardman (Gorton) 2:43:41; 95, W Kelly (Bolton U) 2:43:54; 96, S Hughes (Swinton JF) 2:43:58; 97, B Crowther (Bingley) 2:43:59; 98, T Pinch (Wrexham) 2:44:02; 99, B Light (Leigh H) 2:44:04; 100, P Allan (Salford) 2:44:05; 101, L Irving (Border H) 2:44:13.

4,613 finished.

| **V40** | C Kirkham | (Coventry) | | 2:24:25 |
| **V50** | P Brennan | (Manchester YMCA) | | 2:31:53 |

Women:

1	Lorna Irving	(Border)	V35	2:44:13
2	Maureen Hurst	(Clayton-le-Moors)		2:45:01
3	Jeannie Percival	(City of Hull)		2:58:06;

4, S Exon (Stretford) 2:59:05; 5, M Goodwin (Leigh H) 3:04:29; 6, W Grundy (Heywood R) 3:05:06; 7, L Hardley (Altrincham) 3:05:48; 8, Z Hyde (Manchester University C-C C) 3:13:38; 9, C Walker (Bingley) V35 3:15:46; 10, B Stringer (Manchester YMCA H) V40 3:28:51.

V35	L Irving	(Border)	2:44:13
V40	B Stringer	(Manchester YMCA H)	3:28:51
V45	F Classon	(Deeside)	3:34:44
V50	C Watson	(Swinton JF)	4:18:44
V55	M Hunt	(Unatt)	5:19:09

Clague continued to race and took the veterans trophy in the 1988 Tour of Tameside, clocking 4:50:44 for the double marathon.

Three months later Lorna Irving lost her Glasgow title to Angie Pain (Leeds City) who set a course record of 2:37:06 with Irving second in 2:38:20. That autumn Irving ran 2:47:22 for 23rd woman in New York and the following year turned the tables on Pain in her native Scotland at the Edinburgh Commonwealth Games being fifth, first Briton in the inaugural women's marathon with a lifetime's best of 2:36:34.

Clague, the first of 4,852 finishers, closed another chapter of marathons in Manchester as in early 1986 it was announced that the Piccadilly Radio Marathon would amalgamate with the Bolton Marathon under the title of Piccadilly British Marathon.

PICCADILLY MARATHONS
RANKING OF TOP 50 MEN'S TIMES   1981-85

Rank	Name	Club	Year	Position	Time
1	S Kenyon	(Salford H)	1981	1	2:11:54
2	J Ashworth	(Bingley H)	1983	1	2:15:39
3	I Thompson	(Luton U)	1984	1	2:16:08
4	K R Best	(Bolton U)	1982	1	2:16:22
5	E Williams	(Sale H)	1984	2	2:16:56
6	P Campbell	(Bolton U)	1984	3	2:17:39
7	C Taylor	(Airedale & SV)	1981	2	2:17:56
8	H Clague	(St Helens AC)	1985	1	2:19:31
9	K McDonald	(Bingley H)	1981	3	2:19:34
10	M Critchley	(Bolton U)	1982	2	2:20:10
11	C Woodhouse	(Derby & C)	1985	2	2:20:14
12	J Norman	(Altrincham & D)	1982	3	2:20:23
13	K Best	(Stretford AC)	1984	4	2:20:43
14	P Malcolmson	(L/pool P) V40	1982	4	2:21:23
15	B D Little	(Bolton U) V40	1982	5	2:21:27
16	K Best	(Bolton U)	1981	4	2:21:43
17	C Moxsom	(Haringey AC)	1984	5	2:22:18
18	J Norman	(Altrincham & D)	1984	6	2:22:19
19	K Best	(Stretford AC)	1985	3	2:22:22
20	S Howcroft	(Unattached)	1984	7	2:22:29
21	R Gwilt	(Salford H)	1982	6	2:22:31
22	S Curran	(Salford H)	1983	2	2:22:56
23	M Wakefield	(Salford H)	1981	5	2:23:09
24	N Barlow	(Horwich RMI)	1985	4	2:23:37
25	D Blakeley	(Manchester & D)	1981	6	2:23:39
26	G Huddleston	(Clayton-le-M)	1981	7	2:23:49
27	D Blakeley	(Manchester & D)	1982	7	2:24:00
28	M Coleby	(Gateshead H)	1984	8	2:24:18
29	P Campbell	(Bolton U) '	1985	5	2:24:21
30	D Blakeley	(Swinton AC)	1983	3	2:24:24
31	C Kirkham	(Coventry G) V40	1985	6	2:24:25
32	S Brace	(Bridgend AC)	1984	9	2:24:29
33	G Birkett	(St Helens AC)	1984	10	2:24:32
33	J Alder	(Morpeth H) V40	1981	8	2:24:32
35	B Aspden	(Salford H)	1982	8	2:24:37
36	A Williams	(Un. Doncaster)	1982	9	2:24:59

37	S Howcroft	(St Helens AC)	1985	7	2:25:26
38	G Claff	(Salford H)	1982	10	2:25:35
39	A Ritchie	(Keswick AC) V40	1984	11	2:25:53
40	R Gwilt	(Salford H)	1983	4	2:26:25
41	A Sladen	(Salford H)	1981	9	2:26:28
42	B Knappers	(NETHERLANDS)	1984	12	2:26:31
43	G Woolnough	(Kendal AC)	1985	8	2:26:53
44	K Best	(Bolton U)	1983	5	2:27:01
45	M Martin	(Sheffield AC) V40	1985	9	2:27:10
46	A Robinson	(Sale H)	1985	10	2:27:17
47	S Edmunds	(Sale H)	1983	6	2:27:18
48	G Fairley	(Kilbarchan AC)	1984	13	2:27:25
49	E Ranicar	(Bolton U)	1984	14	2:27:30
50	G Bell	(Halifax H)	1983	7	2:27:32

RANKING OF TOP 20 WOMEN'S TIMES   1981-85

1	L Irving	(Border H)	1985	1	2:44:13
2	M Hurst	(Clayton-le-M)	1985	2	2:45:01
3	L Watson	(London Oly.)	1982	1	2:45:07
4	L Pfeiffer	(Barnet Ladies)	1984	1	2:46:54
5	L Watson	(London Oly.)	1983	1	2:50:56
6	G Markwell	(Leeds City)	1983	2	2:51:15
7	L Shingles	(Middleton H)	1983	3	2:51:29
8	S Catterall	(Bolton U)	1984	2	2:51:56
9	M Hurst	(Clayton-le-M)	1984	3	2:51:58
10	V Hyland	(Unattached)	1984	4	2:55:44
11	V Wallace	(Unattached)	1983	4	2:57:16
12	J Percival	(City of Hull)	1985	3	2:58:06
13	S Exon	(Stretford AC)	1985	4	2:59:05
14	K Fitzgibbon	(London Oly.)	1981	1	3:03:24
15	B Robinson	(Bury AC)	1982	2	3:03:53
16	A Rochester	(–?–)	1981	2	3:05:57
17	S Exon	(Stretford AC)	1982	3	3:06:57
18	L Hardley	(Stockport H)	1983	8	3:07:37
19	Z Hyde	(Epsom & Ewell)	1983	9	3:08:04
20	C Moorat	(London RR)	1983	10	3:10:39

Kevin Best, aged 33 in 1985, and a member of Bolton United, then Stretford, was the only leading runner to have raced all five of these marathons. His record at the end of the series would be: 1981, 4th, 2:21:43; 1982, 1st, 2:16:22; 1983, 5th, 2:27:01; 1984, 4th, 2:20:43; 1985, 3rd, 2:22:22.

STOCKPORT - 14th April 1985

Cold, wet weather greeted the 1600-odd runners for the fourth Stockport Marathon, sponsored by PowerQuip, a Reddish company who made Fork Lift Trucks. The field was lower than in previous years (1,666 entered and 1,078 finished) and the weather kept the spectators indoors. Last year 154 broke three hours against 74 this year.

Bolton's Paul Campbell was a convincing winner in 2:25:14, well clear of Stretford's Dennis Mullings. Coventry's top vet Colin Kirkham had to drop out with cramp.

Results:

1, P Campbell (Bolton U) 2:25:14; 2 D Mullings (Stretford) 2:30:42; 3, M Higginbottom (Salford H) 2:32:46; 4, D Ibbetson (Glossopdale) 2:34:10; 5, M Oldham (ManchesterYMCA) 2:36:19; 6, G Marrinan (Stockport) 2:36:24; 7, P Bates (Bury AC) 2:37:49; 8, P Crookall (E Cheshire) 2:38:05; 9, C Manclarke (Stockport) 2:39:17; 10, F Clayton (Manchester H) 2:39:32.

Veteran men over 40 - P Kilbey (Altrincham) 2:43:02 (13th); 2, P Blagborough (Saddleworth) 2:49:03 (32nd); 3, T Keller (Manchester H) 2:51:03 (35th).

Veteran men over 45 - 1, G Kay (Stone) 2:45:08 (21st); 2, D Atwell (Altrincham) 2:46:07 (25th); 3, R Hill (Clayton-le-Moors) 2:48:51 (31st).

Veteran men over 50 - 1, D Greenwood (Bingley) 2:47:08 (28th); 2, N Houghton, (Winsford) 2:54:26 (47th); 3, B Chalmers (Cheshire T H) 3:06:03 (112th).

Women:

1, M Goodwin V35 (Leigh H) 3:09:25 (134th); 2, P Bethuel (Barnet Ladies) 3:12:47 (173rd); 3, H Broughton (Unattached / Cheadle Hulme) 3:22:50 (269th).

BOLTON - 1st September 1985

This was sponsored by adidas and named the 'British Marathon.' The wet weather on the first day of September did not dampen the competitive spirit of the leading men because at the end less than ten seconds separated the first three men. Jim Dingwall won the race for the line in 2:20:58 with Ian Corrin runner-up 2:21:07 and last year's winner Eric Williams third in 2:21:09. Few foreign athletes were invited: Stoke-based Dutchman Adri Hartveld was fourth (2:21:33) 12 seconds ahead of Belgium's Rene Devos. Sixth was prolific racer Steve Brace (Bridgend) in 2:27:20. Filling the rest of the top ten spots were: 7, Mike Critchley 2:27:28; 8, Nigel Barlow (Horwich RMI) 2:27:31; 9, Gordon Summers 2:28:36; 10, Michael Harrison 2:28:57.

Veronique Marot returned and clocked 2:42:01, ahead of Sandra Lappage 2:46:16 and Ilona Zfilak (Hungary) 2:46:36.

BOLTON - 17th August 1986

The renamed Piccadilly British Marathon, (but also called the Bolton British Marathon) was a success for Mike Neary, now in Salford's colours. He set a personal best of 2:19:22. The next nine were: 2, A Robertson (Torbay) 2:21:15; 3, I Corrin (St Helens) 2:22:11; 4, G Mallirias (Greece) 2:22:34; 5, H Clague (St Helens) Vet 40 2:28:43; 6, N Barlow (Horwich RMI) 2:29:01; 7, I Thompson (Luton) 2:31:42; 8, R Edwards 2:33:37; 9, R Ball 2:34:03; 10, R Robson 2:35:01.

The first three ladies were: 1, G Rimmer (Bolton) V35 3:13:27; 2, J Atkinson (Rochdale) 3:21:46; 3, S Young (Winsford) 3:29:18.

BOLTON - 16th August 1987

The combined race was on again in 1987 and Nigel Barlow (Horwich RMI) won in 2:29:20 from M Moftaquir (2:38:22) and G Shaw (2:40:33). The top three ladies were: 1, B Lennartz 2:59:00; 2, J Danskin 3:00:27; 3, C Gunner 3:19:00.

This was the end of marathons in the Greater Manchester area for nine years.

Chapter 27

The 27th Manchester Marathon
Sunday 16th October 1996

THE GLYCOSPORT MANCHESTER MARATHON

After a break of 11 years the Marathon returned to Manchester.

Manchester had bid to host the 2000 Olympic Games, but in the end lost out to Sydney, Australia. In November 1995, Manchester was confirmed as the host city for the 2002 Commonwealth Games, but even before this the City Council had wanted to put on a marathon to prove to the citizens of Manchester that they could organise a great event. Now with the Commonwealth Games on the horizon a city marathon was even more important and Paul Mee of Manchester Leisure, part of Manchester City Council was appointed race organiser.

Paul was extremely fortunate in enlisting the help of most of the clubs in the Greater Manchester area, who looked after specific sections of the course in terms of marshalling and feed stations. These clubs were: Middleton Harriers AC, Radcliffe AC, Manchester YMCA Harriers, Rochdale Harriers & AC, Oldham and Royton Harriers AC, Swinton RC, Horwich RMI Harriers, East Cheshire Harriers and Tameside AC, Stockport Harriers, Belle Vue Racers, Manchester Harriers, Bury AC, and Sale Harriers Manchester.

During the Manchester Olympic bid I was asked to design a course for use if Manchester had won the nomination, and I proposed a one lap route, taking in the city centre at first, then visiting many boroughs, mainly to the south of Manchester, and covering part of the old Maxol course. This same course could have been used for the Commonwealth Games of 2002, as Manchester had won the right to host these Games, and I felt that runners needed a gimmick to get them to do a marathon and to compete on the course to be used for the Commonwealth Games would be perfect.

In the end it was decided that my proposal would cause too much disruption to motorway access and exit roads, and a course was plotted in conjunction with the police authorities, which ran from Heaton Park in north Manchester to Wythenshawe Park, south Manchester. Although this involved a favourable overall descent of around 53 metres (174 feet), the athletes would be heading in a south south west direction, perhaps into the prevailing south

westerly wind. The separation between start and finish was approximately
14½ Km (9 miles).

The full route was as follows: leave Heaton Park by St Margaret's gate, St
Margaret's Road, Bury Old Road (A665), Middleton Road (A576), Victoria
Avenue (A6104), Hollinwood Avenue, Broadway (A663), Oldham Road (A62),
Hulme Hall Lane, Alan Turing Way, Ashton Old Road, Chancellor Lane,
Devonshire Street, Hyde Road (A57), Mount Road, Matthews Lane, Stockport
Road (A6), Albert Road, Moseley Road (A6010), Kingsway (A34), School Lane,
Parrs Wood Road, Wilmslow Road, Palatine Road, Sale Road, Orton Road,
Wythenshawe Road to finish in Wythenshawe Park.

From an entry of around 2,700 the pre-race favourite was Bashir Hussain,
the local man from Stockport Harriers and a Congleton schoolteacher. Born in
Manchester on 20th December 1964, the thirty-one-year-old had a solid
reputation. He had triumphed in the 1990 Skiddaw Fell race from Keswick,
Cumbria, and as a result gained an England vest for fell running. He had won
the Northern Counties Cross-Country Championships at Pontefract, West
Yorkshire in 1993 and had two victories in the six-day, double marathon,
Brother Tour of Tameside, 1994 and 1995.

On the road he had a 47:55 10 mile time set en route to a 63:01 half-
marathon in Holland in 1992 to his credit, but he had never succeeded at the
marathon, indeed he had struggled to get round a marathon in Sacramento,
1995, clocking a lowly 2:26:56, and he did not finish the 1996 London
Marathon.

There was a wheelchair section in the marathon and things had moved on
considerably for these athletes since the *Piccadilly Radio* series of the 1980s.
Most noticeably chairs were aerodynamically-designed in terms of frame and
large cycling wheels, some models incorporating carbon fibre. The result was
that the two hour marathon barrier was broken regularly.

On a bright and sunny morning, five wheelchair athletes started just ahead
of the 9:30 main race, but a troublesome headwind bothered all the
competitors for much of the way. Jack McKenna (British Wheelchair Racers
Association), a 41-year-old British Paralympian who had been third in the
1996 London Marathon in 1:45:18, took the finish line officials by surprise,
powering up the finishing straight to cross the line in 1:47:25. The sole female
wheelchair racer Rachel Potter (Belle Vue Racers) finished in the midst of the
able-bodied runners in a time of 3:01:23. At the 2002 Commonwealth Games

ROUTE MAP

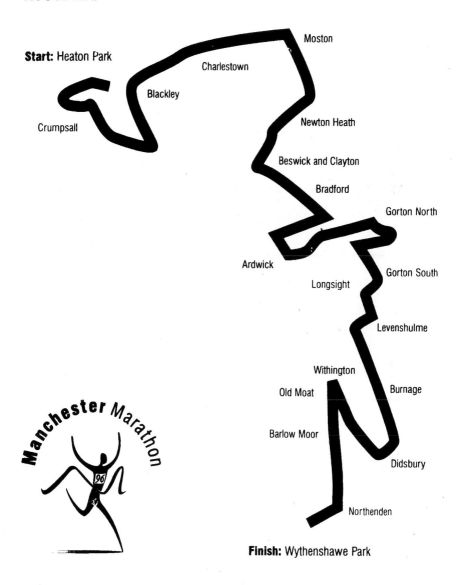

Start: Heaton Park

Moston

Charlestown

Blackley

Crumpsall

Newton Heath

Beswick and Clayton

Bradford

Gorton North

Ardwick

Longsight

Gorton South

Levenshulme

Withington

Old Moat

Burnage

Barlow Moor

Didsbury

Northenden

Finish: Wythenshawe Park

Manchester Marathon

96

Route map for 1996-98 Marathons. (Courtesy Manchester Leisure.)

199

she placed 7th (2:07.37) in the 800m Final of the wheelchair event in the City of Manchester Stadium.

The main race boasted a pace-maker in the person of Des Gibbons (Altrincham & D AC). Des did his job well, passing the half-way point in 1:10:28, before retiring and leaving Bashir Hussain and Gregor Booth from Edinburgh out on their own.

No1 Bashir Hussain. (Picture: Neil Shuttleworth.)

The pair ran together until Hussain sensed that Booth was beginning to flag and speeded up to 5:25 and 5:21 for the 17th and 18th miles. Booth had to let go, but kept Hussain in sight until around 20 miles, when he hit the wall. He later said, "I felt terrible and there was no danger of catching up." Bashir increased his lead to just over two minutes, and crossed the line for his first ever marathon victory in a time of 2:23:32. After the race, he commented, "The course was quite good, but the headwind meant times were generally going to be slow. I'm surprised how comfortable I felt. I would have liked to have gone faster, but the important thing today was to win the race. I've felt worse after a half-marathon so I know I can go faster." He was very happy with his prize of £500.

Booth crossed the line in 2:25:34, well ahead of third man, Bingley Harrier,

Stewart MacDonald who recorded a personal best of 2:30:53 saying, "It's eight years since my personal best, so even though conditions were not good, I had trained well and hard. About 80% of the race was into a head-wind. I knew I was never going to stay with the leaders so I let them go."

There was a big gap to the fourth runner, local man, Gary Matthews of East Cheshire Harriers, 2:36:21, and a scant 30 seconds covered fourth, fifth and sixth. Joey Parkinson of Liverpool Harriers was fifth in 2:36:25. First veteran home in sixth position was Pete Johnson of Thurrock Harriers in a time of 2:36:51.

Janice Moorkite.

Despite suffering an attack of cramp near the end, Janice Moorkite (Invicta East Kent), took the women's title finishing 38th overall, in a time of 2:48:50. She had been coached by 1983 London Marathon winner, Mike Gratton, and crossed the line three minutes ahead of Carolyn Hunter-Rowe (Knavesmire) who recorded 2:51:38.

Third woman home was marathon débutante Kerrie Wood of the Manchester YMCA club in 2:56:17. The 30-year-old was a primary schoolteacher in Salford and a member of Manchester YMCA Harriers. She had competed for the club at all disciplines and was delighted with her first time effort.

Results:

1	Bashir Hussain	(Stockport H)		2:23:32
2	Gregor Booth	(Mizuno)		2:25:34
3	Stewart MacDonald	(Bingley H)		2:30:53
4	Gary Matthews	(E Cheshire H)		2:36:21
5	Joey Parkinson	(Liverpool H)		2:36:25
6	Pete Johnson	(Thurrock)	V40	2:36:51
7	Richard Kerr	(Steel City)	V40	2:37:18
8	Lee Harris	(Wigan P)		2:37:37
9	Peter Bates	(Bury)		2:38:08
10	Nigel Grant	(Unattached)		2:38:36

11, S Leverton (N Derbyshire) 2:38:47; 12, P Packer (Louth) 2:39:33; 13, M Heaton (Lincoln) 2:39:56; 14, W Cruickshank (Lincoln) 2:40:49; 15, P Lewin (Salford) 2:41:16; 16, S Cordell (Manchester H) 2:41:54; 17, I Newcombe (Swinton Jog Fit) 2:42:19; 18, C Manclarke (Stockport) V45 2:42:27; 19, J Price (Liverpool RC) V40 2:42:36; 20, D Clark (Leeds) 2:42:49; 21, I Price (Liverpool H) 2:43:14; 22, P Brady (Middleton) 2:44:18; 23, A Carroll (E Cheshire) V45 2:44:31; 24, J Derbyshire (Stockport) 2:44:46; 25, K Tilson (Trafford) 2:45:43; 26, L Footitt (Buxton) 2:45:58; 27, T Ogden (Unatt) 2:46:31; 28, D Andrew (Unatt) 2:46:36; 29, L Pilkington (Unatt) 2:46:45; 30, P Cuthbert (Wallasey) 2:46:47; 31, S Davies (Blackburn) V45 2:47:00; 32, Stephen ? (Unatt) 2:47:36; 33, B Peacock [C & S] 2:47:47; 34, N Pearce (Ilkley) V40 2:47:55; 35, P Fletcher (E Cheshire) 2:47:59; 38, Janice Moorkite (Invicta East Kent) V35 2:48:50; 39, P Derbyshire (Wigan Phoenix) 2:49:08; 40, J Byers (Trafford AC) 2:49:10; 41, A Clarkson (Clayton-le-Moors) 2:49:19; 42, C Loxam (Stockport) 2:49:51; 43, J Howard (Longwood H) V45 2:49:55; 44, K Moffat (Swinton Jog Fit) 2:50:18; 45, R Thomas (Belle Vue Racers) 2:51:04; 46, R Wayne (Unatt) 2:51:37; 47, Carolyn Hunter-Rowe (Knavesmire H) 2:51:38; 48, D Hanson (Vale Royal) 2:51:45; 49, S Jones (RAF) V40 2:51:47;

50, G Shaw (Unatt) V40 2:51:48; 51, C Beadle (Holmfirth) 2:52:02; 52, D Tann (100 Marathon) V45 2:52:34; 53, P Douglas (Stafford H) 2:52:42; 54, E Edward (Chorley AC) 2:53:03; 55, A Cunliffe (Clayton-le-Moors) V40 2:53:16; 56, W Davies (Unatt) V45 2:53:19; 57, I Brown (Pitreavie AAC) 2:53:28; 58, E Burke (Manchester YMCA) V40 2:53:35; 59, D Panayiotou (Unatt) V40 2:53:45; 60, No 684 (----) 2:53:49; 61, S Marland (Burnden RR) 2:53:57; 62, J Burton (Unatt) 2:53:59; 63, B Worthington (Birchfield) V40 2:54:32; 64, G Leotondeur (Unatt) 2:54:46; 65, A Fitzpatrick (Manchester YMCA) V40 2:54:51; 66, A Weatherby (Manchester H) 2:55:18; 67, P Pickup (Barton AC) 2:55:22; 68, K Parkinson (Todmorden H) V40 2:55:25; 69, A Harris (Radcliffe AC) V40 2:55:27;

70, J Downes (Spectrum Str) V45 2:55:42; 71, C Wilson (Wigan Phoenix) 2:55:44; 72, D A Walton (Altrincham DAC) V50 2:55:49; 73, R Bailey (Unatt) V40 2:55:56; 74, C Murdoch (Hallamshire H) V45 2:56:09; 75, Kerrie Wood (Manchester YMCA) 2:56:17; 76, D Patterson (Blackburn H) 2:56:19; 77, J Spillane (Leigh H) V40 2:56:24; 78, F Hughes (Liverpool RC) V50 2:56:24; 79, G Willden (Blackpool & F) V40 2:57:12; 80, D Nuttall (Sheffield AC) 2:57:19; 81, J MacLachlan (Giffnock N AC) 2:57:20; 82, G Mitchell (Sale H Manch) 2:57:21; 83, A Dunn (Stockport H) V60 2:57:25; 84, A Caddick (Unatt) V45 2:57:31; 85, P Dowson (Lincoln Well) V40 2:57:32; 86, D Milner (Holme Valley Squ) 2:57:51; 87, T Gristwood (Cleethorpes AC) 2:57:53; 88, A Appleby (Preston H) V45 2:57:56; 89, J Parry (Steel City Str) V45 2:57:58; 90, J Freeman (Amman Valley H) 2:58:11; 91, Eleanor Robinson (Border HAC) V45 2:58:18; 92, B Zakrocki (Trafford AC) V45 2:58:20; 93, S Thompson (Humberside Pol) 2:58:21; 94, B Greaves (Oldham & Royton) V40 2:58:31; 95, R McDonald (Fraserburgh RC) V45 2:58:32; 96, F Fielding (Glossopdale) V45 2:58:35; 97, T Holmes (Bury AC) 2:58:40; 98, J Noon (Worsley H) V40 2:58:41; 99, D Utton (Altrincham) 2:58:43; 100, T Stock (Macclesfield H) 2:58:49.

V40	P Johnson	(Thurrock)	2:36:51
V45	R Kerr	(Steel City Str)	2:37:18
V50	D A Walton	(Altrincham)	2:55:49
V55	A Wheddon	(Cleethorpes)	3:06:46
V60	A Dunn	(Stockport H)	2:57:25
V65	A Rees	(Unattached)	4:11:19

Women:

1	Janice Moorkite (Invicta EK)	2:48:50
2	Carolyn Hunter-Rowe (Knavesmire)	2:51:38
3	Kerrie Wood	(Manchester YMCA)	2:56:17;

4, E Robinson (Border) V45 2:58:18; 5, K Kaiser (Valley) V45 3:06:04; 6, J McGee (Lancaster & M) 3:08:57; 7, V Hamlet (Rossendale) 3:09:38; 8, S Exon (Trafford AC) V40 3:09:54; 9, S Cherel (Unatt) 3:11:48

V35	J Moorkite	(Invicta EK)	2:48:50
V40	S Exon	(Trafford AC)	3:09:54
V45	E Robinson	(Border H & AC)	2:58:18
V50	V Leigh	(Unatt)	3:58:37
V55	K Garnett	(Clayton-le-Moors)	4:06:15
V60	E Blackledge	(Winston Runners)	5:42:10

Wheelchair

Men:

1	Jack McKenna	(BWRA)	1:47:25
2	Dean Cavanagh (Unatt)		2:21:25
3,	D Alcock (Unatt)		3:14:40;
4,	M Marten (Unatt)		3:17:00

Women:

1	Rachel Potter	(Belle Vue R)	3:01:33

5 finished.

A total of 1,686 finishers were recorded. Of the 192 females four were under three hours, 21 were under 3:30, and 54 broke 4 hours. Race Director Paul Mee of Manchester Leisure was delighted with the success of the day.

Janice Moorkite never returned to the Manchester Marathon.

Shortly after her Manchester victory she went to hospital to have a disc removed. Things went wrong, an artery was severed resulting in six weeks off work and running. Recovery was slow but in 1998 she ran 2:54:48 in the London Marathon. She followed this in August 1999 with a second place, 3:00:38 in the World Veterans Championships at Gateshead. The night before Gateshead she broke her finger and during an operation in November to repair this she picked up a "super-bug" infection, which has bothered her ever since. The London Marathon of 2000, where she placed third in the 40-plus age group, in a time of 3:01:01, was her last marathon. However, she still loves her running and recorded a sub-40 minute 10 Km in 2002.

Carolyn Hunter-Rowe also did not run Manchester again. She had begun running in 1991 with Pudsey and Bramley, a fell running club near Leeds. It was said that she was not very good at descending and turned her attention to ultra-distances with much success. Virtually in her first year of running she won the women's race in the London to Brighton finishing 30th overall in 7:18:09. In 1993 she became British 100 Km Champion, in one track race set world bests for 30 miles, 50 Km and 40 miles, won the World 100 Km Championship at Torhout, Belgium, in a personal best time of 7:27:19, and two months later won the London to Brighton finishing sixth overall in 6:34:10.

Seven weeks before Manchester the 32-year-old took the European 100 Km title in Cleder, France with 7:41:29.

Crossing the Pennines she joined Horwich RMI Harriers in 1997. That year she finished fifth British woman in the London Marathon, running

2:40:32, (four seconds short of her personal best set at London in 1994), as a result of which she represented Great Britain in the World Championships held over the classic course from Marathon to Athens. She finished 47th in 3:01:01. In October 1998 she regained the World 100 Km title in Nakamura City, Japan taking 8:16:07.

Eleanor Robinson (nee Adams), like Hunter-Rowe, an ultra-distance specialist, has had a long and distinguished career. She won the Stockport Daffodil Marathon in 1984, (2:56:21) but this distance was nothing to her. She celebrated her fiftieth birthday in 1997 with a 1,000 mile World Best on the track! She is currently the World Track 24 Hour record holder with 149 miles 142 yards, and she was entered in to the Guinness Book of Records Hall of Fame for setting the most world records by any one person in any sport.

Chapter 28

The 28th Manchester Marathon
Sunday 12th October 1997

BASHIR HUSSAIN AGAIN

The second edition of the revived Manchester Marathon attracted an entry of over 2,000. The course of the previous year was retained.

Favourite for the men's title was 1996 victor Bashir Hussain of Stockport Harriers. During the summer he had won the *Brother* Tour of Tameside six stage double marathon for the third time on this occasion from Graham Hill of Stockport Harriers. Hill was also down for the Manchester Marathon.

Hussain had been training for the Berlin Marathon which was held two weeks before Manchester. His preparation had included a win in a mountain race in the Pyrenees, a 64:13 21 Km race in Briancon, France, followed by another mountain race, the Stellina Challenge in Susa, Italy, where representing England he finished seventh and first Briton home. He then linked up with the Italian Mountain Running Squad for a week's altitude training in Sestrierre, Italy, close to the French border.

This month before Berlin had seen training weeks of between 105 and 115 miles, much of it at altitude. With the three races plus quality speed sessions this was a heavy four week's work. His aim in Berlin was 2:14 and in the race he went through 20 miles in 1:42-43, on target; but at 23 miles he blew up and dropped out. In Manchester, still in good shape, he wanted to atone for this failure.

Another local runner on the start line was 41-year-old Tony Duffy who lived in Salford. Originally a member of Manchester YMCA Harriers, he was now running for Bolton United Harriers. Ten years previously he had run 2:18:44 for seventh place in the Paris Marathon and went on to gain three British vests with Marathon races in Majorca (1988), 11th, 2:20:52; Warsaw (1989), 1st, 2:18:32 and Kuala Lumpur (1990), 5th, 2:35:37. His best time had been set in September 1989 at the Commonwealth Games Marathon Trial in Liverpool when he recorded 2:17:09 for third place, gaining a reserve spot for the English team. Alas, he was not called upon to run. His form continued in 1997 when he recorded 2:21:33 in the London Marathon finishing 47th overall and second veteran overall, and first British veteran. This time compared favourably with Bashir Hussain's 1996 Manchester winning time of

2:23:32. Duffy too had been training for Berlin, but a torn calf muscle in July had caused him to refocus on Manchester.

Second place man from 1996 Gregor Booth of the Edinburgh-based Mizuno Running Club, who had run stride for stride with Hussain until 17 miles was entered again.

In the women's race, last year's third placer, Kerrie Wood was back, but an interesting entry was that of Sarah-Jane Heatley, daughter of Basil Heatley. Heatley had won a brilliant silver medal in the 1964 Tokyo Olympic Games Marathon behind Ethiopian Abebe Bikila. Sarah-Jane had never run a marathon before.

The wheelchair race boasted two superstar competitors. David Holding had a formidable record on the track and road with four wins in the London Marathon, the latest being earlier in 1997 when he recorded 1:42:15, his fastest for that course. Tanni Grey from Cardiff had won London three times, 1992, 1994 and 1996 and had been runner-up in London in the spring with the fast time of 1:49:15. The 27-year-old had represented Great Britain on the track at distances of 100m to 800m, and had competed at the Paralympics of 1988, 1992 and 1996. She was appointed MBE in 1993.

It was a cool day 10° C (50° F), mainly cloudy with a light wind coming from the north west, a side wind mainly on the right hand side of the runners.

No1, Bashir Hussain battlees it out with Gregor Booth.
(Picture: Peter Downing.)

207

The start was fast, like a 10K race. By 4 miles only Bashir Hussain and Gregor Booth were at the head of the field with a larger group behind clicking along at 5 minute 15 seconds per mile pace, this bunch including Tony Duffy, Graham Hill and Gary Matthews (East Cheshire Harriers). No-one was willing to head the pursuing pack for long, as the leading pair matched strides for 15 miles.

Along Broadway, between eight and nine miles Hill surged, but not long after dropped back to the group, talking. Both Hill and Matthews surged again, but at 14 miles Duffy was leading the race for third place, but suffering a bad patch having gone through half-way in a respectable 69 minutes.

Just after 15 miles, Hussain ran away from father of two Booth, who decided to just forget about the lead and concentrate on second place. By 20 miles, Hussain still felt capable of a 2:15-16 finish. However, for the second time in his career he was about to "hit the wall." Booth kept on at a steady pace and towards the end realised he was not too far behind. Nearing the finish he could see Hussain "rocking," but each time he tried to catch him, he didn't feel too clever himself. Hussain slowed to a 6:30 mile at the end, but realised in the last 400 metres that Booth was catching. Although he felt like he was "running through treacle," he managed to hold on for a two second victory in 2:19:00, a new course record and a £750 prize.

Meanwhile behind, up Hyde Road at around 16 miles, Graham Hill ran away to build up a 150 to 200 metre lead over the rest of the pursuers. Tony Duffy was next in line at Albert Road, around 19½ miles, he began to sense that Hill was in trouble; he was not taking the shortest line on the road. About half a mile later Duffy passed Hill, who did not respond. Duffy's legs stiffened and he began to tire. At 25 miles his objective became to break his London time, and he picked up the pace, which was fortunate for him as Darren Hale of the Army had also passed Hill, and closed to within 17 seconds. The London time goal slipped away and he pushed himself to clock under 2:22, which he did (2:21:52) with Hale still 17 seconds adrift.

Hill had slowed to walk for a mile giving the opportunity for Matthews to pass and take fifth place, 2:30:26, 18 seconds ahead of Hill.

In the women's race Northern Ireland fell running international Tricia Sloan (Salford H) who came into the race with a best of 3:03:15, led the race up to eight miles, with Kerrie Wood (Glossopdale H), third place last year in 2:56:17, lying in second place. Sarah-Jane Heatley (Sheffield AC), a 33-year-old researcher, was in her debut marathon, and started out steadily, running in around fifth place for three miles then picking off her competitors one by one.

Sarah-Jane Heatley.

At eight miles Wood injected some pace and soon left Sloan behind. However, she had probably gone too fast, and by 18 miles lost the lead to Heatley. Wood also fell victim to the fast-finishing Sloan and was overtaken on Palatine Road at Northenden Bridge, around 24 miles. Sloan gained almost two minutes on Wood in the last two miles. Heatley had recorded 2:53:05 and her proud father was there at the finish to see her take first place and a £500 prize. Sloan recorded 2:57:13, a personal best'by over six minutes.

In the wheelchair race David Holding, clearly the favourite in Manchester, showed that fast times are achievable taking 1:43:33, 12 minutes in front of Anthony Booth from Clayton, 1:55:38. Tushar Patel, a promising 18-year-old youth from London was third just inside two hours, 1:59:12. Missing this mark by 25 seconds was Dean Cavanagh of the British Wheelchair Racers Association. Tushar Patel was one of the few from outside Greater Manchester who would return to Manchester. He next appears in the Millennium Marathon in Manchester.

Tanni Grey had something of an off-day compared to London and was 7th overall, winning the women's title in 2:08:28. Fourteen men and five women finished.

Results:

1	Bashir Hussain	(Stockport)		2:19:00
2	Gregor Booth	(Mizuno)		2:19:02
3	Tony Duffy	(Bolton U)	V40	2:21:52
4	Darren Hale	(24 AFA, Army)		2:22:09
5	Gary Matthews	(E Cheshire)		2:30:26
6	Graham Hill	(Stockport)		2:30:48
7	Andrew Doel	(Police AA)		2:31:20
8	Steve Leverton	(N Derbys)	V40	2:32:24
9	Martin Farran	(Longwood)		2:33:14
10	Mark Lane	(Police AA)		2:33:24

11, M Burke (Unatt) 2:33:35; 12, P Bates (Bury) V40 2:33:55; 13, P Aspinall (Stockport) 2:34:25; 14, T Leibrick (ATR, Pirb, ARMY) 2:35:01; 15, E Wilson (Blackburn) V40 2:35:13; 16, P Harewood (Bad Kineton, ARMY) 2:35:18; 17, J Parkinson (Liverpool H) 2:35:18; 18, N Bateson (HQ4, Div, ARMY) 2:35:26; 19, D Clamp (Bolton) 2:35:32; 20, B Gardner (Lancaster) 2:35:39; 21, P Dewhurst (Chorley) 2:35:48; 22, R Simpson (Rowntree) 2:36:10; 23, R Jackson (Horwich) 2:36:20; 24, K Bowers (Horsforth) 2:36:24; 25, S Riley (Leamington) 2:37:07; 26, L Footitt (Buxton) 2:37:25; 27, I Wallace (Police AA) 2:37:34; 28, C Earl (Barnsley) 2:37:51; 29, P Allen (Police AA) 2:37:59;

30, R Butterfield (Horsforth) V40 2:38:44; 31, S Peacock (City of Hull) 2:38:59; 32, P Aston (Bad Kineton, ARMY) 2:40:07; 33, R Strempel (Manchester Univ) 2:40:27; 34, S Cordell (Stockport) 2:40:46; 35, D Unwin (E Cheshire) 2:40:57; 36, I Newcombe (Swinton Jog Fit) 2:41:05; 37, W Crook (South Ribble H) 2:41:08; 38, D Burke (Manchester YMCA) V45 2:42:09; 39, J Thompson (Police AA) V40 2:42:18; 40, H Young (Police AA) V40 2:42:36; 41, I Brown (Pitreavie AAC) 2:42:45; 42, P Garside (Middleton H & AC) V40 2:42:53; 43, S Boynton (Knavesmire H) V40 2:43:02; 44, C Patton (ARMY - 7 Royal Irish) 2:42:38; 45, G Gilhooley (Livingston AAC) 2:42:45; 46, S Shaw (Unatt) 2:44:07; 47, D McGill (ARMY - Dpt Royal Irish) 2:43:38; 48, P Shirley (Moray RR) 2:44:43; 49, S Lonnen (Bad Kineton) 2:44:46;

50, N Beever (Wigan Phoenix) 2:44:47; 51, N Strange (Knavesmire H) 2:44:47; 52, P Taylor (Rossendale H) 2:45:42; 53, C Manclarke (Stockport) V45 2:45:48; 54, S Brooks (Unatt) 2:46:05; 55, A Martin (ARMY) 2:46:11; 56, R Grey (Road Runners Club) 2:46:18; 57, A Yates (Sale H Manch) 2:46:20; 58, C Ireland (Sale H Manch) V40 2:46:21; 59, P Douglas (Stafford H) V45 2:46:31; 60, F Hughes (Liverpool RC) V50 2:46:44; 61, A Caddick (Unatt) V45 2:46:47; 62, S Hulme (Unatt) 2:46:47; 63, J Ashton (Horwich RMI) 2:47:02; 64, G Swan (Huncote H) V40 2:47:12; 65, D Matthews (E Cheshire) 2:47:13;

66, M Lavelle (Sale H Manch) 2:47:20; 67, P Fraser (ARMY) 2:47:28; 68, S Anderton (Todmorden H) 2:47:42; 69, E Sweeney (Manchester YMCA) 2:48:08; 70, A Booth (Knavesmire H) 2:48:30; 71, T Williams (Picton RC) V40 2:48:31; 72, P Bailey (Unatt) V45 2:48:41; 73, B Horrocks (Clayton-le-Moors) 2:48:49; 74, R West (Police AA) V40 2:48:57; 75, P Crookall (Trentham AC) V40 2:49:08; 76, P Marsh (ARMY) V45 2:49:23; 77, P Prescott (Unatt) 2:49:29; 78, T Price (Police AA) 2:49:38; 79, M Barnes (Bolton UH) V55 2:49:44; 80, J Howarth (Longwood H) V45 2:49:46; 81, K Lewis (Clayton-le-Moors) V45 2:49:59; 82, K Hill (St Helens Str) V40 2:50:22; 83, I Rowland (Dunbar RC) 2:50:55; 84, R George (Salford) 2:51:21; 85, P Mellon (Unatt) 2:51:34; 86, D Horrocks (Clayton-le-Moors) 2:52:11; 87, G Power (Salford) V40 2:52:30; 88, C Laycock (ARMY) 2:52:37; 89, P Foley (Road Runners Club) 2:52:46; 90, Sarah-Jane Heatley (Sheffield AC) 2:53:05; 91, I Stainthorpe (Rochdale H) 2:53:04; 92, M Mattison (Mercury Tri) 2:53:15; 93, S Butler (Unatt) 2:53:56; 94, J Brooker (Police AA) 2:54:33; 95, C Bayliss (Wirral AC) 2:54:41; 96, J Kuterescz (Todmorden H) 2:54:46; 97, T Daniels (Salford) V45 2:54:49; 98, D Hanson (Vale Royal) 2:54:52; 99, J Walker (Penny Lane Str) V45 2:54:57; 100, A Taylor (Clayton-le-Moors) 2:55:02. 1,338 finished.

V40	S Leverton	(N Derbys)	2:32:24
V45	D Burke	(Man YMCA)	2:42:09
V50	F Hughes	(Liverpool RC)	2:46:44
V55	M Barnes	(Bolton)	2:49:44
V60	P Brennan	(Salford)	3:07:51
V65	A Rees	(Unatt)	3:40:07
V70	R Marsden	(Lancs WC)	4:51:23

Women:

1	Sarah-Jane Heatley	(Sheffield)	2:53:05
2	Tricia Sloan	(Salford)	2:57:13
3	Kerrie Wood	(Glossopdale)	2:59:36

4, J Jackson (Unatt) V40 3:04:07; 5, L Yates (ARMY) 3:07:34; 6, P Spurr (Police AA) V35 3:08:20; 7, L Knights (Police AA) 3:09:08; 8, L Owen (Belle Vue Racers) V40 3:10:03; 9, G Glynn (Middleton H & AC) 3:13:43; 10, C Rawlings (Police AA) 3:14:07.

V35	P Spurr	(Police AA)	3:08:20
V40	J Jackson	(Manchester Univeristy)	3:04:07
V45	J Nicholls	(Middleton)	3:26:33
V50	J Hemmings	(Denby)	3:50:32
V55	J Manners	(Cleveland)	3:21:20
V60	K Garnett	(Clayton-le-M)	3:49:06

Army Championships
Men: Darren Hale 2:22:09   Women: Lisa Yates 3:07:34

Police Championships
Men: Andrew Doel 2:31:20   Women: Pauline Spurr 3:08:20

Wheelchair
Men:

1	David Holding	(BWRA)	1:43:33
2	Anthony Booth	(Unatt)	1:55:38
3	Tushar Patel	(BWRA)	1:59:12;

4, D Cavanagh (BWRA) 2:00:25; 5, I Thompson (Manchester Kes) 2:05:35; 6, E Grazier (BWRA) 2:06:59; 7, T Grey (Cardiff AAC) F 2:08:28; 8, J Hanks (Woking BWRA) 2:13:06; 9, N Jarvis (BWRA) F 2:13:06; 10, M Kettrick (BWRA) V40 2:13:08; 11, B Cooper V45 (BWRA) 2:13:34; 12, G Allen V50 (Stratford AC) 2:22:22; 13, R Cassell V45 (BWRA) 2:57:29; 14, K Lewis (Red Star AC) 3:02:12; 15, A Holt (Mansfield H) 3:06:33; 16, D Alcock (Unatt) 3:24:45; 17, W Fox V50 (Unatt) 3:33:40.

Women:

1	Tanni Grey	(Cardiff)	2:08:28
2	Nicola Jarvis	(BWRA)	2:13:06
3	Karen Lewis	(Red Star AC)	3:02:12
4	Tracy Gill	(BWRA)	3:48:39
5	Jackie Wagstaff	(Radcliffe AC)	4:15:00

Sarah-Jane Heatley did not return to Manchester. She had planned to come back in 1998, and as preparation won the Wolverhampton Marathon on 6th September in 3:01:21. Unfortunately in that race she aggravated a back injury which kept her out of Manchester. This injury plagues her to this day. She ran the Sheffield Marathon in 1999 finishing second in 3:04:59 to Eleanor Robinson's 2:59:39 and taking the Yorkshire title. Since then she has moved south to Colchester and was content to run the three or four miles to work and back. At the end of 2000 she started to run cross-country for Colchester Harriers and in 2002 decided to give the marathon another go. A 2:53:05 in Berlin just behind her twin sister Ruth (2:52:53) was the result.

Tanni Grey, another not to return to Manchester, became a household name. She had three more wins in London and won four Gold Medals in the Sydney 2000 Paralympics. She was appointed OBE in 2000. At the Commonwealth Games in 2002 she placed fourth (1:55.71) in the Final of the 800m wheelchair event held in the City of Manchester Stadium.

Chapter 29

The 29th Manchester Marathon
Sunday 11th October 1998

HAT TRICK FOR HUSSAIN

Around 1,600 runners entered the third Manchester Marathon to be run over the now established course from Heaton Park to Wythenshawe Park.

Once more the favourite for the race was Stockport Harriers' Bashir Hussain, victor in 1996 and 1997, but he might not have it all his own way as Andy Arrand, a 32-year-old soldier based in Germany, was entered and was looking to beat 2:19. Other returning runners were Darren Hale of Rotherham AC, fourth last year and East Cheshire Harrier Gary Matthews, fourth in 1996 and fifth last year.

In the women's race the favourite on paper was Jackie Newton, a 33-year-old primary schoolteacher based in Cheshire, and like her boy friend, Bashir Hussain, a member of Stockport Harriers. Also like Hussain she had three wins in the classic Tour of Tameside, a six stage double marathon, her victories coming in 1994, 1995 and 1996. Her marathon debut had been in the 1996 Dublin Marathon where she clocked 2:47:28, soon after recording a 1:17:31 half-marathon in Holland. She had entered the race in 1996 and 1997 but did not start; in fact she nearly didn't make it to the start line again as she had been full of a cold all week "and didn't know whether to bother." However, she decided to run and go as far as she could and see what happened. Tricia Sloan of Salford Harriers, a National Health Service executive in Manchester, second in last years race, was running again and she had set a personal best of 2:54:42 in the London Marathon in the spring. In addition, three weeks before this race, the 33-year-old had represented Northern Ireland in the World Cup for Mountain Running on the Indian Ocean island of Reunion. Third placer from 1997 was also on the start line. Kerrie Wood, the Salford schoolteacher, and a member of Glossopdale Harriers was improving year by year. Last year she took third place in the Tour of Tameside, this year she was second.

The wheelchair race had 14 athletes, some attracted possibly by David Holding's fast 1:43:33 in 1997. Now 29-years old, Holding was returning to Manchester. In the spring he had been the first Briton in the London Marathon recording 1:46:07 for fourth place. One place behind him in

London, as he had been in 1997 also, was Ivan Newman (Saffron Striders) and he was on the start line in Manchester.

The temperature was good for marathon racing, 10° C (50° F), but the wind was awful, blustery and in the faces of the athletes for much of the way.

This must have affected the fourteen wheelchair racers as Holding was over four minutes slower than the previous year, crossing the line in 1:47:42 to Newman's 1:51:13. Close behind in third place was Chris Madden (British Wheelchair Racers Association) (1:52:20) with local man Anthony Booth of Clayton taking fourth place in virtually the same time as he did in 1997 (1:55:14). For Madden the Marathon was a mere sprint as he had travelled in his chair from London to Edinburgh, and also the full length of Japan. Deborah Brennan (Birchfield Harriers) (2:54:23) was the only female wheelchair athlete to finish.

In an attempt to crack 2:19 and get a course record Paul Freary, the British Half-Marathon Champion was invited to the race to be a pace-maker. Paul was the son of Bolton United Harrier, Mike Freary who recorded times of 2:17:10 and 2:17:54 in the 1971 and 1972 Manchester Maxol Marathons. Paul did his job well leading Hussain through half-way in 68:30, with Arrand not too far behind and the record definitely on. At 17 miles, his task over, Freary pulled over to leave Hussain alone at the head of the field. He continued solo, but found the conditions "very blowy" and it soon became apparent that he was not going to break 2:19. Meanwhile the army man Arrand clawed back the gap until just entering Didsbury at around 21 miles he went into the lead.

Bashir Hussain. (Picture: Peter Downing.)

Hussain was glad to track Arrand and take shelter from the gusty conditions. Three miles later, in Northenden, Hussain broke away and struck for home. It was a painful last two miles. Unbeknown to his rivals, Hussain had badly sprained his ankle the previous Saturday. So bad was the injury that he had to have three days off work and despite intensive treatment he felt he should probably not have run. But here he was, and in agony from the ankle he could wrest only 13 seconds out of Arrand. However, it was enough to win the race in 2:23:23. As Trevor Baxter of the *Manchester Evening News* put it, "Maths teacher Hussain came up with a winning formula for the third successive year." Hussain commented, "It's still nice to complete the hat trick, but may be it's someone else's turn next year." Arrand took the Army Championship succeeding for that title third man home Darren Hale who had left the army and joined the police force. Salford Harrier Mike Higginbottom was first veteran in fifth place.

Jackie Newton. (Picture: Peter Downing.)

In the women's race Jackie Newton and Tricia Sloan contested the lead for around three miles until Newton decided to let Sloan go. Kerrie Wood meanwhile was running at her own even pace content to let the two ahead fight it out. In fact Sloan ran away and for most of the race was out of sight. Newton "didn't feel too clever" at the half-way point, but at around 20 miles began to pick up the pace. Eventually she saw Sloan in the distance and encouraged by spectators comments that she was slowing, Newton bore down on her. Sloan had "blown up" in Northenden, 24 miles, and half a mile later Newton went past and on to victory in 2:53:56. To add to Sloan's discomfort

Kerrie Wood passed her within sight of the Wythenshawe Park gates, going onto clock 2:55:28. Sloan gamely hung on to third place with 2:56:06, only 1:24 slower than her best. Wood now had fourth, third and second places to her credit in this race.

Results:

1	Bashir Hussain	(Stockport)		2:23:23
2	Andy Arrand	(ARMY)		2:23:36
3	Darren Hale	(Rotherham)		2:26:30
4	Darren Bilton	(City of Hull)		2:30:17
5	Mike Higginbottom	(Salford)	V40	2:30:40
6	Alex Rowe	(Wesham)	V40	2:32:11
7	Gary Matthews	(E Cheshire)		2:32:36
8	Paul Kinsella	(Cheltenham)		2:32:40
9	Kenneth Butler	(ARMY - 5 AB)		2:33:32
10	Jimmy Bell	(Elswick)	V50	2:34:32

11, P Lowery (Lancaster & M) 2:34:47; 12, T Coyle (Scottish Vets) V40 2:36:10; 13, J Parkinson (Liverpool H) 2:36:30; 14, S Leverton (N Derbys) V40 2:36:59; 15, S Peacock (City of Hull) 2:38:01; 16, B Goldsmith (ARMY AA) 2:38:14; 17, W Birchall (Stockport) 2:38:22; 18, P Deaville (Stockport) 2:38:27; 19, A Carroll (E Cheshire) V50 2:38:29; 20, M Lee (Bury) 2:38:54; 21, P Bates (Bury) V40 2:38:54; 22, K Wilding (Wesham) V40 2:40:34; 23, R Jackson (Salford) 2:41:34; 24, J Sproson (Middleton) 2:41:45; 25, G Bergin (Spectrum Striders) 2:41:55; 26, D Speake (Bildeston Bounde) 2:42:46; 27, E Sweeney (Manchester YMCA) 2:43:36; 28, H Roberts (Horsforth) V40 2:43:44; 29, C Patton (Ballydrain H & ARMY) 2:43:58;

30, W Crook (South Ribble H) 2:44:06; 31, G Felton (ARMY) 2:44:23; 32, S Marland (Burnden RR) 2:44:39; 33, P Reynolds (ARMY) 2:44:40; 34, P Dewhurst (Chorley AC) 2:44:58; 35, M Nester (Blackburn RR) V40 2:45:08; 36, N Corken (Civil Service AA) 2:45:16; 37, M Quinn (Sheffield AC) 2:45:32; 38, A Brown (Unatt) 2:45:35; 39, D Burke (Manchester YMCA) V45 2:45:35; 40, J Docherty (ARMY) 2:46:36; 41, R Ironmonger (Notts AC) 2:47:10; 42, P Harwood (ARMY) 2:47:44; 43, J Fletcher (E Cheshire) 2:47:54; 44, M Traynor (GPT Harriers) 2:48:07; 45, P Butterworth (Clayton-le-Moors) V40 2:48:37; 46, F Royle (Salford H) V45 2:48:43; 47, C Booth (Hull Springhead) 2:49:26; 48, P Douglas (Stafford H) V45 2:49:38; 49, A Martin (ARMY) 2:49:56;

50, D Kirkland (Birmingham Univ) 2:50:07; 51, S Davis (ARMY) 2:50:15; 52, P Marsh (Barnet & D) V40 2:50:20; 53, W Taylor (Finch Coasters) V45 2:50:30; 54, I Stainthorpe (Rochdale H) 2:50:39; 55, C Manclarke (Stockport) V45 2:50:51; 56, P Crookall (Northern Vets) V40 2:51:13; 57, J Thompson (Humberside Police) V40 2:51:44; 58, T Williams (Penny Lane Str) V40

2:52:02; 59, T Ashelford (Aireborough Tri) 2:52:29; 60, J Lingard (St Helens Str) V50 2:52:34; 61, D Horrocks (Clayton-le-Moors) 2:52:37; 62, A Greenhough (Macclesfield H) V45 2:52:39; 63, M Elliot (Kidderminster) 2:53:28; 64, D Hydon (Reading RR) V40 2:53:54; 65, T Brown (Unatt) 2:53:55; 66, Jackie Newton (Stockport) 2:53:56; 67, C Nightingale (Wigan Phoenix) 2:53:59; 68, D Matthews (E Cheshire) 2:54:03; 69, Keith Burgess (Unatt) 2:54:12;

70, A Jacobs (Great Western R) V45 2:54:23; 71, J Breen (Civil Service AA) V40 2:54:58; 72, J Pratt (Macclesfield H) 2:55:08; 73, K O'Neill (Belle Vue Racers) V45 2:55:14; 74, Kerrie Wood (Glossopdale H) F 2:55:28; 75, F Hughes (Liverpool RC) V50 2:55:34; 76, G Ardern (Wigan P) 2:55:46; 77, G Ryan (Inland Revenue A) 2:55:54; 78, S Stennett (Civil Service AA) 2:56:05; 79, Tricia Sloan (Salford) F 2:56:06; 80, S Fitzpatrick (Liverpool RC) V55 2:56:22; 81, P Arpey (Unatt) 2:56:24; 82, S Watson (Billingham MH) V45 2:56:25; 83, K Worrall (Trafford AC) 2:56:33; 84, B Williams (ARMY AA) 2:56:40; 85, B Benson (West Cheshire RC) 2:56:48; 86, N Cobb (Redhill RR) 2:56:51; 87, P Addison (100 K Assoc) 2:56:53; 88, P Gillespie (Redhill RR) 2:56:56; 89, J Howarth (Longwood H) V45 2:57:01; 90, J Whilcock (Staffs Moors) 2:57:07; 91, R Nash (Civil Service AA) 2:57:44; 92, A Clarkson (Clayton-le-Moors) 2:57:55; 93, B Gardner (Lancaster & M) V40 2:57:55; 94, M Searle (Helsby FR) 2:58:00; 95, I Sharples (Wesham) 2:58:34; 96, P Quick (Hadleigh Hares) 2:58:48 A; 97, R Miller (Wigan P) 2:59:07; 98, D McCarthy (Unatt) 2:59:09; 99, R Harris (Bank of England) V50 2:59:23; 100, M Jones (Altrincham & DAC) V40 2:59:39. 1,338 finished.

V40	M Higginbottom	(Salford)	2:30:40
V45	W Taylor	(French Coasters)	2:50:30
V50	J Lingard	(St Helens Str)	2:52:34
V55	S Fitzpatrick	(Liverpool RC)	2:56:22
V60	T Thompson	(Horsforth H)	3:13:20
V65	G Dawson	(Valley Strider)	3:35:38
V70	A Hodgson	(IOM Vet Athletes)	4:23:56

Women:

1	Jackie Newton	(Stockport)	2:53:56
2	Kerrie Wood	(Glossopdale)	2:55:28
3	Tricia Sloan	(Salford)	2:56:06

4, K Kaiser (Valley Str) V45 3:00:27; 5, S Cariss (Bingley H) V45 3:07:25; 6, D Corrigan (Gade Valley H) 3:14:36; 7, C Dixon (Salford H) 3:19:44; 8, B Carter (Chorley H) 3:20:34; 9, B King (Hull Springhead) 3:22:16; 10, S Walker (Police AA) 3:25:00.

V35	K Hatton	(Eryri H)	3:39:41
V40	M Hart	(Leeds City)	3:25:11
V45	K Kaiser	(Valley Str)	3:00:27
V50	M Wilson	(Horsforth H)	3:34:01
V55	G Thompson	(Barrow & F)	3:45:59
V60	M Caldwell	(RRC)	4:39:20

Army Championships
Men: Andy Arrand   Women: Sonia Hurst (SEME) 3:25:14

Civil Service Championships
Men: Paul Kinsella   Women: Sue Cariss (Bingley) V45 3:07:25

Wheelchair
Men:
1	David Holding	(BWRA)	1:47:42
2	Ivan Newman	(Saffron Str) V45	1:51:13
3	Chris Madden	(BWRA)	1:52:20

4, Anthony Booth (Unattached / Clayton) 1:55:14; 5, K Papworth (Unattached) 1:58:40 6, J Hallam (BWRA) 2:20:18

Women:
| 1 | Deborah Brennan (Birchfield H) | 2:54:23 |

12 men and 1 woman finished.

Chapter 30

The 30th Manchester Marathon
Sunday 10th October 1999

NEW CHAMPIONS ALL ROUND

For the 1999 *Manchester Evening News - Magic 1152* Manchester Marathon the course was changed. This involved new loops in the Openshaw and Levenshulme areas, with the start in Heaton Park moving back 103 metres and the finish being more direct from Sale Road. The exact route was: leave Heaton Park by St Margaret's gate, St Margaret's Road, Bury Old Road (A665), Middleton Road (A576), Victoria Avenue (A6104), Hollinwood Avenue, Broadway (A663), Oldham Road (A62), Hulme Hall Lane, Alan Turing Way, Gibbon Street, Ashton New Road, Croft Street, Clayton Lane, Parkhouse Street, Victoria Street, Ashton Old Road, Chancellor Lane, Devonshire Street, Hyde Road (A57), Mount Road, Broom Lane, Stockport Road (A6), Albert Road, Moseley Road (A6010), Kingsway (A34), School Lane, Parrs Wood Road, Wilmslow Road, Barlow Moor Road, Palatine Road, Sale Road, Rackhouse Road to finish in Wythenshawe Park.

The weather was overcast and the temperature was around 16° C (60° F). Once more there was a stiff breeze, mainly facing the athletes for most of the way.

Favourite for the men's title had to be the three times winner Bashir Hussain. Six weeks earlier the Stockport Harrier had won his fourth Tour of Tameside, six stage double marathon, but by race day he had been suffering from a cold and never really intended to go the full distance.

Second favourite was Tony O'Brien was a 28-year-old field service engineer with United Utilities. He was from Liverpool and joined Liverpool Harriers at 15, but now was with Morpeth Harriers. He was a useful cross-country runner finishing runner-up in the Lancashire Junior Cross-Country Championships in 1990. He had a brief spell away from the sport, playing football, but soon returned to running and made a name for himself on the roads. He set a 10 Km best of 29:21 in 1995. Competing in his home city, the same year, he gained an England vest for half-marathon. In the Liverpool International Half-Marathon, on a boiling hot day, he placed eighth (third Briton) in 67:59. He gained a British vest in 1997 representing his country in the Ekiden Relay in Japan. In 1999 he had his best ever cross-country season, 14th in the Inter-Counties and 15th in the National, which paved the way for his marathon debut in London. At stake were places in the World Cup and World Championships with a standard of 2:16 to be achieved. With this in mind he aimed for 2:15 and was on pace to 20 miles (1:43:45), but faded over the last four miles to end up with a 2:20:20, sixth Briton and 33rd place overall.

However, recently he had been under a lot of stress. A family illness had forced him to withdraw from the Puma Edinburgh Marathon two weeks previously and he was not sure how the strain would affect his latest race plans.

Also in the 1999 London was O'Brien's club-mate Alan Shepherd, who recorded 2:22:15 for 39th place. Shepherd was a soldier and had just returned from a tour of duty in Kosovo, Yugoslavia. He was the favourite for the Army title.

A wild card was Martin Rush of Bideford AC, now working at the University of Manchester as their Sport Development Officer. Rush had competed for Great Britain in the 1992 Barcelona Olympics in the 20 Km walk and had taken 24th place.

Finally, there was veteran Emlyn Roberts of Eryri Harriers, a Welsh running club based in Llanberis. His apprenticeship included a 41st place, 2:37:02, in the 1981 Manchester Charity Marathon. Roberts had won the tough Snowdon Marathon in 1991 in 2:31:41, not that far off the course record, 2:28:02 set by Altrincham ACs Jeff Norman, marathon Olympian in 1976 and himself a consistent Manchester Marathon performer: 1971, 2:16:45; 1972 2:19:22; 1982 2:20:23; and 1984 2:22:19. How would Roberts fare on a flat course?

In the women's race 1998 Champion Jackie Newton had made a late bid to enter after a disappointing run in Edinburgh (11th woman, 2:57:20) two weeks previously, but was refused by the organisers. The only woman with any kind of form was Stockport Harrier, mother of three, Estelle McGuire from Buxton. She had won the White Peak Marathon in 3:11:49. This is a point-to-point off-road marathon on the Tissington Trail in Derbyshire. This year she had finished third woman in the same race, despite the fact that she had given birth to twins less than a year before the Manchester date. McGuire had a totally relaxed attitude to running: no training programme, no pressure, no expectations. She raced with a Walkman running in her own world oblivious to what was happening around her.

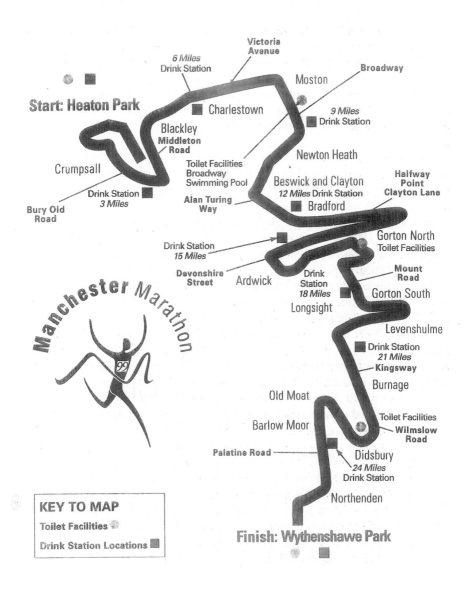

Route map for 1999 Marathon. (Courtesy of Manchester Leisure.)

In the wheelchair race there were eight starters, the favourite being Anthony Booth (Unattached) from Clayton in Manchester who had been fourth last year.

The race had a total of around 1,200 entrants and the wheelchair section went to the formbook with Booth leading all the way. His journey was not without incident as he had a puncture and had to go from about 7 miles with a flat tyre until someone sorted it out for him. This was reflected in his time of 2:07:51, almost 13 minutes down on his 1998 time. It was almost a sprint for second place as Paul Hunt edged out James Hallam, 2:15:20 to 2:15:54, Hallam's time being almost 5 minutes faster than the previous year. Local woman Jackie Wagstaff from Radcliffe was the first and only woman in 4:18:56.

In the main race Rush lived up to his name and dashed off alone. O'Brien was happy to run with Hussain, feeling the pace was "nice and easy" and having no desire to chase Rush. At nine miles the three times Manchester Champion decided to call it a day and dropped out.

Tony O'Brien.

223

At the half-way point on Clayton Lane, Openshaw, Rush was timed at 69:32 with O'Brien next, 1:48 down at 71:20. This gap hardly changed in the next couple of miles and stood at 1:45 passing the 15 mile point. Rush's pace then began to fall inexorably with successive miles of 5:37, 5:46, 5:59, 5:53, then a 5:56 to the 20 mile point (1:49:20) where O'Brien caught him. Swooping into the lead, O'Brien thought he now had it in the bag and perhaps became complacent. His next miles were 5:52, 5:51, then a 5:58. At 23 miles he heard he was being challenged and looked behind to see Alan Shepherd "coming like a train." He upped the tempo slightly with a 5:49 mile, then kicked in the 25th mile, a 5:21 to finish off Shepherd. Both were extremely tired by then and O'Brien's 26th mile was a 6:05, but he hung on to victory with a 2:25:18 to 2:25:56. Emlyn Roberts kept his head, he too passing Rush in the later stages for a 2:29:26 finish and third place.

Hussain was at the finish in Wythenshawe Park to see O'Brien break the tape and take the £750 first prize. He was the first to congratulate the emotional Morpeth Harrier who had entered the previous years race but never made it to the start line. O'Brien was close to tears at the end and admitted: "It's been an emotional few weeks for me and I've had a lot of stress. I've done it against the odds really and this makes the all effort worthwhile."

It was a satisfying run for Shepherd and second place was sufficient to give him the Army title incorporated into the main race.

Third man Emlyn Roberts was also the leading veteran and could hardly have been happier if he had he won the event. He collected a £200 prize and joked: "Usually all I get is a bottle of wine."

Estelle McGuire.

Estelle McGuire became the fourth new women's champion crossing the line in 2:52:34. And taking the £500 prize. She was the only woman to break three hours and her margin of victory was over 12 minutes. Her time ranked her 21st in the Britain in 1999 and her relaxed style, Walkman and all, led her to be portrayed in Reebok advertisements. Second woman home was Ruth Whitehead of Bingley Harriers in 3:04:59, whilst third woman was in the V45 category, Jennifer Adams of Red Rose Runners recording 3:10:14.

Results:

1	Tony O'Brien	(Morpeth)		2:25:18
2	Alan Shepherd	(ARMY)		2:25:56
3	Emlyn Roberts	(Eryri)	V40	2:29:26
4	Martin Rush	(Bideford)		2:31:12
5	Ian Kelly	(Bolton U)		2:31:37
6	Keith Worrall	(Trafford)		2:35:37
7	Jim Rose	(Altrincham)		2:36:56
8	David Ardern	(Goyt V)		2:37:28
9	Charles Thurstan	(Coldstream G)		2:37:32
10	Dave Carrington	(Sale)	V40	2:38:19

11, D Speake (Martial Arts) 2:38:29; 12, S Lund (Unatt) 2:38:30; 13, S Downes (ARMY) 2:38:41; 14, Phil Derbyshire (Wigan P) 2:39:33; 15, J Bell (Elswick) V50 2:39:52; 16, C Downs (Middleton AC) 2:39:59; 17, P Blanchfield (ARMY) 2:40:46; 18, P Dobson (Leeds City AC) 2:41:12; 19, R Brewster (Clayton-le-Moors) V40 2:41:17; 20, R Jackson (Salford) 2:41:27; 21, A Pead (Stockport) 2:41:38; 22, I Newcombe (Middleton) V40 2:42:00; 23, C Patton (7 Royal Irish & ARMY) 2:42:29; 24, S Curran (Salford) V50 2:42:46; 25, A Clarkson (Clayton-le-Moors) V40 2:42:59; 26, S Shaw (Burnden RR) V40 2:43:50; 27, J Fletcher (E Cheshire) V40 2:44:37; 28, P Bates (Bury AC) V40 2:44:54; 29, A Caddick (Unatt) V50 2:46:21;

30, N Cobb (Redhill RR & CS) 2:46:47; 31, M Higginbottom (Salford) V45 2:47:20; 32, P Nesbitt (ARMY) 2:47:43 A; 33, J Baird (E Lothian) V40 2:47:47; 34, G Matthews (E Cheshire) 2:48:15; 35, J Callaghan (Keighley & Craven) 2:48:52; 36, N Rickard (Darwen Dashers) 2:49:05; 37, R Hunter (Upavon) V40 2:49:18; 38, D Mellor (E Cheshire) V45 2:49:36; 39, J Sproson (Middleton) 2:50:27; 40, S Davis (ARMY) 2:50:30 A; 41, J Duffy (Shettleston H) 2:50:39; 42, A Brown (Unatt) 2:51:03; 43, G Shufflebottom (Worsley H) V50 2:51:42; 44, D Burke (Manchester YMCA) V45 2:51:58; 45, M Schofield (Middleton) V50 2:52:03; 46, E McGuire (Stockport) F 2:52:34; 47, S Stennett (Unattached - CIVIL SERVICE) 2:53:09; 48, D Palmer (Wreake R) V50 2:53:53; 49, G Walsh (Spenborough AC) V50 2:53:59;

50, Philip Derbyshire (Wigan Phoenix) V40 2:54:18; 51, B Duncalf (North Staffs RR) V40 2:54:34; 52, M Nester (Blackburn RR) 2:54:36; 53, P Douglas (Stafford H) V45 2:54:43; 54, D Clarke (ARMY) 2:55:41; 55, H Bottger (Unatt) 2:55:42: 56, J Plumridge (Holmfirth H) 2:55:58; 57, M Elliot (ARMY) 2:55:59 A; 58, B Daniel (ARMY) 2:56:06; 59, B Russell (Tipton H) V50 2:56:18; 60, M Haire (Celestica AC) 2:56:39; 61, J Lingard (St Helens Str) V50 2:56:39; 62, M Platt (Macclesfield H) 2:57:37; 63, C Manclarke (Stockport) V45 2:57:50; 64, T Evans (Unatt) 2:58:08; 65, J Whilock (Staffs Moors) 2:59:07; 66, M Durcan (Stockport) V55 2:59:21; 67, S Ellis (Swinton RC) 2:59:54; 68, S Taylor (ARMY) 3:00:07; 69, P Westwood (Unatt) 3:00:56;

70, N MacGregor (Shettleston H) V50 3:01:09; 71, G Cunliffe (Clayton-le-Moors) V40 3:01:25; 72, D Cawdron (Newcastle) 3:01:34; 73, C Price (Swinton RC) 3:01:59; 74, R Hobbs (ARMY) 3:02:10; 75, P Mellon (Unatt) 3:02:18; 76, M Schofield (Unatt) 3:02:30; 77, T Daniels (Salford H) V50 3:02:30; 78, I Rowland (Unatt) 3:02:55; 79, D Parry (Steel City Str) V45 3:02:56; 80, A Smith (Darwen D) 3:02:58; 81, K Tuzio (Wigan P) 3:03:33; 82, P Deaville (Stockport) 3:03:35; 83; D White (ARMY) 3:03:38; 84, T Galpin (Bournemouth AAC) 3:04:06; 85, D Cockburn (Saddleworth R) 3:04:28; 86, D Drury (Serpentine) 3:04:30; 87, T McCrave (Rivacre R & J) V40 3:04:34; 88, R Blake (Unatt) V45 3:04:39; 89, G Kueberuwa (Unatt) V40 3:04:47; 90, I Brown (Pitreavie AAC) 3:04:56; 91, D Matthews (Sale H Manch) V40 3:04:57; 92, Ruth Whitehead (Bingley) F 3:04:59; 93, D Tinsley (Wirral AC) V40 3:05:02; 94, B Williams (ARMY) 3:05:03; 95, D Hanson (Vale Royal) V40 3:05:08; 96, T Lawlor (Marconi H) 3:05:09; 97, S Normandale (Unatt) 3:05:38; 98, P Denmore (St Helens Str) 3:06:07; 99, H Jones (Unatt) 3:06:45; 100, N Floyd (Unatt) 3:06:47. 907 finished.

V40	E Roberts	(Eryri H)	2:29:36
V45	M Higginbottom	(Salford H)	2:47:20
V50	J Bell	(Elswick)	2:39:52
V55	M Durcan	(Stockport H)	2:59:21
V60	D Matthews	(Unattached)	3:39:14
V65	A Dunn	(Stockport H)	3:10:28
V70	E Lloyd	(Penny Lane St)	4:19:48

Women:

1	Estelle McGuire	(Stockport)	2:52:34
2	Ruth Whitehead	(Bingley)	3:04:59
3	Jennifer Adams	(Red Rose) V45	3:10:14

4, S Crehan (Sale) V40 3:10:51; 5, E Rest (Serpentine) 3:14:04; 6, L Diggle (West Cheshire RC) V40 3:18:45; 7, S Welsh (Unatt) 3:24:53; 8, L Richardson (Newquay RR) V35 3:28:07; 9, S Cariss (Bingley) V45 3:28:40; 10, H Sandelands (Wigan Ph) V35 3:28:40.

V35 L Richardson	(Newquay RR)	3:28:07
V40 S Crehan	(Sale H)	3:10:51
V45 J Adams	(Red Rose R)	3:10:14
V50 V Sutcliffe	(Red Rose R)	3:39:16
V55 S Whyte	(Unattached)	5:49:03
V60 J Geraghty	(Manchester H)	4:53:20

Army Championships
Men: Alan Shepherd 2:25:56 Women: none finished.

Civil Service Championships
Men: Jim Bell 2:39:52   Women: Sue Cariss V45 (Bingley) 3:28:12

Wheelchair
Men:

1	Anthony Booth	(Unattached)	2:07:51
2	Paul Hunt	(Birchfield)	2:15:20
3	James Hallam	(BWRA)	2:15:54

4, A Kenneth (Red Star AC) V55 2:44:32; 5, D Johnson (Unatt: Bury) 2:48:49; 6, D Alcock V60 (Unatt) 2:48:49; 7, M Marten V40 (BWRA) 4:03:56

Women:

| 1 | Jackie Wagstaff | (Unatt: Radcliffe) | 4:18:56 |

7 men and 1 woman finished.

None of the first three men returned to Manchester.

Tony O'Brien dropped out of the 2000 *Flora* London Marathon with a calf injury and acted as a pace-maker for the 2001 *Flora* London Marathon. This latter was a prelude to his best ever track season when he ran a 3:50.38 1,500m; 14:01.38 5,000m and 29:28 10,000m. He was also a member of the successful medal-winning Morpeth Harriers road relay six and 12 man squad, in 2000 and 2001 at regional and National level.

Alan Shepherd improved his best time in London the following spring, recording 2:19:29 for 27th place.

None of the first three women returned to Manchester.

Estelle McGuire ran in the *Peli Products* Millennium Tour of Tameside, 2000, finishing third to Jackie Newton's first place and helping Stockport Harriers to the team prize.

Chapter 31

The 31st Manchester Marathon
Sunday 12th October 2000

CHAMPIONS ALL CHANGE ONCE MORE

As usual the marathon was organised by Manchester Leisure under the direction of Paul Mee. The race was supported by New Balance, the running shoe company with a UK manufacturing base.

The 2000 course involved a change to that used in 1999. The first three miles of the race were run in Heaton Park and from there it was probably the most direct route that had been used to arrive at Wythenshawe Park.

The details were: after completing the first three miles in Heaton Park leave Heaton Park by St Margaret's gate, St Margaret's Road, Bury Old Road (A665), Middleton Road (A576), Victoria Avenue (A6104), Hollinwood Avenue, Broadway (A663), Oldham Road (A62), Hulme Hall Lane, Alan Turing Way, Ashton Old Road, Chancellor Lane, Devonshire Street, Hyde Road (A57), Mount Road, Broom Lane, Stockport Road (A6), Albert Road, Moseley Road (A6010), Kingsway (A34), School Lane, Parrs Wood Road, Wilmslow Road, Barlow Moor Road, Palatine Road, Sale Road, Rackhouse Road to finish in Wythenshawe Park.

At 9:30 am on race day the weather was cool, and the temperature would average around 10° C (50° F) throughout the competition but with occasional downpours of rain. Although the wind would again be partly against the runners, it was the least breezy of the series so far.

Around 1400 runners had entered, up on 1999. Once more Bashir Hussain was the favourite. He had to drop out of the classic double marathon, *Peli Products* Millennium Tour of Tameside. Now in its 20th year, it was the final time the event would be run. Going for his fifth win he had had to abandon the opening stage with a metatarsal tunnel syndrome injury. By October, although he reckoned he was behind on his training schedule, he felt that his injury had recovered and he was fit enough to win his fourth title.

Andy Arrand, from Newton, Hyde, Cheshire was second to Hussain in the 1998 Manchester Marathon, a mere 13 seconds behind. Here, the 34-year-old army sergeant based at Aldershot with the Royal Logistics Corps was hoping

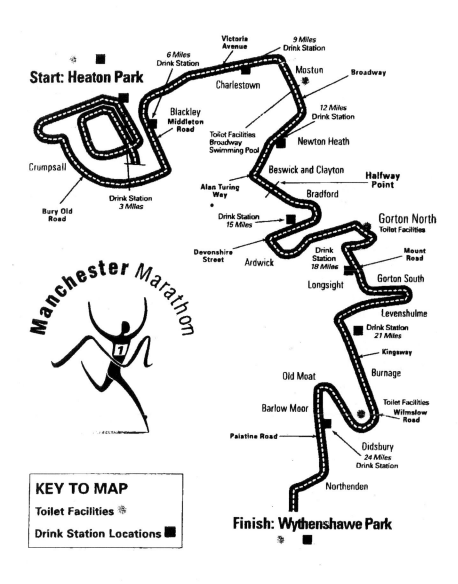

Route map for 2000 Marathon. (Courtesy of Manchester Leisure.)

to go one better. His training had included up to 100 miles a week for five months, but he too would have to pull out of the 2000 Tour of Tameside with a kidney infection. He was starting training with the Parachute Regiment soon and felt he may not have the time to enter this race again.

Tony Duffy (Bolton United Harriers) third in the 1997 Manchester Marathon was back to compete again. Since becoming a veteran in 1996 he had been very selective with his marathons, running only four, but with tremendous success. Second veteran in London in 1997, third place and first veteran in Manchester the same year, first veteran in London in 1998, 2:25:42, and finally a gold medal in the World Veterans Marathon Championships in Gateshead, August 1999, in a time of 2:23:25. Duffy had changed jobs from sign painter and poster writer to a bus driver and a late shift the day before the race did not help his chances.

In the women's race only one previous champion had returned, Jackie Newton of Stockport Harriers, winner in 1998, and it looked like she was the woman to beat.

The wheelchair race had only two contestants, and one was 21-year-old Tushar Patel from Fulham, a member of the Velocity club, who had been third in the 1997 Manchester race and fifth in this year's London Marathon. Patel came home first in 2:07:45, surprised at the lack of competition. His time was almost half an hour worse than his best due to a collision in the opening mile. Michael Marten (BWRA) was second in 4:35:51.

In the main race Andy Arrand of the Army shot off from the start and soon established a big lead. Behind him a big group formed running at a serious but relaxed pace. The group included Bashir Hussain, his club-mate Warren Birchall, Rob Deakin (Staffordshire Moorlands), Ronnie Adams (Portsmouth Joggers), Tony Duffy, Nathan Vengdasalam (Liverpool Pembroke Sefton) plus Chris Cariss and Stewart MacDonald, both of Bingley Harriers.

Just after six miles, with Heaton Park on the left and just before the turn to the uphill of Victoria Avenue, Rob Deakin, the 33-year-old newsagent from Stoke-on-Trent shot off the front of the chasing group.

For a moment Duffy followed, then remembering the gaps in his training, he "chickened out" and fell back to the group. But he knew that that was the significant break.

At the half-way point on Hulme Hall Lane Arrand passed in 71:28 with Deakin 10 seconds behind. But the latter was closing inexorably and where the Alan Turing Way crosses Ashton New Road at 14 miles, the two came together. They ran stride for stride for one mile, then on Ashton Old Road,

Rob Deakin. (Picture: Peter Downing.)

Deakin, whose marathon debut had been in London in 2000 with a 2:26:10, began to move ahead. Arrand did not give up and three miles later he was only 20 seconds behind, but their relative paces did not change and the gap at 21 miles was 30 seconds, at 24 miles 40 seconds growing to 47 seconds at the finish, when a jubilant Deakin recorded 2:23:53 for his first ever victory and £750 prize.

Even though picking up a £500 prize and a second Army title to add to his 1998 award, Arrand was not happy saying, "If you're going to make a break it might as well be a decisive one. Second to me is first loser's spot. I entered to win it, but once again got my tactics wrong and suffered."

At 15 miles the following bunch was two minutes down, Duffy tried to push on but no one else in the group wanted to work. In Burnage, on Kingsway, at the 21 mile point Hussain felt his hamstrings tighten as they swung up a hill and he decided to call it a day. He later stated, "I could have finished, but was not excited by a slow time like 2:30 odd."

A mile further down Kingsway, Duffy lost contact and from that point was hanging on, as Adams, Vengdasalam and Cariss left him behind. Adams, who had a 2:22:49 marathon to his credit from the 1999 London, probably underestimated his own ability and with a late charge got to within 17 seconds of Arrand with a 2:24:57. Vengdasalam was 17 seconds further back in fourth with 2:25:14, and Cariss 36 seconds after that with 2:25:50. Duffy hung onto sixth taking the veteran's prize once more in 2:26:38.

In mixed competitions it must be difficult for the women to know in their own race. In this particular case Wigan Phoenix's 38-year-old Kath Charnock finished runner-up in 2:47:44, slightly slower than the 2:47:28 she had run in Dublin the previous year.

At the finish Charnock said, "I was just planning to go for an extension of my normal Sunday training run, but felt great and to be honest at one stage I thought I was in the lead. I didn't think Shona was in front of me."

Exactly five minutes in front was the winner, 29-year-old Shona Crombie-Hick from London, a member of the Mornington Chase club. Her time was almost 16 minutes better than her 1999 winning debut of 2:58:51 in Lanzarote, and set a new course record.

Shona Crombie-Hick. (Picture: Peter Downing.)

The health club worker finished 18th overall and after the race revealed, "I was going to run the Nottingham Marathon two weeks ago but I had a problem with my Achilles and pulled out. I was worried that the injury might flare up again, but it didn't." After this success she had ambitions to get in the Commonwealth Games marathon team for Scotland in Manchester 2002, for which the qualifying time was 2:40:00

Third in the women's race was Sam Bretherick of Preseli Harriers.

Jackie Newton dropped out of the race at the half-way point with stomach problems which had been bothering her all week. She had been with the chasing group of women including Charnock and Bretherick, and had a novel way of getting to the finish. Newton jogged to Piccadilly Railway Station, and because she was in her running gear and had no money, the guard took pity on her and allowed her to catch the train to Manchester Airport from where she ran back to Wythenshawe Park.

Results:

1	Rob Deakin	(Staffs. Moors.)	2:23:53
2	Andy Arrand	(Army)	2:24:40
3	Ronnie Adams	(Portsmouth J)	2:24:57
4	Nathan Vengdasalam	(Liverpool P S)	2:25:14
5	Chris Cariss	(Bingley H)	2:25:50
6	Tony Duffy	(Bolton U) V40	2:26:38
7	Warren Birchall	(Stockport)V40	2:29:42
8	Stewart MacDonald	(Bingley H)	2:33:16
9	Sebastian Boncler	(Unattached)	2:36:08
10	John Howarth	(Leigh H)	2:36:10

11, E Cook (Blackburn) V45 2:36:20; 12, J Hartley (Clayton-le-Moors) V40 2:36:23; 13, R Jackson (Salford H) 2:37:50; 14, J Duffy (Shettleston) 2:40:33; 15, A Caddick (Unatt) V50 2:40:47; 16, N Pickard (Darwen Dashers) 2:41:42; 17, K Povey (ARMY) 2:42:16; 18, Shona Crombie-Hick (Mornington Chase) F 2:42:44; 19, T Berg (Mornington Chase) 2:42:46; 20, A Hough (Unatt) 2:43:04; 21, P Blanchfield (ARMY) 2:43:09; 22 D Unwin (E Cheshire H) 2:43:29; 23, A Brown (Salford H) 2:43:30; 24, D Lockett (Salford H) 2:45:08; 25, J Docherty (ARMY) 2:45:40; 26, N Jones (ARMY) 2:46:02; 27, C Routledge (ARMY) 2:46:16; 28, J Fletcher (E Cheshire H) V40 2:46:28; 29, Kath Charnock (Wigan Phoenix) V35 2:47:44;

30, M Haire (Celestica AC) 2:47:58; 31, D Bolton (Trafford AC) 2:48:01; 32, S Stennett (Unatt) 2:48:26; 33, R Knox (ARMY) 2:49:42; 34, J Creak (ARMY) 2:50:00; 35, S Davis (ARMY) 2:50:16; 36, D Lane (Spenborough AC) 2:50:23; 37, S Crampin (Road Runners Club) V40 2:50:38; 38, A Mahoney (Scottish Vets) 2:50:54; 39, D Vaughan (E Cheshire H) 2:51:15; 40, I Sharples (Wesham) 2:51:32; 41, G Pendlebury (Wesham) V45 2:51:32; 42, C Thompson (Edmonton R) 2:52:08; 43, M Platt (Macclesfield H) V45 2:52:13; 44, Sam Bretherick (Preseli H) F 2:53:37; 45, T Stock (Macclesfield H) 2:53:49; 46, D Cairns (Unatt) 2:53:54; 47, J Bebbington (Liverpool RC) V50 2:53:54; 48, Angela Allan (Tipton H) F 2:53:54; 49, D Constance (Stafford H) 2:54:09;

50, G Taylor (Darwen Dashers) 2:54:11; 51, C Pass (E Cheshire H) V40

2:54:16; 52, G Poulton (Trafford AC) 2:54:18; 53, S Backhouse (Scarborough AC) 2:54:20; 54, W Willmitt (Liverpool RC) V50 2:54:26; 55, M Ostermeyer (Fairlands Valley) 2:54:38; 56, P Welch (Scunthorpe AC) V40 2:54:41; 57, H Bingham (Tynedale H) 2:54:53; 58, D McKenna (Unatt) 2:54:58; 59, J Worthington (Wigan Phoenix) 2:55:06; 60, J Spillane (Leigh H) V45 2:55:07; 61, C Johnson (Unatt) 2:55:18; 62, D Blazier (Abergele H) 2:55:19; 63, H Issatt (Unatt) 2:55:34; 64, R Miller (Wigan AC) V50 2:55:44; 65, D Dickson (Unatt) V45 2:55:58; 66, N Holdsworth (Knavesmire H) 2:56:19; 67, J Wamsley (Billingham MH) V55 2:56:24; 68, S Normandale (Unatt) 2:56:34; 69, M Frampton (ARMY) 2:56:42;

70, K Uzzell (Stone Master Mar) V50 2:56:49; 71, C Leith (Unatt) 2:57:02; 72, H Jones (Unatt) 2:57:16; 73, M Nester (Blackburn RR) V45 2:57:29; 74, O Andersen (Unatt) 2:57:34; 75, P Waine (Unatt) V40 2:57:39; 76, A Bolton (Unatt) V40 2:57:45; 77, M Heath (Unatt) 2:57:53; 78, M Conroy (Leigh H) 2:58:22; 79, A Wade (Ilkley H) V35 2:58:24; 80, J Howarth (Longwood H) V45 2:58:26; 81, Helen Barber (Horsforth H) F 2:58:40; 82, D Reeve (Clayton-le-Moors) V40 2:58:40; 83, S Almond (Stockport H) 2:58:47; 84, G Felton (ARMY) 2:59:03; 85, P Brown (Unatt) 2:59:12; 86, B Grant (ARMY) 2:59:13; 87, K Boardman (Leigh H) V40 2:59:32; 88, T Kay (ARMY) 2:59:38; 89, P Aird (Dee Striders) V40 2:59:46; 90, B Clementson (Unatt) 2:59:59; 91, S Weston (Unatt) 3:00:00; 92, P Crookall (Northern Vets) V45 3:00:13; 93, J Colley (ARMY) 3:01:10; 94, ?? (Unatt) 3:01:25; 95, M Elliott (ARMY) 3:01:38; 96, C Smith (Eccleshill RR) 3:01:51; 97, A Gristwood (Cleethorpes AC) 3:01:58; 98, D Horrocks (Clayton-le-Moors) 3:02:06; 99, T Daniels (Salford H) V50 3:02:11; 100, A Welsh (Unatt) 3:02:12. 888 finished.

V40 T Duffy	(Bolton U)	2:26:38
V45 E Cook	(Blackburn H)	2:51:32
V50 A Caddick	(Unatt)	2:40:47
V55 J Walmsley	(Billingham)	2:56:24
V60 B Everett	(Wolds Vets)	3:45:26
V65 L Moss	(100 Marathon)	3:42:44
V70 M Aimable	(Stubbington G)	5:10:58

Women:

1	Shona Crombie-Hick	(Mornington Chase)		2:42:44
2	Kath Charnock	(Wigan Phoenix)	V35	2:47:44
3	Sam Bretherick	(Preseli H)		2:53:37

4, A Allan (Tipton H) 2:53:54; 5, A Wade (Ilkley H) V35 2:58:24; 6, H Barber (Horsforth H) 2:58:40; 7, S Cariss (Unatt) V50 3:04:33; 8, J Myatt (Unatt) V35 3:05:17; 9, J Coleman (Chorley H) V40 3:10:47; 10, A Sedman

(Unatt) V35 3:14:39.

V35	K Charnock	(Wigan Phoenix)	2:47:44
V40	J Coleman	(Chorley H)	3:10:47
V45	G Williams	(Picton RC)	3:21:41
V50	S Cariss	(Unatt)	3:04:33
V55	J Tomlinson	(East Cheshire)	4:31:47
V60	K Garnett	(Clayton-le-Moors)	4:01:40

Army Championships
Men: Andy Arrand 2:24:40   Women: Paula Waites 3:22:58

Civil Service Championships
Men: J Duffy (Shettleston) 2:40:33   Women: Charnock (Wigan Ph)

Wheelchair

1	Tushar Patel	(Velocity)	2:07:45
2	Michael Marten	(BWRA)	4:35:51

2 finished.

Tushar Patel did not return to Manchester. In autumn 2000 he recorded 1:36:00 in the Berlin Marathon and was second in the 2002 London Marathon, 1:41:17.

None of the first three men returned to Manchester.
Rob Deakin improved his best to 2:23:29 in 2001 in the Dublin Marathon coming 15th.
Bashir Hussain did not run Manchester again, but still competes regularly. He was fourth in the recently resurrected Tour of Tameside.
None of the first three women returned to Manchester.
Although Shona Crombie-Hick won the 2001 Copenhagen Marathon in 2:45:23, she never did get selected for the Commonwealth Games.

After the event, race director Paul Mee expressed a hope that the 2001 race could be held on the proposed route for the Commonwealth Games in 2002, in which case he expected a record number of entries.

Chapter 32

The 32nd Manchester Marathon
Sunday 23rd September 2001

WOOD COMPLETES HER SET OF MEDALS

Race Director Paul Mee, of Manchester Leisure, got his wish and the course used in the 2001 Manchester Marathon was as close as possible as that to be used in the 2002 Commonwealth Games. This was a natural enough development as it would serve as a useful rehearsal for the big races themselves the following year.

The course was nothing like that of the previous races and was two laps starting in front of the Town Hall and taking in many of Manchester and Salford's famous landmarks. The route as issued was: The athletes leave Albert Square and go along Cross Street and Corporation Street, turn left onto Todd Street and then along Victoria Station Approach into Hunts Bank and Victoria Street. The route then goes along Deansgate, over the Bridgewater Viaduct to Chester Road, along Bridgewater Way (A56) to turn right at the roundabout onto Trafford Road.

In Salford the athletes turn left onto Broadway, go straight on at the roundabout to The Quays following the road to the Lowry Centre, and continue along the waterside round the back of the Lowry Centre, and the retail development. The front of the Water Sports Centre is passed and then around its back, to turn right onto The Quays Road to traffic lights when a right turn is made at the next set of lights into Trafford Wharf Road.

The route is down Trafford Wharf Road to the roundabout with the junction of Churchill Way where, after going around the roundabout the route returns towards the city centre along Trafford Wharf Road. At Waters Reach there is a right turn, then through the traffic lights onto Sir Matt Busby Way. At Warwick Road the route is straight on and then left onto Talbot Road, left at the White City Way and left onto Chester Road to the junction. After a left turn down a bus lane for approximately 25 metres there is a right turn onto the A56, Bridgewater Way and straight onto Chester Road.

When the city centre is reached *via* the Bridgewater Viaduct and Deansgate, a right turn into Peter Street is made and at Mount Street a left into Albert Square allows the lap to Salford Quays and Old Trafford to be repeated. On reaching the Mancunian Way for the second time the athletes

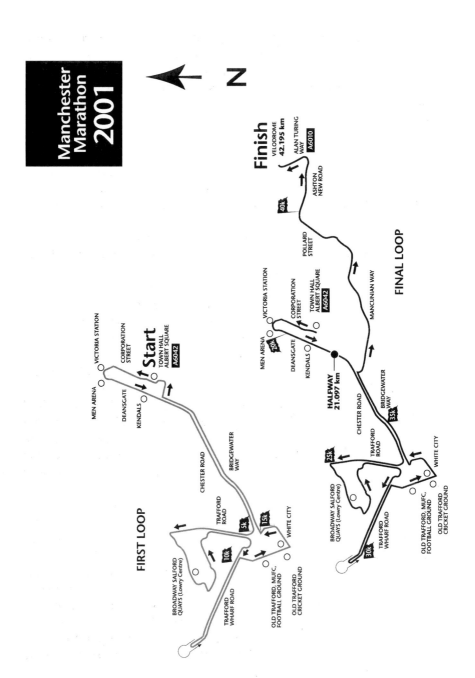

Route map for 2001 Marathon. (Courtesy of Manchester Leisure.)

turn right onto the Mancunian Way and go along it to Great Ancoats Street. Turning right into Pollard Street the athletes continue along to Merrill Street and then onto Ashton New Road until Alan Turing Way is reached. Then a left turn along Alan Turing Way until Gibson Street where a right turn is made, then a left onto Stuart Street. A right turn is made into the "Velodrome" where the race finishes.

The weather was favourable for marathon running, with a temperature of around 9° C (50° F) for most of the race, dry, overcast, and little wind except for an easterly breeze, hitting the runners for the last 5 kilometres (3 miles) including the elevated section of the Mancunian Way. The fact that this was the marathon course for the Commonwealth Games had not dramatically affected the entries which stood at 1,500, up around 100 on the previous year, and no potential Commonwealth Marathon contender from the home countries had been tempted into testing the route.

In the men's race no previous winner had entered. Fastest on paper was Ian Fisher of Otley AC, Yorkshire. He had a best of 2:20:27 from London 2000. Another Yorkshire runner, Chris Cariss, Bingley Harriers was back. His fifth place time of 2:25:50 had been his personal best. That had been his sixth marathon, all five others being London.

As well as being an open race, the 2001 marathon included British Veterans, Army, Police and Civil Service Championships. Defending his police title, gained when finishing third in the 2000 Glasgow Marathon was Salford Harrier Darren Hale, who already had a useful record in Manchester with a 2:22:09 for fourth place in 1997 and third place in 1998, 2:26:30. Vying for victory in the British Veterans Championships was Andy Wethrill of Redhill Road Runners who had been ranked number one veteran in 2000 with 2:24:31.

In the women's race, fastest on paper was 37-year-old Melanie Ellis from the Shaftesbury Barnet Athletic Club. In 1997 she had run 2:48:51, but bettered this in 1999 with a 2:46:55 in the famous Boston Marathon, 18th woman home. She followed Boston with a 2:49:06 in Sacramento, USA, the same year.

The local favourite was Kerrie Wood, Stockport Harriers, who was renewing her rivalry with Salford Harriers' Tricia Sloan who had second position in the 1997 Manchester and third in 1998. Wood had third in 1996 and 1997, and second in 1998. If Wood could win this year, she would have the full set of medals. Since her last Manchester she had won a AAA silver medal in London, 1999. Actually, she was third in the AAA's section of the race, but second placer Jackie Newton, our Manchester winner in 1998, was disqualified for not wearing her club colours. Wood missed Manchester in 1999 in favour of the Dublin Marathon, but before that race she had not been sleeping well and dropped out at 10 miles. She was absent from Manchester 2000 having just given birth to a daughter, Abagail, in August of that year. With time constraints due to the arrival of her child her training had to change. Advised by her partner, Dr Mike Doyle, she switched from a moderately high mileage, 70 - 80 miles a week, to a medium volume high quality workload, 40 - 50 miles a week. This seemed to pay off. In 2001 London Marathon she set a personal best of 2:49:12. She followed this with five months of solid training, much of it on the track, then tapered down for Manchester, aiming for a time of 2:45.

Another female with the credentials to feature well in this race was Lisa Knights of the Police AA club. A policewoman in Derbyshire, she had taken the police title and seventh place in the 1997 Manchester with 3:09:08. She had a personal best from 1998 of 2:48:59 and in this year's London, her 2:51:43 gave her 35th place behind Kerrie Wood's 31st.

As last year the men were competing for a £750 prize and the women £500.

Only two competitors contested the wheelchair race.

The race was scheduled to start at 8:00 am with the men and women running together. This would correspond to the start time of the women's race in the Commonwealth Games the following year with the men programmed to start 20 minutes later.

The idea this year was for most of the runners to park at the "Velodrome," the National Cycling Centre, as the Commonwealth Stadium was nowhere near finished. Buses would then take competitors to the start. Unfortunately, the car park designated for the athletes did not open as advertised at 6:00 am, and many cars were parked on nearby side streets. This resulted in people being ordered off the buses, to retrieve their vehicles and park them up in the now open official parking area. The final outcome was a 15 minute delay and probably some worried moments for many competitors fearing missing the start.

Before the starter's signal a minutes silence was observed in remembrance of those who had died in the terrorist attacks on the Twin Towers of the World Trade Centre in New York, and at the Pentagon in Washington, DC, in Pennsylvania on 11th September 2001.

The wheelchair contestants departed a few seconds before the main race,

Jerry Forde from Blarney, Ireland came home first in 3:20:14, whilst Michael Marten, British Wheelchair Racers Association was second. Marten was nothing if not tenacious and had Manchester finishes of 3:17:00, 1996; 4:03:56, 1999; and 4:35:51 in 2000.

It was a reasonably quick start and by $1^1/_2$ Km Joey Parkinson was leading Chris Cariss and Tony O'Brien, an unattached runner and not the 1999 Manchester winner. Parkinson was no stranger to Manchester, having, as a Liverpool Harrier, finished fifth in 1996 (2:36:25), 17th in 1997 (2:35:18) and 13th in 1998 (2:36:30). Twenty metres behind this trio was Andy Wethrill who had missed this initial break, and a further 40 metres back was a group of a dozen or so, headed by Darren Hale and including Steve Littler from Blackpool, Ian Fisher, Simon Edney (Bideford AC), Chris Downs (Swansea Harriers), and Mark McDonald (Lowfell RC).

By $2^1/_2$ Km Parkinson was gone and ultimately did not finish the race, whilst Cariss and O'Brien had been joined by Wethrill. Five kilometres was passed in 16:21, 2:18 pace, with the three running together. A second 5 Km in 16:52 saw O'Brien falling behind by 30 metres, which became 200 metres by $12^1/_2$ Km. By 15 Km, after a third 5 Km in 17:01, the pair of Cariss and Wethrill were away on their own sharing the pace. Another 17:01 5Km took them back through Albert Square and round by Victoria Station to Deansgate where the half-way point was passed in 71:10, with Cariss "still feeling strong."

Further down the field, Fisher had moved through to third and in Albert Square was leading O'Brien and Edney by 45 metres. Darren Hale had had to dive off the road at around 16 Km for a pit stop and once back in the race was in no-man's land. At 23 Km he had a back spasm which forced him to stop and abandon the race, a problem which was to afflict him in a later marathon in Utrecht. He eventually recovered and in 2002 won the Sheffield Marathon, making it a hat trick of wins in that city.

Up front the pace was remarkably even with the pair working together after one more 5 Km in 17:01, and reaching 25 Km in 84:16. It was Cariss' turn to lead. He was later to say, "I didn't put in an effort; he (Wethrill) just dropped. Till then we had worked well together and took it in turns, then when I'm in front at 27 / 28 Km I hope he'll stay." In fact the sixth 5 Km was 16:21, the fastest, along with the first 5 Km, of the race, and the damage had been done. By 31 Km Wethrill was 50 metres down and Fisher now had him in his sights.

Despite slowing to 5 Km splits of 18:00 and 18:23, possibly due to the head wind, Cariss took three minutes out of Wethrill over the last 12 Km as he cruised in to a personal best of 2:25:23 and his first victory. Fisher stormed through and himself finished nearly two minutes ahead of Wethrill, the latter taking the veterans title.

One interesting athlete finishing in 2:45:12 was Hugh Marsden running in the colours of Exmouth Harriers. He had represented the Falkland Islands in the last two Commonwealth Games. He had lived and worked there following post-graduate studies at Manchester University in 1986. He was hoping to make a third appearance in the Commonwealth Marathon but unfortunately his length of residence in recent years did not qualify him for selection.

Chris Cariss finishes the 2001 race. (Picture: Neil Shuttleworth.)

In the women's race Kerrie Wood had planned to run each 5 Km of the beginning of the race in 20 minutes, but she went with the fast early pace set by Melanie Ellis and ended up running the first 5 Km in 18:50. After the race she was critical of the absence of individual kilometre markers, which would have indicated her pace right from the start, and allowed for an adjustment. As it was she eventually ran away from Ellis, passing half-way in just under 81 minutes, and covering the last half in over 90 minutes to record 2:51:26, more than three minutes ahead of Ellis, 2:54:35 in second place. Tricia Sloan, Wood's training partner also misjudged the early pace and did not finish. Lisa Knight in 2:59:30 was third.

Kerrie Wood on the Mancunian Way. (Picture: Phil McCann.)

In sixth place in the women's race was 51-year-old civil servant Sue Cariss, the mother of Chris. In her 18th marathon she recorded 3:05:40 close to her best of 3:04:30 and took the V50 title in the British Veterans Championship.

Results:

1	Chris Cariss	(Bingley H)		2:25:23
2	Ian Fisher	(Otley AC)		2:26:45
3	Andrew Wethrill	(Redhill RR)	V40	2:28:42
4	Simon Edney	(Bideford AC)	V40	2:30:22
5	Steve Littler	(Unattached)		2:30:54
6	Chris Booth	(Unattached)		2:35:13
7	Des Murney	(Army)		2:36:48
8	Gary Matthews	(E Cheshire)	V40	2:37:31
9	Martin Slevin	(Police AA)		2:38:56
10	John Hartley	(Clayton-le-M)	V40	2:39:19

11, M McDonald (Lowfell RC) 2:39:34; 12, D Lockett (Salford H) 2:39:39; 13, A Lammali (Unatt) 2:40:04; 14, P Kilgallon (Wirral AC) V45 2:40:11; 15, R Jackson (Horwich RMI) 2:40:33; 16, J Creak (ARMY) 2:40:39; 17, M Eustace (Tipton H) V40 2:40:56; 18, I Tindale (ARMY) 2:41:36; 19, S Thirkell (Bingley) V45 2:41:42; 20, D Vaughan (E Cheshire) 2:42:07; 21, G Farmer (Chase H) V50 2:42:16; 22, C Rigby (Horwich RMI) 2:43:16; 23, A Brown (Salford H) 2:44:39; 24, H Marsden (Exmouth H) V40 2:45:12 B; 25, S Smith (Preston H) 2:45:39; 26, A Bruce (British Library) V40 2:45:50; 27, D

Donaghy (Exmouth H) V45 2:46:55 B; 28, C Downs (Swansea H) 2:46:59; 29, S Stennett (Unatt) 2:47:08 C;

30, M Baylis (Wirral AC) V40 2:47:29; 31, W Crook (S Ribble H) 2:48:00; 32, M Bagguley (Trentham RC) V40 2:48:25; 33, S Boynton (British Library) V45 2:48:59; 34, N Grant (S Liverpool) 2:49:08; 35, P Speake (Bildeston Bounde) 2:49:20; 36, M Lewis (ARMY) 2:49:32; 37, A McCarroll (ARMY) 2:49:36; 38, J Fletcher (E Cheshire H) 2:50:00; 39, P Butterworth (Clayton-le-Moors) V45 2:50:12; 40, P White (Salford H) V45 2:50:29; 41, R Lees (Clayton-le-Moors) V45 2:50:33; 42, A Dodd (Trentham RC) V45 2:50:35 B; 43, A McDevitt (Wirral AC) V45 2:50:46; 44, C Routledge (ARMY) 2:50:47; 45, K Tulloch (Metro Aberdeen) 2:50:53; 46, C Jeffs (Police AA) V40 2:51:03; 47, A Smith (Darwen Dashers) 2:51:09; 48, Kerrie Wood (Stockport H) V35 2:51:26; 49, J Parsons (Pudsey & Bramley) 2:51:31;

50, M Nester (Blackburn RR) V45 2:51:41; 51, A MacLachlan (Giffnock North) V40 2:51:43; 52, P Orme (Police AA) V40 2:51:49; 53, M Wrench (Valley Str) 2:51:54; 54, T Wood (Tipton H) V40 2:52:31; 55, P Woolley (ARMY) 2:52:33; 56, B Dewhurst (Preston H) 2:53:02; 57, C Howard (ARMY) 2:53:10; 58, C Furse (Newcastle) 2:53:13; 59, S Davis (ARMY) 2:53:15; 60, J Bebbington (Liverpool RC) V50 2:53:38; 61, D Bell (ARMY) 2:54:22; 62, D Clarke (ARMY) 2:54:26; 63, Melanie Ellis (Shaftesbury Barnet) V35 2:54:35; 64, S Almond (Stockport H) 2:54:57; 65, N Crompton (Warrington AC) 2:55:03; 66, D Dowd (Bolton UH) V50 2:55:14; 67, J Thompson (Police AA) V40 2:55:16; 68, M Hood (Unatt) 2:55:27; 69, F Fielding (Glossopdale H) V50 2:55:48;

70, M Haynes (Liverpool RC) 2:55:54; 71, T Kay (ARMY) 2:56:00; 72, A Richards (Tipton H) V40 2:56:29; 73, A Wade (Ilkley H) 2:56:31; 74, D Green (E Cheshire H) V50 2:56:37; 75, M Hammond (Liverpool RC) 2:56:39; 76, J Taylor (Tipton H) V50 2:56:44; 77, R West (Police AA) V40 2:56:46; 78, K Burgess (Altrincham & D AC) V55 2:56:49; 79, B Davey (Southport Waterloo) V45 2:56:59; 80, M Platt (Macclesfield H) V45 2:57:05; 81, H Jenkins (Bromsgrove & Red) 2:57:07; 82, V Spain (Police AA) 2:57:09; 83, C Baker (Peel RR) 2:57:27; 84, R Burton (Scunthorpe AC) V45 2:57:37; 85, A Massey (Unatt) 2:57:42; 86, R Spark (Unatt) V40 2:58:13; 87, M Swannell (Unatt) 2:58:27; 88, P Nesbitt (ARMY) 2:58:27; 89, M Mann (ARMY) 2:59:08; 90, P Price (West Cheshire RC) V40 2:59:24; 91, T Welsh (Unatt) 2:59:28; 92, Lisa Knights F (Police AA) 2:59:30; 93, G Coxon (E Cheshire H) V45 2:59:34; 94, P Cotterill (British Aerospace) 2:59:47; 95, D Law (E Cheshire H)2:59:54; 96, R Flesher (Valley Str) V45 2:59:57; 97, M Elleman (Unatt) 3:00:02; 98, M Pennington (Holmfirth H) V45 3:00:13; 99, T Allen (Unatt) 3:00:28; 100, P Andrews (Norwich AC) V60 3:00:37.   1,085 finished.

V40	A Wethrill	(Redhill RR)	2:28:42
V45	P Killgallon	(Wirral AC)	2:40:11
V50	G Farmer	(Chase H)	2:42:16
V55	K Burgess	(Altrincham)	2:56:49
V60	P Andrews	(Norwich)	3:00:28
V65	W McCaskey	(City Edinburgh)	3:35:17
V70	M Huggins	(Midland Vets)	3:40:13

Women:

1	K Wood	(Stockport H) V35	2:51:26
2	M Ellis	(Shaftesbury B)	2:54:35
3	L Knights	(Police AA)	2:59:30

4, V Perry (Altrincham) V40 3:00:41; 5, A Dennison (Bradford Air.) V35 3:04:10; 6, S Cariss (Bingley H) V50 3:05:40; 7, C Howard (Police AA) 3:12:18; 8, A Sedman (Unatt) 3:13:33; 9, A Webb (Saddleworth) V35 3:13:35; 10, G Fiddes (Unatt) 3:14:01

V35	K Wood	(Stockport H)	2:51:26
V40	V Perry	(Altrincham)	3:00:41
V45	N Bird	(Arbroath Footers)	3:28:19
V50	S Cariss	(Bingley H)	3:05:40
V55	I Bass	(Harrogate Imp)	3:39:59
V60	B Jones	(Bro Dysynni)	3:55:03

Army Championships
Men: Des Murney 2:36:48   Women: Paula Waites 3:18:32

Civil Service Championships
Men: Stan Stennett (Unatt) 2:47:08 Women: Sue Cariss 3:05:40

Police Championships
Men: Martin Slevin 2:38:56   Women: Lisa Knights 2:59:30

British Veteran Athletic Federation Championships
Men:

V40	A Wethrill	(Redhill RR)	2:28:42
V45	P Killgallon	(Wirral AC)	2:40:11
V50	G Farmer	(Chase H)	2:42:16
V55	K Burgess	(Altrincham)	2:56:49
V60	P Andrews	(Norwich AC)	3:00:37
V65	W McCaskey	(City Edinburgh)	3:35:17
V70	M Huggins	(Midland Vets)	3:40:13

Women:

V35	K Wood	(Stockport H)	2:51:26
V40	V Perry	(Altrincham)	3:00:41
V45	N Bird	(Arbroath Footers)	3:28:19
V50	S Cariss	(Bingley H)	3:05:40
V55	I Bass	(Harrogate Imp)	3:39:59
V60	B Jones	(Bro Dysynni)	3:55:03

Wheelchair

1	Jerry Forde	(Blarney)	V50	3:20:14
2	Mike Marten	(BWRA)	V40	3:59:03

Chris Cariss, a 26-year-old insurance underwriter, posted a much-improved personal best in the 2002 *Flora* London Marathon placing 21st and fifth Briton in a time of 2:20:46.

Also in London 2002, Ian Fisher ran 2:22:07.

Kerrie Wood was unable to defend her title in the 2002 open Manchester Marathon, due to the birth of a son, Jacob, the week before.

The number of finishers in this last series of marathons is as follows:

1996	1,686
1997	1,338
1998	1,338
1999	907
2000	888
2001	1,088

A declining trend, apart from 2001, the pre-Commonwealth Games year.

Manchester Leisure Marathons
RANKING OF TOP 50 MEN'S TIMES 1996-2002

Rank	Athlete	Club	Year	Position	Time
1	B Hussain	(Stockport H)	1997	1	2:19:00
2	G Booth	(Mizuno RC)	1997	2	2:19:02
3	T Duffy	(Bolton U) V40	1997	3	2:21:52
4	D Hale	(Army)	1997	4	2:22:09
5	B Hussain	(Stockport H)	1998	1	2:23:23
6	B Hussain	(Stockport H)	1996	1	2:23:32
7	A Arrand	(Army)	1998	2	2:23:36
8	R Deakin	(Staffs Moors)	2000	1	2:23:53
9	A Arrand	(Army)	2000	2	2:24:40
10	R Adams	(Portsmouth J)	2000	3	2:24:57
11	N Vengdasalam	(Liverpool P S)	2000	4	2:25:14
12	T O'Brien	(Morpeth H)	1999	1	2:25:18
13	C Cariss	(Bingley H)	2001	1	2:25:23
14	G Booth	(Mizuno RC)	1996	2	2:25:34
15	C Cariss	(Bingley H)	2000	5	2:25:50
16	A Shepherd	(Army)	1999	2	2:25:56
17	T Abyu	(Salford H)	2002	1	2:25:58
18	D Hale	(Rotherham H)	1998	3	2:26:30
19	T Duffy	(Bolton U) V40	2000	6	2:26:38
20	I Fisher	(Otley AC)	2001	2	2:26:45
21	A Wethrill	(Redhill RR) V40	2001	3	2:28:42
22	E Roberts	(Eryri H) V40	1999	3	2:29:26
23	W Birchall	(Stockport H) V40	2000	7	2:29:42
24	D Bilton	(City of Hull)	1998	4	2:30:17
25	M Higginbottom	(Salford H) V40	1998	5	2:30:40
26	S Edney	(Bideford) V40	2001	4	2:30:22
27	G Matthews	(E Cheshire H)	1997	5	2:30:26
28	M Higginbottom	(Salford H) V40	1998	6	2:30:40
29	G Hill	(Stockport H)	1997	6	2:30:48
30	S MacDonald	(Bingley H)	1996	3	2:30:53
31	S Littler	(Unattached)	2001	5	2:30:54
32	M Rush	(Bideford)	1999	4	2:31:12
33	A Doel	(Police AA)	1997	7	2:31:20
34	A Rowe	(Wesham RR) V40	1998	7	2:32:11
35	S Leverton	(N Derbys) V40	1997	8	2:32:24

36	G Matthews	(E Cheshire H)	1998	8	2:32:36
37	P Kinsella	(Cheltenham C)	1998	9	2:32:40
38	M Farran	(Longwood H)	1997	9	2:33:14
39	S MacDonald	(Bingley H)	2000	8	2:33:16
40	M Lane	(Police AA)	1997	10	2:33:24
41	K Butler	(Army)	1998	10	2:33:32
42	M Burke	(Unattached)	1997	11	2:33:35
43	P Bates	(Bury AC) V40	1997	12	2:33:55
44	P Aspinall	(Stockport H)	1997	13	2:34:25
45	G Matthews	(E Cheshire H)V40	2002	2	2:34:27
46	J Bell	(Elswick H) V50	1998	11	2:34:32
47	P Lowery	(Lancaster & M)	1998	12	2:34:47
48	T Leibrick	(Army)	1997	14	2:35:01
49	E Wilson	(Blackburn H) V40	1997	15	2:35:13
50	C Booth	(Unattached)	2001	6	2:35:13

RANKING OF TOP 20 WOMEN'S TIMES 1996 - 2002

1	S Crombie-Hick	(Mornington C)	2000	1	2:42:44
2	P Powell	(Blackburn H)	2002	1	2:46:28
3	K Charnock	(Wigan Ph)	2000	2	2:47:44
4	J Moorkite	(Invicta EK)V35	1996	1	2:48:50
5	K Wood	(Stockport H) V35	2001	1	2:51:26
6	C Hunter-Rowe	(Knavesmire)	1996	2	2:51:38
7	E McGuire	(Stockport H)	1999	1	2:52:34
8	S-J Heatley	(Sheffield AC)	1997	1	2:53:05
9	S Bretherick	(Preseli H)	2000	3	2:53:37
10	A Allan	(Tipton H)	2000	4	2:53:54
11	J Newton	(Stockport H)	1998	1	2:53:56
12	M Ellis	(Shaftesbury B)	2001	2	2:54:35
13	K Wood	(Glossopdale H)	1998	2	2:55:28
14	T Sloan	(Salford H)	1998	3	2:56:06
15	K Wood	(Man YMCA)	1996	3	2:56:17
16	T Sloan	(Salford H)	1997	2	2:57:13
17	E Robinson	(Border H) V45	1996	5	2:58:18
18	A Wade	(Ilkley H) V35	2000	5	2:58:24
19	H Barber	(Horsforth H)	2000	6	2:58:40
20	L Knights	(Police AA)	2001	3	2:59:30

RANKING OF WHEELCHAIR ATHLETES' TIMES

MEN - 1996-2002

1	David Holding	(BWRA)	1997	1	1:43:33
2	Jack McKenna	(BWRA)	1996	1	1:47:25
3	David Holding	(BWRA)	1998	1	1:47:42
4	Ivan Newman V45	(Saffron Str)	1998	2	1:51:13
5	Chris Madden	(BWRA)	1998	3	1:52:20
6	Anthony Booth	(Unatt)	1998	4	1:55:14
7	Anthony Booth	(Unatt)	1997	2	1:55:38
8	Kevin Papworth	(Unatt)	1998	5	1:58:40
9	Tushar Patel	(BWRA)	1997	3	1:59:12
10	Dean Cavanagh	(BWRA)	1997	4	2:00:25
11	Ian Thompson	(Manch. Kes)	1997	5	2:05:35
12	Ed Grazier	(BWRA)	1997	6	2:06:59
13	Tushar Patel	(Velocity)	2000	1	2:07:45
14	Anthony Booth	(Unatt)	1999	1	2:07:51
15	John Hanks	(BWRA)	1997	8	2:13:06
16	M Kettrick V40	(BWRA)	1997	10	2:13:08
17	B Cooper V45	(BWRA)	1997	11	2:13:34
18	Paul Hunt	(Birchfield H)	1999	2	2:15:20
19	James Hallam	(BWRA)	1999	3	2:15:54
20	James Hallam	(BWRA)	1998	6	2:20:18
21	Dean Cavanagh	(Unatt)	1996	2	2:21:25
22	Geoff Allen V50	(Stratford AC)	1997	12	2:22:22
23	A Kenneth V55	(Red Star AC)	1999	4	2:44:32
24	Dave Johnson	(Unatt)	1999	5	2:48:49
25	Dave Alcock V60	(Unatt)	1999	6	2:48:49
26	Anthony Holt	(Mansfield H)	1998	8	2:54:24
27	Ric Cassell V45	(BWRA)	1997	13	2:57:29
28	Anthony Holt	(Mansfield H)	1997	15	3:06:33
29	Ric Cassell V45	(BWRA)	1998	9	3:13:16
30	M Marten V40	(BWRA)	1998	10	3:13:17
31	Dave Alcock	(Unatt)	1996	4	3:14:40
32	Mike Marten	(Unatt)	1996	5	3:17:00
33	Jerry Forde V50	(Blarney)	2001	1	3:20:14
34	Dave Alcock	(Unatt)	1997	16	3:24:45
35	William Fox V50	(Unatt)	1997	17	3:33:40
36	Dave Alcock	(Unatt)	1998	11	3:51:34

37 William Fox V55	(Unatt)	1998	12	3:56:41
38 Mike Marten V40	(BWRA)	2001	2	3:59:03
39 Mike Marten V40	(BWRA)	1999	7	4:03:56
40 Alan Kenneth V55	(BWRA)	1998	14	4:33:16
41 Michael Marten	(BWRA)	2000	2	4:35:51

WOMEN - 1996-2002

1	Rachel Potter	(Belle Vue R)	2002	1	2:05:56
2	Tanni Grey	(Cardiff AAC)	1997	1	2:08:28
3	Nicola Jarvis	(BWRA)	1997	2	2:13:06
4	Deborah Brennan	(Birchfield H)	1998	1	2:54:23
5	Rachel Potter	(Belle Vue R)	1996	1	3:01:33
6	Karen Lewis	(Red Star AC)	1997	3	3:02:12
7	Tracy Gill	(BWRA)	1997	4	3:48:39
8	Jackie Wagstaff	(Radcliffe AC)	1997	5	4:15:00
9	Jackie Wagstaff	(Unatt)	1999	1	4:18:56

Chapter 33

The 33rd Manchester Marathon
Sunday 28th July 2002

THE COMMONWEALTH GAMES WOMEN'S MARATHON
CLEAN SWEEP FOR AUSTRALIA

The Commonwealth Games had started in 1930 as the British Empire Games, and the name had changed over the years to reflect the developing political situation. The venues and names were as follows:

Year	Venue	Name
1930	Hamilton, Canada	British Empire Games
1934	London, England	British Empire Games
1938	Sydney, Australia	British Empire Games
1950	Auckland, New Zealand	British Empire Games
1954	Vancouver, Canada	British Empire and Commonwealth Games
1958	Cardiff, Wales	British Empire and Commonwealth Games
1962	Perth, Australia	British Empire and Commonwealth Games
1966	Kingston, Jamaica	British Empire and Commonwealth Games
1970	Edinburgh, Scotland	British Commonwealth Games
1974	Christchurch, New Zealand	British Commonwealth Games
1978	Edmonton, Canada	Commonwealth Games
1982	Brisbane, Australia	Commonwealth Games
1986	Edinburgh, Scotland	Commonwealth Games
1990	Auckland, New Zealand	Commonwealth Games
1994	Victoria, Canada	Commonwealth Games
1998	Kuala Lumpur, Malaysia	Commonwealth Games

The scope and popularity of the Games had increased with time. In 1930, eleven countries were represented, contesting six sports, with over 400 competitors including more than 165 in athletics. By 1970, forty-two countries were competing in nine sports with 1,744 competitors including 545 in athletics. 2002 showed a grand total of 72 countries with 17 different sports providing around 4,000 competitors and almost a quarter of these, 973, athletes.

The women's marathon had only been introduced in 1986 in Edinburgh, Scotland, and has never attracted a massive field, the largest turnout having been in 1994, Victoria, Canada, when 16 females started. The complete statistics are shown below:

Games	Starters	Finishers
1986	12	11
1990	15	14
1994	16	15
1998	11	9

This year, 15 female athletes would toe the line. The consistency of the number is probably accounted for by the fact that in 1986 there were not as many female marathon runners as now, whereas today many full-time athletes are not as keen to run in championship races when they can have a pay day in a big city marathon.

The 2001 course required some minor adjustments. Instead of ending at the "Velodrome" the finish was in the newly-built stadium on the opposite side of Alan Turing Way. The stadium finish line would be used and the final 200 metres run in the stadium on the track. To ensure the correct distance a notable change included a loop around the outside of Manchester United Football ground at Old Trafford.

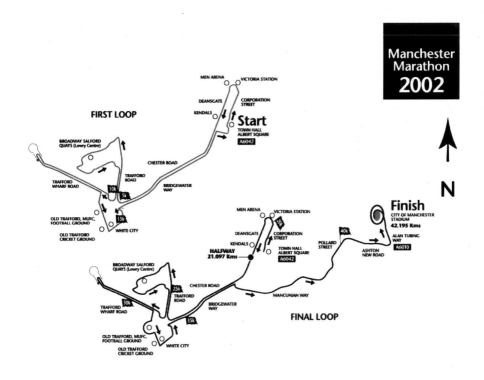

Route map for 2002 Commonwealth Games Marathon.

Every kilometre was marked and the intermediate timing at 5 Km intervals (plus half-way) was both manual and electronic. The blue line usually applied to the road indicating the optimum route and seen in high profile championships and big city marathons was absent.

Australians had dominated this race with three wins out of four: Lisa Martin, 1986, 2:26:07, and 1990, 2:25:28; and Heather Turland, 2:41:24 in 1998. The athlete preventing a clean sweep was Canada's Carole Rouillard in 1994 winning in 2:30:41.

On this occasion Australia had sent their best three, and England's trio was the full complement allowed. Lesotho also sent three. Namibia had two with single athletes from Guernsey, Malta, Northern Ireland and Kenya.

The fastest woman in the field was 35-year-old Esther Maina Wanjiru of Kenya. She had been the 10,000m Champion in Kuala Lumpur, 1998 and her best marathon time of 2:23:39 had been set in Osaka in 2000. On the downside, she had only managed a lowly 17th place in this year's Boston Marathon, 2:44:32, more than 23 minutes behind the winner, O'Kayo of Kenya, 2:20:43 She was living and was coached in Japan.

Next fastest was Australian Kerryn McCann, also 35-years-old, whose best was 2:25:59 achieved in London, 2000. She had qualified for her team by running 2:28:30 in Osaka, this year, which gave her the season's fastest time of all the runners.

The only other runner with a best time of below 2 hours 30 minutes was England's Marian Sutton. The 38-year-old had run 2:28:42 in the Chicago Marathon in 1999, a race which she had won in 1996 and 1997. Her selection had come about by virtue of her winning time of 2:31:33 in February's Austin, USA, Marathon.

Of the rest, the most promising was Elizabeth Mongudhi of Namibia. She had a best time of 2:36:44, but more to the point she was Commonwealth Games bronze medallist in the heat of Kuala Lumpur in 1998, recording 2:43:28.

The prestigious magazine *Athletics Weekly* predicted a win for Marian Sutton, with Kerryn McCann second and Teresa McCluskey of Northern Ireland, third. Thirty-three-year-old McCluskey, a Beechmount Harrier from Belfast, had a lifetime's best of 2:35:27 from the 2001 London Marathon, but had only managed 2:50:33 for second place in this year's Belfast Marathon.

The race start position was a break with tradition with the finish being in a different place. Here in Manchester it ended at the stadium and began in Albert Square in front of the town hall. A big crowd was there to see the race get under way promptly at 8:00 am with an electronic "beep." Cloudy and overcast, the weather was surprisingly warm for the time of morning, 21° C (70° F), but not warm enough to trouble the runners. Only a stiff, south westerly breeze could possibly affect performances.

After only two minutes of running, Penny Buckingham, representing Guernsey was off the back. The 35-year-old with a best of 2:58:57 was running her own pace.

At 2 kilometres, heading down Deansgate, the rest of the field were still together, but significantly Mongudhi in the blue vest of Namibia, Wanjiru in the red fronted vest of Kenya and McCann in the green and gold colours of Australia were running abreast at the head of the bunch. These three were making the pace and as they headed in to the wind along Chester Road then Bridgewater Way they began to draw away. Surprisingly, with the breeze in their faces, they raced side by side, toughing it out.

On Deansgate - one mile down, 25 to go

left to right – Galea (Malta); Mongudhi (112); Wanjiru (108); behind her McCluskey and in sunglasses Stanton; Hartigan; McCann (102); Robinson (105); Sutton (106); and Lechela (110). Gallagher is in the sunglasses behind Robinson. (Picture: Ron Hill.)

Turning right into Trafford Road and the 5 Km point, McCann on the left did not seem to mind running the long way round. Five kilometres was reached in 17:49 (2:30 pace) and already this trio had a substantial lead. Ominously, the next two through this point, 23 seconds down in 18:12, were the other two Australians, again running side by side, and not sharing the pace. Of this pair, 34-year-old Jackie Gallagher was an ex-triathlete with seven World Championship medals to her credit including gold in 1996 and silver in 1995, 1997 and 1999. She was also World Duathlon Champion in 1996 and 1999, and her only marathon was a highly respectable 2:35:46, for 11th place in Boston only months before. Gallagher's team-mate, 36-year-old Krishna Stanton had a best of 2:38:11 from the 2001 Sydney Marathon, her only race at this distance.

A further 11 seconds behind (18:23) was a group of seven including the British quartet of Sutton, McCluskey, Debbie Robinson and Bev Hartigan of England, plus Carol Galea of Malta, Beata Naigambo of Namibia, and Matsepo Angelina Sephooa of Lesotho. Mamokete Lechela (18:42) and Mpho Kholobeng (18:49), both 21-year-olds from Lesotho were now well behind and faced a lonely journey to the finish.

Shortly after 5 Km all three of the leaders had taken drinks then continued to run side by side, through Salford Quays to the 10 Km mark on Trafford Wharf Road, reached in 35:20 with the two Australians now 69 seconds in arrears but still running together. The third group began to break up just before 10 Km as Debbie Robinson moved ahead to pass in 36:49, 20 seconds down on the Australian pair. The 34-year-old mother from Sutton-in-Ashfield, Nottinghamshire had qualified for her England berth by winning the Dublin Marathon, October 2001 in 2:35:40. Now she was in sixth place ahead of her team-mate 35-year-old Bev Hartigan (36:52), the Birchfield Harrier. Hartigan had had an interesting career taking the bronze medal at 1,500 metres 12 years previously in the Auckland Commonwealth Games. She had won the Peli Products Millennium Tour of Tameside, six day double marathon and earned her place in England's team on the strength of a 2:36:02 finish for seventh place in the 2001 Berlin Marathon. Hartigan was running with McCluskey, and Sutton (36:56) was beginning to fade. The 39-year-old Maltese runner with a best of 2:36:53 was gone (37:21) as was Naigambo (37:21) and Sephooa (37:51).

As the runners passed Old Trafford, Manchester United's Football ground for the first time Mongudhi, the Namibian record holder at 5,000m, 10,000m and marathon began to loose contact. In this next 5 Km section, Robinson consolidated her sixth place. At 15 Km the times were: McCann and Wanjiru, 52:59; Mongudhi, 53:17; Stanton, 54:44; Gallagher, 54:45; Robinson, 54:53;

McCluskey, 55:37; Hartigan, 55:40 and Sutton, struggling further back in ninth place, 55:51. Sutton had withdrawn from the World Half-Marathon in May due to a calf injury.

At 16 Km (10 miles), Gallagher, was beginning to struggle a little too and coming back down Chester Road quickly lost ground to her team-mate Stanton. Both Australians, as with McCann, the joint leader, were wearing sunglasses, despite the absence of sun. Robinson put in her fastest 5 Km split over this section, 17:43, (2:30 pace) to overhaul Gallagher at 18 Km and move into fifth position.

At 20 Km, after passing through Albert Square, McCann and Wanjiru were still together, side by side, in 1:10:35, but the Australian had been testing the Kenyan since 17/18 Km. Mongudhi was almost $1^{1}/_{2}$ minutes behind in 1:12:02, just half a minute ahead of Stanton, 1:12:32 and Robinson, just four seconds after that, 1:12:36. Gallagher was still close, 1:12:44, with the next three McCluskey, 1:14:04, Hartigan, 1:14:42 and Sutton, 1:14:53. At the back of the field Buckingham, 1:21:03, had overtaken Kholobeng, 1:21:35, so was no longer last.

The temperature on this overcast morning had risen 1° C. Most used the drinks stations, some taking two, the first their own special one and the second, plain water mostly used to cool the body externally.

The runners reached the feed station outside Victoria Station just after 20 Km, then ran downhill to Hunts Bank, followed by a testing uphill to Deansgate and the half-way point near the imposing sandstone-built John Rylands Library. McCann and Wanjiru reached mid-way in 1:14:33, but Wanjiru seemed to be weakening. She had an unusual running style, with hardly any knee lift at all, but still could cover the ground at a good pace.

At 22 Km McCann started to leave Wanjiru, but the Kenyan came back. Gallagher passed Robinson, whose burst of speed in the fourth 5 Km had been a little too ambitious, and Stanton was rapidly closing on Mongudhi in third place. At 23 Km, just before the end of the Bridgewater Way, Stanton moved in to third place. At 24 Km, McCann opened up a gap of three to four metres and this began to grow, but not long after Wanjiru had fought her way back. She dived for her drink on the right and momentarily headed McCann. Also at 24 Km Gallagher passed the rapidly-tiring Mongudhi and moved in to fourth place. By 25 Km, Robinson had also passed Mongudhi to give her fifth place. Times at this point were: McCann, 1:28:55, Wanjiru, 1:28:57, Stanton, 1:31:08, Gallagher, 1:31:22, Robinson, 1:31:54, Mongudhi, 1:31:57, McCluskey, 1:33:29, Hartigan, 1:34:16, Sutton, 1:34:59.

Shortly after 25 Km on an uphill section, McCann moved away from

Wanjiru, who seemed to give up and allow the gap to open up very rapidly. Also around this point Stanton appeared to be going through a bad patch, showing signs of distress and not using the road, cutting the bends. On the other hand Gallagher, Australian Sports Woman of the Year in 1996, looked determined and aggressive in the chase. But Stanton recovered and ran this 5 Km split to 30 Km in 18:16 to Gallagher's 18:26. Times at 30 Km, on Trafford Wharf Road were: McCann, 1:46:18, Wanjiru, 1:47:51, Stanton, 1:49:25, Gallagher, 1:49:49, Robinson, 1:51:08, McCluskey, 1:52:32, Mongudhi, 1:52:48, Hartigan, 1:53:40, Sutton, 1:55:04, Galea with Naigambo, 1:55:45.

It was obvious that Wanjiru was in trouble, she was barely jogging. Emerging from the gloom of a tunnel alongside Old Trafford, Stanton passed the Kenyan. Five minutes later, now out of the medals, Wanjiru stopped, walked for a bit then jogged on. The Kenyan was passed by Gallagher just after 32 Km, then along Bridgewater Way at around 34 Km she was overtaken by Robinson.

Now, heading for home, the times at 35 Km were: McCann, now well ahead, 2:04:06, Stanton, 2:07:57, Gallagher, 2:08:42, Robinson, 2:10:47, Wanjiru, 2:11:01, McCluskey, 2:11:55, Hartigan, 2:13:12, Mongudhi, 2:14:21, Sutton, 2:15:33, Naigambo, 2:16:03 and Galea 2:16:05. Wanjiru's 5 Km split between 30 and 35 Km was a desperate 23:09 compared with McCann's 17:48, and somewhere in the next 5 Km she dropped out. Between 30 and 35 Km Lesotho's Mamokete Lechela dropped out whilst in 14th position.

From 35 Km McCann continued to increase her lead, the regular 2 hours 40 minutes Sunday runs and two months training in London with Ireland's Sonia O'Sullivan obviously had prepared her well and she looked to be running easily right to the end. It was a great run, leading from start to finish, and her time of 2:30:05 put her four minutes and 47 seconds ahead of the second athlete. This was her first victory in sixteen marathons.

Nothing could stop a clean sweep for the Australians, Stanton herself running away from the rest in second place. The strain was showing on her face as she entered the stadium; but at the finish she was overjoyed with her silver medal and a personal best of 2:34:52, improving by 3:19 on her only other marathon.

With Jackie Gallagher taking the bronze medal it meant that of the fifteen medals on offer since the women's marathon started in 1986, eight had been won by Australians including four golds out of five.

The Australian women were justly proud to represent their country so well.

England's trio all finished despite being below their best. It appeared

Debbie Robinson's hope of splitting the Australians disappeared at around half-way when she suffered cramp in her calf. The English contingent was split by the other Briton, Teresa McCluskey who was fifth less than a minute behind Robinson.

Results:

1	Kerryn McCann	Australia	2:30:05
2	Krishna Stanton	Australia	2:34:52 **PB**
3	Jackie Gallagher	Australia	2:36:37
4	Debbie Robinson	England	2:39:42
5	Teresa McCluskey	North. Ireland	2:40:29 **SB**
6	Beverley Hartigan	England	2:41:27
7	Carol Galea	Malta	2:45:48
8	Marian Sutton	England	2:45:55
9	Beata Naigambo	Namibia	2:47:22 **SB**
10	Elizabeth Mongudhi	Namibia	2:49:19
11	Matsepo A Sephooa	Lesotho	2:52:06
12	Penny Buckingham	Guernsey	2:58:40 **PB & NR**
13	Mpho Kholobeng	Lesotho	3:16:36 **SB**

Did not finish:

Esther Maina Wanjiru (Kenya); Mamokete Lechela (Lesotho).

Only Krishna Stanton and Penny Buckingham ran personal bests and on average the runners were four minutes 56 seconds slower than their bests.

Kerryn McCann's next marathon was New York where she finished seventh in 2:27:51. Her husband, Greg, had represented Australia at surfing. Their son Bento was five and he usually got mum's medal, but McCann said, "He can read now and his response will be 'where's my name?' "

Krishna Stanton began her international career a decade before when she was eliminated in the heats of the 3,000m at the 1992 Olympic Games. About selection she reflected, "The selectors had faith in us. We were grateful to be given the opportunity as we were the only ones to run to form." Stanton confessed to training only 90 Km a week.

Jackie Gallagher holds a Masters degree in cardiac rehabilitation and exercise physiology from the Eastern University of Illinois. She commented, "I was beaten by two mothers, and have done alright for an old girl."

Chapter 34

The 34th Manchester Marathon
Sunday 28th July 2002

THE COMMONWEALTH GAMES MEN'S MARATHON
NAALI LEAVES THEM ALL BEHIND

Fifty minutes after the women had started their 2002 Commonwealth Marathon race, twenty-three men were on the start line for this the 17th men's Commonwealth contest at this distance. The original schedule had indicated an 8:20am start, but this was changed to 8:50am, we understand for the benefit of Australian television.

England had had an excellent record in the '60s and '70s, but after that the Australians and Africans dominated as shown by the list of winners:

1930 Duncan McLeod Wright	Scotland	2:43:43
1934 Harold Webster	Canada	2:40:36
1938 Johannes Coleman	South Africa	2:30:49.8
1950 Jack Holden	England	2:32:57
1954 Joseph McGhee	Scotland	2:39:36
1958 David Power	Australia	2:22:45.6
1962 Brian Kilby	England	2:21:17
1966 Jim Alder	Scotland	2:22:07.8
1970 Ron Hill	England	2:09:28
1974 Ian Thompson	England	2:09:12
1978 Gidamis Shahanga	Tanzania	2:15:39.8
1982 Rob de Castella	Australia	2:09:18
1986 Rob de Castella	Australia	2:10:15
1990 Douglas Wakiihuri	Kenya	2:10:27
1994 Steve Moneghetti	Australia	2:11:49
1998 Thabiso Moqhali	Lesotho	2:19:15.

On this occasion England's current best marathon runners had not made themselves available, though a full complement of three had been selected. Thirty-three-year-old Morpeth Harrier Mark Hudspith was the fastest with a personal best of 2:11:58 set in the 1995 London Marathon. He qualified by running 2:13:13 in the 2001 London Marathon. Next fastest was 34-year-old Dominic Bannister, Shaftesbury Barnet Athletic Club, the 1998 National

Cross-Country Champion. His best, 2:14:39, was set in his debut, the 2000 Hamburg Marathon, and he got in the team with his 2002 season's best of 2:16:18 in the Vigarano Marathon, Italy. England's final representative was 37-year-old Stuart Hall, Tipton Harriers. He qualified with a personal best of 2:16:23 in the Seville Marathon, Spain, run in February 2002. Why the London Marathon had not been the official trial is a mystery.

The only other Briton in the race was Scotland's Simon Pride. The 35-year-old, a member of the Metro Aberdeen Club, was the UK 100 Km record holder at 6:24:05, set when winning the 1999 World 100 Km Championships in Chavagnes, France. His best marathon time was set in the 2001 London Marathon, 2:16:27, and he had won the Scottish Trial race in Moray, September 2001, in 2:28:34 which guaranteed his place. Being an ultra-runner, a winning 2:22:21 in Belfast on May Day 2002 should not have taken anything out of him.

The outstanding favourite for the men was the Kenyan Eric Wainaina. The 28-year-old had set his best of 2:08:43 in February 2002, winning the Tokyo Marathon in Japan where he is based. He was proven championship material as shown by his Olympic medals: bronze in Atlanta, 1996, 2:12:44, and silver in Sydney, 2000, 2:10:31.

Next quickest in terms of lifetime bests was the Namibian national record holder Luketz Swartbooi. He had run 2:09:08 in Boston in 1994, but at age 36 and with 48th place in the Sydney Olympics 2000, 2:22:55, and 28th place in the Edmonton World Championships, 2001, 2:25:40, he was perhaps past his best.

A third athlete with a sub-2:10 clocking was Tanzania's Francis Robert Naali. His best was 2:09:33 set in Berlin in 1996, and we know nothing of his marathon career after that, though he was a regular on the road running circuit at shorter distances. He was one of four brothers, two of them marathon runners. One, Simon, had finished third in the 1990 Commonwealth Games in Auckland, New Zealand in 2:10:38, and only 11 seconds behind the winner. Sadly he died after being hit by a car whilst out training in 1994. The other brother Thomas was famous for his run in the 1992 London Marathon. Both he and Francis had been signed up as "rabbits," pace-makers, with the task of taking the field through to the half-way distance in a good time; which they did. Francis, then 20, slowed and eventually came home in 2:36:13, but Thomas, the elder by three years, kept going to pick up third place with 2:10:18!

The Australians had sent their full complement of three, two of whom were 2:10 men. Lee Troop had graduated from 5,000m and 10,000m on the track to record a best of 2:10:04 for eighth place in Rotterdam, 2001. Shaun Creighton's best was 2:10:22 set when he placed tenth in the 1997 Berlin Marathon, and the 35-year-old had run a 2:11:54 in October of 2001 finishing sixth in Chicago. The third Australian did not seem to be in the same class as his best was 2:15:06, over three minutes behind Creighton in the 2001 Chicago race, for 15th place.

Amazingly the Kenyans had only two at the start. Wainaina was an obvious choice, but the second athlete Joshua Chelanga was not ranked in the World top 50 for 2001, whereas 18 other Kenyans were. Nevertheless his best was still a useful 2:10:29 set in his debut marathon, Boston 2001, where he took third place. His seasons best was again set in Boston where he finished 11th in 2:12:40, with six Kenyans ahead of him including the winner Rodgers Rop, 2:09:02.

The reigning Commonwealth Champion could not be discounted. Lesotho's Paul Thabiso Moqhali had a best of 2:10:55 set when finishing seventh in the 1992 London Marathon paced by the Naali brothers, but he had taken Commonwealth gold in Kuala Lumpur with 2:19:15. However, he too had not fared well in the Edmonton World Championships finishing two places behind Swartbooi in 30th in 2:25:44. His season's best time was quoted on the start list as 2:18:27.

The only other man with a 2:10 best was 23-year-old Salaho Ngadi of Tanzania who was recorded on the start list as having a lifetime's best of 2:10:36 and a season's best of 2:16:56.

Australia, England, Lesotho and New Zealand had three starters, Kenya, South Africa and Tanzania had two, with one apiece from Malawi, Namibia, Norfolk Island, Scotland and St Vincent and the Grenadines.

At 8:50 precisely, there was an audible "beep," but only one athlete, No 7, the Kenyan, Chelanga, ran forward. For some reason it was a false start! Chelanga returned to the line and at 8:50 and 27 seconds a second "beep" sounded and the race commenced. It appeared to be a relaxed start, but after a couple of minutes one man was trailing. Twenty-four-year-old James Donaldson from the tiny Norfolk Island in the Pacific Ocean, over two hours by air from Brisbane in Australia, had a stated best of 3:26:00. To make things worse he had been suffering from a torn calf muscle for the last 2½ months, and special arrangements had had to be made to escort him along the Mancunian Way at the end of his race, when it had been opened to traffic. He would run the race entirely alone.

It was still overcast as the large group made the right turn off Bridgewater

Way at the 5 Km point. Only two seconds covered a phalanx of 18 runners, as Ngadi in the pale blue vest of Tanzania led in 15:41. Lebohang Mahloane of Lesotho whose best was 2:30:26, Hall, Pride, and Mpesela Ntlotsoeu, also of Lesotho with a best of 2:36:44, had just been dropped.

Ngadi continued to hold his place at the head of the group as they charged round the Salford Quays area to reach 10 km in 31:10 with again just a couple of seconds covering 17 athletes. The second 5 Km had taken 15:29 and the pace was 2:11/2:12 for the full distance. Bannister was now off the back in 18th position, with Hall 19th and Pride 21st. Mark Hudspith was right up there for England, but at around 12 Km he began to experience breathing problems, shortness of breath, and his arms and legs felt so tired his pace dropped dramatically and he had to abandon the race. He was taken to Manchester Royal Infirmary and kept in over night. Tests had not solved the mystery, but had revealed no heart disease.

As the group circled Manchester United Football Club and passed Old Trafford cricket ground the tempo increased ever so slightly again with a 15:21, 5 Km split to 15 Km, reached in 46:31. Ngadi was still at the head of the proceedings with Chelanga, Wainaina, and Swartbooi more or less alongside and followed closely by the rest of the bunch including the 27-year-old South African Josaia Bembe in the dark green vest of his country. His best of 2:11:49 was set in 2001. Moqhali was there, Troop, and in the black and white vest of New Zealand, 29-year-old Jonathan Wyatt who was running at a pace much faster than his previous best of 2:14:55 set in Berlin 2001. At the rear of the group was Letherby and Malawi's 30-year-old Rodwell Kamwendo, who had a reported personal best of 2:17:18, and who had finished 13th in the Games 10,000m only 36 hours earlier, setting a national record of 29:11.13. The next four at 15 Km were Joseph Maqala, South Africa, 46:44, ten seconds down on Kamwendo, Creighton, 46:44, New Zealand's 32-year-old Phil Costley, best time of 2:13:36, 46:53 and Pamenos Ballantyne in the yellow vest of St Vincent and the Grenadines, 47:06. Twenty-eight-year-old Ballantyne was an experienced marathoner who had competed in the Olympics and World Championships and had a best of 2:15:37. Bannister was now 16th, 47:10, Craig Kirkwood, the fastest of the New Zealanders at age 27, with 2:13:18, 47:15, Hall was 18th, 48:15 and Pride 19th in 48:38.

From 15 Km the pace was cranked up even further. First the current title-holder, Lesotho's Moqhali dropped behind at 17 Km leaving the group now numbering ten. At 18 Km Kamwendo and Wyatt began to drop. Shortly afterwards all the athletes took sponges, and refreshed, Wyatt fought his way back. Ngadi and Chelanga led, as they received encouragement from the city centre crowds. Troop, Letherby and Wyatt fell back, but by 19 Km and passing through Albert Square these three antipodeans were back with the leaders. On Cross Street at around 19¹/₂ Km the tightly-knit bunch passed over two unmarked anti-speed bumps and unsighted Naali tripped and fell. He rolled over on his back and was up quickly to rejoin the vanguard by 20 Km. That 5 Km segment had taken 15:12, and at 20 Km four seconds covered the nine leaders headed by Swartbooi, Chelanga and Bembe in 61:44. Bannister had moved up to 15th, 63:11, with Hall 18th, 64:33 and Pride 19th, 65:19.

Drinks station just after 20 Km
left to right – Naali (22); Bembe (17); Swartbooi (12); and Chelanga (7).
(Picture: Ron Hill.)

At the feed station outside Victoria Station, just after 20 Km, Ngadi abruptly quit the race. Had he been acting as pace-maker for his compatriot Naali? We do not know. Up on to Deansgate, and at the half-way point the five Africans were given a time of 65:09, one second ahead of Wyatt, Troop and Letherby who had been dropped and again had found their way back. Someone would have to run a "negative split" to take Ian Thompson's Games Record of 2:09:12 set 28 years previously. Just after half-way the New Zealander Craig Kirkwood dropped out.

These leading eight athletes now stayed together along Chester Road, Bridgewater Way and right turn down to Trafford Road with Naali now bravely leading into the wind. Eight hit 25 Km in 77:37/38 with a 5 Km split of 15:52.

Around the Salford Quays a lot began to happen. At 27 Km the South African, Bembe was dropped and Troop seemed to be struggling at the back of the remaining seven. All the athletes took sponges again, but at 28 Km, with Naali still forcing the pace, Troop was gone. At 29 Km, Wyatt had to let go and shortly after that Letherby too. In that last 10 Km the leading group of eight had been whittled down to four.

Passing 30 Km, Swartbooi was leading, 93:06 with Chelanga, Naali and Wainaina, 93:07, on his heels. This 5 Km split had been 15:28. Following them were Letherby, 93:13, Wyatt, 93:14, and Troop, 93:21. Bannister remained 13th, 96:31, Hall, 98:09 had overtaken Moqhali to move into 15th, whilst Pride, 1:40:25, was still 17th. The sun had just come out.

Circling Manchester United for the second time and back on to Bridgewater Way, the four leaders stayed together and passed 35 Km in 1:49:03/04. Wainaina had sat in for most of the later part of the race and must now have been a danger. That 5 Km split of 15:56 meant the pace was slowing and Ian Thompson's record was safe. Troop made an effort and moved in to fifth place, 1:49:29 with Letherby sixth, 1:49:36 and Wyatt, seventh, 1:49:39.

At almost exactly 36 Km Naali put in a burst. Swartbooi was dropped, but the two Kenyans slotted in behind Naali. But only momentarily, as Naali began to draw away. After a sharp right turn on to the Mancunian Way, the Tanzanian surged again. By 37 Km, Chelanga was beginning to pull away from Wainaina. But from 38 Km onwards, Naali was looking back anxiously and appeared to be straining. The athletes were assigned to the fast lane of the elevated section of the traffic-free Mancunian Way and here Naali's progress continued apace. His lead had grown to 20 seconds by 40 Km, 2:04:43 to 2:05:03, with Wainaina third, 2:05:24, Swartbooi, fourth, 2:05:55, Letherby closing rapidly fifth, 2:06:07, and Wyatt, 2:06:41, now up to sixth due to Troop struggling and falling away.

Naali was now in charge and over the last 2.195 Km increased his lead by 26 seconds. He entered the stadium to the applause of more than 30,000 spectators and crossed the line in 2:11:58. Unfortunately, there was no tape nor a finishing clock, and Naali continued around the track dodging the hurdles set out for the men's 400m semi-finals. He was angry when he reached the finish line again to see Chelanga, who had not made the same mistake, standing there! Eventually he calmed down saying that he was very happy with his first marathon victory. The Kenyan had taken silver in 2:12:44. Shortly after 41 Km, the little-fancied Letherby had passed Swartbooi to move in to fourth place. He continued his charge, running at exactly the same pace as the winner, and on entering the stadium saw Wainaina. The Kenyan was shattered and had no response when Letherby sprinted past him with only 60 metres to go, to take bronze in a personal best time of 2:13:23. Wainaina was fourth, 2:13:27, Swartbooi, fifth 2:13:40, and Wyatt, the least favoured of the New Zealanders, sixth, 2:14:20, a lifetime's best.

England's Bannister and Hall were rewarded for their perseverance with 10th and 12th places respectively while Scotland's Pride came home 16th in 2:23:56.

James Donaldson did have a lonely journey, ".. .. .. but it was great out there," he said after receiving a standing ovation. "It was really inspiring out there. The support was first class." From a population of 1,800, Norfolk Island sent a team of 13 including lawn bowlers, triathletes and a hammer thrower who was ninth and last. Donaldson's time was slowest ever recorded Marathon in a Commonwealth Games.

Results:

1	Francis Naali	Tanzania	2:11:58	
2	Joshua Chelanga	Kenya	2:12:44	
3	Andrew Letherby	Australia	2:13:23	**PB**
4	Eric Wainaina	Kenya	2:13:27	
5	Luketz Swartbooi	Namibia	2:13:40	
6	Jonathan Wyatt	New Zealand	2:14:20	**PB**
7	Lee Troop	Australia	2:16:44	
8	Josaia Bembe	South Africa	2:18:16	**SB**
9	Shaun Creighton	Australia	2:18:19	
10	Dominic Bannister	England	2:19:31	
11	Pamenos Ballantyne	St Vincent	2:19:36	
12	Stuart Hall	England	2:19:53	
13	Rodwell Kamwendo	Malawi	2:20:10	
14	Joseph Maqala	South Africa	2:21:03	
15	Paul Moqhali	Lesotho	2:23:10	
16	Simon Pride	Scotland	2:23:56	
17	Phil Costley	New Zealand	2:28:16	
18	Mpesela Ntlotsoeu	Lesotho	2:29:21	**PB**
19	James Donaldson	Norfolk Island	3:30:20	

Did not finish: Mark Hudspith (England); Salaho Ngadi (Tanzania); Craig

Kirkwood (New Zealand); Lebohang Mahloane (Lesotho).

Three men set personal bests - Letherby by 1:43, Wyatt by 0:35 and Ntlotsoeu by 7:23. On average the men ran four minutes 59 seconds slower than their best.

Like McCann in the women's race this was Naali's first marathon victory. He said, "It was a difficult race, but it went well for me."

From being fourth in the 1999 World Cross-Country Championships, Joshua Chelanga has moved up distance with much success winning the Lisbon Half-Marathon 2002 in 61:01.

Andrew Letherby's mother represented Australia on the road and country in the early 1980s, her best probably being in the World Cup Marathon in Hiroshima in 1985 when she was 38th, 2:48:43. Letherby who was currently studying in America, represented his country in the 2000 World Half-Marathon in Veracruz, Mexico placing 37th in 67:38. His 2:15:06 in Chicago was achieved by running 125 miles a week "including $2^1/_2$ hours on a Sunday."

Jonathan Wyatt stayed in Europe and went on to win the World Mountain Running Trophy in Innsbruck, Austria in September. The uphill only event suited him as he had had three wins in the Sky Tower Vertical Challenge, a race up the Sky Tower in Auckland.

Chapter 35

The 35th Manchester Marathon
Sunday 13th October 2002

FIRST TIMERS WIN BY MILES

The open Manchester Marathon, the seventh in the Manchester Leisure series reverted to the 2000 course from Heaton Park to Wythenshawe Park. Despite the possible inspiration of the recent Commonwealth Games, the entries were down.

In the men's field two regulars were entered: Gary Matthews, the 42-year-old Club Captain of East Cheshire Harriers had competed in all bar the 2000 race consistently around the 2:30 mark. His Manchester best was 2:30:26 for fourth place in 1996. Peter Bates, Bury Athletic Club, had run all of the first four of this series and had a best of 2:33:55 from the 1997 race. He held the course record at 2:33:40 for the off-road White Peak Marathon set in 1994.

For the first time in the history of Manchester Marathons there was an Ethiopian entrant. Twenty-four-year old Tomas Abyu had arrived from Arrusi in central Ethiopia, seeking political asylum in 1999. He was now a member of Salford Harriers but had been racing in Ethiopia from the age of 15. Before he left his home country he had done some training with Gezahegne Abera, the Sydney Olympic marathon champion, though he himself had not attempted the distance until now.

The ladies race had an international cross-country runner who was head and shoulders above the rest. Pauline Powell, a 29-year-old Burnley shopkeeper, and a member of Blackburn Harriers, had begun running as a ten-year-old and, coached by her father, had made steady progress. She excelled at cross-country and had three England vests. On the road she had 34 minutes 10 Km speed and had clocked 77:48 for a half-marathon (Great North Run 2001). Training weeks of 70-80 miles, including runs of 20 miles, led her to expect a time of around 2:48.

The weather was ideal for marathon running, windless and cool.

The start was not without a mishap as one of the buses ferrying competitors from the finish area in Wythenshawe got lost. This led to some delay, not good for the runners' warm-up routines, and the race finally got under way at 9:30, 30 minutes late.

Colin Patton, an Army Physical Training Instructor, led a large group through the opening three miles of 5:57, 5:22, and 5:57, a modest pace, before the red-vested Abyu took control. Successive miles of 5:33 and 5:30 gave him a lead of 100 yards at the 5 mile point (28:09). He continued to increase that lead, passing 10 miles in 56:13, 15 in 83:22 and 20 in 1:51:09 to eventually win by almost 8 1/2 minutes, and claim the £750 prize. His 2:25:59 was the slowest winning time of this Manchester Leisure series, but a club-mate said, "Tomas has been working up to 70 hours a week at Rathbone's bakery and hadn't been able to train as much as he wanted."

Patton remained in second place until 21 miles, where he was passed by Gary Matthews, and lost $2^{1}/_{2}$ minutes over the last 5 miles, but still hung on to third place.

In the ladies race Pauline Powell's race plan was to concentrate on keeping a steady pace and not go too fast in the early miles. It was so cold, she ran in gloves. The start delay had unsettled her somewhat, as also did the fact that her sports drinks, in specially marked bottles, put round the course by her family early in the morning were not there when she reached the feed station tables. She had to rely on water alone, and ran with a group of four or five men until half-way, when, feeling the pace slowing, she struck out on her own. "I just kept up the pace, tired a bit and found the last two miles hard, but not as hard as I expected." She came 19th overall with a time of 2:46:58, winning £500. She was pleased with the time, which could have been even faster had she had competition in the later miles.

Helen Fines from the Forest of Dean club was second $14^{1}/_{2}$ minutes behind, but slashing 90 minutes off her personal best with 3:02:59, just one second ahead of Jeanette Coleman of Chorley Harriers. Sue Cariss, mother of the 2001 men's winner Chris, set a personal best of 3:04:28 to take fourth place.

Tomas Abyu   *Pauline Powell*
(Pictures: Steve Bateson – www.runningpix.co.uk)

In the wheelchair event the sole competitor, Rachel Potter of Belle Vue Racers returned to the race for the first time in six years. In 1996 she recorded 3:01:23; this year the 27-year-old from New Moston, Manchester raced to a lifetime's best of 2:05:56.

Rachel Potter

Results:

1	Tomas Abyu	(Salford H)		2:25:58
2	Gary Matthews	(E Cheshire)	V40	2:34:27
3	Colin Patton	(ARMY)		2:36:58
4	Jonathan Crook	(ARMY)		2:37:45
5	David Warner	(ARMY)		2:38:09
6	Mark Thompson	(ARMY)	V40	2:39:12
7	John Duffy	(Shettleston)		2:39:50
8	Stuart Shaw	(Burnden RR)	V45	2:40:30
9	Peter Bates	(Bury AC)	V45	2:42:06
10	John Hartley	(Clayton-le-Moors)	V45	2:42:48

11 S McMyler (Salford) V40 2:42:51; 12 R Whitehall (Goodyear RC) 2:43:19; 13 C Howard (ASPT) 2:44:09; 14 B Wells (RRC) V55 2:45:11; 15 C

Areba (Unatt) 2:45:30; 16 A Brown (Salford) 2:45:36; 17 R Bamsey (Neath) V45 2:45:42; 18 S Almond (Stockport) 2:46:09; 19 P Powell (Blackburn H) 2:46:28; 20 A Carroll (E Cheshire) V55 2:47:13; 21 G Ramsay (Barnsley) 2:47:32; 22 P Speake (Bideford) 2:47:34; 23 D Anderson (Unatt) 2:47:58; 24 M Clapp (Holme Pierpoint) 2:49:10; 25 M Kuronen (E Cheshire) V40 2:49:35; 26 S Allen (Colchester H) 2:49:53; 27 A Smith (Darwen) 2:49:54; 28 S Davis (ARMY) 2:50:05; 29 B Nolan (Unatt) 2:50:31; 30 S Stennett (Unatt) V40 2:50:44; 31 L Chownsmith (Unatt) 2:51:31; 32 T Courage (ARMY) 2:53:45; 33 D Breen (Giffnock N) 2:54:04; 34 B Greaves (Oldham & Royton) V45 2:54:06; 35 H Jones (Unatt) 2:54:29; 36 D Wright (Colchester H) V40 2:55:01; 37 D Goss (Unatt) V40 2:55:24; 38 K Breen (Civil Service) V45 2:55:26; 39 J Littler (Unatt) 2:55:43; 40 M Platt (Macclesfield) V45 2:55:45; 41 P Mallison (Unatt) 2:56:11; 42 A Massey (Unatt) V40 2:56:27; 43 M Bates (Wesham) V45 2:57:11; 44 M Flatley (Middleton) 2:57:24; 45 M Grath (Knavesmire) V50 2:57:37; 46 G Poulton (Trafford) 2:58:14; 47 R Hunt (ARMY) 2:58:19; 48 J Barry (Boalloy) V50 2:58:32; 49 J Bebbington (Liverpool RR) V50 2:58:34;

50 R Bowd (Tri UK) 2:58:52; 51 P Sinnott (Northern Vets) V45 2:59:33; 52 N McCallum (ARMY) 2:59:07; 53 S Moseley (Unatt) 2:59:10; 54 C Walker (Unatt) V40 2:59:15; 55 J Kelly (Unatt) 2:59:32; 56 D Murphy (Unatt) 2:59:33; 57 J Bradshaw (Unatt) 2:59:53; 58 G Woolmington (Unatt) 2:59:57; 59 K Child (Tamar) 3:01:23; 60 G Carracher (Carnethy Hill RC) V40 3:01:32; 61 S Eggleton (NICSAC) 3:01:43; 62 M Gold (ARMY) 3:01:47; 63 J Pares (Road Runners Club) 3:01:56; 64 C Nightingale (Wigan Phoenix) 3:02:07; 65 D Bell (ARMY) 3:02:28; 66 M McCauley (Civil Service AA) V45 3:02:39; 67 C Donoghue (ARMY) 3:02:41; 68 F Martin (Unatt) V45 3:02:52; 69 B Macfadyen (Macclesfield H) V45 3:02:53; 70 C Carroll (Unatt) 3:02:55; 71 Helen Fines F (Forest of Dean) 3:02:59; 72 Jeanette Coleman (Chorley H) F45 3:03:00; 73 K Hickman (ARMY) 3:03:17; 74 D Brisco (ARMY) V45 3:03:52; 75 A Clark (ARMY) 3:03:57; 76 C Smith (ARMY) 3:04:14; 77 R Byers (Trafford AC) 3:04:27; 78 V Booth (Trafford AC) 3:04:27; 79 Sue Cariss (Bingley H) F50 3:04:28; 80 J Coulomb (Unatt) 3:04:29; 81 W Lord (Unatt) 3:05:38; 82 T Hurn (Darwen Dashers) V45 3:05:54; 83 J Smithson (Accrington RR) V50 3:06:07; 84 D Roberts (Bridgnorth AC) 3:06:55; 85 ??? (Unatt) 3:07:02; 86 C Webb (Chris Lane) V45 3:07:13; 87 B Cumpsty (Unatt) 3:07:37; 88 A Turnbull (Wigan Phoenix) V50 3:07:50; 89 M Humphreys (Unatt) V45 3:07:53; 90 M Elson (Unatt) 3:08:02; 91 J Colley (ARMY) 3:08:33; 92 G Best (ARMY) 3:08:50; 93 A Collodel (Unatt) V45 3:09:05; 94 P Crookall (Northern Vets) V45 3:09:07; 95 D Durnin (Spectrum Striders) V45 3:09:09; 96 D Lord (Clayton-le-Moors) V45 3:09:15; 97 A Ivory (Unatt) V45 3:09:18; 98 C Gell (Unatt) 3:09:37; 99 G Chesters (Middleton H&AC) V45 3:09:54; 100 B Penhale (Manchester Tri) V45 3:09:58. 639 finished.

V40 G Matthews   (E Cheshire)   2:34:27
V50 M Grath   (Knavesmire)   2:57:37
V60 E Sidebottom   (Strathern H)   3:23:37

Women:

1	Pauline Powell	(Blackburn H)		2:46:28
2	Helen Fines	(Forest of Dean)		3:02:59
3	Jeanette Coleman	(Chorley H)	V45	3:03:00

4 S Cariss (Bingley H) V50 3:04:28; 5 A Sedman (Unatt) V35 3:10:36; 6 L Clarkson (Darwen Dashers) 3:11:56; 7 E Sowter (Swaledale RRC) V40 3:17:17; 8 J Murray (Unatt) 3:22:25; 9 A Tucker (Quaker RC) 3:25:18; 10 H Walker (Unatt – Civil Service) V45 3:27:04.

<u>Army Championships</u>
Men: Colin Patton 2:36:58   Women: Sarah B-Walker 3:49:11

<u>Civil Service Championships</u>
Men: Stan Stennett (Unatt) 2:50:44   Women: Hilary Walker 3:27:04

Wheelchair
1   Rachel Potter   (Belle Vue R)   2:05:56

Abyu was unpressed when he won at Leeds in 2:24:54 in May 2003 with 13^1/$_2$ minutes spare. In June he won the Sheffield Marathon in 2:27:42, a mile (5 minutes) clear. When the Tour of Tameside was revived in July 2003 he was the 21st Tour Champion.

Powell placed 11th and second Briton in the 2003 Cinque Mulini in Italy. She now hopes to gain further international honours and achieve the Olympic qualifying time (2:35) in the 2004 London Marathon.

The number of finishers was 639, down on all of the previous years in this last series, see page 245.

This was the end of marathons in Manchester for the present time.

APPENDIX I
MANCHESTER MARATHON WINNERS

Year	Winner	Club	Time
1908	Frederick T Lord	(Wibsey Park H)	1:50:23 *
1909	James Roberts	(Sefton H)	2:40:28.8
1923	Ernie Leatherland	(Polytechnic H)	2:51:25
5/1924	Ernie Leatherland	(Polytechnic H)	2:48:43.8
8/1924	D McL Wright	(Shettleston H)	2:35:25 * *
8/1924	Samuel Ferris	(Royal Air Force)	2:47:44 * *
1925	D McL Wright	(Shettleston H)	2:44:07.8
1926	Harold Wood	(Makerfield H)	2:43:51.8
1927	Samuel Ferris	(RAF Uxbridge)	2:48:46.4
1928	Harold Wood	(Makerfield H)	2:39:29.2
1931	Harold Wood	(Makerfield H)	2:43:18.4
1932	Harold Wood	(Makerfield H)	2:36:12
1933	A C Chamberlain	(Sheffield U)	2:56:37
1934	Harold Wood	(Makerfield H)	2:56:11
1935	George P Birchall	(Warrington AC)	3:01:20
1936	Harold Wood	(Makerfield H)	2:40:02
1947	John A Henning	(Duncairn N)	2:45:37
1969	Ron Hill	(Bolton U H)	2:13:42
1970	Akio Usami	(JAPAN)	2:13:45
1971	Ron Hill	(Bolton U H)	2:12:39
1972	Lutz Philipp	(W GERMANY)	2:12:50
1973	Eckhard Lesse	(GDR)	2:12:24
1981	Steve Kenyon	(Salford H)	2:11:54
1982	Kevin R Best	(Bolton U)	2:16:22
1983	James Ashworth	(Bingley H)	2:15:39
1984	Ian Thompson	(Luton U)	2:16:08
1985	Harold Clague	(St Helens AC)	2:19:31
1996	Bashir Hussain	(Stockport H)	2:23:32
1997	Bashir Hussain	(Stockport H)	2:19:00
1998	Bashir Hussain	(Stockport H)	2:23:23
1999	Tony O'Brien	(Morpeth H)	2:25:18
2000	Rob Deakin	(Staffs Moors.)	2:23:53
2001	Chris Cariss	(Bingley H)	2:25:23
2002	Tomas Abyu	(Salford H)	2:25:58
Commonwealth Games			
2002	Francis Naali	(TANZANIA)	2:11:58

Note:

* The 1908 trial was over 19 miles.

* * Ferris was the first to take the full route. In fact he ran further, as he was mis-directed. Wright ran short. (See Chapter 5.)

1981	Katie Fitzgibbon	(London Oly.)	3:03:24
1982	Leslie Watson	(London Oly.)	2:45:07
1983	Leslie Watson	(London Oly.)	2:50:56
1984	Libby Pfeiffer	(Barnet Ladies)	2:46:54
1985	Lorna Irving	(Border H)	2:44:13
1996	Janice Moorkite	(Invicta E Kent)	2:48:50
1997	Sarah-Jane Heatley	(Sheffield AC)	2:53:05
1998	Jackie Newton	(Stockport H)	2:53:56
1999	Estelle McGuire	(Stockport H)	2:52:34
2000	S Crombie-Hick	(Mornington C)	2:42:44
2001	Kerrie Wood	(Stockport H)	2:51:26
2002	Pauline Powell	(Blackburn H)	2:46:58

Commonwealth Games

2002	Kerryn McCann	(AUSTRALIA)	2:30:05

Wheelchair athletes

MEN

Year

1996	Jack McKenna	(BWRA)	1:47:25
1997	David Holding	(BWRA)	1:43:33
1998	David Holding	(BWRA)	1:47:42
1999	Anthony Booth	(Clayton)	2:07:51
2000	Tushar Patel	(Velocity)	2:07:45
2001	Jerry Forde	(Blarney)	3:20:14
2002	no male finished		

WOMEN

1996	Rachel Potter	(Belle Vue R)	2:53:25
1997	Tanni Grey	(Cardiff)	2:08:28
1998	Deborah Brennan	(Birchfield)	2:54:23
1999	Jackie Wagstaff	(Radcliffe)	4:18:56
2000	no female finished		
2001	no female finished		
2002	Rachel Potter	(Belle Vue R)	2:05:56

APPENDIX II
ALL-TIME MANCHESTER MARATHONS
RANKING TOP 100 MEN'S TIMES

Rank	Athlete	Club	Year	Position	Time
1	S Kenyon	(Salford H)	1981	1	2:11:54
2	E Lesse	(GERMAN DR)	1973	1	2:12:24
3	R Hill	(Bolton U)	1971	1	2:12:39
4	L Philipp	(W GERMANY)	1972	1	2:12:50
5	R Hill	(Bolton U)	1972	2	2:12:51
6	T Wright	(Hallamshire H)	1971	2	2:13:27
7	Y Kitayama	(JAPAN)	1973	2	2:13:29
8	B Armstrong	(CANADA)	1973	3	2:13:30
9	R Hill	(Bolton U)	1969	1	2:13:42
10	A Usami	(JAPAN)	1970	1	2:13:45
11	F Le Grange	(S AFRICA)	1973	4	2:13:58
12	J Busch	(GERMAN D R)	1971	3	2:14:03
13	Y Morita	(JAPAN)	1973	5	2:14:06
14	D Macgregor	(Edinburgh S H)	1972	3	2:15:06
15	C Kirkham	(Coventry G)	1972	4	2:15:17
16	J Julian	(NEW ZEALAND)	1971	4	2:15:19
17	C Kirkham	(Coventry G)	1971	5	2:15:21
18	J Ashworth	(Bingley H)	1983	1	2:15:39
19	D Clayton	(AUSTRALIA)	1969	2	2:15:40
20	J Alder	(Morpeth H)	1971	6	2:15:43
21	S Badgery	(Herc Wimb AC)	1971	7	2:15:44
22	D Faircloth	(Croydon AC)	1972	5	2:15:52
23	E Austin	(Worcester YMCA)	1972	6	2:15:59
24	Y Unetani	(JAPAN)	1970	2	2:16:00
25	A J Wood	(Aberdeen AC)	1971	8	2:16:06
26	L Philipp	(W GERMANY)	1973	6	2:16:07
27	I Thompson	(Luton U)	1984	1	2:16:08
28	B Plain	(Cardiff AC)	1972	7	2:16:18
29	F Le Grange	(S AFRICA)	1972	8	2:16:19
30	K R Best	(Bolton U)	1982	1	2:16:22
31	S Edmunds	(Sale H)	1973	7	2:16:24
32	E Austin	(Worcester YMCA)	1971	9	2:16:24
33	P Angenvoorth	(W GERMANY)	1973	8	2:16:27
34	C Perez	(SPAIN)	1972	9	2:16:27
35	D Faircloth	(Croydon AC)	1973	9	2:16:32
36	P Angenvoorth	(W GERMANY)	1972	10	2:16:44
37	M Steffny	(W GERMANY)	1972	11	2:16:45
38	J Norman	(Altrincham & D)	1971	10	2:16:45
39	D Holt	(Herc Wimb AC)	1972	12	2:16:53
40	M Rowland	(Thames V H)	1972	13	2:16:53
41	E Williams	(Sale H)	1984	2	2:16:56
42	J Busch	(GERMAN D R)	1970	3	2:16:57
43	M Freary	(Bolton U)	1971	11	2:17:10
44	A Moore	(Hillingdon AC)	1972	14	2:17:18
45	M A Child	(Wakefield H)	1973	10	2:17:18
46	N Deakin	(City of Stoke AC)	1972	15	2:17:20
47	A Domleo	(Derby & C)	1973	11	2:17:33
48	P Campbell	(Bolton U)	1984	3	2:17:39

49	H Leeming	(Derby & C)	1971	12	2:17:44
50	J W Craven	(Rowntree AC)	1971	13	2:17:48
51	R Richardson	(Blackheath H)	1972	16	2:17:51
52	M Freary	(Bolton U)	1972	17	2:17:54
53	C Taylor	(Airedale & SV)	1981	2	2:17:56
54	L Austin	(City of Stoke AC)	1971	14	2:17:56
55	C Leigh	(Salford H)	1972	18	2:18:08
56	W v Renterghem	(BELGIUM)	1973	12	2:18:15
57	J Alder	(Morpeth H)	1969	3	2:18:18
58	L Austin	(City of Stoke AC)	1972	19	2:18:38
59	G Brockbank	(Manchester & D)	1971	15	2:18:51
60	P Angenvoorth	(W GERMANY)	1971	16	2:18:57
61	C Kirkham	(Coventry G)	1970	4	2:18:59
62	A Wood	(Aberdeen AC)	1972	20	2:19:00
63	B Hussain	(Stockport H)	1997	1	2:19:00
64	G Booth	(Mizuno RC)	1997	2	2:19:02
65	R G Sercombe	(Newport H)	1973	13	2:19:04
66	J Norman	(Altrincham & D)	1972	21	2:19:22
67	S Taylor	(Aberdeen AC)	1971	17	2:19:28
68	J Newsome	(Wakefield H)	1973	14	2:19:30
69	R Richardson	(Blackheath H)	1971	18	2:19:31
70	H Clague	(St Helens AC)	1985	1	2:19:31
71	M Critchley	(Cardiff AC)	1972	22	2:19:33
72	D Macgregor	(Edinburgh S H)	1971	19	2:19:34
73	K McDonald	(Bingley H)	1981	3	2:19:34
74	Y Unetani	(JAPAN)	1969	4	2:19:37
75	C T Leigh	(Salford H)	1971	20	2:19:38
76	B Watson	(Cambridge H)	1973	15	2:19:42
77	B Plain	(Cardiff AC)	1971	21	2:19:49
78	C Woodward	(Leamington & C)	1973	16	2:19:50
79	A Fernandez	(SPAIN)	1972	23	2:19:56
80	A Wight	(Edinburgh S H)	1972	24	2:19:59
81	M Critchley	(Bolton U)	1982	2	2:20:10
82	P Talkington	(USA)	1973	17	2:20:12
83	S Curran	(Salford H)	1973	18	2:20:13
84	W Adcocks	(Coventry G)	1969	5	2:20:13
85	C Woodhouse	(Derby & C)	1985	2	2:20:14
86	A Aldegalega	(PORTUGAL)	1972	25	2:20:21
87	J Norman	(Altrincham & D)	1982	3	2:20:23
88	M Steffny	(W GERMANY)	1971	22	2:20:33
89	M Craven	(Kendal AC)	1972	26	2:20:35
90	K Best	(Stretford AC)	1984	4	2:20:43
91	P Krebs	(GERMAN D R)	1970	5	2:20:45
92	L Carroll	(Wirral AC)	1973	19	2:20:47
93	H Hellbach	(W GERMANY)	1971	23	2:20:53
94	M Craven	(Kendal AC)	1970	6	2:21:05
95	K Angus	(Sheffield AC)	1972	27	2:21:12
96	S Edmunds	(Sale H)	1972	28	2:21:17
97	P Malcolmson	(L/pool P) V40	1982	4	2:21:23
98	B D Little	(Bolton U) V40	1982	5	2:21:27
99	I MacIntosh	(Ranelagh H)	1972	29	2:21:30
100	A Byrne	(Bolton U)	1971	24	2:21:32

Note: This list does not include the 2002 Commonwealth Games.

APPENDIX III
RANKING TOP 50 WOMEN'S TIMES   1981-2002

1	S Crombie-Hick	(Mornington C)	2000	1	2:42:44
2	L Irving	(Border H)	1985	1	2:44:13
3	M Hurst	(Clayton-le-M)	1985	2	2:45:01
4	L Watson	(London Oly.)	1982	1	2:45:07
5	L Pfeiffer	(Barnet Ladies)	1984	1	2:46:54
6	P Powell	(Blackburn H)	2002	1	2:46:58
7	K Charnock	(Wigan Ph)	2000	2	2:47:44
8	J Moorkite	(Invicta EK) V35	1996	1	2:48:50
9	L Watson	(London Oly.)	1983	1	2:50:56
10	G Markwell	(Leeds City AC)	1983	2	2:51:15
11	K Wood	(Stockport H) V35	2001	1	2:51:26
12	L Shingles	(Middleton H)	1983	3	2:51:29
13	C Hunter-Rowe	(Knavesmire)	1996	2	2:51:38
14	S Catterall	(Bolton U)	1984	2	2:51:56
15	M Hurst	(Clayton-le-M)	1984	3	2:51:58
16	E McGuire	(Stockport H)	1999	1	2:52:34
17	S-J Heatley	(Sheffield AC)	1997	1	2:53:05
18	S Bretherick	(Preseli H)	2000	3	2:53:37
19	A Allan	(Tipton H)	2000	4	2:53:54
20	J Newton	(Stockport H)	1998	1	2:53:56
21	M Ellis	(Shaftesbury B)	2001	2	2:54:35
22	K Wood	(Glossopdale H)	1998	2	2:55:28
23	V Hyland	(Unattached)	1984	4	2:55:44
24	T Sloan	(Salford H)	1998	3	2:56:06
25	K Wood	(Man YMCA)	1996	3	2:56:17
26	T Sloan	(Salford H)	1997	2	2:57:13
27	J Percival	(City of Hull)	1985	3	2:58:06
28	E Robinson	(Border H) V45	1996	5	2:58:18
29	A Wade	(Ilkley H) V35	2000	5	2:58:24
30	H Barber	(Horsforth H)	2000	6	2:58:40
31	S Exon	(Stretford AC)	1985	4	2:59:05
32	L Knights	(Police AA)	2001	3	2:59:30
33	K Wood	(Glossopdale H)	1997	3	2:59:36
34	K Kaiser	(Valley Striders)	1998	4	3:00:27
35	V Perry	(Altrincham) V40	2001	4	3:00:41
37	S Catterall	(Bolton U)	1983	5	3:01:34
38	C Borrill	(East Hull)	1983	6	3:01:46
39	H Fines	(Forest of Dean)	2002	2	3:02:59
40	J Coleman	(Chorley H)	2002	3	3:03:00
41	K Fitzgibbon	(London Oly.)	1981	1	3:03:24
42	B Robinson	(Bury AC) V35	1982	2	3:03:53
43	J Jackson	(Unatt)	1997	4	3:04:07
44	R Cornou	(Paris)	1983	7	3:04:28
44	S Cariss	(Bingley H)	2002	4	3:04:28
46	M Goodwin	(Leigh H)	1985	5	3:04:29
47	S Cariss	(Unatt) V50	2000	7	3:04:33
48	L Hardley	(Altrincham & D)	1984	5	3:04:49
49	R Whitehead	(Bingley H)	1999	2	3:04:59
50	W Grundy	(Heywood R)	1985	6	3:05:06

BIBLIOGRAPHY

BOOKS

Athletics of Today – History, Development and Training; F A M Webster, (F Warne, London, 1929).

Borrowed Time - Salford Harriers 1884-1984; D Scott and C Bent; (Manchester; 1984).

Honour of Empire, Glory of Sport – The History of Athletics at the Commonwealth Games; Bob Phillips; (Parrs Wood Press, 2000).

Irish Marathon Legends; Noel Henry; (Irish Runner, 1992).

Leigh Harriers - 50 years of Athletics 1909-1959; E Roberts & R Sutton; (published privately; 1959).

Manchester Athletic Club - Jubilee Souvenir 1886-1936; F W Hatton; (published privately; 1936).

Marathon and Chips - Biography of Jim Alder, World Record Holder by A T McKenzie; (Alder Sports (Dadwill Ltd) 1981).

Northern Cross Country Association - A Centenary History; Dr P Thomas; (1982).

The Encyclopaedia of Athletics, M Watman, (R Hale, 1973).

The First Hundred Years of Ranelagh Harriers, Founded 1881; R D Callis; (published privately; 1981).

The Ghost Runner, John Tarrant's Own Story, ed M Watman; (Rochester, 1979).

The Guinness Book of Athletic Facts and Feats; P Matthews; (Guinness Superlatives, 1982).

The Guinness Book of the Marathon; R Gynn; (Guinness Superlatives, 1984).

The Long Hard Road - Part One: Nearly to the Top; R Hill; (Hyde, 1981).

The Long Hard Road - Part Two: To the Peak and Beyond; R Hill; (Hyde, 1982).

The Marathon Footrace; D Martin & R Gynn; (Charles Thomas, USA, 1979).

The Olympic Marathon; D Martin & R Gynn; (Human Kinetics, 2000).

The Salford Harriers Club - Jubilee Season 1933-1934; J H Hardwick; 1934.

Who's Who of UK and GB Internationals 1896-1939; Ian Buchanan, (NUTS, 1999).

William Penny Brookes and the Olympic Connection; M Furbank, H Cromarty and G McDonald; (Wenlock Olympian Society, 1996).

MAGAZINES

Athletics; Athletic Review; Athletics Weekly; Road Runners Club Newsletter; Running Review.

NEWSPAPERS

Athletic News; Bolton Evening News and their sports paper - Cricket and Football Field; Crewe Chronicle; Daily Dispatch; Manchester Evening News; Manchester Evening Chronicle; Sheffield Star; Sporting Chronicle; The Manchester Guardian; The Times; Wigan Observer.

INDEX

Cormack, Joseph Norman, 3
Cranny, Martin, 129
Craven, Jim, 132, 134, 137, 159, 273
Craven, Martin, 119, 121, 126, 127, 128, 129, 146, 274
Critchley, Mike, 146, 147, 156, 159, 168, 170, 171, 193, 196, 274
Crombie-Hick, Shona, 232, 233, 235, 247, 272, 275
Crossland, George, 8
Curran, Stan, 153, 161, 167, 175, 176, 178, 180, 181, 193, 225
Cusack, Neil, 181, 187

Darcy, Mike, 154
Darius, King of Persia, 1
Davies, Dai, 121, 122, 137, 147
Davis, T C, 11
Day, William H, 6, 7, 9, 14
de Coubertin, Baron Pierre, 2, 3
Deakin, Norman, 146, 159
Deakin, Rob, 230, 231, 233, 235, 246, 271
Dodd, Sam, 96
Doggett, Geoff, 87
Doggett, Harold, 84, 85, 86, 87
Domleo, Alan, 121, 151, 153, 156, 159, 273
Donaldson, James, 260, 264
Dorando, Pietri, 17, 18, 19, 25, 26, 27
Doyle, Mike, 239
Drayton, Jerome, 125
Duffy, Tony, 206, 208, 210, 230, 231, 233, 246
Duncan, Alexander, 6, 7, 9, 13, 16, 17, 22

Edmunds, Steve, 137, 146, 151, 152, 153, 155, 156, 158, 172, 176, 177, 178, 184, 194, 273, 274
Edney, Simon, 240, 242, 246
Eglington, R, 12, 14
Ellis, Bob, 121, 122, 147
Ellis, H, 12
Exon, Sue, 172, 173, 174, 192, 194, 203, 275

Faircloth, Don, 125, 126, 132, 140, 143, 144, 145, 146, 151, 152, 153, 158, 273
Farrimond, Arthur, 34, 35, 36, 40, 41, 42, 43, 44, 45, 47, 48, 50, 51, 52, 67, 70, 74, 79
Farrington, John, 156
Fernandez, Agustin, 142, 143, 144, 146, 148, 159, 274
Ferris, Sam, 45, 47, 48, 50, 51, 52, 53, 59, 60, 64, 65, 66, 68, 69, 73, 75, 76, 77, 85, 86, 88, 106, 108, 271
Fewery, John, 117, 118, 119, 120, 121, 126, 127, 129, 130
Fines, Helen, 267, 270, 275
Fish, D, 102

Fisher, Ian, 238, 240, 241, 242, 245, 246
Fitzgibbon, Katie, 163, 166, 194, 272, 275
Forde, Jerry, 240, 245, 248, 272
Forshaw, Joseph, 19
Forshaw, Robert, 81, 82, 89, 91, 95, 96, 102, 105, 109
Foster, J W, 38, 45, 57
Foster, Jack, 125, 156
Franklin, Ron, 121, 122, 137, 147
Freary, Mike, 136, 139, 146, 147, 159, 215, 273
Freary, Paul, 215
Freeman, Walter, 32, 34, 35, 43

Gailly, Etienne, 109
Galea, Carol, 254, 256, 257
Gallagher, Jackie, 254, 255, 256, 257
Gartlon, Cyril, 81
Gold, Arthur, 114
Goodyear, Ralph, 129, 130
Grainey, John W, 95
Grant, Alan, 121, 122, 126, 129
Green, Harry, 20, 29
Grey, Tanni, 207, 209, 212, 249, 272
Griffiths, Leslie, 106, 107, 108
Grove, Ron, 117, 118
Gwilt, Ricky, 171

Haines, Chris, 121, 137, 138, 146, 147, 154
Hale, Darren, 208, 210, 212, 214, 216, 217, 238, 240, 246
Hall, Stuart, 259, 261, 263, 264
Hallam, James, 223, 227, 248
Halsey, Joseph G, 89
Hampton, Phil, 121, 122
Hardwick, Harry, 85
Haro, Mariano, 141, 142, 143, 144
Harper, Ernie, 59, 76, 77, 102
Harris, Dawn, 173
Hartigan, Bev, 254, 255, 256, 257
Haslam, Eric, 147
Haslam, Jack, 122
Hatton, Fred, 18
Hayes, J J, 19, 27
Heatley, Basil, 114, 207
Heatley, Sarah-Jane, 207, 208, 211, 212, 247, 272, 275
Heeley, T, 65, 66, 68
Hefferon, Charles, 17, 18, 19
Hellbach, Hans, 137, 138, 274
Henning, John, 106, 107, 108, 109, 110, 271
Herodotus, 1
Hicks, Thomas, 3, 11
Hidalgo, Juan, 142, 143, 144
Hiles, Leslie F, 132
Hill, Graham, 206, 208, 210, 246

McDonald, Kim, 163, 165, 166, 193, 274
McGuire, Estelle, 221, 225, 226, 227, 247, 272, 275
McKenna, Jack, 198, 204, 248, 272
McKenna, John, 45, 47, 48
McShane, J, 99
Mee, Paul, 197, 204, 228, 235, 236
Melville, Frank, 6, 7, 9, 12, 13, 24, 25
Mills, A R 'Bobby', 45, 47, 48, 59
Miltiades, 1
Moir, Dr E, 26, 34, 54, 62
Mongudhi, Elizabeth, 252, 253, 254, 255, 256, 257
Moore, Ken, 148
Moorkite, Janice, 201, 202, 203, 204, 247, 272, 275
Moqhali, Paul Thabiso, 258, 260, 261, 263, 264
Morita, Yoshiaki, 150, 151, 152, 153, 158, 273
Morris, E J, 34, 36, 39, 42, 55, 56, 74, 79, 95
Morris, Frank, 119
Moxsom, Colin, 183, 184, 193
Murray, Fergus, 125

Naali, Francis Robert, 259, 260, 262, 263, 264, 265, 271
Naigambo, Beata, 254, 256, 257
Nan, Shoryu, 102
Neary, Mike, 166, 181, 187, 196
Newman, Ivan, 215, 219, 248
Newsome, John, 132, 133, 134, 137, 146, 151, 153, 155, 159, 274
Newton, Arthur, 110
Newton, Jackie, 214, 216, 218, 221, 227, 230, 233, 239, 247, 272, 275
Ngadi, Salaho, 260, 261, 262, 264
Nicholls, Reg, 95
Norman, E V, 12
Norman, Jeff, 132, 134, 136, 146, 148, 149, 158, 159, 168, 170, 171, 181, 182, 184, 193, 273
Norris, Bertie, 95, 102
Ntlotsoeu, Mpesela, 261, 264, 265

O'Brien, Tony, 220, 225, 227, 271
O'Leary, Dave, 122, 129, 130, 157
Orr, Tom, 106
Otsuki, Kenichi, 150, 151, 154
Ouafi, El Boughera, 77

Papworth, Kevin, 219, 248
Parry, Edward W, 8, 44
Patel, Tushar, 209, 212, 230, 235, 248, 272
Patton, Colin, 210, 217, 225, 266, 267, 268, 270
Payne, Harry, 75, 76, 77, 83, 86
Perez, Carlos, 142, 143, 144, 145, 146, 148, 158, 273

Perkin, H S, 6, 7, 9, 24
Peters, Jim, 83, 110
Pfeiffer, Libby, 183, 185, 194, 272, 275
Pheidippides, 1, 2
Philipp, Lutz, 141, 142, 143, 144, 146, 148, 150, 151, 152, 153, 158, 271, 273
Phillipedes, 1
Pirie, Gordon, 135
Plain, Bernie, 132, 133, 134, 135, 136, 137, 141, 142, 143, 144, 145, 146, 147, 156, 158, 159, 273, 274
Plutarch, 1
Popel, Brian, 132, 137
Porter, Mike, 108, 122, 130, 138
Potter, Rachel, 198, 204, 249, 268, 270, 272
Powell, Pauline, 247, 266, 267, 270, 272
Price, Jack, 14, 15, 17, 18, 21
Pride, Simon, 259, 261, 262, 263, 264
Pryce, W, 147

Radcliffe, Paula, 155
Ranicar, Eric, 174, 184, 194
Rawlinson, Teddy, 66, 67, 70
Renterghem, Walter van, 150, 151, 152, 153, 274
Reyes, Manuel Plaza, 77
Richards, Tommy, 108
Richards, Wilf, 102, 105
Richardson, R, 137, 138, 146, 147, 159, 274
Rimmer, J T 'Jack', 25, 26
Ristimaki, A, 141, 142, 143, 161
Ritchie, Alan, 184, 185, 186, 194
Roberts, Emlyn, 191, 221, 224, 225, 246
Roberts, James, 24, 25, 26, 27, 28, 271
Robertson, Donald McNab, 64, 86, 87, 95, 102
Robinson, Brenda, 172, 173, 275
Robinson, Debbie, 254, 255, 256, 257
Robinson, Eleanor, 167, 187, 203, 205, 212, 247, 275
Robinson, John, 156
Roelants, Gaston, 123
Rostrum, B, 125
Rouillard, Carole, 252
Rowland, Mike, 146, 159, 273

Sarafis, P, 155
Schneider, Strimatter, 150, 154
Semple, Jock, 78
Sercombe, Bob, 151, 153, 156, 159, 274
Serekwane, Ovid, 150, 155
Shahanga, Gidamis, 149, 258
Shepherd, Alan, 221, 224, 225, 227, 246
Sheridan, John, 151, 154
Sherring, William, 3, 11
Shingles, Lynn, 177, 179, 181, 194, 275
Shorter, Frank, 148, 155, 160

ABOUT THE AUTHORS

Ron Hill

Ron Hill won two Manchester Marathons, 1969 and 1971, the first of which was a breakthrough in his marathon career. Competing in 115 marathons, he is a former European (1969) and Commonwealth Champion (1970) where he set a best time of 2:09:28. He won the Boston Marathon in 1970 in the then record time of 2:10:30. A GB International athlete for over a decade and a AAA medallist from 1962 to 1974, he was appointed MBE in 1971. In 1983 he passed the 100,000 milestone and now has recorded more than 143,000 miles. He competed at the highest level in three Olympics, four Europeans and three Commonwealth Games. Hill's last marathon was at the 100th Boston in 1996. A member of Clayton-le-Moors Harriers, he still races frequently and travels extensively. To follow his progress see his column on www.realrunner.com

Neil Shuttleworth

Neil Shuttleworth, who competed in the Maxol Marathons as a Bolton United Harrier, is a veteran of 24 marathons and nine Karrimor two day Mountain Marathons. He came third in the 1972 Karrimor with partner Peter Walkington, a former Fell Runners Association Secretary. A member of the Bob Graham 24 Hour Club and the Road Runners Club, he is a former Club Champion with Keswick AC, and his present club Glossopdale Harriers. His most noteworthy race was in 1997 when as a post-graduate student at Manchester University he was the first Present member home in the annual Past v Present cross-country race, a competition Hill won countless times when he was younger.